The Quinoa Bust

CALIFORNIA STUDIES IN FOOD AND CULTURE

Darra Goldstein, Editor

The Quinoa Bust

THE MAKING AND UNMAKING OF AN ANDEAN MIRACLE CROP

Emma McDonell

UNIVERSITY OF CALIFORNIA PRESS

University of California Press
Oakland, California

Library of Congress Cataloging-in-Publication Data

Names: McDonell, Emma, author.
Title: The quinoa bust : the making and unmaking of an Andean miracle
    crop / Emma McDonell.
Other titles: California studies in food and culture ; 84.
Description: Oakland : University of California Press, [2025] | Series:
    California studies in food and culture ; 84 | Includes bibliographical
    references and index.
Identifiers: LCCN 2024033962 (print) | LCCN 2024033963 (ebook) |
    ISBN 9780520401709 (cloth) | ISBN 9780520401716 (paperback) |
    ISBN 9780520401723 (epub)
Subjects: LCSH: Quinoa industry—Peru—Puno (Puno) | Quinoa—
    Peru—Puno (Puno)
Classification: LCC HD9049.Q552 P46 2025 (print) | LCC HD9049.Q552
    (ebook) | DDC 338.1/731—dc23/eng/20241101
LC record available at https://lccn.loc.gov/2024033962
LC ebook record available at https://lccn.loc.gov/2024033963

34 33 32 31 30 29 28 27 26 25
10 9 8 7 6 5 4 3 2 1

publication supported by a grant from
The Community Foundation for Greater New Haven
as part of the *Urban Haven Project*

CONTENTS

NOTE ON NAMES AND PLACES

As is conventional in ethnographic research, I have chosen to use pseudonyms for people who are not widely known public figures to protect the identities of my interlocutors. I also use toponyms for specific places below the region level that could reveal individuals' identities. For the quinoa producer associations, cooperatives, and businesses I worked with closely, I have also created pseudonyms to help protect these organizations from facing consequences for participating in this research. This book tells a complex story about the quinoa boom and bust that diverges from familiar portrayals of villains and victims in the global food system. It examines the complicated day-to-day calculations of actors in dynamic and difficult situations that occasionally led individuals to resort to dishonesty and deceit. My intention in this book is to provide an assessment of the ways quinoa industry actors were caught in extremely difficult, sometimes morally fraught situations, not to point out "bad behavior."

1932   Argentine researchers find bread made with quinoa flour to be more nutritious than wheat bread.

1935   First known quinoa experimental trial conducted outside the Andes takes place in Kenya using seeds obtained from Britain's Kew Royal Botanical Gardens.

1950   Researchers discuss a "little known grain" (quinoa) at the UN Food and Agriculture Organization's conference on nutrition in Latin America.

1953   Collaborations between Peruvian scientists and researchers at Harvard University and University of Iowa commence with funding from the Inter-American Affairs of the Foreign Operations Administration, finding quinoa's nutritional content superior to cow's milk.

1956   The US Department of Agriculture funds (unsuccessful) experimental quinoa plots in Colorado.

1965   Efforts to "improve" quinoa commence in 1965 in Patacamaya, Bolivia's Experimental Station, with funds from the UN's program against hunger and OXFAM.

1968   First Chenopod Convention takes place in Puno, Peru.

1975   The National Academy of Sciences publishes *Underexploited Tropical Plants with Promising Economic Value*, featuring a chapter on quinoa.

1976   Potosí, Bolivia, hosts second Chenopod Convention.

1979   Fondo Simón Bolivar and Inter-American Institute of Agricultural Sciences fund study on feasibility of quinoa commercialization in Puno, Peru.

1983   Quinoa Corporation is formed and begins importing small quantities of Bolivian quinoa into the United States.

1983   Quinoa trials begin in the United Kingdom.

1984   Quinoa trials begin in Denmark and Tibet.

1985   Quinoa trials begin in India.

1984   Quinoa trials begin in The Netherlands.

1988   Quinoa trials begin in China.

1989   Quinoa trials begin in Brazil and Cuba.

1989   The National Academy of Sciences publishes *Lost Crop of the Incas: Little-Known Plants of the Andes with Promise for Worldwide Cultivation*, featuring quinoa among other Andean crops.

1993   The European Union launches quinoa field trials in England, Denmark, The Netherlands, and Italy, as well as laboratory tests in Scotland and France.

1996   The International Quinoa Trial, a joint venture between the Danish International Development Agency and the International Potato Center, initiates trials of quinoa in numerous countries.

2008   The SWUP-MED project develops extensive quinoa trials in the Mediterranean Sea region.

2011   The FAO publishes *Quinoa: An Ancient Crop to Contribute to World Food Security*, a report that foreshadows the declaration of the UN International Year of Quinoa.

2012   The UN announces 2013 will be the International Year of Quinoa.

2013   Coastal farmers in Peru aggressively take up quinoa production.

2014   Quinoa's farm-gate price peaks.

2014   Peru's national-level quinoa production figures double in a single year, largely due to record yields in coastal areas.

2014   Between May and December, a number of containers of Peruvian quinoa are rejected at US ports of entry for exceeding allowable levels of agricultural chemicals.

2015   Quinoa prices fall almost 40 percent from 2014's peak.

2015   Peru surpasses Bolivia as world's chief quinoa-producing country.

2015   A group of industry actors in Puno begin discussing possibility of a collective brand for the region's quinoa.

2016   Quinoa prices continue to fall an additional 20 percent.

2018   Proponents of a collective brand declare the project a failure.

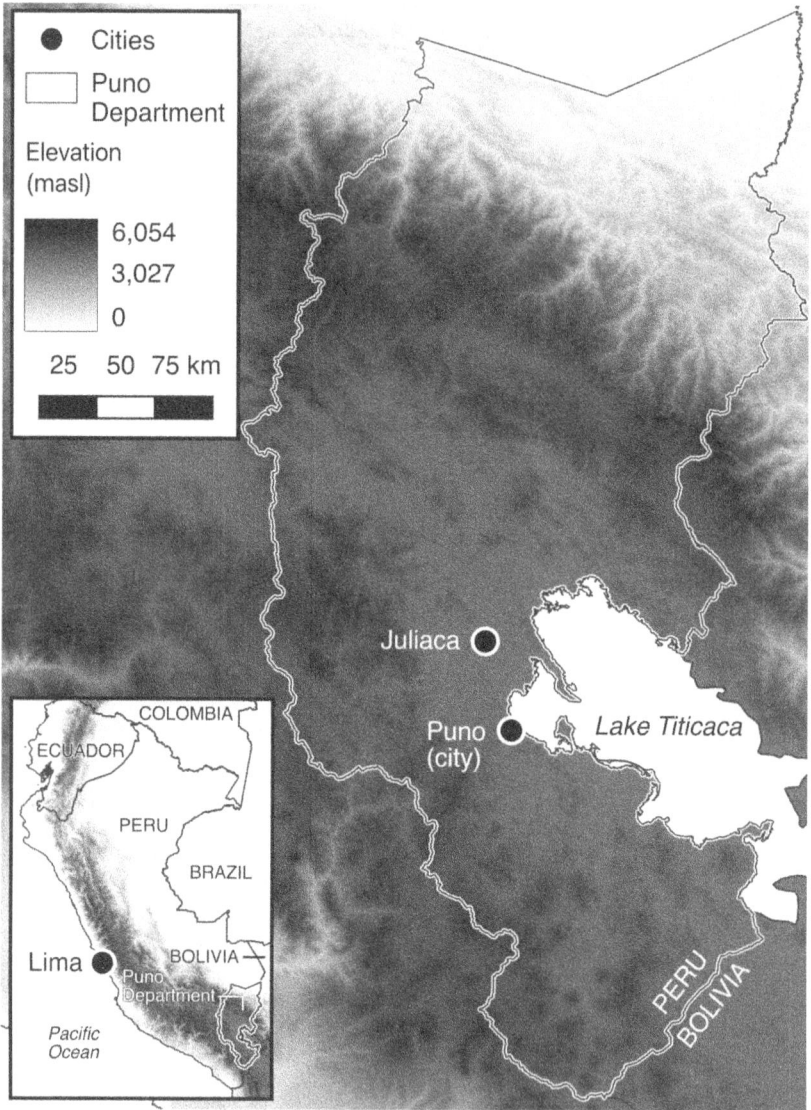

Map of Puno Department. Produced by Jordan Blekking.

Introduction

QUINOA'S PROMISE

IN MAY 2013 Nadine Heredia, Peru's First Lady, made a public appearance at the "Quinua Mama" Festival in Calaya, a small farming community on the Peruvian side of the Andean altiplano, the massive high-altitude plateau that covers much of western Bolivia and southern Peru along with slivers of northern Chile and Argentina. In anticipation of the day's proceedings, a temporary stage with an overhead tent had been set up in front of the seventeenth-century Catholic Church anchoring Calaya's Plaza de Armas. It was a good day for a festival—the start of the dry season meant cloudless skies, midday warmth, and no chance of rain. Thick red ribbons and a vinyl banner printed with the logo of Peru's Ministry of Agriculture decorated the stage.[1] Calaya's typically sleepy town plaza was full of life: a marching band played booming music and a balloon artist twisted colorful animal figures for a line of children as a large crowd gathered.[2]

Just over a year earlier, the United Nations had declared that 2013 would be the International Year of Quinoa, initiating a yearlong series of UN-sponsored events that collectively sought to promote quinoa as a sustainable development tool. Heredia, President Ollanta Humala's wife, had been selected as a "special ambassador" for the International Year of Quinoa, a position she would share with Bolivian president Evo Morales. This largely symbolic role entailed presiding over events like this one. With the main speeches about to begin, Heredia stood on the stage flanked by officials from the Ministry of Agriculture and representatives from the municipal and regional governments, the shade tent protecting them from the unrelenting altiplano sun. Atop crisp blue jeans and hiking boots, Heredia wore a *traje típico* (traditional outfit), a common gesture Peruvian politicians make when visiting highland communities.[3] The bright red *pollera,* embroidered wool jacket, and a thick garland of roses and greenery made her stand out beside the muted suits and slacks of adjacent officials.[4]

After a brief introductory address, the minister of production passed Heredia the microphone. "I've come here to Calaya to express to you the pride President Humala and I feel for the work that you're doing to preserve our quinoa and to transform it into not only an object of national pride but one of international pride," Heredia told the crowd as a gust of wind blew her long dark hair across her face. "My husband and I have started a massive campaign to make sure that our indigenous Andean products will be revalorized." The audience clapped. "We are not only going to grow our domestic quinoa markets but we're going to conquer international markets," Heredia continued as fierce altiplano wind muffled the audio. "With quinoa, we are going to create jobs and we are going to begin to reduce poverty." Quinoa exports, Heredia declared, would usher Peru's "most remote, most vulnerable populations" along the road to progress and bring modernity to Calaya. "Through all this," she promised, "we will accompany you."

For the hundreds of people gathered in the plaza, primarily farmers from the area, Heredia's speech provoked a palpable sense of excitement. Calaya is the kind of out-of-the-way place that rarely attracts the attention of national-level politicians.[5] Tiny Calaya is about six square blocks (town blocks, not city blocks) of mostly dirt roads. An able-bodied person can walk from one end of town to the other in just over five minutes. For public figures based in Peru's coastal capital city of Lima, visiting Calaya also means braving the altiplano's hypoxic environment. A trip to the altiplano, where altitudes average about four thousand meters above sea level, often includes twenty-four hours of *soroche,* the local term for the violent altitude sickness that overcomes many visitors shortly after arrival. Yet Calaya's farmers, who had organized Peru's first quinoa cooperative in 2010, had earned a reputation for being some of the country's most serious commercial quinoa producers. These farmers were playing a key role in the transformation of this humble Andean grain into a high-value export crop. A growing number of people saw Calaya as a model for the future of agriculture in the Peruvian altiplano. A hand-painted concrete sign on the outskirts of town read, in fresh paint: "Welcome to Calaya: ancient birthplace of the world's organic quinoa."[6]

The First Lady's trip to Calaya marked the crescendo of quinoa's building promise in the Andean highlands and beyond. At the time of Heredia's 2013 visit, export demand for quinoa was skyrocketing. In less than a decade, quinoa had been transformed from a local staple, produced and consumed

FIGURE 1. First Lady Nadine Heredia threshing quinoa for a photo op as part of the "Quinua Mama" Festival in 2013. *Source:* Presidencia Perú Flikr / Creative Commons BY-NC-SA 2.0.

almost exclusively in the Andes, into a globally circulated commodity. Quinoa's price increased sevenfold between 2008 and 2014, with the most dramatic price surge taking place between 2013 and 2014. As wealthy consumers across the globe integrated this new "superfood" into their diets, quinoa producers, middlemen, and hopeful entrepreneurs across the Andes scrambled to take advantage of this rare windfall.

The quinoa boom was both an "economic" phenomenon of surging prices and a moment when a collective sense of possibility was harnessed. It's difficult to exaggerate the excitement surrounding quinoa at that point in time. In the Puno region of Peru, the quinoa production hub for the world's chief quinoa-producing country, the grain's booming popularity abroad offered hope for a better future. Heredia's speech emphasized these aspirations. For the Peruvian altiplano, a region largely left out of the country's decade of dramatic economic growth and commonly dismissed by Peruvian elites as a cultural backwater, quinoa's rise to global stardom was considered an unparalleled rural development opportunity. This is a region where over a third of the population lives on less than PEN 250 (approximately US$75.00) per month.[7] The Puno Region has one of the highest poverty rates in the country, and in some years the highest. While 70 percent of homes in Peru have electricity and running (though not drinkable) water, only 40 percent of homes in Puno have access to these services, and about half of the homes in the region rely on open pits or open fields to dispose of sewage.[8] Steady income opportunities are scarce here. The industrialization that twentieth-century development theorists thought would free people from land-based livelihoods never materialized in Puno.[9] Agriculture remains the region's dominant economic activity, though informal gold mining and a massive contraband economy based in the city of Juliaca offer additional prospects.[10]

Quinoa promised something better. Puno's farmers had been left out of Peru's high-value agricultural export sector, an industry comprised of large-scale chemical- and capital-intensive farms along Peru's coast that produce asparagus, mango, blueberries, and avocados destined for Northern Hemisphere consumers who seek fresh produce year-round.[11] Only a handful of native crops can grow in the altiplano's harsh conditions, meaning Puno's farmers could not simply adjust their crop portfolios to take advantage of demand for crops like asparagus.[12] While coastal agribusinesses benefited from profitable "nontraditional agricultural exports," Andean agriculture remained oriented toward home consumption and regional markets. The sudden transformation of quinoa—a crop specifically adapted to the highland environment—into a cash crop offered the potential of a *lucrative* Andean agriculture, promising income opportunities beyond the region's dominant mining sector and informal economy. It heralded a brighter future for rural communities devastated by decades of rural-urban migration, civil war, and neglect by state institutions: a long-awaited answer to the yearning for a better life.[13]

Like many commodity booms, the quinoa boom was used to leverage narratives of progress and visions of modernity.[14] The grain's rise to global stardom signaled the potential of a development model in which cultural difference was not an obstacle to progress but a means to achieve it. For some, this was a moment of reckoning. A native crop long denigrated as "Indian food" by Peruvian elites, quinoa's popularity abroad presaged a new era in which indigenous Peruvians would be recognized as more than relics of a bygone past.[15] This was an opportunity to convert the Andes' rich natural and cultural endowment into economic development for all.[16] Quinoa's revalorization came to stand in for a hopeful vision of Peru's future as a multicultural society in which diversity was an economic asset rather than a source of tension. This new perspective dovetailed with a growing culinary nationalism in Peru, an outward- and inward-facing project that repackaged Peruvian identity around culinary traditions. The "gastronomic revolution," so dubbed by some of its leading proponents, was pitched as an unprecedented opportunity for "inclusion" of those previously left out of the country's record economic growth. Importantly, this project centered around repackaging native ingredients (such as quinoa) for new audiences.[17] Quickly, quinoa became a poster child for a broader refashioning of Andean indigeneity for modernity in Latin America and beyond, a revalorization based around commodification. The particularities of quinoa's promise in Peru—the broader context of the gastronomic revolution, the layered histories of racism and marginalization, the unique agricultural landscape—shaped the collective sense of hope quinoa crystallized.

Quinoa's rise marked a shift in the treatment of so-called neglected crops. Farming communities across the world produce unique crops and crop varieties that are deeply embedded in local meaning systems and agroecologies but do not circulate in global markets.[18] In the radical simplifications that characterized the modernist gaze of twentieth-century statist and developmentalist projects, unique crops like quinoa were inefficient vestiges of the past, and those who produced them were considered "stubbornly" set in their ways.[19] But many of these unique species remain firmly rooted in local identities, cultural rituals, crop rotations, and diets even as they have been systematically devalued over the course of European colonialism, capitalist expansion, and international development paradigms that see them as antiquated and of marginal use.

The very crops long assumed to be neglected, disappearing, or obsolete are increasingly coveted by discriminating eaters. Wealthy eaters across the world now prize foods "with stories behind them."[20] Gone are the days when upper-class eating sensibilities centered around conspicuous consumption in expensive steak houses, French haute cuisine, and white tablecloth restaurants.[21] Instead, today's sophisticated eaters convey cultural capital by wielding knowledge about foods considered exotic or authentic.[22] Cosmopolitan consumers' desire for distinction has helped drive the transformation of a number of marginalized foods into delicacies in recent years.[23] Quinoa's transformation into a global commodity fits into a larger project that seeks to exploit Peru's "culinary resources." Imagining the nation as a melting pot of unique and (bio)diverse culinary traditions, leaders of the gastronomic revolution have framed Peru as a pantry of ingredients awaiting revalorization.[24] In 2016, Peru's Ministry of Export launched the Superfoods Peru campaign at product expositions around that world, framing the country as the "land of superfoods." Peru's superfoods would "conquer" global markets. Superfoods Peru sought to build exports of products like maca, kañiwa, and aguaymanto.[25] Meanwhile, Peru's upscale restaurants increasingly lured tourists with discourses around trying Peru's lost foods. Marginalized foods were the new business frontier.

With shifting consumer preferences in mind, by the early 2010s a growing number of powerful international development organizations were rethinking their understandings of neglected crops. Perhaps these crops were not relics of the past, but tools to help usher in a more sustainable future. The World Bank, the International Fund for Agricultural Development, Biodiversity International, and the UN Food and Agriculture Organization (FAO) funneled funds into commercializing so-called neglected crops.[26] A growing number of development organizations began framing the transformation of local crops into export goods as an unparalleled sustainable development opportunity. In theory, this was a win-win that would provide an income source for struggling smallholder farmers while incentivizing them to maintain their cultural traditions and safeguard the world's agricultural biodiversity for future generations. Many saw it as an environmentally friendly and culturally sensitive approach to poverty reduction. The promise of neglected crops is also at times framed through the lens of climate change adaptation, with native crops theoretically being better adapted to local ecologies than non-native ones, making them less susceptible to pest outbreaks and unforeseen weather events. This new attitude marked a shift away from the "green revolution" model of agricultural development, wherein international development organizations sought to replace "unproductive" local crops with "improved" varieties. Simultaneously, it represented a pivot away from destroying traditional knowledge and cultural traditions in the name of progress and toward a newfound esteem for local knowledge and the wisdom of traditional agricultural systems. As excitement about the prospect of so-called neglected crops grew, quinoa was heralded as a prodigy.

The Quinoa Bust traces the social, ecological, technological, and political work that went into transforming a humble Andean grain into a development miracle crop—and the unintended consequences of this project.[27] Quinoa's simultaneous constructions as a development miracle crop, on the one hand, and an altiplano cash crop, on the other, were inextricable from one another and illuminate the grain's boom-bust trajectory. One could study each of these dynamics separately—development discourses surrounding quinoa, the commodification of an indigenous staple crop, the formation of a new global commodity chain, still another commodity boom in Latin America—yet it is the connections among these dynamics that lie at the heart of this book. Transforming quinoa into a global commodity was a collective project, one that enrolled diversely positioned social, technical, and material actors. Nutrition scientists, agronomists, plant breeders, chefs, politicians, journalists, development practitioners, entrepreneurs, processors, exporters, and of course farmers all collaborated in this effort. Being imbued with the aspirations outlined earlier helped quinoa forge these connections. However, the project lacked a unitary goal, and quinoa's transformation was produced in and through the interactions between actors with competing interests, diverse social positions, distinct worldviews, and differing moral imperatives. Making quinoa into a global commodity required building links between and translating across diverse social worlds. These encounters took place across vast and often asymmetrical social, cultural, racial, and class distances. Such power differentials were not incidental; they profoundly shaped quinoa's commercialization and its effects. Transforming a local staple crop into a widely circulating superfood was not only a "social" process in a traditional sense. While humans are at the heart of this story, quinoa's boom and bust were constituted within and through encounters between people and complex ecologies. Quinoa's biophysical properties, the idiosyncrasies of the altiplano climate, and the materiality of agricultural chemicals, among other nonhuman factors, also played roles in the making and unmaking of quinoa as a miracle crop. I pay close attention to the frictions animating this process, tracking how quinoa's transformation articulated with specific local histories of land tenure, ideologies of race, and agroecologies.[28]

While this is a story of quinoa's rise to stardom, it is also a tale about the aftermath that attends to the unraveling of a set of promises, growing contradictions between visions of quinoa's future, and unintended consequences. That is, the bust. The sense of hope quinoa crystallized would ultimately prove to be what Lauren Berlant called cruel optimism, an attachment to fantasies of the good life that are out of reach. The drama of the bust resides not only in the plummeting prices but also in the unraveling of quinoa's "cluster of promises."[29] The bust foreclosed the sense of possibility quinoa had helped foster and fractured the set of relationships the promise of quinoa had helped assemble. It forced actors invested in quinoa to acknowledge that the better future quinoa was supposed to usher in was still out of reach. The quinoa miracle was a mirage.

From a culinary standpoint, quinoa (*Chenopodium quinoa*) is often associated with grains like wheat, rice, oats, barley, or corn, but agronomically it is very distinct from these crops. While all cereal crops—rice, oats, wheat, barley, and corn—are annual grass species, quinoa is not a grass at all, but rather a relative of spinach and beets, and like those plants it has edible and highly nutritious leaves.[30] Quinoa is part of the Chenopod or "goosefoot" genus, a group of plants known for their oddly shaped leaves, which resemble the webbed feet of geese. Many goosefoots are considered weeds. In an article in *Nature Magazine* in 1954, Elizabeth Parry described quinoa's appearance as distinctly weedy: "The average layman would doubtless describe Chenopodium quinoa in one scornful word—weed. It stands three to five feet tall with triangular leaves not unlike those of a mallow, a stout, furrowed, and much-angled stem, inconspicuous flowers, and a multitude of tiny, varicolored seeds. It is certainly no ornament to a garden."[31] An annual, quinoa has a woody stalk reaching up to two meters high, with many short, thin branches known as *panicles*.

Quinoa was domesticated in the Andean altiplano some eight thousand years ago, likely along the shores of Lake Titicaca.[32] It is one of only a handful of crops that can survive in the rugged altiplano environment. Quinoa thrives at thirty-five to forty-five hundred meters above sea level in a climate defined by frequent drought and extreme diurnal temperature fluctuations, and it grows well in saline soils common throughout the region.[33] There are hundreds of varieties of quinoa, ranging from bright magenta to jet black and varying in size, shape, taste, and, perhaps most critically, agronomic characteristics such as vulnerability to temperature extremes and average yields. As quinoa fields reach maturity each year in April, shocks of bright yellow, red, and maroon dot the vast altiplano landscape. I disagree strongly with Parry's assessment of quinoa's attractiveness—in a largely monochromatic landscape, mature quinoa fields are a sight to behold.

Quinoa has historically played a key role in an ingenious Andean cropping system that includes some combination of potatoes; native tubers like *oca* and *ulluco*; the closely related *kañiwa*; *tarwi*, a nitrogen-fixing native lupin; and maize at lower altitudes.[34] Andean crop rotations can extend over a decade, with each farmer tending multiple small fields. Livestock—like llamas, alpacas, sheep, cows, and guinea pigs—are essential for these agricultural systems, recycling nutrients back into the soil. The weediness Parry

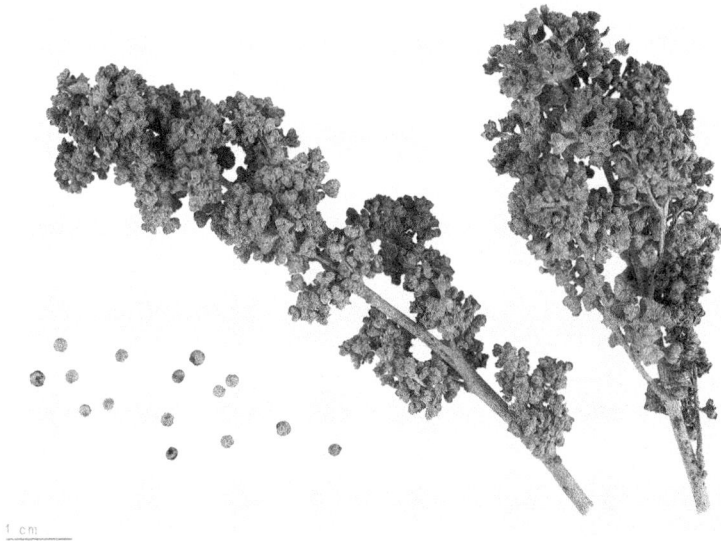

FIGURE 2. Close-up of branch of dried quinoa panicle. *Source:* Roger Culos, Muséum de Toulouse. *Source:* Wikimedia, https://commons.wikimedia.org/w/index.php?curid =43329432 / Creative Commons BY-SA 3.0.

commented on is an agroecological asset: quinoa can be grown with little effort, allowing farmers to attend to other aspects of their farms, although as chapters 3 and 4 make clear, producing *commercial* quinoa requires farmers to invest considerable time, energy, and capital. Like most grains, quinoa is not ready to eat upon harvest. The quinoa seed has a hull that needs to be removed and, even beyond that, a bitter coating called saponin that deters pests but also causes indigestion in humans. As explored in chapter 4, this quinoa processing influences industry power dynamics.

While quinoa is a plant, we often use the term to refer to the small oblong edible seeds it produces. Eighteenth-century Spanish explorer Antonio de Ulloa thought the quinoa seed resembled a very small lentil and marveled at the way the seed, "when boiled, opens and out of it comes a spiral fibre [*sic*] which appears like a small worm, that's whiter than the husk."[35] These seeds are exceptionally nutritious, especially when compared to dominant staple grains like wheat and rice. Rich in protein, quinoa is considered a "perfect protein" because it has an amino acid profile very rarely seen outside animal products.[36] Quinoa is high in fiber, B vitamins, and several minerals including manganese, iron, and zinc. Perhaps because of this profile, it has evolved into a versatile ingredient in highland cuisine, used in soups, especially a savory porridge called *p'esque*; as a base of a beer-like drink called *chicha*; and as quinoa flour, combined with water and sugar to make calorie-dense snacks called *k'ispiña*.

Miracle crops like quinoa are not born, they are made. Though quinoa does have remarkable features, the crop is not intrinsically miraculous. At a specific historical juncture, quinoa came to be seen as such. Crops have tangible agronomic and nutritional elements, but these characteristics only take on meaning and power within specific social, material, and political conjunctures. I use the term *miracle crop* to situate quinoa within a class of crops that, at different moments, have come to be seen as potent solutions to what are often called "development problems." International development agencies enlist them in alleviating poverty, combating malnutrition, helping adapt global food systems to the global climate crisis, or otherwise bringing about desired social changes.[37] Unlike development miracle *foods*, the potential of miracle *crops* lies in their nutritional *and* agronomic features. I use the concept as an analytical tool to direct attention to the social, symbolic, material, and political work that goes into transforming a crop into a miracle crop. The term also gestures toward such crops' spectacular nature, suggesting exaggeration.

The miracle crop draws inspiration from two conceptual kin. Historian Lisa Haushofer showed how the convergence of nutrition science and commercial worlds at the turn of the twentieth century generated a host of "wonder foods," food products produced through technological wizardry that promised to remedy individual and social ills alike.[38] These new products provoked wonder with visions of modernity, efficiency, and scientific progress not unlike the way quinoa harnessed dreams of a brighter future. The narratives constructed around quinoa differed from wonder food discourses, however, because the future quinoa promised was inclusive and attentive to cultural traditions, while the meanings attached to those earlier wonder foods were based in exclusionary logics of exploitation. Anthropologist Aya Kimura's analysis of the successive waves of "charismatic" nutrients in international nutrition policy is also instructive.[39] Certain nutrients, like protein or vitamin A, she argued, are not innately powerful and instead become "charismatic" only when powerful sociopolitical networks are formed around them. Like charismatic nutrients, different development paradigms have had their own miracle crops. For example, the high-yield, disease-resistant wheat varieties Norman Borlaug developed in the mid-twentieth century were projected to usher in a world without famine. The utopian quality of these visions should not obscure the fact that these crops do sometimes produce tangible and positive impacts on people's lives. Borlaug's wheat strains were adopted by millions of farmers across the world. However, the spectacle of the promised miracle can distract us from the processes, effects, and contingencies that lent the crop charisma, and it can obscure unintended consequences.

PERU'S QUINOA HEARTLAND

Get in your helicopter and come up here, if you can . . .
The hundred quinoa flowers I sowed on the summits boil in color under the sun. The black wing of the condor and the small birds have become a flower.
It's midday; I'm together with the sacred mountains: the great snow with flashes of yellow, reddish stains, throws its light to the heavens.
In this cold land, I plant quinoa of a hundred colors, of a hundred kinds, of powerful seed. The hundred colors are also my soul, my inexhaustible eyes.

—JOSÉ MARÍA ARGUEDAS, "Llamado a algunos doctores"
[Call to some professors], 1966

Nestled in the southeastern corner of the country, the Puno Region contains the entirety of Peru's portion of the Andean altiplano.[40] This enormous high-altitude plateau lies at the widest point of the Andean mountain range, which runs north-south across almost the entire western side of South America. The altiplano is an interlude in the cordillera's dramatic reliefs. To the west, the Andes plunge down to the shores of the Pacific Ocean, while to the east the mountains descend into the immense green jungles of Amazonia. The starkness of the altiplano landscape is difficult to put into words. Not only do few crops survive here; other kinds of vegetation struggle to grow in the hypoxic environment. Because of this, this massive plain is largely treeless. For most of the year, it is a vast golden expanse of flatlands punctuated by occasional ridges and low-growing shrubs. During the rainy season, the hills gain a faint green hue as the mature potato and quinoa fields add splashes of color. On a clear day, the plateau is ringed by snowcapped mountains in all directions. These mountain peaks, many of which rise over six kilometers into the sky, are considered powerful and agentive in Andean belief systems. But those who have spent their lives here will tell you the white caps are receding, and the glaciers shrink a little each year.

This is Peru's quinoa heartland. Until 2014, the region consistently produced about 80 percent of the nation's quinoa.[41] Agricultural livelihoods dominate, with over half of the "economically active" population primarily engaged in farming. Puno's farmers practice some of the highest altitude agriculture in the world. The Andean highlands have long been considered a laboratory for studying how humans survive in rugged mountain environments. These altitudinal gradients fascinated German geographer Alexander von Humboldt during his travels through the Andes at the turn of the nineteenth century. His influential cross-sectional map of Ecuador's Chimborazo volcano inspired generations of geographers, archaeologists, and anthropologists to study the "vertical" orientation of Andean social and ecological worlds. In the 1970s the Andean highlands became a hub of cultural ecology research, a paradigm that saw Andean culture as a set of adaptations to the unique high-altitude environment.[42] Numerous studies delineated ingenious adaptations to the "formidable" climate, including terracing fields strategically across an altitudinal gradient.[43] Indeed, cultural ecology's underpinning idea—that cultural traits can be in large part explained as adaptations to the environment—made the most sense in extreme environmental contexts.

Beyond understanding the altiplano's social and ecological geography, Puno's position in the nation's imagined geography shaped the stakes of the quinoa boom and bust. Historian José Luis Renique argued Puno is the "counter-story" of Peru. "It is the most Indian region. It is the other face of the *limeñizada* history of our country.[44] It's the challenge of the Peruvian republic; a borderland . . . a backyard, a burden, an obstacle for Peru's development."[45] Within Peru, ideas about development and modernity are interwoven with the imperialist logics of "the Indian problem." For centuries, many of the country's elites have framed the primary obstacle to national progress as the vaguely defined but ever powerful idea of "the Indian problem." What exactly defines the "problem," and thus the solutions to that problem, has varied from moment to moment and context to context. Sometimes the problem was framed as a uniquely "stubborn" Andean culture. At other times the problem has been a "lack of education." The element uniting these narratives is the location of blame for Peru's national situation in indigenous peoples. The rhetoric pathologizes indigeneity while obscuring structural causes for the country's striking social inequities.[46]

Peruvian geography is commonly imagined as a tripartite schema of coast/ Andes/Amazon. These regions are considered "environmental"—reflecting general patterns of landscapes and weather patterns—while also spatializing social and racial difference.[47] Throughout the Andes "'race' is regionalized, and regions are racialized."[48] The "urbanized coast, the majestic Andean mountains, and the impenetrable Amazonian forest" are not neutral descriptions of difference but manifestations of a hierarchical logic based in old colonial metrics of civilization.[49] The coast is coded as white, modern, and civilized. The Amazon is dark and backward. The Andes occupies an unsettled in-between position. The Inca Empire's capital was located in the highland city of Cusco, making the Cusco region the symbolic heir to the Inca legacy. And yet not every region in the sierra, or all residents of the highlands, have equal claim to Inca heritage. While Cusco is the undisputed hub of all things Inca, with the temples and tourist traffic to prove it, Puno occupies a rather awkward place in this three-part national imaginary. Puno is located squarely in the highlands, but it is also the only highland region in the country not fully conquered by the Inca—something evidenced today by the many speakers of Aymara (as opposed to Quechua, which was the Inca Empire's language). This peculiarity was raised many times by *limeños* surprised or preoccupied to learn I (a white North American woman) was living in Puno.[50] I was told that *puneños* were uniquely closed, very strange, and even dangerous, and this was sometimes directly attributed to the absence of the Inca's "civilizing" influence.[51] If Cusco embodies the majestic Incaic symbolism and the lucrative possibilities of commodifying cultural difference, Puno symbolizes the "Indian problem" that has defined national conversations about progress and national identity since the inception of the Peruvian nation-state.[52]

In Peru, commercializing indigenous foods presents the newest solution to the "Indian problem." José Carlos Mariátegui, Peru's most famous Marxist intellectual, sharply critiqued the "Indian problem" logic in his 1928 work, *Seven Interpretive Essays on Peruvian Reality*. He declares, "Any treatment of the problem of the Indian—written or verbal—that fails or refuses to recognize it as a socio-economic problem is but a sterile, theoretical exercise destined to be completely discredited."[53] Mariátegui understood that, at its heart, the so-called Indian problem was a mask for the continued exploitation of the masses by the elites. The gastronomic revolution has sought to "refashion" (both in terms of remaking and rendering fashionable) indigeneity for modernity by rendering social difference commodifiable (read:

lucrative). Crops like quinoa have long been seen as relics of the past and their continued use in the Andes as an emblem of the stubborn nature of Andean peasants. This attitude is apparent in decades of state-directed projects to "modernize" agriculture in the Andes through developing commercial milk production and other income-generating opportunities. Farming crops like quinoa, kañiwa, or tubers like ulluco is from a productivist mindset an illogical and very inefficient use of land. But recently these "problems" have been reframed as solutions. Andean indigeneity and the associated crops are increasingly big business.

FOLLOWING QUINOA BEYOND PUNO

Though the quinoa boom and bust's consequences for socionatural worlds in the Andean altiplano are at the heart of this tale, it is not a unidirectional story of "effects" or a top-down one of the monolithic influence of global capital. On the contrary, this is a story that transcends scales. Understanding the work that goes into making a local good into a global commodity and how this shapes socioecological dynamics in the Peruvian altiplano required me to stay rooted in place while remaining attentive to processes and interactions beyond Puno. *The Quinoa Bust* forges links between multiple vantages and actors that have at best been only partially connected in previous scholarship. I combine a firm commitment to the specificities of Puno with the requirements of multisited ethnography. In other words, I locate my research in the Peruvian altiplano while tracing out ties to individual and institutional actors—restaurateurs in Lima, agro-exporters, international development agencies, and Peru's Ministry of Agriculture—connected to but not lying "within" the altiplano.

My approach to understanding the quinoa boom and bust combined a commitment to in-depth ethnographic fieldwork among the key network of actors who formed Puno's quinoa industry with an attention to a larger web of relations beyond the region.[54] Members of one particular producer association within Puno's largest and oldest quinoa cooperative, which I call QCOOP, and a small and relatively new quinoa producer association northwest of Juliaca were generous enough to allow me to conduct participant observation during daily farm tasks and welcomed me in producer association meetings where collective challenges and internal issues came to the fore.

Many of these farmers also sat for interviews, through which I gained an understanding of their life trajectories, experiences with quinoa markets, and the evolving challenges that defined life as a quinoa farmer during the boom and bust. I also spent considerable time with management and employees of a Puno-based quinoa-buying and -processing business I call CIMA, following along on quinoa buys and technical assistance visits. Attending QCOOP's cooperative-wide events and cooperative leadership meetings along with CIMA's company meetings offered me a contrasting perspective on the rapidly shifting struggles to keep Puno's industry afloat. *Técnicos* served as key mediators between farmers and a host of development initiatives, state-funded projects, and especially buyer-processors, helping connect farmers to wider commodity circuits.[55] I followed técnicos on routine visits to farmers related to technical assistance, quinoa buys, and organic certification dealings, and I attended the various técnico-led trainings. While the técnicos with whom I worked most closely were employed by buyer-processors or the cooperative, I also built relationships with the regional agricultural board and foreign-funded development projects' técnicos. I interviewed quinoa processing plant owners at different moments during the quinoa boom and bust and also toured processing facilities. Attending the monthly Mesa Técnica de la Quinua meetings, at which all of Puno's quinoa industry actors were invited to discuss problems and ideally forge collaborations to help solve them, provided me with yet another vantage point on the industry's collective challenges and defining tensions.

The story is at once based in the Peruvian altiplano, attending to the distinct positionalities of industry actors, while also tracing the threads beyond the altiplano—especially to Lima. In the capital, I interviewed exporters, chefs, culinary influencers, academic agronomists, and policymakers in Peru's Ministry of Agriculture and Ministry of Exterior Commerce. This diverse set of actors helped illuminate the ways quinoa export was made possible by, and enrolled in, larger political, economic, cultural, and epistemological dynamics. To better understand the quinoa industry before my arrival, I spoke with people who had been involved in the industry since the 1970s and conducted archival research on development project reports from the 1990s and 2000s, activities that inform chapter 1. I also collected packaging, restaurant menus, and other material related to quinoa's marketing in Lima, which further evidenced the transformation of quinoa's symbolic importance. This work forms the basis for chapter 2.

Quinoa used to be cheap. Before 2008, its price oscillated minimally, with quinoa's farm-gate price hovering around US$0.30/kg in Peru.[56] Part of what made quinoa a dietary staple in the region was its low cost. It was a poverty food, providing economical sustenance.[57] Between 2005 and 2010, consumers outside the Andes took a decided interest in quinoa, and prices began to rise steadily. The year 2008 was often referenced as an inflection point in Puno, when an industry focused on export began to emerge, and demand outside the Andes inched up. In 2008 quinoa's price jumped almost 50 percent from a year prior, from US$0.38/kg to US$0.56/kg. In 2009 it doubled to US$1.13/kg—and this was just the beginning. The price skyrocketed in 2013 and 2014. Prices peaked at around US$3/kg in 2014—a 700 percent increase from 2005—though some farmers received as much as US$4.37 for their quinoa (see figure 17 in appendix).[58] Rising prices incentivized Puno's farmers to intensify quinoa production and attracted the attention of farmers outside the Andean highlands, who began to experiment with the now lucrative grain. (For detailed maps that display how quinoa's production geography changed in Peru over the course of the quinoa boom and bust, see www.emmamcdonell.com/quinoa-boom-bust-maps.) In Puno, quinoa production increased from 22,700 to 36,200 tons between 2008 and 2014 (60%), jumping 7,000 tons just between 2013 and 2014.[59] While domestic demand was increasing, much of this quinoa was destined for export. Peru's quinoa exports were negligible in the early 2000s, totaling just 210 tons in 2002. In 2008 they increased dramatically, to 2,100 tons, and grew each year until 2017, when they plateaued (see figure 18 in appendix). In 2014 an estimated 36,224 tons were exported from Peru, and 2016's export data shows 44,340 tons.[60] The bust, which I trace in part III of the book, was equally dramatic. Prices peaked in 2014 and began plummeting in early 2015. By 2016 many in the industry were reevaluating the risks and rewards of quinoa export, with some individuals and organizations leaving the quinoa business altogether.

This is in part a story about hope and disappointment at the margins of global capitalism. Quinoa's boom and bust is in some sense quite an ordinary, even predictable, tale. The grain's rise and fall can be read as the most recent chapter in a longer Peruvian history defined by dramatic booms and busts. Contemporary Peru has its origins as an extractive zone for the Spanish Empire. The colonial era silver booms defined the region's value to the Spanish crown, providing a massive injection of wealth to the global economy that arguably helped jump-start global capitalism.[61] The mid-nineteenth-century guano boom (and subsequent bust) reshaped global agriculture by supplying nitrates to increasingly fertilizer-dependent agricultural systems while also laying the foundation for Peru's enduring economic dependency.[62] At the turn of the twentieth century, surging demand for alpaca fiber abroad created a new class structure in the highland regions and solidified the tenant labor regime that would dominate rural Peru into the 1970s.[63] Booms in rubber, petroleum, and fish meal followed similar paths. After a prolonged civil war and economic lull, Peru's neoliberal structural adjustment in the 1990s generated unprecedented foreign investment in mineral extraction, leaving behind widespread environmental crises.[64] Neoliberal restructuring also spurred massive growth in nontraditional agricultural exports like asparagus, mango, blueberries, and roses along Peru's coast, products that are especially prone to market volatility.[65] The boom-bust cycle is the rhythm to which the "open veins of Latin America" flow.[66]

Like many economic concepts, *boom* and *bust* are subjective designations that depend on one's position within a larger web of relations. While quinoa's price plummeted in Puno, business was good on the other side of the commodity chain. Retailers in the United States saw demand continuing to grow, and they welcomed the price drop that allowed them to sell more quinoa. From this perspective six thousand kilometers away from Puno, there was no quinoa "bust." Puno's "bust" also coincided with opportunities elsewhere, as new quinoa production operations in North America and Europe raced to take advantage of growing demand. This book defines the boom and bust from the standpoint of Puno's quinoa industry.

Part of the subjective nature of booms and busts has to do with the way they are never simply "economic" phenomena. Price signals did help drive dramatic reorganizations of social and ecological relations in quinoa-producing regions. Surely the relationships between supply, demand, and the ways these factors shaped the interests, material circumstances, and daily lives of those in the quinoa industry are a central part of this story. The quinoa boom was also made possible by and itself generated dreams, hopes, and aspirations.[67] Dreams of sending children to university. Hope for a better life. It was an affective experience as much as an "economic" one.[68] While an economist might define the quinoa boom and bust around price signals, as an anthropologist, I foreground the inseparability of the economic reality of the quinoa boom from power relations, structures of meaning, and moral imperatives. This book takes an ethnographic approach to understanding the quinoa boom and bust, bringing in shifting ideas about national identity, long-term struggles between Peru's coast and highlands, and the ways changing prices altered day-to-day life. Value does not innately inhere in a given object—it must be produced through social relations. Demand shifts, supply changes, and price surges are not phenomena unto themselves; they are symptoms of complex social, political, and ecological processes. Growing Peru's quinoa exports ("increasing supply") required the formation of new social relationships, themselves laden with power asymmetries. It meant collaborating to generate and apply new sets of conventions about what defined export-quality quinoa. It demanded remaking deeply ingrained ideas about "good farming" and reworking agroecological relations to emphasize quinoa productivity over competing farm priorities.

Agricultural economists tend to focus on the macroscale impacts of commodity booms. Marc Bellemare and colleagues, for instance, sought to understand the aggregate effects of the quinoa boom on household welfare in Peru. Using national data from surveys of household consumption (as a proxy for "welfare") at different geographical levels, they sought to understand whether the boom had been a good thing or a bad thing for Peruvians. The quinoa boom, they conclude, had "not been harmful to household welfare in Peru."[69] These macro claims, however, are not only oversimplifications but are also unsatisfying, as they fail to contribute to a more nuanced understanding of everyday realities. How does a boom shape people's daily lives? Who benefits, and who loses out? What is the affective or emotional experience of a boom? What are the risks for different actors? Beyond the individual level, how does a boom impact social ties, kinship relations, and agroecologies? Pursuing a more detailed picture of *how* people navigate the rapidly changing risks and opportunities of a commodity boom illuminates the ways these booms fit into, and remake, the larger moral, symbolic, and ecological world.

Ethnographic research on commodity booms has mostly prioritized a local scale, looking into how larger market changes shape conditions in one particular area. This research is largely concerned with impacts on producer communities. Tania Li, for instance, demonstrated how the cacao boom generated local class divisions and rearranged land tenure systems in Sulawesi, Indonesia.[70] While economists likely would have found that the cacao boom generated positive effects in terms of local incomes, Li painted a multilayered picture of the boom's effects that involved a dramatically uneven distribution of access to markets and a rapid shift away from local land tenure arrangement towards an exclusionary private property mode. Similarly, James Ferguson's study of the Zambian Copper Belt tracked the gaps between stories of resource extraction as "national progress" and miners' experiences of this "progress."[71] In the agricultural sector, studies of boom markets for coffee, cacao, bananas, rubber, cloves, ginger, and vanilla have repeatedly reinforced that bonanzas are never simply "economic" in nature. They drive—and sometimes are driven by—migrations, livelihood changes, new consumption patterns, shifting land tenure arrangements, local class relations, labor arrangements, land tenure, and ecological crises.[72]

But what about the bust? With few exceptions, scholars have paid more attention to growth than decline.[73] While booms tend to be fleeting, busts often last. A longitudinal approach helps us attend to temporality. As Li showed, we need to pay attention to the variability of impacts, tracking uneven impacts among different groups and resisting imagining monolithic categories like "producers." A boom-bust is by definition a rapidly changing situation that generates uneven effects: incentives change, new actors arrive, risks and opportunities shift. The quinoa case reveals that the winners at the onset of the boom are not always the winners at its apex, nor at its nadir. A longitudinal frame leads us beyond questions of consequences for local producers. I am deeply concerned with impacts, and indeed much of the book emphasizes those impacts. But this book expands the scope of analysis in time and space to consider how the quinoa boom and bust was produced within and through larger processes and patterns.

The Quinoa Bust tracks a boom-bust *trajectory*, analyzing the broader arc of a boom and bust. When I began this project in 2013, I believed I was studying a commodity boom. Two years later, it became clear that I was investigating a boom-bust trajectory. I conducted my fieldwork over four separate research trips between 2014 and 2018, totaling eighteen months. Each of these data collection trips took place at a different moment along quinoa's boom-bust arc. The longitudinal nature of the project helps us see not a snapshot, but a portrait evolving over time. The rapidly changing nature of the quinoa industry in Puno made this fieldwork especially challenging. For example, CIMA, the organization with which I had built trust and rapport in 2014 and 2015, was crumbling by mid-2016, a dynamic that undermined my access to the day-to-day operations. These kinds of changes meant that the book could not (indeed, does not) provide a clean, linear depiction of a select group of people over a defined unit of time. Instead, it focuses on a dynamic assemblage of actors whose daily tasks, anxieties, and interests shift.[74] The changing "cast" reflects the unstable nature of fortunes during the quinoa boom and bust. The form and structure of the book are thus an intentional result of my particular ethnographic approach, which reflects the volatility of quinoa's varied entanglements.

PUTTING COMMODITY CHAINS IN CONTEXT

In 1977 Terrence Hopkins and Immanuel Wallerstein developed the commodity chain concept as part of their larger effort to challenge the then-dominant modernization theory.[75] Modernization theorists posited that countries' economies were at different stages of development, some more and some less "developed," which explained larger inequalities among them. Hopkins and Wallerstein formed part of a growing chorus of modernization theory critics who argued that this way of understanding the world fundamentally misrecognizes what is an interrelated "world system" as many detached, individual national economies. World-system theory sees the world as a stratified and interconnected world *system* that at once relies on and reproduces structural inequalities. Countries like Peru are not "underdeveloped" and instead are located in a position of structural dependency; they are being exploited. The commodity chain concept was meant to help operationalize this research agenda, providing a tool to provide insight into how, in practice, a stratified world system was reproduced in specific industries. For Hopkins and Wallerstein, a commodity chain was "a network of labor and production processes whose end result is a finished commodity," a sometimes long and winding chain that linked producers on one end to distant consumers on the other.[76]

Political and economic action do not just occur at the ends of the chain as in many economic models (e.g., producers who create supply and consumers who generate demand) but also at various points along the chain. While Hopkins and Wallerstein used the commodity chain to understand the historical development of capitalism, some scholars have adapted the chain metaphor to understand today's global economy. Sociologist Gary Gereffi pioneered the *global* commodity chain approach, which draws on organizational sociology and focuses on the "inter-firm" relationships that link manufacturers, suppliers, and subcontractors to each other and to global markets.[77] Gereffi used this concept to interrogate how, in today's complex and sprawling global economy, goods like clothing and computers are made and marketed.[78] Another adaptation of the commodity chain is the global *value* chain approach, which draws on international business literature and transaction cost economics. This model envisions a chain in which value is added to a commodity at each step, a framing that has helped generate typologies of different kinds of value chains (e.g., bottom-up versus top-down).[79] These approaches have provided policy-relevant insights into how certain firms can be made more competitive or even come to dominate a given sector. But they also offer a narrower view that prioritizes "internal" chain dynamics and generates a model of commodities disembedded from the political economies, historical processes, institutional and regulatory factors, social and cultural systems, and physical landscapes that shape them.[80]

Building on these approaches, a growing number of scholars are working to reorient attention to the ways these chains are "articulated within and through the larger social, cultural and political-economic environments in which they operate."[81] Sociologist Jennifer Bair, for instance, has suggested that scholars of global commodity chains focus on "the factors external to chains that shape their geography and configuration, and strongly affect the extent to which different actors benefit from participation in them."[82] Commodity chains are not circumscribed patterns of exchange but culturally mediated "sites of encounter" that are shaped by broader social histories and relations of power.[83] The global circulation of commodities requires social actors to negotiate commodities' economic values and to negotiate distinct cultural and social meanings.[84] Quinoa's commercialization was neither a smooth nor a linear transition from local good to global commodity, but rather an uneven process that emerged at the "sticky materialities of practical encounters" between diversely positioned people, histories, and ecological realities, and that in turn, reworked these same relationships.[85] Responding to Bair's call for deeper understandings of the contextual factors that shape commodity chains, the locus of action in this book is the specific set of encounters that constituted Puno's quinoa industry rather than the more obscure global marketplace.

Centering regional dynamics made clear the oversimplifications and erasures that a more standard global commodity chain analysis of quinoa would have generated.[86] Quinoa produced in Puno travels through many sometimes obscure market channels; it is an industry characterized by multiple intermediaries. Adding to this complexity, farmers tend to sell small amounts of quinoa at a time and may sell to multiple different intermediaries. Some farmers sell to local companies with processing plants, which in turn may sell to brokers or directly to agroexporters. These buyers often have multiple clients and channel some of their quinoa toward export and some into domestic markets. Farmers also sell to small-scale *acopiadores*, or collectors, who buy directly at the farm or collect quinoa in local markets and then channel it into larger urban markets or elsewhere.[87] Some farmers are organized into cooperatives, which buy their quinoa. These cooperatives generally sell to international clients. Some of Puno's quinoa is trafficked across the nearby border with Bolivia, though more Bolivian quinoa comes in illegally to Peru and enters Puno's quinoa stocks as "Peruvian quinoa." One study estimated that in 2012 almost a quarter of Peru's total quinoa production was actually grown in Bolivia, then smuggled into and commercialized in Peru.[88] Zooming in on the regional dynamics reveals that there is no single "quinoa commodity chain" from Puno. Instead, quinoa follows a dizzying array of sometimes circuitous routes on its journey from farm to table.

This book attends to quinoa's multiple market channels and chains while emphasizing the interests, aims, and limitations of regional actors—traders, nongovernmental organization (NGO) staffers, state agency officials, and others. A more traditional commodity chain analysis might follow quinoa's path from a farm in Peru to a distant table in North America, taking note of the steps along the way and relationships between these various actors who "transform" quinoa. This attention to regional dynamics also reveals the critical roles actors who do not figure into formal commodity chain analyses play in mediating and creating quinoa's value. While commodity chain models focus on the actors who "transform" the good between production and consumption (e.g., processors, exporters, retailers), a host of figures also contributed to the rearticulation of quinoa's value: chefs in Lima, who used their cultural capital to disseminate new narratives about the grain; técnicos, who guided the reorientation of agroecologies toward quinoa export; and scientists, who provided evidence for quinoa's utility and advocated for rethinking neglected crops. The formal "transformation" of quinoa on its way to consumers is critical to how a local staple crop is made into a global commodity, but so too are the roles played by chefs, técnicos, and scientists.

My framing centers not only the essential relationship *building* that made possible Puno's quinoa export industry during the boom, but also the processes of rupture and disconnection that undid many of these relationships during the bust. Though literature on commodity chains has overwhelmingly emphasized incorporation, understanding how actors and or entire regions are expelled from commodity circuits can help us better understand how global commodity chains reproduce uneven geographies.[89] This is a tale of inclusion: the inclusion of new farmers in global commodity chains and the formation of relationships that constituted the fledgling quinoa export industry. But it is simultaneously one of exclusion: how new quality standards pushed some farmers out of quinoa export and how an increasingly competitive global quinoa market sidelined Puno's industry.

The Quinoa Bust bridges work that understands capitalist processes in general and commodity chains in particular as disjunctive, culturally embedded practices *and* a long tradition in anthropology of food that focuses on a single global food commodity, to provide insight into larger cultural, political, and economic processes. Following in the footsteps of Sidney Mintz's classic analysis of sugar in *Sweetness and Power*, this book is at once both about quinoa and not only about quinoa.[90] Quinoa is the object of inquiry, *and* it is a tool to elucidate relationships between race/racism, coloniality, commercial processes, international development paradigms, and the encompassing agrifood system.

ORGANIZATION OF THE BOOK

Each chapter in *The Quinoa Bust* focuses on a distinctive moment and unique social and ecological conjuncture in the quinoa boom-bust trajectory. The first two chapters track the social, political, and symbolic work that went into reimagining quinoa as a development miracle crop and a symbol of Peruvian identity. In part I, chapter 1 traces the longer history of efforts to define and realize quinoa's "potential" over the course of the twentieth century. It analyzes the roles nutrition scientists, agronomists, and development practitioners played in enrolling quinoa in a set of larger institutional networks and constructing compelling stories about quinoa's significance that, taken together, helped produce quinoa as a development miracle crop. This chapter draws on the idea of the boundary object—a concept from science and technology studies originally used to study scientific collaboration—to analyze the ways distinct and sometimes incompatible visions for quinoa's future intermingled. Chapter 2 examines the symbolic work that went into repackaging quinoa for new eaters, especially middle- and upper-class audiences within the Andes. Revalorizing a so-called Indian food was an innovative attempt to subvert neocolonial culinary hierarchies. But this process also reproduced some of those same radicalized structures of power. Making quinoa palatable to new audiences required creating new narratives about the grain and erasing old ones. This chapter develops the concept of culinary bioprospecting and shows how prominent chefs, marketing agencies, and the Peruvian state generated and disseminated new narratives about quinoa that collectively distanced the grain from living indigenous peoples.

Part II positions the analysis more squarely in Puno. These chapters track the transformation of socioecological landscapes that the quinoa bonanza (2013–15) set in motion. Chapter 3 analyzes quinoa's commercialization in Puno as a contested ecological and political project. Chapter 4 foregrounds the role quality standards played in facilitating quinoa's circulation beyond the region. Drawing on anthropologist Tania Li's idea of "rendering technical," I demonstrate how quality standards transformed power struggles into neutral questions of grain quality, though never completely.

Part III charts the quinoa bust, following the foreclosure of opportunities, the rupturing of relationships, and attempts to salvage what remained of Puno's promise. Chapter 5 tracks how plummeting price and growing competition reshaped the power dynamics animating Puno's quinoa industry. Chapter 6 explores how secrecy and distrust reverberated along the commodity chain in the wake of scandals around toxic residues on Peruvian quinoa, intensifying existing frictions and power asymmetries. During the quinoa boom, quality standards were used to collapse difference—to transform diverse quinoa varieties into one uniform "golden stream." Making quinoa from one farm identical with that of another—one region mixable with that of another—was the goal. With the onset of the bust, a number of actors involved in Puno's quinoa industry sought to employ standards for the opposite purpose—to differentiate Puno's quinoa from the common "*quinua commodity*." Chapter 7 explores how industry actors with competing interests attempted but failed to differentiate Puno's quinoa from the increasingly homogenous "commodity quinoa" *and* from other differentiation projects, like the Bolivian state's effort to brand Quinua Real (Royal Quinoa).

PART ONE

Miracle Crop

ONE

Reimagining the Future of a Neglected Crop

IN 1918 the *Bulletin of the Pan American Union* published a feature article about a little-known South American grain. Sandwiched between an obituary for "the patriarch of Chilean diplomats" and a story lauding the growth of copper mining in the Americas, "Quinoa: A South American Cereal" introduced readers to an "exceedingly hardy" crop that had been "almost completely ignored by our modern alimentary experts." Staff writer Edward Albes, who primarily wrote the *Bulletin*'s city profiles, compared quinoa to tomatoes and potatoes, expressing bewilderment about why such a useful crop as quinoa would have received so little attention outside the Andes: "How it happens that the white man has taken so kindly to some of these [native American crops] and spread their use all over the world, while others have been almost entirely neglected, is something of a mystery."[1]

Albes marveled at quinoa's sturdiness in the high Andean climate and the results of the first study of quinoa's nutritional composition. But he lamented the current state of affairs: "Quinoa is still being cultivated in the countries to which it is indigenous in much the same primitive manner employed by the Indians when the Spaniards conquered the Inca. The surface of the ground is scratched over with a rude substitute for a plow, and the seed scattered broadcast and lightly covered with a layer of the soil."[2] In the hands of "the natives," in his view, quinoa's potential was not being realized.[3]

Modern science, Albes suggested, could unlock quinoa's possibilities. He urged "the white man" to turn his attention to the "ancient crop," reasoning that, as was the case in the improvement of "Indian corn," scientific techniques applied to quinoa "may produce results fully as wonderful." While Albes envisioned a bright future for quinoa as a major global crop, in the immediate term he suggested that quinoa flour could provide a much sought after substitute for wheat flour to ease World War I's strain on the North American wheat supply.[4] "The world is clamoring for additions to its cereal foods," he declared, urging researchers to direct their energies to improving quinoa and introducing the grain to North America and Europe in order to fully harness quinoa's potential.[5]

While Albes envisioned quinoa primarily as a wartime substitute for wheat, in the century that followed his article, development practitioners, state bureaucrats, entrepreneurs, nutritionists, and agronomists came to imagine quinoa as a solution to myriad social, ecological, and economic problems. During that time, quinoa gained a small but dedicated following of advocates who saw the grain as a miracle crop that could help solve issues increasingly framed as problems of "underdevelopment." Some saw quinoa as an answer to malnutrition in the Andes. Others imagined a global hunger curative that could alleviate food insecurity outside the region. Toward the end of the twentieth century, a growing number of experts envisioned a lucrative export crop that could relieve Andean poverty, and in the early twenty-first century, quinoa gained acclaim as a climate change adaptation crop that might keep agriculture viable in increasingly arid regions across the world. A one-size-fits-all development miracle crop, quinoa seemed capable of solving myriad complex development dilemmas. While numerous development actors saw unrealized potential in quinoa, what exactly that potential was—what problems it ought to solve—varied widely.

This chapter traces the historical construction of quinoa as a development miracle crop. It examines the multiple "promissory narratives" that emerged over the course of the twentieth and early twenty-first centuries that imagined quinoa as a curative for a host of social, economic, and ecological problems.[6] These narratives of possibility helped mobilize the formation of a sociotechnical network surrounding the grain that in turn made possible quinoa's changing status. New visions of quinoa's potential did not replace existing visions. They coexisted, at times awkwardly, and built upon each other in complicated ways.[7] Critically, some visions of quinoa's potential were incompatible. For instance, if quinoa were to solve malnutrition in Andean countries, its price would need to be low enough that urban poor people could afford to buy it. For quinoa to alleviate poverty among small farmers in the Andes as a high-value export crop, the price would need to be high. And if farmers in the highlands were to earn sufficient income from quinoa production, expanding production outside the Andes in the name of climate change adaptation would likely undermine this goal, foreclosing Andean farmers' competitive advantage in global markets.

Miracle crops follow what Julie Guthman calls a "solutionist logic," wherein the solution itself precedes the search for an applicable problem.[8] Anthropologists who study international development have long argued that the fetishization of clean, technical, charismatic, and commodifiable "solutions," at the expense of deep understanding of problems, is a hallmark of international development work.[9] A discrete set of vetted solutions appear as the answers to wide-ranging problems in drastically different contexts. The miracle crop is a particularly potent example of solutionism because of the simple curative metaphor it invokes. Miracle food and miracle crop fantasies reify conceptions of malnutrition as a biomedical pathology in need of a nutritional antidote.[10] They promote an illusion that malnutrition is solvable without disturbing the structures of power that produce undernourished bodies. This is the key distinction between the superfood and the miracle food: one purports to act on the individual (consumer) body, and the other promises change to the social body.[11] Quinoa's story and the assemblages that have produced it as a miracle crop in different times and places are unique. Yet quinoa also represents one case in a longer history of cycles of development miracle foods, from fish flour and brewer's yeast to Plumpynut® and kuli kuli bars.[12] The miracle *crop* expands this logic beyond nutrition (i.e., miracle *foods*) to include agronomic variables and in doing so incorporates a larger array of development problems. Solving problems like malnutrition, poverty, and climate change, it seems, does not demand overhauling power structures or controversial policy interventions but instead requires the right crop.

Albes's article is noteworthy as one of the first English-language articles on quinoa with an audience beyond the Andes *and* for the way it articulates what would become a dominant theme in quinoa's construction as a miracle crop: a celebration of quinoa's potential to solve world problems alongside a lament of its neglect.[13] Quinoa promotors with disparate ideas about the specifics of the grain's potential and conflicting worldviews came together around a common belief in quinoa's lamentable underuse and its miraculous potential. This sense of mission helped form the set of partially connected sociopolitical networks made this crop into a miracle crop.[14] The idea that quinoa had profound unrealized possibilities helped build enthusiasm for quinoa's future among disparate individuals and organizations who did not all actually see quinoa's future similarly. This belief in unrealized potential made quinoa into a boundary object that allowed communities of practice with disparate interests and worldviews to collaborate across difference. Boundary objects are "simultaneously concrete and abstract, specific and general, conventionalized and customized" such that they facilitate translation across multiple social worlds.[15] It is the vagueness of boundary objects, their plasticity and openness to interpretation, that makes them useful for connection building. Yet this boundary object quality also stymied discussion of the incompatibilities between the various visions of quinoa's future.

Boundary objects are central to international development work. While science studies scholars Susan Star and James Griesemer developed the concept to analyze how scientists with divergent viewpoints develop scientific agreement, international development work requires similar kinds of collaboration and consensus building. Actors from disparate social worlds often work together on "projects" and must come to rough agreements about needs and priorities. Boundary objects facilitate this translational work. Miracle crops are especially potent boundary objects because of their future orientation and their physical tangibility. They help generate momentum by building expectations and pointing toward a better future, though what that future will be is ultimately up to interpretation. And while a miracle crop is an idea, a story, it also appears as a very real and tangible "thing" that we can hold in our hands.

While subsequent chapters primarily focus on the quinoa boom-bust period in Peru generally and Puno specifically, this chapter positions the boom-bust within quinoa's longer history as an object of interest for scientists and development experts. It traces the growth of an international community of quinoa boosters and analyzes the multiple, often conflicting, narratives of potential that animated their interest in the grain. Unlike later chapters, this one draws primarily on analysis of historical documents and reports from development institutions rather than firsthand ethnographic accounts. The first section tracks the growing interest in quinoa among a small group of vanguardist Andean nutrition scientists and agronomists in the early twentieth century. Results of the first studies of quinoa's nutritional content surprised researchers who were steeped in a dietary imaginary that left the nutritional supremacy of wheat, milk, and eggs unquestioned. While early advocates envisioned a bright future for quinoa, the lack of an existing narrative slot for quinoa or powerful sociopolitical networks surrounding it prevented the grain from gaining much traction outside the Andes until decades later. The next section traces the rise of the neglected and underutilized species discourse, one of the alternative development models that arose in the 1970s and 1980s. Among a small number of progressive US-based development experts, quinoa came to be understood as one of a number of neglected crops with untapped potential to solve development problems. While there was consensus that quinoa was *under*utilized, there was no agreement about the precise contours of the grain's potential, that is, which problems quinoa should remedy. Instead, different individual and institutional actors had disparate views of quinoa's potential as a development tool. The next four sections tease out the dominant narratives of quinoa as development solution: quinoa as malnutrition palliative in the Andes, quinoa as global hunger curative, quinoa as poverty alleviation in the Andes, and quinoa as climate change adaptation tool. While these visions conflicted in some ways, enthusiasm about quinoa's potential—its boundary object quality—obscured contradictions. The final section explores the UN International Year of Quinoa as the moment when quinoa's boundary object status peaked and then began to disintegrate as contradictions between visions of quinoa's future became more visible.

EARLY INTEREST IN A "PRIMITIVE GRAIN"

While nutrition science and agronomy saw major advances in the nineteenth century, these fields mostly ignored crops like quinoa. At the time, agronomists focused their attention on finding ways to cultivate existing commercial crops more rationally. Grain research centered around the undisputed reigning cereal crops (wheat, maize, and rice). Meanwhile, nutrition scientists worked to delineate the basic nutritional components of foods common in the dairy-laden and wheat-based Western diet, a diet presumed to be far superior to all others, let alone the eating practices of indigenous South Americans.[16] And while nutritional magic bullets did loom large in the nineteenth-century nutritional imaginary, it was believed that these foods would come about through technological wizardry, certainly not from the diets of indigenous peoples.[17] Within this context, it made little sense to study a crop produced and consumed almost exclusively by indigenous Andeans. By definition, so-called Indian foods were connected to the past, not the future.

Quinoa began to capture the interest of a handful of unconventional Andean nutrition scientists in the early twentieth century. Bolivian researchers conducted the first study of quinoa's nutritional content in the 1910s, but it wasn't until the 1930s and 1940s that quinoa caught the attention of more researchers.[18] Two influential studies found quinoa to be surprisingly nutritious. Argentine researchers found bread made from a mix of wheat and quinoa flour to be more nutritious than wheat bread.[19] Studies conducted in Peru in the 1940s documented quinoa's amino acid profile, demonstrating the high protein quality in the grain even when compared to dairy products.[20] Bolivian agricultural researcher Jorge Alcázar, who chaired the Bolivian delegation at the UN's 1948 conference on nutrition in Latin America, stated that research on quinoa "consistently gave the most flattering results." Quinoa, he declared, "is a top quality cereal, quite superior to wheat, corn and barley."[21]

It's difficult to exaggerate the degree to which these findings went against nutrition science dogma at the time. The nutritional supremacy of milk and wheat were taken for granted as common sense. Ideas about proper diets in Latin America had been used to justify social hierarchies since colonial times: it was of course wheat-eating Europeans who ruled the world, leading some to wonder whether their "superiority" stemmed in part from their milk- and wheat-based diets.[22] Historian Rachael Laudan has contended that milk and wheat were the quintessential foods of European empire in the twentieth century, making them yardsticks from which to measure the value of other foods.[23] This was a time when Wonder Bread was considered the pinnacle of nutritional innovation, and milk was "nature's perfect food."[24] Finding a little-known grain consumed by indigenous Andeans with protein quality akin to that of milk and eggs that was overall nutritionally far superior to the dominant grain crops contradicted basic tenets of the mid-twentieth-century nutritional imaginary. While one might assume that the results of these studies would quickly turn quinoa into an international nutritional sensation, only a small community of mostly Andean researchers were paying attention. The assumed superiority of the "Western diet" and the emphasis on expanding this diet globally meant there was no existing narrative frame that quinoa could fit into.[25]

In 1954 Carlos Collazos, head of Peru's Ministry of Health and Social Assistance Nutrition Department, penned an article called "The Indian Diet." In it, Collazos laid out what he saw as a puzzle: "[Peruvian] Indians have violated all nutritional laws" and yet "the species" had not gone extinct.[26] The reason, he argued, was quinoa. Collazos suggested that native populations in the high Andes had survived largely because they ate quinoa: "The diet of the Peruvian Indian is very poor according to modern standards. The high biological value of quinoa seeds and a possible adaption mechanism to low protein intake are proposed as possible explanations for the survival of the population on the mentioned diet."[27] A nutrition scientist who conducted early studies of quinoa's nutritional content, Collazos struggled to reconcile his low regard for living indigenous populations with the impressive characteristics of their staple grain. He resolved the dissonance between his growing esteem for quinoa and his disdain for "Indians" by emphasizing quinoa's role in keeping indigenous populations alive while ignoring the role they played in domesticating, cultivating, and valuing the crop. Early quinoa researchers in the Andes wrestled with deep-seated prejudices as the results of their studies increasingly revealed quinoa to be an excellent source of nutrition. Notably, many of these Andean nutrition scientists and agronomists became passionate advocates for quinoa as a solution to malnutrition in the Andes.

By the late 1960s, a robust enough Andean scientific community had coalesced around quinoa to warrant a conference. The first event to convene researchers working specifically on quinoa took place in Puno, Peru, in 1968. The Chenopod Convention brought together researchers from Peru and Bolivia who had studied the crop.[28] The goal was to develop a collective research agenda focused on improving basic knowledge about quinoa's biological and nutritional characteristics and to forge institutional collaborations to carry out this work.[29] At the same time, attendees sought to create strategies to promote quinoa's potential as a tool to combat malnutrition in the Andes. At a time when fortifying staple foods and increasing the productivity of wheat, rice, and corn were seen as the solutions to malnutrition in poor countries, a scientific meeting about a crop seen by many in the Andes as an "Indian food" was progressive if not radical.[30]

Scientific interest in quinoa gradually expanded outside the Andes through research collaborations between Andean and US-based scientists. In the 1940s the US National Research Council (NRC) funded a collaboration between Peruvian scientists and researchers at Harvard.[31] The US Department of Agriculture also funded (unsuccessful) experimental quinoa plots in Colorado.[32] Yet the larger international development community was slow to take notice, and quinoa research remained a primarily Andean affair.

Even with a growing body of research demonstrating the grain's unique agronomic and nutritional features, the grain's role was unclear in the midtwentieth-century's development zeitgeist. Between World War II and the 1980s, agricultural development work in so-called developing countries revolved around a model that would come to be called the green revolution. This paradigm focused on breeding "improved" versions of major commodity crops, disseminating these seeds and associated "technology packets" (fertilizers and pesticides) to farmers across the world, and introducing yield-centric agricultural management practices. The miracle crops of that era were hybridized varieties of corn and wheat, which would indeed lead to dramatic increases in agricultural productivity across the globe but also generated a host of other social and environmental effects.[33] Quinoa did not appear as a solution within this framing of "development problems" because there was no existing narrative into which a crop like quinoa could be inserted. At the time, the future of food appeared to lie in science, technology, and innovation. Native crops without strong markets were precisely the kind of crop species the development apparatus was looking to replace.

THE RISE OF THE NEGLECTED
AND UNDERUTILIZED SPECIES

Quinoa began to garner more attention outside the Andes when a group of mostly North American vanguardist development experts frustrated with the failures of the green revolution created the idea of the neglected crop.[34] In the early 1970s the NRC convened an ad hoc panel of US-based researchers, including development practitioners, botanists, pharmaceutical researchers, and biochemists, who shared concerns about the dominant agricultural development model and its reliance on a small number of species. In 1975 they published *Underexploited Tropical Plants with Promising Economic Value*, an influential book that introduced the concept of the underexploited species. The book opened by declaring that the reliance on a limited number of crop species was not only misguided; it begged a catastrophe of epic proportions: "Throughout human history man has used some 3,000 plant species for food. . . . But over the centuries the tendency has been to concentrate on fewer and fewer."[35] Noting that most of the human population is fed by a mere twenty crops, the authors declared that these species are "the main bulwark between mankind and starvation."[36] They began with a familiar neo-Malthusian crisis narrative commonly invoked to justify the green revolution that depicted an exploding global population and insufficient food supply. But they arrived at a novel solution, arguing that scientists should be focusing less on rice and wheat and instead on "neglected"

FIGURE 3. Cover of *Underexploited Tropical Plants with Promising Economic Value* (1975). *Source:* National Academy of Sciences.

or "underexploited" species that "show promise for improving the quality of life in tropical areas."[37] These were plants that had received little prior attention from scientific researchers and the international development community but that appeared to have substantial potential to solve development problems.[38]

For these reformists the same agricultural systems that the green revolution was destroying in the name of progress contained the key to humanity's survival. Indigenous farming landscapes were not primitive vestiges of a bygone era but critical reservoirs of underexploited plants. The underexploited species campaign critiqued the ways understandings of the world born from European colonialism continued to shape food systems and influence research priorities in the late twentieth century. Advocates saw the dominance of certain crop species as arbitrary in agronomic terms. For them, a small number of crops dominated agricultural research because of prejudice: "The apparent advantages of staple plants over minor tropical plants often result only from the disproportionate research attention they have been given. Many indigenous species may possess equal merit, but were disregarded during the colonial era when consumer demands in European countries largely determined the cultivation (and research) priorities in tropical agriculture."[39]

Hybrid maize and high-yielding wheat varieties had social capital, whereas neglected crops by definition lacked powerful sociopolitical networks. The compelling narrative of the neglected crop helped quinoa gain some traction among development experts. Emphasizing the possibility that these crops would be lost forever generated a moral imperative to study quinoa's possibilities.

While the NRC book featured thirty-six underexploited plants, the authors saw quinoa as a particularly "striking case." Emphasizing its neglect, they suggested that quinoa "is virtually unknown outside the Andes" despite being "one of the most productive sources of plant protein." They also suggested that the agronomy of quinoa had "advanced little in the past four centuries," blaming this on "the Spanish," who focused agricultural research only on wheat and barley. Neglected crop advocates heralded crops devalued in colonialist and developmentalist social and agricultural hierarchies as part of the future. In doing so, they implicitly questioned the legitimacy of the very systems that led to the devaluation ("disappearance") of these crops and inverted the previous linkage of non-Western ways of being with the past.[40]

The idea was that more research—more bioprospecting—would yield crop species equipped to solve the twin issues of increasingly vulnerable monocultural agricultural systems and food shortages that the authors saw as defining global dilemmas. "Man has only just begun to take stock of the chemical and genetic possibilities in the plant kingdom," and the solutions to problems like malnutrition and poverty may lie in crops that researchers knew little about. The authors called for reorienting research priorities away from overstudied plants like wheat and focusing instead on understudied plants: "Now we must scrutinize the thousands of plant species, many of which are still untested and some as yet unidentified."[41] The authors insisted that this matter was pressing, as these plants would "otherwise become extinct."[42] In other words, we might find critical antidotes to development ills that high-yield varieties had not provided, but only if we acted fast.[43] Generating this fear of loss and endangerment activated potentiality, creating a sense of urgency around cataloging these crops.[44]

Collecting these plants was only the beginning. While neglected species advocates marveled at the plants' attributes, they considered them insufficient in their current states. Crops like quinoa needed to be improved to reach their potential. "The agronomy of quinua has advanced little in the past four centuries," declared the authors of the 1975 NRC volume, calling for North American researchers to study the grain and to develop quinoa breeding programs.[45] They envisioned quinoa as a sort of raw material with potential that North American researchers could unlock.

Calling a crop "neglected" begs some questions: neglected by whom? And what utility was not being employed sufficiently? The claim that quinoa was neglected would puzzle anyone familiar with Andean foodways, given that the grain comprises a core element of Andean diets and millions of people eat it daily. The NRC report authors suggested at one point that quinoa was "eventually displaced by" European crops but later in the volume admitted that quinoa remains a staple for millions.[46] In the 1989 volume *Lost Crops of the Incas: Little Known Plants with Promise for Worldwide Cultivation*, the authors specified that the featured crops were "not truly lost" and instead asserted that "international science and people outside the Andes" had overlooked them.[47] Yet framing these crops as underutilized made evident that quinoa's existing use as an Andean staple food did not really count. As a dietary staple for Andean populations, quinoa was not reaching its full potential.

The underexploited plants discourse gained some traction in progressive agricultural development circles in the 1980s, consolidating under the concept of the "neglected and underutilized species" (NUS). The NUS model was one of several emergent alternative approaches to development that attempted to address growing concerns that development had wrought environmental destruction and ignored local perspectives. The model caught on amid mounting worry about biodiversity loss and growing concern about the degree to which the green revolution's impacts on local food systems had been positive. As the discourse spread into US-based development institutions and research networks across the "developing world," a community of researchers began to think about their research through this framework by the mid-1980s. For instance, in 1986 the University of Minnesota Agricultural Experiment Station published a report titled "Amaranth, Quinoa, Ragi, Tef, and Niger: Tiny Seeds of Ancient History and Modern Interest"—a convergence of crops that only makes sense if one sees them as having in common a quality of underutilization.[48] That same year, the FAO organized a meeting about underexploited Andean crops of nutritional value in Santiago, Chile, and by 1988 the International Centre for Underutilized Crops (ICUC) was established in London.[49] In 1998 Purdue University began hosting a semiannual symposium on "new crops," at which in 1995 participants would enjoy a banquet "prepared entirely from new crops, including ostrich, quinoa, buckwheat, kiwi fruit, Indiana duck, pearl millet, tempeh (a soy-based food similar to tofu) and new varieties of mushrooms."[50]

NUS researchers identified the Andean region as a hotbed. Just a year after the National Academy of Sciences's 1989 publication of *Lost Crops of the Incas*, the FAO and Peruvian agronomist Mario Tapia published *Underexploited Andean Crops and Their Contribution to Nutrition*, which made the case for the potential of quinoa and a handful of other Andean crops.[51] By the end of the decade, the NUS discourse was mainstream enough to warrant the attention of Norman Borlaug, the agricultural scientist who in 1970 had won a Nobel Prize for developing the high-yield dwarf wheat that helped spark the green revolution. Commenting on the prospect of quinoa and other "lost crops of the Incas" in a 1989 *New York Times* article, he said, "'I think they're fascinating, myself. . . . Given reasonable research . . . [some of these plants] might turn up to have a lot of potential."[52]

But what exactly was the promise of these crops? If they were *underex-ploited*, what would it look like to properly exploit their potential? The early NUS texts were unclear and at times contradictory. In *Underexploited Tropical Plants with Promising Economic Value*, quinoa was at once pitched as underutilized for income generation in developing countries (i.e., a potential export crop), malnutrition alleviation in the Andes, and global hunger relief.

The authors agreed that quinoa was not sufficiently exploited, but they had multiple visions of quinoa's prospects. Quinoa's potential was open to interpretation, allowing diverse constituencies to get behind its promotion. Quinoa's framing as a neglected and underutilized crop—the vagueness of its proclaimed development *potential* underutilization implied—allowed stories about its development applications to multiply.

While Andean researchers had been studying quinoa for decades, the NUS discourse helped quinoa attract the attention of development experts and researchers outside the Andes. The compelling tale of neglect and potential motivated the formation of a nascent international network of quinoa advocates and generated a sense of urgency for research on the grain. Enthusiasm for quinoa's potential as a development tool brought together expert communities who usually operated in separate institutional realms: nutrition scientists, agronomists, entrepreneurs, biodiversity experts, rural development experts, Latin America–oriented development organizations like the Inter-American Development Fund, US-based research institutions like the NRC, and globally oriented ones like Biodiversity International. And beyond quinoa, the story created a meaningful narrative slot that myriad species across the world could fit into, from millet varieties and amaranth to moringa trees. Though the NUS discourse never became dominant in development circles, it helped quinoa gain nascent charisma as a development miracle crop.

A HOMEGROWN PROTEIN: QUINOA AS MALNUTRITION PALLIATIVE IN THE ANDES

In 1948 the recently formed FAO held a special conference on the status of nutrition in Latin America in Montevideo, Uruguay. At the conference, a grain barely recognized outside the Andes garnered surprising attention. "Latin Nations See New Food in Quinoa" announced a *New York Times* report on the event. In response to the "enormous areas of hunger in South America" revealed at the conference, the Bolivian delegation urged UN officials to create a "scientific mission" to study quinoa's "possibilities."[53] The possibilities they envisioned were rather specific. "It [is] conceivable that some day quinoa, through modern cultivation, might occupy a major role in feeding the Upland Indians, whose needs are among the greatest in the Americas," continued the article.[54]

The concept and practice of international development consolidated after World War II largely around the issue of hunger.[55] Though colonial malnutrition had been "discovered" between the world wars, during the 1940s and 1950s reports surfaced documenting startling numbers of hungry individuals in areas of the world increasingly understood as "underdeveloped." Latin America at large and the high Andes in particular came to be problematized as malnourished regions in need of intervention.[56] Experts diagnosed the nutrition problem in the high Andes as a protein issue. Eduardo Viñas, one of the first Peruvian nutrition scientists to study quinoa, suggested that the Andean population's "nutritional deficiencies and particularly the ingestion of protein substances are always so notorious." He called for the Peruvian government to disseminate "propaganda of quinoa's nutritional virtues" and to promote quinoa production and consumption as official policy.[57] In an article in *Nature* published two decades later, Edward Weber, the senior program officer for the Latin American International Development Research Centre's regional office in Bogotá, also noted an "acute shortage of locally produced food protein" in the high Andes and suggested quinoa was the answer.[58]

The prevailing strategies for addressing malnutrition in the mid-twentieth century, such as food fortification, food aid, and the green revolution, all generated dependence on outside experts and institutions.[59] Quinoa, by contrast, presented a homegrown solution to the region's malnutrition. Since the earliest accounts of quinoa's nutritional prowess, quinoa promoters imagined the grain as a uniquely Andean tool to combat the region's malnutrition. It attracted the attention of Andean researchers and development experts precisely because it did not originate outside South America, as did food aid and fortified foods, and quinoa use did not involve overhauling existing agricultural systems. Yet the same characteristics that appealed to some prevented quinoa from taking on a prominent role as a tool for alleviating malnutrition in the region until much later.

This idea of a uniquely Andean grain interested Peru's and Bolivia's leftist governments in the 1970s. This was the heyday of import substitution industrialization, an economic model that sought to reduce dependence on imports from abroad. In Peru, Juan Velasco Alvarado's presidential administration blamed wheat imports from the United States for undermining Andean food systems and tasked the Ministry of Agriculture with studying the prospects for increasing quinoa production in the name of alleviating malnutrition.[60] In neighboring Bolivia, Hugo Banzer's administration passed a law in 1974 obligating bread flours to contain a minimum of 5 percent quinoa flour.[61] While bolstering quinoa production and consumption made some sense amid the interest in Andean self-sufficiency that characterized that decade, these efforts proved ineffective. Banzer's flour requirement was never enforced, and Peru's Ministry of Agriculture studied the possibilities for increasing quinoa production for the first time without generating clear policies.

The idea that quinoa could solve malnutrition in the high Andes presented a paradox: quinoa was already a key element of highland food systems. How could malnutrition exist in the quinoa heartland? Some suggested that native populations no longer ate as much quinoa as they had in the past. The authors of *Lost Crops of the Incas* asserted that Andean indigenous populations had "forsaken their indigenous crops."[62] So-called dietary modernization had led to the replacement of foods like quinoa with less nutritious staples in general and cheap imported US wheat in particular.[63] Advocates called for nutrition education campaigns that would educate Andean poor people about the virtues of quinoa and encourage them to turn away from rice and cheap noodles. And while the idea that the Andean poor ought to be eating more quinoa became a common lament by the early 2000s, little had been done to actually encourage this. Peru's nutritional assistance program did purchase quinoa in the 1990s, and in 2013 the country revamped the national school breakfast program, Qali Warma, utilizing quinoa in its effort to offer more culturally appropriate meals and educate children in proper nutrition. Yet the stigmatization of quinoa consumption meant that this was less an access issue or one of nutrition education and more in part one of racism. As long as quinoa was disparaged as Indian food, increasing its consumption would be an uphill battle.

Fears that quinoa's popularity abroad was further undermining Andean diets renewed enthusiasm for this problem-solution narrative during the height of the quinoa boom. The *Atlantic*, the *Guardian*, and the *New York Times* all published stories in the early 2010s reporting that quinoa's high price was leading Andean farmers to give up eating quinoa in order to sell it for export.[64] While the degree to which quinoa farmers were forgoing quinoa was exaggerated in journalistic accounts, quinoa's high price during the boom did affect the urban poor in the Andes, for whom quinoa was suddenly inaccessible.[65] International media attention inadvertently highlighted the contradictions between different visions of quinoa's potential. If quinoa were to prevent malnutrition in the Andes, the price needed to remain low.

If it were to help alleviate dire poverty among rural Andean farmers, the price needed to be high.

A NEW TOOL IN THE FIGHT
AGAINST GLOBAL HUNGER

Potatoes and maize had "revolutionized the world's dietary customs, improving them considerably," declared Bolivian agronomist Jorge Alcázar in 1948. But "the continent's contribution to humanity does not stop there." Quinoa, he suggested, could dramatically improve diets across the globe, "especially for those with scarce resources."[66] While some early advocates thought quinoa should play a regional role in solving malnutrition, others had global ambitions for the grain. Alcázar envisioned quinoa as a global hunger curative. For him, quinoa's potential was too great to be confined to the Andes. The grain could make an "enormous contribution" to humanity at large, and it was the responsibility of researchers like him to help expand quinoa production into new regions of the world.[67]

Interest in expanding quinoa production beyond the Andes first developed at the turn of the twentieth century, but these initial efforts were not explicitly justified in relation to hunger. Quinoa was among the four hundred "charming botanical strangers" the US Department of Agriculture introduced in 1913 as part of a program encouraging home gardeners to "try out" the new plant varieties.[68] The first known experiments with quinoa outside the Andes took place in Kenya in 1935 with seeds obtained from the Kew Royal Botanical Gardens.[69] Noting quinoa's nutritional profile, adaptability to high altitude, and ability to withstand bird pests, the agricultural officer who started the Kenyan experiments declared, "Quinoa will become an important crop here in time to come, I feel sure."[70]

A growing number of quinoa enthusiasts began to view the grain as a tool to fight global hunger in the 1970s. The organizers of the second Chenopod Convention in Potosí, Bolivia, in 1976 justified a conference dedicated to the grain by positioning quinoa within the global food crisis. Grain prices were soaring at the time as a result of dramatic changes in the world grain market. Meanwhile, famines in Senegal, Ethiopia, and Cambodia were making international headlines. The conference proceedings opened with a firm declaration: "The global crisis in food production, particularly with respect to cereals and the demographic explosion, constitutes imminent danger for the wellbeing of humanity and thus requires us to find new food supplies."[71] Invoking neo-Malthusian fears of a population bomb and situating the conference in global affairs, the conference suggested that quinoa could be just the new grain food the world needed: "[Quinoa] is called to complete an important role in the solution of the world's nutritional problems."[72]

Researchers experimented with quinoa production in new locales in the 1970s and 1980s, and by 1989 experimental quinoa production had taken place in eleven countries outside the Andean region.[73] But it wasn't until the 1990s that more systematic efforts to expand quinoa production began. Two projects in the 1990s—The American and European Test of Quinoa and a collaboration between the International Potato Center in Lima and the Danish government's Development Agency—pioneered extensive quinoa trials across Europe. Program organizers articulated their goals in direct relation to global malnutrition but also combined this emphasis with a concern about climate change, stating that their chief aim was to improve the nutrition of the general population "above all in areas with climactic challenges."[74] By the end of the decade, thirteen more countries had engaged in experimental quinoa production.[75] With these trials in mind, the FAO declared quinoa "one of humanity's most promising crops" for food security in 1996.[76]

It was not only quinoa's nutritional profile that made it a candidate for global expansion in the name of malnutrition alleviation. Quinoa's hardiness and ability to adapt to new environments made it not only a miracle food but a miracle crop. A large genetic base—the many varieties farmers across the Andes had created—offered plant breeders ample material for adapting varieties to non-Andean environments. European researchers began breeding varieties adapted to northern latitudes in the 1990s, and a growing chorus of researchers began calling for more breeding programs in the name of global food security.[77] "I want it out of the health food section," declared Mark Tester, the leader of a team of researchers who sequenced the quinoa genome in 2017.[78] Justifying their work, which would enable genetically modified quinoas in the future, the researchers claimed that their main objective was to "[enhance] global food security for a growing world population."[79]

While quinoa promotors increasingly saw the grain's future outside the Andes, calls for expansion often overlapped with other goals in confusing ways. The NRC's *Lost Crops of the Incas* explicitly advocated "worldwide cultivation" and discussed at length the potential of cultivating these plants in the United States and Europe. Yet the authors at one point claimed that their ultimate goal was to relieve malnutrition in the Andes. Moreover, the degree to which efforts to breed quinoa and sequence its genome (the first step in creating genetically modified quinoas) would benefit global food security was dubious. Instead, plant genetic resources tended to be extracted from the Global South, "improved" in the Global North by researchers seeking intellectual property protections for the varieties they created, and then sold back to poor farmers for profit.[80] Agreement about quinoa's unrealized potential—its boundary object status—concealed these kinds of contradictions.

A NOVEL SOLUTION TO ANDEAN POVERTY

At the 1948 Conference on Malnutrition in Latin America, Bolivian delegates made a strong case for quinoa's capacity to address the region's malnutrition. But reports also noted that the same quinoa advocates "tended to regard the plant as an eventual export commodity."[81] While other conference attendees "felt that this opinion was premature" and suggested focusing on quinoa's role in feeding local populations, the idea of quinoa as a cash crop has animated some quinoa advocates since at least the 1940s.[82] But it was not until the 1980s that quinoa production in the high Andes came to be seen as a viable poverty alleviation strategy. At this time, a growing consensus among quinoa advocates emerged that saw the development of robust quinoa export markets as a novel answer to rural poverty in the Andes.

Quinoa made sense as a tool for addressing rural poverty in the high Andes in part because the unique highland ecology prevented the standard mid-twentieth-century strategies for dealing with rural poverty from working effectively. The extreme Andean climate presented a conundrum for development experts working within the green revolution paradigm. While agricultural development initiatives were replacing local crops with improved wheat varieties and hybridized corn across the globe, these crops could not survive in the high-altitude environment. Few non-native crops could reliably fully mature in the highlands. Development projects did introduce new cattle breeds, improved potato varieties, and technology packets to the region with limited success, but the green revolution model proved mostly unfeasible here.[83] The untenability of the standard development agricultural agendas in the Andean highlands compelled a small group of Andean agronomists and rural development actors to look into the potential of native crop and quinoa in particular, as a cash crop.[84]

Several obstacles prevented this vision from coming to fruition at the time. In the 1970s the Simón Bolivar Foundation and the Inter-American Institute of Agricultural Sciences funded a multiyear "diagnostic" study of quinoa commercialization in Puno that sought to delineate the issues preventing the development of a commercial quinoa industry.[85] Although the study authors saw developing more formalized quinoa markets as a way to increase farm incomes while improving nutrition of Peruvians, they documented manifold difficulties. Existing commercial relationships were characterized by informality, unstable market channels, and highly uneven power dynamics. There was no industrial quinoa-processing infrastructure. Quinoa varieties were not standardized, and the authors reported that the end product often contained sticks and rocks. In addition to these obstacles, they found little demand for quinoa among urban Peruvians, who by and large viewed the grain as an Indian food.

To add to these challenges, the 1970s and 1980s were tumultuous times for Peru's rural areas. In 1969 President Alvarado launched an agrarian reform that initiated a major transformation of the rural land tenure system. In an effort to put an end to the semifeudal land tenure arrangements that predominated in the Andean countryside and generated massive race-based inequities, the reform expropriated *hacienda* land and turned this land into massive state-run cooperatives.[86] But in 1975, partway through the implementation of the reform, General Francisco Morales Bermúdez took over the presidency (1975–80) and walked back many of these policies. The subsequent president, Fernando Belaúnde Terry (1980–85), further dismantled the reform and instead reworked land tenure based on the neoliberal paradigm that favored land privatization, undermining collective land management systems Andean communities had devised.[87] Then, in 1980, Peru erupted in a bloody, protracted civil war that devastated rural communities in the high Andean regions of the country in particular.[88] The war was an obstacle to quinoa's commercialization in Peru on multiple fronts and generated fear of outsiders. The fear the war created undermined cooperation among Peruvians and generated distrust of outsiders, especially in the rural areas most impacted. At the same time, the instability and violence interfered with support from international aid agencies, which did not want to send personnel to dangerous areas or invest in zones where they could not monitor their projects.

As quinoa's commercialization stalled in Peru, a small export market developed in neighboring Bolivia. In the early 1980s three Americans founded Quinoa Corporation, a small quinoa import-export business based in Boulder, Colorado, that would eventually become Ancient Harvest (one of the main quinoa purveyors in the United States).[89] US health food markets were a "logical" place for quinoa, explained David Cusack, who has an international development PhD and was one of Quinoa Corporation's founders: "[The market] is made up of a clientele which values nutrition, is receptive to new products, and is intrigued by the unfamiliar and exotic. This market has been the starting point for the entry of many new products into the mainstream US market."[90] But Quinoa Corporation founders saw their venture as more than just a business. While developing quinoa exports in the name of rural development was their primary focus, they also saw addressing Andean malnutrition and developing quinoa production outside the Andes as secondary aims. "We were on a mission for quinoa," founder Steven Gorad remarked decades later.[91] Quinoa Corporation founders were quinoa enthusiasts who saw incredible potential in the grain and a lamentable neglect. They saw their work within the NUS discourse, and in fact Cusack participated in the NRC's *Lost Crops of the Incas* seminar.[92] In a 1984 article in the *Ecologist*, Cusack argued that "the shortest marketing route for quinua from Cuzco (the former capital of the Inca Empire) to Lima (the modern capital of Peru) may be through the US health food market."[93] In a roundabout way, the best way to increase quinoa consumption in the Andes, he contended, was to develop quinoa exports. Though the founders saw quinoa exporting as a poverty alleviation tool, Quinoa Corporation became instrumental in developing quinoa production outside the Andes. They began planting quinoa experimentally in Colorado in the 1980s and have since developed commercial production at scale in Colorado.

In 1992 Peru's internal conflict concluded, officially speaking. Development actors attuned to Peru perceived an urgent need for programs that could revive the country's devastated rural economies. Some nonprofit organizations working on agricultural development in the Puno region began focusing their attention on quinoa in the early 1990s, seeing a much-needed agricultural development tool that could provide income to impoverished farmers. These groups sought to organize farmers into quinoa producer associations and link them with domestic buyers, with an eye toward eventual exporting. Over the course of the next decade, local organizations made major strides in training farmers in commercial quinoa production and organizing farmers into production associations that could conceivably allow them some bargaining power and make the process more efficient for buyers. But limited demand for quinoa among Peruvians meant that quinoa production and processing were not profitable endeavors at the time. Instead, these organizations relied on grants from international agencies and state funding, while working to create a future in which quinoa production could be a viable income strategy.

Quinoa's prospects as an income strategy for farmers in the high Andes improved around 2008 when foreign demand for quinoa began to climb. As quinoa's price ticked up, growing quinoa began to appear as a potentially lucrative endeavor. Existing organizations and programs working with Puno's farmers began to prioritize training farmers in commercial quinoa production, and new quinoa-related development projects found funding. Within Puno, this vision for quinoa—as poverty alleviation for rural farmers and a new era for altiplano agriculture—would come to dominate visions for quinoa's future by the 2010s. Yet quinoa's role as a poverty alleviation tool conflicted with its potential for alleviating regional malnutrition. A growing export market and high price was good for poor farmers, but it would also make the grain less accessible to Peru's urban poor, therefore undermining its malnutrition alleviation potential in the Andes. And expanding quinoa production globally, as advocates for quinoa as a global hunger curative would push for, would likely undermine the competitive advantage Andean farmers had as the main quinoa production region.

A "FUTURE-PROOF" CROP

In the early 2000s agricultural development organizations increasingly turned their attention to climate change. At the time, it was becoming evident that intensifying climate uncertainty and more frequent climate extremes posed an urgent problem for agricultural development. Those practicing land-based livelihoods, like farming and fishing, were especially vulnerable to extreme weather events and longer-term changes in regional climate patterns. At the same time, many past agricultural development initiatives focused on intensifying production of a small number of commodity crops had made farmers more vulnerable to these changes. The agricultural development initiatives started to focus on "adapting" local food systems to a present and future defined by climate change.[94] International development organizations began generating predictions of the specific ways regions would be affected and sought out strategies to maintain food supply in climate change hot spots.

While quinoa had been acclaimed for its hardiness in Andean contexts for decades, a growing number of researchers saw it as a climate change adaptation tool beyond the region.[95] Quinoa is a "model crop for tomorrow's agriculture" argued one group of researchers.[96] Agricultural chemist Fan Zhu suggested that quinoa "can help us survive climate change."[97] Quinoa's low water needs, hardiness in extreme cold, and ability to tolerate saline soils led researchers to see it as a new crop for increasingly drought-prone regions.[98] A growing number of researchers and institutions framed quinoa as a "climate-smart" or even "future-proof" crop that could withstand the newly challenging climactic conditions that were generating crop failures in other species.[99] While efforts to introduce quinoa production to new regions were already underway in the name of malnutrition alleviation, quinoa's potential was more and more understood through a climate change lens.

Several quinoa initiatives in the name of climate change focused on the Mediterranean and North Africa.[100] While the region is known as the world's cradle of wheat production, water scarcity and saltwater intrusion threaten existing production systems. In 2008 the SWUP-MED project (2008–13), funded by the European Commission, began working to introduce quinoa production (and consumption) in Mediterranean countries as a way to address water scarcity.[101] The project sought to breed quinoas specifically adapted to Mediterranean conditions and train farmers in quinoa production. In 2022 Quinoa4Med (2022–25) was launched, aiming to build on the work of the SWUP-MED project. In 2019 yet another partnership between the International Center for Biosaline Agriculture and the International Development Research Center was formed, focusing on introducing quinoa in Morocco to smallholder farmers.[102]

Meanwhile, plant breeders and biotechnologists are working to further concentrate quinoa's climate-resilient characteristics. Researchers at Brigham Young University are developing hybrid quinoas that are more heat tolerant, salt tolerant, and capable of growing in even more arid conditions. A number of region-specific breeding projects are underway that seek to generate quinoas specifically adapted to, for instance, the Mediterranean or East Africa. And after quinoa's genome was sequenced in 2017, some biotechnologists began to see quinoa as a source of genes that could be applied beyond it.[103] "Not only was quinoa itself resilient to climate change, it might be able to make other crops more resilient to climate change.

Climate change adaptation complements preexisting narratives about quinoa's potential while adding a sense of urgency. For instance, a 2013 article combines a Malthusian crisis narrative of exploding population growth amid dwindling arable land with climate change to make the case for quinoa's importance.[104] Similarly, a 2020 FAO report on the prospects for quinoa utilization in Eastern and Southern Africa suggests that quinoa "is expected to significantly reduce food and nutrition insecurity and help farming communities adapt to climate change."[105] And while reports and projects combining emphases on global malnutrition and climate change adaptation are most common, some projects see quinoa production as a way to increase farm incomes in regions outside the Andes, for instance in Morocco.

2013, INTERNATIONAL YEAR OF QUINOA: THE PEAK AND FALL OF A BOUNDARY OBJECT

Un future sembrado hace miles de años.
A future sown thousands of years ago.
—slogan for the UN International Year of Quinoa

In October 2013, as farmers across the Andes prepared to sow quinoa seeds for the upcoming growing season, a quinoa harvest was taking place in the center of Rome, Italy. In celebration of World Food Day, the FAO Headquarters hosted First Lady Nadine Heredia along with Nemecia Achacollo Tola, Bolivia's minister of land and rural development, at a daylong series of events promoting quinoa as a tool in the fight against global hunger. The World Food Day programming was part of the agenda for the UN International Year of Quinoa (IYQ), a yearlong series of events that took place across the world with the goal of promoting quinoa's capacity to contribute to sustainable development. The IYQ was carried out, in similar fashion to many UN-commemorated "years," through UN-sanctioned events and projects. It would include culinary competitions showcasing inventive dishes made with quinoa; promotional events for prospective quinoa farmers; innovative product contests; biodiversity competitions; a "World Congress on Quinoa" to convene researchers; a symposium to convoke "diverse

FIGURE 4. First Lady Nadine Heredia manually threshing quinoa for a photo op at the FAO headquarters in Rome as part of World Food Day and the 2013 International Year of Quinoa. *Source:* FAO/ Giuseppe Carotenuto.

stakeholders"; and a traveling exhibition detailing quinoa's history, use, and production that visited FAO offices across the globe.[106]

One of the main events on the World Food Day agenda was a symbolic quinoa harvest. In the FAO Headquarters's large entry hall, Heredia, Achacollo, and the FAO's director general, José Graziano da Silva, stood before a table draped in purple linens and set with two terracotta bowls alongside a stack of dry quinoa panicles. A crowd of onlookers—composed of FAO officials as well as representatives of organizations like Biodiversity International and the UN Development Program—watched as these powerful figures attempted to theatrically thresh and winnow quinoa, two critical steps in preparing quinoa for consumption. As da Silva and Achacollo awkwardly pulled grains from the panicle, Heredia picked up a handful of the threshed quinoa in her hand to "winnow" it, intermittently blowing on the quinoa between smiles for the flashing cameras.

If quinoa had struggled to gain the backing of powerful sociopolitical networks during much of the twentieth century, the IYQ marked a dramatic reversal of this trend. The IYQ was a self-conscious project to foster and strengthen the sociopolitical webs necessary to consolidate quinoa's role as a global "miracle plant."[107] It featured numerous venues explicitly intended to kindle partnerships among international NGOs such as Biodiversity International and Slow Food International, development institutions including the World Bank, local development organizations both within and beyond the Andes, national governments, private companies along nascent global quinoa supply chains, and research institutions, an objective made explicit in the IYQ's goal to "encourage partnerships between public, private and nongovernmental organizations related to the cultivation of quinoa."[108]

Quinoa's emergence as a darling of the global development world coincided with changing ideas about development that positioned sustainability, culture, and the ever more pressing issue of climate change as critical development issues. By the 2000s development practitioners were wrestling with the pernicious environmental and social impacts of earlier agricultural development paradigms. How could agricultural development incorporate environmental sustainability and utilize rather than undermine cultural traditions? How could agricultural systems encourage rather than destroy biodiversity? And how could agricultural systems based on one set of climate conditions adapt to changing patterns? Within this altered zeitgeist, so-called neglected crops broadly and quinoa in particular gained new traction.

While quinoa's association with indigenous agriculturalists prevented it from receiving much attention throughout most of the twentieth century, its non-Western roots were front and center in IYQ rhetoric. The symbolic harvest at the FAO, for instance, was intended to underscore quinoa's Andean origins and highlight quinoa's "cultural" aspects. The opening paragraph of the IYQ Master Plan made this evident: "The year 2013 has been declared 'The International Year of Quinoa', in recognition of the indigenous peoples of the Andes, who have maintained, controlled, protected and preserved quinoa as a food for present and future generations thanks to their traditional knowledge and living practices which are in harmony with nature and Mother Earth."[109] The IYQ website and media materials were plastered with photographs of women sporting "traditional" Andean skirts and long braids, evoking a common image of Andean indigeneity. Even the IYQ's slogan, "a future sown thousands of years ago," referenced tradition and culture as the source of quinoa's power. Quinoa's basis in "tradition" was also its connection to environmental sustainability. IYQ documents noted that quinoa had long been grown in a sustainable fashion in biodiverse farms, the result of traditional ecological knowledge. The grain's low water needs and ability to adapt to new environments further supported quinoa's environmental credentials.

The IYQ marked the apotheosis of quinoa's boundary object status. It combined the previously mentioned visions of quinoa's potential into one single, highly contradictory agenda. In official documents, the goal was "to focus world attention on the role that quinoa's biodiversity and nutritional value play in food security, nutrition, and poverty eradication, and in support of the achievement of the internationally agreed development goals including the Millennium Development Goals."[110] IYQ materials emphasized the role quinoa could play in alleviating poverty in the Andes and globally, the potential for quinoa to help alleviate hunger across the world, and the increased relevance of quinoa in a world increasingly shaped by climate change. The IYQ's success in bringing together diverse institutional actors with disparate interests attested to the power of quinoa as a boundary object.

But latent tensions between different visions of "quinoa development" became evident over the course of the year. Boundary objects are unstable, as are the networks that they help cohere. Boundary objects follow patterned trajectories. Over time, groups attempt to control boundary objects and in doing so, provoke outright disagreement. As dissonance increases, new categories and alternative boundary objects can proliferate.[111] Over the course of the IYQ, quinoa's unrealized potential began to lose its power as a boundary object. The inconsistencies between the disparate visions of quinoa's future became increasingly visible. While official IYQ documents prioritized a vision of quinoa as a globally produced commodity that would help alleviate hunger at that scale, the heterogenous events that comprised the IYQ program show a latent struggle to define the future of quinoa. Proponents of the different visions saw the IYQ as an opportunity to push forward their own agendas, while the collective goal of "promoting quinoa" helped disguise division. During the IYQ, it became clear to some that the collaborations inspired by agreement about quinoa's potential were on shaky footing.

Though IYQ rhetoric celebrated quinoa's Andean origins, the IYQ agenda prioritized a future for the grain beyond the region. The majority of IYQ events took place outside the Andean region and focused on introducing quinoa production to new areas, generating quinoa varieties adapted to new regions, and creating an ever-expanding global consumer base. In Peru, coastal Lima hosted dozens of events, and only four official IYQ-sponsored events took place in the Peruvian highlands. Although IYQ rhetoric underlined the role "traditional peoples" played as "custodians," it stopped short of attributing indigenous people agency in quinoa's creation. Andean agriculturalists were framed as passive "stewards," not authors or creators.[112] In the IYQ rhetoric, quinoa was a "natural" product that indigenous people preserved: a gift from the Andean peoples to the world. This language of sharing and stewardship was strategic. Quinoa's global expansion relied on the free availability of quinoa germplasm to plant breeders working on new varieties that could grow in non-Andean regions. This framing of Andean farmers as stewards was explicitly not framing them as proprietors.[113]

Discrepancies between visions for quinoa's future were revealed through both the work of the IYQ and sudden price fluctuations, which undermined quinoa's boundary object quality. Industry actors in Puno, including farmers, voiced discontent about the expansion of quinoa production beyond the Andes, and many blamed the IYQ. While IYQ documents framed Andean farmers as "beneficiaries" of the IYQ, in practice it became clear that Andean smallholders would gain little from the IYQ, which would help remake quinoa's production geography in a way that undercut the region's quinoa industry. The program was not intended to help Andean farmers, but to thank them. Moreover, the price spike was a boon for farmers in the Andes *and* a problem for poor Peruvian quinoa consumers, something that made visible the awkward relationships between the different visions for quinoa's potential. The incompatibility of the different narratives of quinoa's development potential became more and more evident by the end of 2013.

CONCLUSION

"We have more than fulfilled our goal," declared Director General Graziano de Silva during the IYQ's closing ceremony in December 2013. "Leaving behind centuries of neglect, it is with renewed strength that quinoa begins a new phase as a food for the future."[114] For early quinoa enthusiasts who struggled to get quinoa the attention they felt it deserved, the state of affairs in 2013 would undoubtably feel like a triumph. A plant long ignored by mainstream agronomy, science, and development policymakers, quinoa had won the endorsement of a long list of powerful individual and institutional actors. The United Nations was parading quinoa around the world as a virtuous plant that could help address the world's most pressing problems: hunger, poverty, and climate change.

This chapter demonstrated the role quinoa's boundary object status alongside changing development discourses played in enabling this dramatic transformation. Over the course of the twentieth century, a small community of scientific researchers and development experts came to see quinoa as an underexploited crop with much more to offer the world. Some quinoa promotors saw quinoa export as an answer to rural Andean poverty. Others focused on quinoa's nutritional accolades: it could solve Andean "protein shortages" and even alleviate malnutrition across the world. As climate change became a defining problem for agricultural development, a growing number of quinoa boosters argued that quinoa could help farmers across the world adapt to an era defined by fickle climates. These narratives about quinoa motivated the formation of a small assemblage of dedicated researchers, whose work would ultimately make possible quinoa's commercialization.

But quinoa promotors' efforts to demonstrate the crop's virtues went largely unheard before the 2010s. At this time, ideas about the role of indigenous knowledge and sustainability in development had changed dramatically while agricultural development policymakers searched for ways to address the ever more pressing issue of climate change's impact on agricultural systems across the globe. It was within this new discursive milieu that quinoa was able to form a powerful sociopolitical network of advocates. Vague agreement about quinoa's unrealized potential helped generate collaborations between distinct institutions and diversely located individuals. The IYQ both indexed the social capital quinoa had acquired and was itself intended to further bolster quinoa's sociopolitical ties. Quinoa's agronomic and nutritional characteristics by themselves did not make quinoa a miracle crop. The creation of a powerful narrative of lamentable neglect and boundless potential helped forge the sociopolitical networks around quinoa that, in turn, brought the grain into the limelight.

But the story does not end with triumph. "The International Year of Quinoa was a sham; just a spectacle," Victor, a Puno-based técnico told me in 2015. By then, the contradictions between different visions for quinoa's future were plain to see for those involved in Puno's quinoa industry. Consensus about quinoa's incredible potential had obscured contradictions between the interests of different quinoa advocates and the disparate visions for the grain's future. Quinoa's boundary object quality began to disintegrate in the aftermath of the IYQ as it became clear that different visions for quinoa's future competed with rather than complemented each other. The miracle crop, like the network surrounding it, is precarious. The IYQ's global ambitions for quinoa would undermine the goals of Puno's industry actors, like Victor. While the next chapter continues to explore the reimagining of quinoa for new audiences, the remainder of the book tells the story of the breakdown of quinoa's miracle crop status from the perspective of Puno, Peru.

TWO

Whitening a Comida de Indios

CULINARY BIOPROSPECTING
AND THE INCA SUPERFOOD

"I STILL REMEMBER the smell of [my grandparents] cooking quinoa and sweet potato to feed to the dogs," Pedro Miguel Schiaffino told me as we chatted in the bar of his restaurant in the wealthy San Isidro neighborhood of Lima one afternoon. "Honestly, I feel a little embarrassed sharing this now but that's how it was. I grew up thinking quinoa was for animals." When I interviewed him in 2017, Schiaffino had become one of Lima's most renowned chefs. The *New York Times* had reported on his restaurants, Anthony Bourdain had met up with him in *Parts Unknown*, and a steady stream of culinary tourists and wealthy locals were requesting reservations at his two high-end restaurants, Malabar and Ámaz.[1] Schiaffino was part of a cadre of elite Lima-based chefs who had helped reimagine the country's cuisine over the previous decade. The gastronomic revolution, as Peru's culinary leaders called it, had remade perceptions of Peruvian food and transformed Lima into a global culinary destination. Malabar's approach typified the new upscale Peruvian cuisine that had captured the imaginations of cosmopolitan foodies across the world. The restaurant's seasonally updated prix-fixe menu showcased ingredients that until recently would not have been found in a white tablecloth restaurant. Guinea pig, Amazonian river prawn, *queso andino*, *kiwicha*, and quinoa—foods Peru's upper classes had long associated with poverty and desperation—were all reinterpreted using formal French cooking and plating conventions.[2]

At the crux of the project to reinvent Peru as a global culinary capital lie the reappraisal and reinvention of marginalized foods like quinoa. The pursuit of novelty in high-end culinary worlds and health food markets alike has generated the rise of what I call *culinary bioprospecting*. Bioprospecting refers to the search for plant and animal species along with associated traditional ecological knowledge that can generate commercially valuable material, especially medicinal drugs. Following Cori Hayden, we can understand bioprospecting as a "new term for an old practice."[3] In the 1990s (pharmaceutical) bioprospecting became a beacon of hope for deforestation and rural poverty alike. It was pitched as a win-win that would incentivize rural communities in biodiverse areas to protect that diversity while providing valuable new raw materials for pharmaceutical companies. Perhaps unsurprisingly, pharmaceutical bioprospecting did not live up to its anticipated potential, as valuable compounds proved very rare; as a result few communities received sustained benefits from their cooperation with international researchers.[4]

Today, *culinary* bioprospecting has garnered a similar reputation as a win-win business opportunity and development project. Culinary bioprospecting refers to the search for commercially valuable edible (in contrast to pharmaceutical) ingredients, concentrating on foods marginalized communities have produced and consumed. Because of their marginality, many socially, economically, and/or politically marginalized communities have created and maintained distinctive culinary traditions and crop varieties even without market value.[5] In a world where food markets increasingly run on fashion cycles, marginalized communities are an attractive source of novelty. The appeal of the "exotic" only intensifies this dynamic, as wealthy consumers willingly pay premiums for more "authentic" foods.

While Schiaffino did not grow up eating quinoa, he had become an unapologetic quinoa advocate. "Quinoa is always on my menu [at Malabar]; always. Since the very beginning we've always put quinoa on the menu," Schiaffino declared, his enthusiasm evident in his animated nodding. The day I spoke with him, he had just introduced an elaborate new dessert: a chia crisp atop *guanábana* and kefir ice cream, *pasankalla* quinoa, and kiwicha with almond milk.[6] "The tourists always loved quinoa," Schiaffino told me. "It was the Peruvians that I had trouble with." As two employees prepared for the dinner service, spreading crisp tablecloths across the restaurant's round tables, Schiaffino told me about the days before quinoa was widely accepted. In the early 2000s he was head chef at Huaca Pucllana Restaurant, a well-regarded establishment beside a pre-Inca archaeological site in the middle of Lima, one of the early restaurants to serve upscale Peruvian cuisine, known then as *novoandino* (New Andean) cuisine. "I had to be creative. I had to put quinoa in the plate in creative ways for them to like it, and honestly, I still do." By the time Shiaffino and I spoke, in 2017, Lima's high-end restaurants featured quinoa on their menus almost without exception. Peru's supermarkets offered a growing array of value-added products prominently advertising their quinoa content in highly designed packaging, including granola bars, breakfast cereals, chocolates, and candies. Entrepreneurs in Lima had launched new quinoa ventures, creating quinoa-based liquors and beauty products. Peru's upper and middle classes—populations that had long shunned quinoa—now consumed it conspicuously. Peruvian government figures show that between 2000 and 2014, per capita consumption of quinoa in Peru increased 129 percent, from 1.10 to 2.54 kg/person.[7] And recent studies of consumers in Lima have found that higher education levels and higher income levels are positively correlated with quinoa consumption.[8] In 2014 the Peruvian central bank introduced a quinoa-themed coin into circulation.[9] Quinoa had become an object of pride for Peruvians and a symbol of national progress.

Like quinoa's interpellation as a development miracle crop, the grain's new position as a national food resulted from conscious efforts to develop new narratives and strategic network building.[10] By the time quinoa "boomed," a powerful sociopolitical web of chefs, journalists, entrepreneurs, and state entities had coalesced around quinoa in Peru.[11] This network was different from, though partially connected to and enabled by, the development practitioners and scientists analyzed in the previous chapter. These quinoa advocates were focused on promoting quinoa as part of a culinary project. For them, quinoa's "miraculous" potential lay in its presumed ability to remedy massive social fissures in Peruvian society and to create business opportunities at the same time.[12] Quinoa's success abroad and growing acceptance across social strata in Peru had made quinoa an emblem of the gastronomic revolution's success and the potential of revalorizing Peru's underappreciated gastronomic riches.

Over the same period, quinoa was finding new audiences outside Peru as well. Global demand for quinoa skyrocketed during the first two decades of the twenty-first century as quinoa caught the attention of wealthy, health-conscious consumers across the globe. In 2002 Peru exported about 200 tons of quinoa, mostly to the United States. By 2008 that figure had risen over 1,000 percent, to 2,100 tons. Six years later, in 2014, the country was exporting over 36,000 tons, sending shipping containers full of quinoa to dozens of countries across the globe (see figure 18 in appendix).[13] The UN launched the IYQ in 2013, and that same year Peru declared quinoa the tenth official "flagship product." The grain joined Pisco and Peruvian silver in the pantheon of products that "represent the image of Peru abroad."[14] In 2014 the Ministry of Exterior Commerce began promoting Peru as the "land of superfoods" at product expositions across the world. A country long known for its rich mineral deposits, Peru now branded itself as a land singularly abundant in superfoods.

We tend to think of a boom as an economic phenomenon. Yet changes in supply and demand are symptoms of more complex social, political, and material processes. Price signals can index changing desires, new ideas, complex reconfigurations of identities, shifting power dynamics between industry groups, and changes in day-to-day calculations about the meaning and import of particular objects. And in today's globally connected economy, changing dynamics among consumers in one locale can generate far-reaching consequences for the lives of a distant population of producers. From an anthropological perspective, recognizing this growing demand for a product like quinoa generates more questions than it answers. Understanding the quinoa boom anthropologically requires explaining how quinoa became attractive to new audiences in the first place. This, I argue, is largely a story about the circulation of new narratives about the grain and the formation of powerful sociopolitical networks invested in disseminating them.

For decades, social scientists have pointed to connections between diet and social hierarchies across diverse contexts. Pierre Bourdieu's study of French consumer preferences in the 1960s illuminated how taste preferences mapped onto and reinforced social class distinctions.[15] "Taste classifies and classifies the classifier" he famously stated, pointing out how an individual's taste preferences were not arbitrary but based in a larger classificatory system.[16] What one chooses to eat betrays their own status within a social order. But models like Bourdieu's tend to be static; they do not help us explain change over time. At the same time, the main models of change in consumer culture suggest linear relationships. The ideas of Georg Simmel and Thorstein Veblen, both thinkers at the turn of the twentieth century, shaped our understandings of how consumer preferences change. Their work suggested that lower classes imitate the behavior of elites; elites introduce a practice, and others copy it.[17] But clearly the opposite can occur as well: How, for instance, does an Indian food become a superfood? The relationship between food and social boundaries can be complex and indirect.[18] Here, the story of quinoa's evolution offers insight into how and why scorned foods associated with poverty can become coveted foods that mark upperclassness.[19]

In some sense, quinoa's path from poverty staple to fashion food is well-trodden. Served to prisoners during the early nineteenth century, lobster was associated with poverty and criminality in the United States before becoming a symbol of wealth and gluttony. Collard greens have long been a staple in rural households in the US South. This changed when Whole Foods Market began featuring collards as "the new kale" in 2015.[20] Similarly, kale was known as "peasant cabbage" in the United States before becoming a staple of middle- and upper-class diets.[21] In fact, before 2012 Pizza Hut was the largest US purchaser of kale, as a salad bar garnish. Açaí berries, historically a peasant staple in parts of Amazonia, transformed into a global fashion food in the early 2000s.[22] Ramen, commonly associated with college student desperation in the United States, became the focus of foodies in the last decade as upscale ramen restaurants opened in cities across the country. Similar processes have occurred with littleneck clams, caviar, and eels in various European countries, and scholars have documented a number of related cases in Latin America.[23]

Some scholars read the recent commercialization of marginalized foods as a hopeful trend, a long overdue reassessment of the ways colonial legacies shape contemporary ideas about "good food." Indeed, the difference between a delicacy and a food that provokes disgust is both culturally mediated and deeply entangled with histories of oppression. Revalorizing products connected to indigenous peoples, specifically, and marginalized populations, broadly, can be read as an effort to remake the symbolic legacies of colonialism that have led to the systematic devalorization of all things non-European.[24] In this perspective, such an approach might contribute to the reversal of what Aníbal Quijano has called the coloniality of power: the ways colonial logics of categorizing people and lifeways have endured long after colonialism's formal end.[25] In other words, resignifying an "Indian food" as a "superfood" is also an attempt to respect undervalued lifeways and cultural practices in a small but meaningful way. Increasing how much attention consumers, chefs, and journalists pay to marginalized crops can be one tiny part of a larger project to "decolonize" diets and revitalize local cultural traditions.[26] It exposes how coloniality informs ideas about edibility/inedibility and deliciousness/disgustingness. In other words, revaluing foods like quinoa is an entry point to a more radical emancipatory project.[27]

In popular discourse and in messaging from gastronomic leaders and institutions, quinoa has undergone a process of "revalorization." Revalorization frames this dynamic as a wholly positive trend, involving restoring the rightful value of a previously undervalued product. But revalorization is a slippery concept. The confusion stems from the multiple meanings of the root word: *value*. Sometimes when people talk about the revalorization of a food, they are speaking in mostly monetary terms, about a good's growing price or market value. At other times they are referring to a more nebulous cultural value or esteem: the increasing appreciation for a good that was previously "underappreciated." While social value and economic value are entangled, the slippage can also elide complexity. Quinoa's revalorization as a lucrative business opportunity *and* an emblem of a more inclusive Peruvian national identity might appear to be coincident. However, given that foods like quinoa have long been valued by those communities for whom they provide vital sustenance, it would be appropriate to ask, revalorized for whom? Characterizing these dynamics as revalorization can obscure the uneven politics and multiple erasures that can underlie these transformations.

The concept of food gentrification, in contrast, draws our attention toward the extractivist dynamics at play, highlighting the ways in which a food can be "refurbished" to make it palatable to new (elite) audiences in much the same way a working-class neighborhood is transformed to make it attractive to wealthier homebuyers. While its humble origins may offer "character" to the food, much as neighborhoods with old industrial buildings are favored in gentrification, Soleil Ho has argued that the process is ultimately one of appropriation that can, if prices increase, make the food inaccessible to its original eaters.[28] In other words, while some see revalorization as a challenge to colonial legacies, others argue that it can actually exacerbate these dynamics.[29]

Food studies scholars have pointed to how physical and aesthetic transformations of food stuffs have been critical to making indigenous foods acceptable to mainstream (read: white, elite) palates. Hi'ilei Hobart's examination of poi in Hawai'i showed how extracting and commercializing indigenous foods have often relied on the use of technology to transform foods "from abject to acceptable."[30] Sociologist Raul Matta pointed to a related dynamic in the Peruvian context.[31] Roasted *cuy* (guinea pig) has long been an Andean delicacy, though it's traditionally served whole, with the face intact and legs splayed out. Cuy's entrance into Lima's high-end restaurant scene, by contrast, entailed dismembering the carcass to distance it from its origins as an animal and, more importantly, as an Indian food. These physical transformations are intended to domesticate and "civilize" these "uncivilized" foods.

Making a food like cuy valuable to elite audiences in Peru meant remaking its aesthetics to align with European culinary values.

While aesthetic transformations are in many cases critical to this distancing, I argue that retelling quinoa's origin stories enabled changing middle- and upper-class perceptions of quinoa.[32] I underscore the central role narrative and mythmaking play in rebranding marginalized foods and foreground the role different kinds of tastemakers played in repackaging quinoa. The symbolic work carried out by journalists, chefs, and marketing teams remade quinoa's image and effectively whitened quinoa by severing its connection to contemporary indigenous people. Making quinoa into "good food" for middle- and upper-class Peruvians was not just about creating new narratives; it was about erasing old ones. Transforming quinoa from a racialized poverty food into a globally circulated health product and object of national pride entailed repackaging quinoa in ways that made it attractive to new audiences. Quinoa's increased popularity within Peru was not an inevitable, "natural" progression. It resulted from the deliberate construction and dissemination of new stories about quinoa by key cultural figures. Celebrity chefs, such as Schiaffino, home cooks, journalists, entrepreneurs, and state institutions actively remade quinoa in the eyes of Peruvians through constructing new stories about quinoa and obscuring old ones.

Construction and erasure go hand in hand.[33] Making quinoa attractive to middle- and upper-class Peruvians entailed constructing new associations with quinoa *and* eliminating old ones. Specifically, it required actively distancing quinoa from its roots as a poverty food. For quinoa to become palatable to elite *limeños*, it needed to be decidedly less "Indian." The construction formation of new narratives about quinoa's origins and merits, I argue, helped retool quinoa's association with indigeneity. Taken together, connecting quinoa to the majestic Inca, invoking ideas of self-discovery, and emphasizing quinoa's nutritional content worked to distance quinoa from associations with Peruvian indigenous populations and to "whiten" quinoa.

Quinoa's sudden popularity abroad, specifically with North American and European consumers, further reinforced this disassociation. Quinoa's growing favor among foreign consumers articulated with evolving ideas about quinoa within Peru in complex ways. Yet the meanings quinoa acquired in Peru were notably different from those it took on in the United States or France, for example. This chapter interrogates changing ideas about quinoa and the intersection of Peruvian perceptions of quinoa with growing demand abroad. It examines how quinoa was reimagined for new audiences, especially middle- and upper-class Peruvians. Scholars have explored the ways Northern consumers' shifting desires and changing values drive transformation of distant producer livelihoods.[34] But how the globalization of a once locally embedded good affects consumers "back home" remains less thoroughly studied.

Existing interpretations tend to frame culinary revalorization either as a "decolonial" project that seeks to upend colonial culinary regimes or as a "neocolonial" enterprise that can only reify dynamics of exclusion. But reading these projects as wholly neocolonial risks oversimplifying the complex motivations and moral imperatives that guide actors like Shiaffino. Proponents of quinoa's revalorization genuinely upset the colonial culinary hierarchies that had made quinoa an Indian food, *and* in doing so, they reinforced the white supremacy in utilizing narratives that collectively distanced quinoa from actually living indigenous peoples. Remaking an indigenous staple was an innovative and genuine attempt to challenge racialized status hierarchies, *and* the emancipatory potential of this project was always already limited. Peru's gastropolitical leaders were themselves caught within structures of power and limited in the ways their work could challenge the enduring matrices of race and power in Peru. This chapter suggests that reimagining quinoa was at once a progressive move to remake culinary hierarchies *that also* reinforced some power asymmetries. A more nuanced understanding of how these processes work, who benefits, and who has control over the process can give us more insight into the promises and pitfalls of culinary revalorization projects.

COMIDA DE INDIOS

> Thirty years ago, if you went to a wedding, they would serve you little French puff pastry rounds [vol-au-vents] with cans of mushrooms that they just opened in the kitchen. And if you said you were going to serve quinoa, they would say "what's up with you? This is chicken scratch. You're crazy dude, this is *serrano* [someone from the Peruvian highlands, often used derogatorily] food."
>
> —BERNARDO ROCA REY, president of the Peruvian
> Association for Gastronomy, 2013

In 1968 José María Arguedas penned an essay about Violeta Parra, the influential Chilean folk musician whose music had gained a large following beyond Chile. One of Peru's most famous authors to this day, Arguedas was deeply concerned with the plight of Peru's indigenous populations and their representation in Peruvian society. Scholars at the time tended to perceive popular art and culture as something that helped unite a society through generating collective identity and pride. But Arguedas saw precisely the opposite in his native Peru. "The art that Blacks, Indians, and mestizos make is considered an inferior art. Art serves to differentiate these groups, to segregate them, and even devalue them."[35] This dynamic, he argued, was not unique to art; it included other elements of culture such as food. The status of quinoa in Peru was his case in point: "If I asked a gentleman (in Lima we only call high-class men gentleman) if he ate quinoa, he would look at me truly horrified as if I had offended him."[36] Arguedas argued that far from uniting Peruvian society, quinoa was used to differentiate Peru's social strata.

Over the course of Spanish colonialism, quinoa became a stable marker of indigeneity in Peru. Initially, Spanish conquerors showed interest in the grain. Garcilaso de la Vega, the son of an Inca noble and a Spanish conquistador who became Peru's most famous colonial chronicler, noted in 1608 that some Spaniards ate quinoa leaves braised in stews. Garcilaso himself even sent samples of the grain back to Spain. After this early period of symbolic instability during which quinoa's meaning to Spaniards was not yet defined, colonists of European descent came to denigrate quinoa as a food that marked a person as racially Other—as Indian.

In some sense, none of this is surprising. For decades, social scientists have pointed to the connections between diet and social hierarchies.[37] Although this body of work centers tastes (e.g., this social group tends to like such and such a dish), *dis*taste can be an equally or even more salient site of identity making, something quinoa's history bears out.[38] With this in mind, a growing number of food studies scholars now study so-called marginalized foods. These are foods that dominant classes avoid because of their associations with marginalized populations. These foods are not necessarily marginal in the sense of unimportance. Indeed, they are often dietary staples for some segments of society.[39] Critically, they take on negative connotations because the people who eat them have low social status; they are tools to establish and reinforce social divisions.[40] In other words, Indian foods are Indian foods because Indians eat them. Often these foods are also poverty foods—foods that are cheap and provide sustenance for people without the means to acquire more "luxurious" fare.

Marginalized foods take on prominent roles in colonial and postcolonial contexts as tools to symbolically differentiate colonized from colonizers.[41] Yet the social and symbolic work that marginalized foods do varies by context. Historian Rebecca Earle argues that the humoral medicinal paradigm that was dominant in Latin America during the colonial era made colonists particularly wary of native foods and their effects on the body.[42] During the sixteenth through eighteenth centuries, the question of whether the "dismal state" of the Indians was a result of their diet, and in turn, whether eating native foods would turn Spaniards into Indians, was a pressing dilemma.[43] As a result, numerous foods took on considerable symbolic potency as "Indian foods" in the Andes.[44] People who wanted to avoid "becoming" Indian took care to avoid quinoa along with cuy, alpaca meat, *chicha* (corn beer), and other foods that came to be associated with indigenous populations.[45]

The unique construction of race in the Andes shapes the social work marginalized foods do in this context. The particular forms that colonialism took on in the Andes resulted in configurations of race and class specific to the Andes.[46] During the colonial era, the category of the Indian was both a social classification and a legal category that forced people into servile roles and blocked them from many privileges of citizenship.[47] Yet sexual relations and intermarriage between native Peruvians (usually women) and Spanish colonists (usually men) became common, generating a "racial mixing" that made the situation complex. Powerful men needed heirs for their property and therefore wanted their "mixed" children to have rights. In marked contrast to the US context, where rigid racial categories developed in order to deny African Americans a host of rights and privileges, a complicated set of social and racial categories developed in the Andes based on one's *degree* of whiteness.[48] Rather than clear binary categories, a person's identity was located on a spectrum from whiteness to Indianness (and, occasionally, Blackness). In this hierarchical spectrum, whiteness mapped onto ideas of modernity, progress, urbanity, proximity to Europe, and the coast, while Indianness was backward/ignorant, traditional, poor, rural, and Andean.

To further complicate matters, one's location on this imagined spectrum was only in part dependent on skin color. Although phenotype dominates understandings of race in the United States, in much of Latin America, a person's physical characteristics are just one part of the larger racial calculation.[49] In addition to phenotype, variables that might be seen elsewhere as class based or "ethnic" figure into this equation: one's education level, where they were born or where they reside, the way they dress, their language profile, and—critically for our purposes—their eating practices. Race, class, and culture are inseparable in Peru, which means that racial identity is (to an extent) malleable. At the same time that eating quinoa or cuy could make someone "more Indian," Peru's dominant social classes long favored European fare, as it reinforced their proximity to Europe and therefore their whiteness.[50] Marginalized foods are a common way social hierarchies manifest in quotidian power relations, but the Andean understanding of race makes eating an especially potent site of identity making. In this context, marginalized foods aren't just marginalized; they are marginalizing. Eating marginalized foods like quinoa is not simply a reflection of one's racial or class identity; it can actively shape the way one is classified.

Many limeños I got to know during field research told me stories similar to Schiaffino's. They either did not know quinoa existed as a child or had associated it with animals or lower classes. Many, like Adriana, shared memorable early encounters with quinoa. Adriana, who self-described as middle class, grew up in Lima in the 1990s. She was a graduate student at a US university when I spoke with her and had eaten quinoa occasionally during her adult life. But as a child, her mother and grandmother never served her quinoa. "I think I basically thought that if you were putting quinoa in your soup, it was because you were poor," she explained. The idea that quinoa was not for a girl with Adriana's pedigree was subtly and sometimes not so subtly reinforced during her childhood. She recalled that one of her family's maids, who was from the central Andes, would feed quinoa porridge to her baby instead of oatmeal. "I remember being eight or nine [years old] or so, and my mom saying, 'that must be good for the baby, but it looks disgusting.'" For middle-class limeños in the 1990s, quinoa was an inappropriate food for a decent meal.[51] Surveys of quinoa consumption in Lima in the 1990s confirm that frequency of quinoa consumption was highest in homes with low or very low socioeconomic status and among migrants from rural areas.[52]

In the high Andes, by contrast, quinoa was a dietary staple, but one that people tended to eat in close company.[53] Numerous natives of the Peruvian highlands explained to me that during their upbringing, they ate quinoa primarily in private, in the safety of one's home or among friends and family, for fear of social stigma.[54] We can think of this as the opposite of conspicuous consumption, the highly visible forms of shopping or eating used to publicly display one's wealth or status. Eating quinoa in safe settings protected people from social censure. But the flip side of stigma is solidarity. Like chewing coca leaves or speaking Quechua in this context, eating quinoa also generated a strong sense of collective identity among those who partook. It helped create a sense of Us in opposition to Them, and for some people with roots in the Andes, it helped them feel a sense of connection to their families.[55] In rural Andean communities, quinoa remained central to daily culinary and ritual life throughout the twentieth century.[56] As farmers I spoke with emphasized, it was a central part of their identity. It helped generate camaraderie even in the face of denigration by outsiders.

The culinary status hierarchies formed over the course of European colonialism persisted long after the formal collapse of colonialism in Peru. Until quite recently, quinoa formed part of a symbolic milieu that mapped the grain onto categories of Indianness, backwardness, and poverty. The enduring salience of race in shaping contemporary social and economic lives attests to the "durable" nature of the system. "The racial axis has a colonial origin and character, but it has proven to be more durable and stable than the colonialism in whose matrix it was established," argued Peruvian social theorist Aníbal Quijano.[57] The persistent stigmatization of quinoa consumption and the infatuation with European foods well into the twentieth century attest to this "durability" and index how the coloniality of power pervades culinary imaginaries in Peru. Given this long history, which extends into the late twentieth century, how exactly did quinoa shift from Indian food to national food—from poverty food to superfood? In what follows, I argue for the central place of narratives in remaking quinoa's symbolic position within this wider system of taste. Quinoa's shift was not isolated but part of a larger shift in values around food and nation in Peru.[58]

NUTRITIONAL PRIMITIVISM AND
THE RISE OF A GLOBAL SUPERFOOD

Back then, nobody knew about quinoa. Not in Lima, not in
Europe, not in the US, none of those places.

—PAOLO, Juliaca-based quinoa processor, 2016

The gringos love quinoa.

—MARCO, Puno-based chef, 2017

In the mid-1980s psychologist and New Age spiritual seeker Steven Gorad spent many afternoons staked out at natural food stores. Gorad and his business partners took turns handing out promotional fliers and cooked quinoa samples in "little paper cups" to people who had never heard of the grain, often taking the time to verbally explain quinoa's many virtues to the curious shoppers. Gorad had discovered quinoa while attending a spiritual retreat in Bolivia in 1978. He quickly became enamored with the grain and returned to the United States with a 50 lb sack. Seeing a business opportunity, Gorad began devising a plan to import quinoa to the United States. In 1983 he partnered with a fellow disciple of the Bolivian mystic whom Gorad had followed and a Colorado-based agronomist with a PhD in international development to form Quinoa Corporation, the first and for a long time the only quinoa import venture in the United States. It was a unique marriage of New Age spiritualism, entrepreneurialism, and an interest in alternative development models that generated Quinoa Corporation. "We were on a mission for quinoa," Gorad stated decades later, describing the scrappy beginnings of the company.[59] Lacking funds for commercials or advertisements, they made banners and buttons that said "Quinoa is here"—anything to get the word out about this miraculous grain.[60] Over the next decade, Quinoa Corporation had some success. As a small but growing number of health food enthusiasts across the United States began eating quinoa, the grain slowly became incorporated into North American countercultural cuisine.

Throughout the 1980s and 1990s quinoa remained a marginal commodity in the United States, but it did gain a loyal following at health food stores across the country. Quinoa Corporation sold 3,000 lbs. per month in 1985 and 20,000 lbs. per month in 1986, a growth spurt that resulted from the salesmanship of Quinoa Corporation.[61] Figuring that a standard quinoa eater would eat one-half to one pound of dried quinoa per month, we can estimate that there were about twenty to forty thousand quinoa eaters in the United States in 1986, up from roughly zero just a few years prior. By this time, an array of health food markets born out of the organic food movement had become increasingly institutionalized in cities and towns across the country, particularly those with prominent "ex-hippie" populations.[62] They offered an outlet for quinoa where potential new customers were concentrated. Quinoa was slowly incorporated into the diets of committed health food enthusiasts, alongside a handful of other "nutraceuticals" like spirulina, miso, and chia.

Part of quinoa's allure for New Age eaters was its connection to the "ancient" Inca, something Quinoa Corporation emphasized in its marketing. Quinoa Corporation sold (and continues to sell) quinoa under the label

"Ancient Harvest," with the tag line "modern food from ancient fields."[63] For many years the package containing the red quinoa, "Inca Red," stated: "This important grain has ancient origins, dating back over five thousand years to the vast and mighty Inca civilization of South America. Quinoa was so important to the Inca culture, they referred to it as the mother grain. We call it the supergrain of the future because of its unique qualities." Paige West called the use of images of primitivity to add value to global food commodities "the imagined primitive."[64] Radical Otherness is commodified, rendered comfortable and consumable.[65] Emphasizing quinoa's link to the Inca also played up perceived associations between nutritional wisdom and past societies. Interest in quinoa among health food enthusiasts rested on nutritional primitivism, "a tendency to idealize 'primitive' food cultures as nutritional utopias."[66] It fit squarely into the discourses circulating among New Age health food communities about the problems of the industrial food system and the search for alternatives. Skeptical about "modern foods" and questioning mainstream nutritional authority, New Age health food enthusiasts sought out "lost" or "forgotten" wisdom in "ancient ways."

In addition to this strategic marketing, a handful of journalists began promoting quinoa in mainstream outlets in the United States in the 1980s. In a 1986 *New York Times* article titled "Quinoa, Inca Legacy Arrives," food critic Florence Fabricant explained the virtues of the "tiny ivory colored seed" that was being "rediscovered."[67] By 1989 "whole foods pioneer" Rebecca Wood had published a cookbook dedicated to the grain, *Quinoa, the Supergrain: Ancient Food for Today*.[68] A few years later the *New York Times* food section published a Thanksgiving meal article, "America Embraces Its Native Foods," which highlighted quinoa along with jicama and amaranth.[69] Quinoa's entrance into the pages of the *New York Times* is arguably a key moment in its transition from hippie food to "yuppie chow," because the *New York Times*'s food section plays an outsized role in taste making in the United States.[70] As was the case with the heirloom tomato, these mentions arguably provided legitimacy for quinoa and foreshadowed the ways quinoa eating would be more clearly wrapped up in class differentiation later on.[71]

While quinoa had become a staple in health food circles by the end of the 1980s, another two decades would pass before a larger swath of the US population became interested in the grain. The year 2008 was an inflection point. By that time, vegetarianism and veganism had become increasingly mainstream as fears about meat consumption's health impacts, the ethics of the meat industry, and the industry's contributions to global climate change led a growing number of Americans to reduce or eliminate meat and animal products from their diets. A broader swath of the American public was searching for plant-based proteins. Meanwhile, gluten had transformed into the problematic nutrient of the day, and a growing number of eaters were cutting gluten out of their diets, leading to an increased interest in starches that were not wheat based. This broader context, in which wealthy consumers were seeking out plant-based proteins and gluten-free starches, is critical for understanding quinoa's ascent to superfood stardom.

At the same time, quinoa fit easily into existing ideas about the composition of a meal. Anthropologist Sidney Mintz argued that cultures incorporate novel foods into *existing* meal categories.[72] This issue of compatibility can help explain why some exotic foods become popular and others fall by the wayside after initial interest. How, for instance, did quinoa become a mainstream ingredient in North American kitchens, while spirulina, açaí fruit, and kañiwa, quinoa's close relative, have not? The answer, at least in part, lies with quinoa's ability to substitute for more familiar foodstuffs. Most importantly, quinoa could stand in for rice in the North American culinary imaginary almost seamlessly. Quinoa stir-fries, quinoa bowls, and quinoa sushi became common fare, requiring little additional knowledge to prepare. The ease with which quinoa could enter a "standard" North American diet was made explicit in some promotional materials. For example, the description of quinoa on Ancient Harvest's website in 2021 read: "In our kitchen, ancient never gets old. This quinoa takes a time-tested, plant-based, nutrient-dense ingredient and turns it into a delicious break from rice that's ready for real life's fast pace. It'll make your next dish feel more like 'quin-whoa.'"[73]

But the construction of compelling associations and narratives about quinoa was equally important. Anthropologists have documented how incorporating new food practices is not a simple matter of assimilation.[74] Quinoa's meaning had to be constructed. Quinoa's "health halo" helped catapult the grain to mainstream success at a time when "healthy eating" increasingly signaled class status. But other changes in consumer tastes made quinoa stand out from other "healthy foods." The ways elite consumers in the Global North convey class identity through food was shifting in the 2010s. Fading were the days of the "gourmand," who sought ought French restaurants and other overt signals of wealth. Instead, elite status was increasingly conveyed through "culinary cosmopolitanism": an eclectic and worldly palate that prioritizes "exotic" and "authentic" foods.[75] While frequenting an expensive French restaurant may have historically signaled one's upper-class identity, increasingly, knowing about the "most authentic" dim sum restaurant or introducing friends to a little known mezcal variety now do much of that work. Eaters wanted novelty, and they sought out foods with stories behind them that helped craft a sense of authenticity.

The imagined primitive took on renewed symbolic power in this context. While it was a small segment of the population that sought out nutritional primitivism in the 1980s, by the 2010s mainstream consumers increasingly sought out novelty and authenticity. Images of primitivity were used to market a growing variety of goods, from fair-trade coffee to rooibos tea.[76] Calling quinoa a "lost crop" or associating quinoa with the Inca Empire lent quinoa the exotic and authentic appeal that a growing proportion of North American consumers sought. A Bob's Red Mill brand package of organic quinoa from 2022 stated the following:

> My lifelong fascination with whole grains has taken me to the far reaches of the globe. On these journeys I have discovered many delicious treasures— the mighty grains that nourished the world's greatest ancient civilizations. I call them our Grains of Discovery®, and I've brought their stories home to share with you. Like this story of quinoa. . . . Native to South America, this amazing plant was domesticated thousands of years ago near Lake Titicaca, high on the plateaus of the Andes. It was a mainstay in the idea of the ancient Incas, who considered it a sacred crop. I hope you enjoy exploring the culinary and nutritional wonders of ancient grains with quinoa and with all of our Grains of Discovery®.

In a similar move, Alter-Eco brand uses Quechua words to generate an association with Otherness: *Chisaya Mama*, meaning "mother of all grains" in Quechua, is printed in a large, swooping font across the package. Some packages gesture toward primitivity through references to the poverty of contemporary quinoa producers (often including photos of the producers) and suggest the buyer is helping them through their purchase. Alter-Eco notes that fifty-three families are benefiting from the quinoa cooperative where the company purchases its quinoa and states that they are gaining 23 percent in additional revenue. These moral appeals may sell quinoa, but anthropologist Paige West has argued that these images of primitivity used to sell food commodities often imply that the "backwardness" of the producers causes poverty, obscuring the structural relations and global political economy that actually support poverty in the Andes.[77] Together, quinoa's novelty and origins in the "exotic" Andes helped transform quinoa from granola health food to status symbol.

In the 2010s quinoa demand grew quickly, making its way onto the plates of wealthy, health-conscious "neophiles" within and beyond the United States.[78] In addition to its increase in North America, quinoa consumption increased dramatically among well-off urban populations across Western Europe, Australia, South Asia, East Asia, the Middle East, and Africa. Quinoa was increasingly a staple in the diets of self-consciously cosmopolitan eaters the world round. Consuming quinoa came to signify wealth and sophisticated sensibilities—ironically, the opposite of its historic meaning in the Andes.

This mushrooming interest in quinoa among wealthy eaters in the Global North helped transform its meaning to Peruvian eaters, especially those who had long avoided the grain. Outside the Andes, quinoa's meaning had to be constructed from scratch. There was no symbolic baggage shaping perceptions of it. This was far from the case in the Andes. Long associated with rural poverty and backwardness, quinoa was now being eaten by gringos—the epitome of whiteness, wealth, and modernity that many Peruvians aspired to. The upper echelons of Peruvian society have for centuries sought to emulate consumer tastes in consumer goods from the Global North.[79] It is perhaps the paradigmatic example of the coloniality of power that appreciation for quinoa among wealthy Peruvians required first its appreciation by wealthy white consumers in the Global North. But now these ideas came into direct conflict with the way many Peruvians had been socialized. Could the ever-present yearning for modernity take the shape of eating Indian food?

REDISCOVERING "AUTHENTIC" PERUVIAN FOOD

In 2013 one of Peru's main beer brands, Cuzqueña, began producing a quinoa-based beer. The launch for Cuzqueña Quinua included a full-blown marketing campaign: billboards around Lima and television advertisements encouraged Peruvians to try this unique beer. Cuzqueña Quinoa, these advertisements suggested, was not just another beer. "Our flavor, made into beer," read the billboards. The Cuzqueña Quinua television spot features a sequence of short slow-motion clips set to Andean pan pipe music: a pair of Caucasian hands grasp handfuls of quinoa from a large sack; these same hands slice an orange, then peel a potato; quinoa grains drop into water, making small splashes; and a *lomo saltado* (a common Peruvian dish) sautés in a pan. Halfway through the sequence, a male narrator's booming voice, with a characteristic limeño lilt, declares the following: "Quinoa defines our flavor as Peruvians. And this deserves celebration with a special beer. This is a special blessing: Cuzqueña Quinua . . . *our* flavor, made into beer."[80]

The commercial framed Cuzqueña Quinoa as an homage to the very essence of Peruvianness: a literal distillation of Peruvian identity. Drinking Cuzqueña Quinua, the marketing campaign suggests, could help Peruvians get in touch with their very Peruvianness. By 2013 quinoa's position within the Peruvian culinary imaginary had changed to such an extent that this marketing campaign made sense to a growing sector of the Peruvian population. No longer a marginalized food, quinoa had come to be seen as a key ingredient in Peruvian food *and* a quintessential aspect of Peruvian identity writ large. Idioms of discovery and especially self-discovery, I argue, were a key component of the reimagining of quinoa specifically and Peruvian food generally.[81] This shifting understanding of quinoa among Peruvians was part of an explicit project to transform Peruvian food into a globally relevant cuisine and position food as a core element of Peruvian identity often called the gastronomic revolution. At the same time, it reframed social difference within Peru as benign and commodifiable cultural (culinary) elements, a depoliticized and unhistorical understanding of diversity Peruvian anthropologist Gisela Cánepa has argued: "We only seem comfortable when those 'others' and their cultural manifestations can be appreciated as objects of consumption and aesthetic pleasure."[82]

Throughout much of the twentieth century, the concept of a high-end Peruvian food restaurant was an oxymoron for Peruvians and foreign tourists alike. Lima's expensive restaurants featured European fare, and Peruvian dishes were considered unequivocally inferior to their European counterparts. During the late 1980s, a small cadre of limeño journalists and chefs sought to change this.[83] Driven by a sense of nationalism and an interest in novel business opportunities, they began meeting together in each other's homes with the goal of developing a Peruvian haute cuisine that could compete with the likes of French and Italian food. Bernardo Roca Rey, the late journalist and member of the Miró Quesada family that runs Peru's most powerful newspaper, became a leader in this effort. "All the nice restaurants in Lima were French. That was part of my job. There were about sixty or eighty French restaurants that were the most important restaurants in Lima and today there are only two. Two. That is a battle, not against French cuisine, it is a battle to revalue what is ours," he told me in 2016, reflecting on these early efforts. The resulting novoandino cuisine paired Andean ingredients such as quinoa, oca, ulloco, and Andean potatoes, many of which were widely disparaged or relatively unknown in Lima, with European cooking techniques and plating styles. Quinoa was, from the beginning, central to novoandino cuisine. The ease with which quinoa could be incorporated into familiar forms, combined with its symbolic potency, made it a hallmark of novoandino cooking. Quinoto, for instance, a risotto dish prepared with quinoa instead of rice, became the archetypical novoandino dish.

Novoandino_cuisine was an explicitly elite project intended to produce an exclusive culinary culture that could compete with other haute cuisines. Zilkia Janer critiqued new world "fusion" cuisines like novoandino as neocolonial projects that reinforce Eurocentrism because the resulting cuisine is structured by European culinary values "and incorporates other cuisines only to reduce them to sources of natural ingredients devoid of a culture of their own."[84] Peruvian elites were socially distant enough from Peru's indigenous people that they could experiment with so-called Indian foods without fear that their own social status would be thrown into question. Peru's middle classes, by contrast, were not comfortably far enough from the perceived contamination of indigeneity to allow for this kind of safe experimentation without provoking class and racial anxiety. At the same time, the French plating, upper-class limeño chefs, and expensive menu prices helped further distinguish ingredients like quinoa from their associations with poverty and ensured novoandino would remain an elite pastime. Yet this creation of "gourmet" Andean food also legitimized ingredients like quinoa, helping make them acceptable to more Peruvians.[85]

The scope of this project broadened dramatically in the early 2000s. A small group of native limeños with European culinary training sought to expand the reinvention of Peruvian food beyond high-end cuisine. Gastón Acurio, the son of a prominent politician, would become the unequivocal public face of the "gastronomic revolution," a project that would reinvent Peruvian food in the eyes of Peruvians and foreigners alike. Acurio invokes a trope of self-discovery in his oft-repeated story of his own reappraisal of Peruvian food, which is frequently framed as the beginning of a national reappraisal of Peruvian food. The story goes that Acurio was sent to Spain to study law in the 1980s. While there, he dropped out of law school to follow his childhood dream of cooking professionally. After attending Le Cordon Bleu in Paris he returned to Lima with his German wife, Astrid Gutsche, and opened an upscale bistro serving French food in Lima. But within a few years they had changed over to serving Peruvian food, a shift Acurio has attributed to his "discovery" of Peruvian food: "[At first, we cooked] French food—it's what they taught me. But I then realized that right in front of me was the green pepper, which is super difficult to find, and that I could have four or five Peruvian species of green pepper along with a dozen exotic fruits at my disposal. I began to rediscover my country and to associate all that I had learned in Europe with my surroundings."[86] In other words, once Acurio "discovered" the culinary potential of Peru and its untapped gastronomic resources, he began to incorporate Peruvian dishes and ingredients into Astrid y Gaston's menu.

While "revolution" is arguably a misnomer insofar as the project did not radically remake the sociopolitical structures of the country, it is difficult to exaggerate the degree to which the gastronomic revolution impacted Peruvian national identity. A number of Peruvians explained to me that before the gastronomic revolution, Peru had a "self-esteem problem." A common refrain was that while Brazil had the best soccer players and Argentina had tango, what did Peruvians have to be proud of besides Machu Picchu? In the 2000s and 2010s the answer increasingly became that Peru had the best food. The unequivocal agreement among Peruvians that the country had the best food was the result of a highly intentional social, political, and economic project carried forward by a host of powerful actors. María Elena García calls the set of relationships linking the celebrity chefs, state officials, journalists, and political elites who have actively promoted food as a dominant strategy for economic development and a new form of nationalism Peru's "gastro-political complex." Journalists and chefs played a pivotal role in disseminating new ideas about Peruvian food and locating food at the core of what it meant to be Peruvian. Major newspapers made food journalism central to their lifestyle sections, featuring recipes for Peruvian dishes and interviews with Peruvian chefs. Instead of offering tips on how to cook Italian food, these articles contributed to the increasingly codified sense of Peruvian food as a unique and coherent cuisine.

Tropes of discovery have been central to the marketing of Peruvian food abroad.[87] Peru's celebrity chefs leverage narratives of lost and discovered foods to market the Peruvian food experience to foreign consumers and culinary tourists while positioning themselves as national and global culinary leaders. This language of exploration and mystery, alongside aestheticized depictions of culinary bioprospecting, helps draw culinary tourists to Peru. Yet the meaning of these discovery narratives is dual in nature. While the gastronomic revolution beckoned wealthy foreigners to "discover" the "mystical" and "exotic" country of Peru through food, and spend their tourist dollars while doing it, its significance for Peruvians was in the chance it offered them to rediscover what it meant to be Peruvian. Its significance for Peruvian audiences was distinct from its meaning for foreigners; it was about self-discovery and getting in touch with Peruvian identity. Diego Muñoz, who took over the head chef position at Astrid y Gastón after Gastón stepped down to focus on other ventures, explained this pursuit of the authentic Peruvian identity through cooking: "It's more about looking to what was done in the past. It is about looking for the pure, the autochthonous. It's about searching for oneself."[88] Peruvian chefs and journalists commonly invoke an *us* when discussing Peruvian food; discussion of our food, our recipes, our ingredients, and our heritage is commonplace. In a 2016 interview, Acurio explained the shift from chefs cooking French food to cooking Peruvian food in Peru, "We decided we will cook *as Peruvians* to put a value on *our own* ingredients, culture, traditions."[89] Food was increasingly articulated as something Peruvians shared, something they should take pride in.

Quinoa was one of the "lost" elements of Peruvian identity that warranted revival. Quinoa's significance for the gastronomic revolution was related to the way it fit squarely into the discourses of discovery/self-discovery that lay at the heart of the gastronomic revolution. Yet it was not simply revalorizing what Peruvians already knew; the gastronomic revolution also sought to help Peruvians *discover* Peruvian food in the first place. The gastronomic revolution sought to educate Peruvians about Peruvian food and to generate a sense of pride in it. The gastronomic revolution promoted a form of Peruvian self-discovery and self-actualization through exposure to new dishes and ingredients. Food was an avenue for getting in touch with authentic Peruvian-ness, now a safe way to experience and perform what it meant to be Peruvian. That quinoa was never actually lost—it remained a staple for millions of Peruvians throughout the colonial and postcolonial eras—mattered little. Framing foods like quinoa as "lost" conceals the fact that many of them are not lost but rather poverty foods unknown to cultural elites. These narratives of loss and discovery instead exalt the heroic work of chefs and journalists who transform these "valueless" ingredients into valuable dishes served in Lima's high-end restaurants.[90]

Quinoa acquired outsized symbolic weight within the gastronomic revolution. Quinoa demand abroad dovetailed with the success of Peruvian food as a concept within and beyond Peru. As quinoa increasingly received attention among wealthy consumers abroad, this demand legitimized its value within Peru and underscored the lucrative nature of revalorizing, repackaging, and exporting Peruvian ingredients and products for the rest of the world. Quinoa became an emblem for the commodifiable version of Peruvian national identity promoted by gastronomic revolution proponents.

Since 2010 countless published Peruvian cookbooks have featured numerous quinoa recipes, the vast majority of which use quinoa in ways not common in its native highlands. Quinoa was the only ingredient with its own hall in the 2013 Mistura Food Festival, an annual celebration of food and food products on the outskirts of Lima that boasted an attendance of over one hundred thousand participants. Mundo Quinoa featured booths with chefs cooking creative dishes that used quinoa in new ways (quinoa tamales, quinoa pastas, etc.), along with a wide array of products containing quinoa, such as bars and candy. The sheer quantity of different presentations of quinoa at the festival highlighted the centrality of quinoa in this broader reimaginative project. Not simply an ingredient in the national cuisine, quinoa had become part of the iconography of the Peruvian nation.

In this way, quinoa served as a metonym for a larger nationalist effort. Quinoa's historical marginalization, in which it was long derided as an "Indian food" and "poor people's food," followed by its sudden popularity among wealthy elites at home and abroad offered an allegory for the potential to reconsider undervalued aspects of Peruvian identity. Quinoa's own ascent from poverty food to global superfood dramatized the narrative of self-discovery. As Acurio explained: "So, when we started this movement 20 years ago, one of the amazing reasons why we wanted to do this is we wanted to liberate our people from this fear [of shame]. We wanted to prove to them that it was not true that our culture is inferior to other cultures. That the heritage we have over the years of embracing other cultures is not something worse, or of less value, than the culture of Europe, or Japan, or the United States."

Quinoa offered middle-class Peruvians an opportunity to rediscover an "authentic" Peru in a safe way that did not put their class status at risk. As quinoa dotted the menus of the country's most expensive restaurants and increasingly was featured on the pages of *Somos* and other national publications, eating quinoa no longer connoted the social dangers it once had.

This invocation of value—embracing the value of quinoa alongside and in combination with the value of Peruvian identity—muddles concepts of social value and economic value. Peruvians should be proud of quinoa in part because of its economic value, which lends validity to the changing social value. Quinoa's price on the global market is proof of quinoa's value. Gastronomic revolution rhetoric explicitly draws on the slippage between these ideas of value.[91] This was in some sense a retooling of Max Weber's "gospel of wealth" idea, which suggests that capitalism relies on the idea that economic productivity is morally righteous. Quinoa's growing price suggested its goodness; its economic value justifies and supports its social value. As the next section shows, the use of scientific knowledge about quinoa's nutritional profile served to further rationalize quinoa's value and distance it from connections to indigeneity.

THE INCA'S GOLDEN GRAIN

An ancient Andean pseudo-cereal that was revered by the Incas, quinoa is regarded as a superfood because of its health-promoting properties—packed with protein, it contains most of the essential amino acids, is high in dietary fibre and a good source of iron, potassium, and magnesium. It's also gluten free.

—description in recipe for "quinoa milk,"
VIRGILIO MARTINEZ, *Lima, the Cookbook* (2015)

Before the 1970s, Peruvian supermarkets did not sell quinoa. Buying quinoa entailed going to an open-air public market or a weekly *domingal*, one of the many weekly informal markets where vendors take over the streets of a prescribed section of a town or city for a day. At these markets, vendors sell quinoa alongside other grains, dried pastas, and potatoes from large polypropylene sacks, measuring out a buyer's desired amount and pouring it into a clear plastic bag. In this historically predominant model, there is no glossy "marketing," no catchy labels, slogans, or advertising. Instead, individual market vendors (almost exclusively women) must convince customers to buy their products, relying on their reputations and personal relationships with customers. These markets are not neutral spaces within the Peruvian spatialized racial imaginary. If the new large supermarkets colonizing the country—Plaza Vea and Wong—represent a clean modernity with abundant consumer products, for many, the domingales and municipal markets represent an intrusion of rural Peru (coded as Indian, traditional, and dirty) into urban spaces.[92] Upper-class customers commonly avoid these markets, seeing them as unhygienic and the products within them as questionable in quality. Quinoa, along with other products exclusively available in the markets, took on these associations.

In 1971 Cuzqueño entrepreneur Teodoro Ortiz sought to change how quinoa was sold. He founded what would be the first commercial quinoa-processing operation, which sold quinoa in individual packages under the label IncaSur. This was a turning point for the marketing of quinoa. Ortiz's marketing sought to link quinoa to the Inca in the eyes of Peruvian consumers. All IncaSur products feature the IncaSur logo, a cartoon depiction of Machu Picchu, the famous Inca ruin, with "IncaSur" written in large white text below it. Its slogan, "Revalorizing our Andean grains, an inheritance from our ancestors," gestures toward the (Inca) ancestors while invoking a Peruvian "us." While many Peruvian products have been marketed using Inca imagery (e.g., Inca Kola), Ortiz's project was to reassociate quinoa. Quinoa was not an *Indian* food; it was an *Inca* food—and, by extension, a Peruvian food.

At the same time, IncaSur's use of individual packages was making quinoa available in new kinds of spaces, in supermarkets. Packaging quinoa in individual sacks allowed it to move from markets, long viewed by Peruvian elites with some combination of suspicion and contempt, to more "reputable" (read: whiter, modern) spaces like supermarkets, places where decent folk shopped.[93] Geographer Jennifer Jordan suggested that space plays a pivotal role in the meanings foods take on.[94] Her study of the rise of the heirloom tomato as a status symbol among North American foodies showed that this change was made possible by heirloom tomatoes' appearance in elite spaces: high-end restaurants, the *New York Times* food section, and lifestyle magazines. Quinoa was undergoing a similar respatialization in Peru. IncaSur's packaging of quinoa helped create a symbolic distance between quinoa and open-air markets. Later efforts by Peru's gastropolitical leaders to position quinoa recipes prominently in lifestyle magazines and chefs' use of quinoa in high-end restaurants further respatialized quinoa, helping make it palatable to Peruvian elites.

For more than three decades, IncaSur faced little competition, as demand for quinoa in supermarkets remained relatively low. Quinoa was still primarily sold in Peru's open-air markets. However, starting in the 2010s IncaSur began to face competition as demand for quinoa and products containing quinoa grew. By 2015 quinoa was a staple in Peruvian supermarkets. In addition to quinoa in grain, a host of products emerged featuring quinoa:

cookies, granola, bread, chips, crackers, milk, and chocolate bars. Many of these new products built on the connection of quinoa to the Inca that Ortiz had pioneered. Packaging for these products commonly featured symbols of the Inca—explicit mentions of the Inca (e.g., "golden grain of the Incas") and/or symbolic connections like an Inca crown or Inca tapestry designs.

Reframing quinoa not as an Indian food but as an *Inca* food was critical to quinoa's transformation in the eyes of middle- and upper-class Peruvians. While invoking the Inca on quinoa packaging is likely to generate images of the "imagined primitive" for a North American consumer, in Peru the Inca are not primitive at all. The Inca and Indians have long been seen as quite distinct in the racial imaginary of Peruvian elites.[95] In the 1500s many Inca elites joined forces with Spanish colonists, intermarrying and consolidating political power while working together to subjugate commoners. The figure of the Inca remained central to Peruvian nationalism after independence.[96] During and since the early days of the Republic, Peruvian elites have claimed indigenous (Inca) symbols and often touted explicit ancestral linkages to Inca nobility.[97] The Inca were elites, majestic and civilized. Yet the same consideration was never "extended to existing indigenous peoples, who were seen as dirty and uncivilized." Marisol de la Cadena traced how this differentiation between preconquest Indians and living indigenous peoples has played out among upper-class Cuzqueños.[98] Throughout the twentieth century, Cuzqueño elites fashioned themselves as heirs to the Inca legacy, appropriating Inca symbolism while actively distancing themselves from the indigenous peoples who lived in and around the city. What is stigmatizing for those in marginalized social positions can be authenticating for those in securely elite social positions. While the Inca are considered regal and powerful, today's indigenous communities remain highly marginalized within Peruvian society.

The Inca's symbolic potency, then, has to do with the way it stands in for ideas of civilization, nationalism, and citizenship. After Peru gained independence in the early nineteenth century, nationalist elites sought to create meaningful national histories and myths that would have broad appeal to the newly minted "Peruvians."[99] The Inca (both as in the Inca Empire and the political and spiritual leader of it, "the Inca") featured prominently in these early constructions of Peruvianness, and national narratives about the Inca Empire sit the crux of Peruvian identity today, often to the exclusion of other identities.[100] While the association with the Inca made quinoa exotic and invoked a mystical Other for foreign consumers, for Peruvians the Inca mythmaking invoked modernity and even whiteness. The Inca have always been modern, and have "also always been white," argued Shane Greene.[101] The construction of the Inca is conflated with discourses of modernity, civilization, and whiteness such that associating quinoa with the Inca was a dramatic change from its previous association with Indians.

Using images of the Inca to make a product evoke "Peruvian-ness" is by no means limited to quinoa. The world's only national soda that outsells Coca-Cola in its own country, Inca Kola, invokes the Inca to appeal to Peruvians, but especially white-mestizo Peruvians.[102] Not unlike the Cuzqueña Quinua commercial, with its conspicuously pale hands, advertisements for Inca Kola make explicit the imagined audience's whiteness. The common use of the Inca in marketing products to Peruvian audiences derives from the potency of this symbol of national heritage. Associating quinoa with the Inca helped obscure its connection to living indigenous Peruvians, while at the same time rendering it a "national" food replete with associations of Inca grandeur.

The complex construction of the Inca helps us understand why reimagining quinoa as an Inca food matters. Quinoa's prior association with contemporary indigenous people rendered it an "Indian food" and unfit for consumption by so-called decent folks. Refashioning quinoa as Inca food had the effect of distancing quinoa from its connection to Peru's indigenous population. While it would be tempting to read quinoa's revalorization as indicative of a wholesale reappraisal of indigenous lifeways in this context, the explicit connections forged between quinoa and the Inca undermine that explanation. Linking quinoa to the Inca helped make quinoa acceptable to Peruvian middle and upper classes, many of whom identified with Inca heritage but *not* with existing indigenous populations. This erasure helped divorce quinoa from its long-standing associations with rural poverty, Indians, and backwardness. In other words, it helped whiten quinoa.

AN ANDEAN SUPERFOOD:
WHITENESS AND NUTRITIONAL AUTHORITY

Ecoandino brand's quinoa is packaged more like high-end coffee than a grain. An opaque white plastic sack that is resealable at the top, the quarter-kilogram package features slick graphic design. The bag reads *supergrano* in large print above an image of white quinoa and a list of key nutritional features in maroon text:

Essential Amino Acids
Vitamins and Minerals
0% Saponin
Omega 3 and 6

Almost all quinoa packages available in Peruvian supermarkets today conspicuously display nutritional properties. While linking quinoa to the Inca made quinoa symbolically palatable to middle- and upper-class Peruvians by invoking elite nationalism, emphasizing quinoa's nutritional bona fides offers scientific legitimacy for quinoa's value. Featuring a list of the grain's "charismatic nutrients" became ubiquitous in the 2010s.[103] This list of quinoa's verified nutritional components made its value appear objective and unquestionable. Invocations of nutritional science in quinoa packaging legitimized quinoa consumption and had a similar distancing effect to that of the association with the Inca. While the discourse of quinoa as an Inca food "whitened" quinoa through referencing complex ideas about Inca nationalism, listing nutritional components modernized quinoa by invoking science. This was the opposite of the nutritional primitivism that companies used to sell quinoa to wealthy foreigners. Instead, via this nutrition discourse, quinoa became explicitly associated with "modern" nutritional science.

Quinoa was not just any food; it was a superfood. The superlative further removed quinoa from the general food category. Quinoa did not just shift from a poverty food to an acceptable food; it became a superfood, one with seemingly magical nutritional prowess. While the concept of a superfood is a marketing device, it is also a folk category that people use to make sense of relationships between food and health.[104] Though no agreed upon definition of a superfood exists, the term has come to take on specific meanings in a range of social contexts.

Disaggregating quinoa into its constituent nutritional elements comprises what Gyorgy Scrinis has called *nutritionism*, a paradigm that sees the scientifically identified nutrients within a food as the primary determinants of the food's value.[105] Within this framework, a diet is simply nutrition, and a food is a vehicle for nutrients: an aggregate of a specific set of nutrients. Conceiving of a food's purpose as solely nutritional deemphasizes its connection to cultural practices, symbolic meanings, and identities. Scholars of nutritionism assert that this way of seeing food is severely lacking because a food's cultural meanings, ritualized consumption, and connection to collective memory are rendered unimportant. In other words, nutritionism is

FIGURE 5. Packet of Ecoandino brand quinoa. Photo by author.

a form of erasure that centers the nutritional components of a food over all else. Nutritionism's erasure proved useful in distancing quinoa from its previous associations. Quinoa was an impressive agglomeration of nutritional properties, one that stood out in comparison to other foods. Reinforcing quinoa's nutritional credentials helped disassociate it from previous links with the "backward" and "irrational" beliefs of native peoples quinoa had long been associated with. Quinoa's value was validated by scientific authority and sanitized from older associations.

While Adriana did not grow up eating quinoa, when she was a young adult in the early 2000s her sister introduced her to the idea of quinoa as a "diet food." "It was like quinoa was something you should eat instead of rice. A cup of quinoa instead of a cup of rice because it has more protein or less calories or something." Framing quinoa around its nutritional dimensions contributed to the divorcing of quinoa from its prior connections to Indianness. No longer a symbol of backwardness and ignorance, eating quinoa was modern and rational. Because of how understandings of race intersect with concepts of progress, quinoa also became *whiter*. Scholars have remarked on the whiteness of hegemonic nutritional policies in many contexts.[106] Usually this takes the form of imposing supposedly "universal" nutritional ideals about what a "good diet" looks like, which center a "Mediterranean diet" (read: Greco-Roman) while excluding other nutritionally complete diets.[107] In quinoa's case, reframing quinoa's value within the language of nutritional science offered scientific validation for quinoa's value, with scientific knowledge itself coded as modern and therefore countering its previous associations with indigeneity.

Quinoa offered a model for a growing number of Andean foods that have since been marketed to both Peruvian and foreign audiences as superfoods (maca, lucuma, etc.). The essence of this strategy is to take foods with either negative associations for middle- and upper-class consumers or no associations at all and to reimagine them by fitting them into a new "legible" category. Selling these foods involves making claims of special nutritional prowess beyond what one expects of a normal food and in turn works to distance the food from its past meanings while drawing on and centering scientific authority. This emphasis on nutritional content is not benign in this context but figures into layered and racialized meanings.

CONCLUSION

Discussions of the revalorization of marginalized foods often suggest a wholly positive trend, something universally laudable and worth encouraging, *or* a condemnable neocolonial project that can only generate superficial change. The story of quinoa's transformation from poverty food into an emblem of

Peruvian national identity and staple of middle- and upper-class Peruvians should give us pause. Quinoa's story reveals a complex situation: actors like Schiaffino may have been guided by genuine motivations to foment social change and challenge the racist ideas that led to the concept of an Indian food. Yet larger structures of power limited the possibilities of this revalorization project. Efforts to reinvent quinoa and other so-called Indian foods were caught in an enduring racialized culinary hierarchy, such that remaking the image of quinoa required whitening it. Quinoa became palatable to middle-class Peruvians in part through explicit distancing from living indigenous peoples. Quinoa wasn't just revalued; it was whitened. It was this process that helped give the grain value in the eyes of more Peruvians. Quinoa's revalorization was based in the creation and circulation of new narratives about quinoa *and* the erasure of existing ones. Taken together, connecting quinoa to the majestic Inca and ideas about "authentic" Peruvian-ness, along with emphasizing quinoa's nutritional content, worked to distance quinoa from associations with Peruvian indigenous populations and to "whiten" it. The narratives often overlapped and reinforced each other. As we know from the previous chapter, quinoa's nutritional content was by no means a recent discovery. Throughout the twentieth century, many Peruvians shunned the grain even though its impressive nutritional properties were widely known. Quinoa's acceptance as a healthy superfood—one wealthy and middle-class Peruvian eaters sought out—was based in part on the way emphasis on quinoa's nutritional properties simultaneously interacted with other narratives that distanced quinoa from its indigenous origins. These narratives would not have circulated without the formation of a sociopolitical network of powerful actors to disseminate them. Quinoa was associated with the Inca, Peruvian nationalism, and scientific authority but also with the elite chefs proffering these stories. This too, was racialized. As other scholars have argued, it was not just the prestige of chefs like Acurio and Schiaffino that helped reposition quinoa in the national imaginary: it was their whiteness, their location in Lima, their training in European culinary institutions.

Chapters 1 and 2 tracked the sociopolitical and symbolic work that went into transforming perceptions of quinoa among the international development community and among Peruvian eaters, respectively. These chapters foregrounded actors who operated outside of, though in partial connection to, the Puno Region of Peru. These chapters collectively brought to the fore the diverse kinds of individual actors—chefs, journalists, nutrition scientists, agronomists, development practitioners—and institutional actors—restaurants, media outlets, development agencies, research institutions—that played critical roles in changing quinoa's social status. The remaining chapters explore the quinoa boom and bust from the vantage of Puno, Peru, quinoa's global production hub, while attending to the ways actors based physically in Puno were always already connected to individuals, institutions, narratives, and processes outside the region. The next chapter tracks the social and ecological dynamics animating the nascent quinoa export industry in Puno during the quinoa bonanza (2013–14), demonstrating how the transformation of quinoa into an export crop was also a project of landscape change.

PART TWO

———————

Boom

THREE

———

The Quinoa Frontier

MAKING A PRODUCTIVE
AND ORDERLY LANDSCAPE

> A frontier is an edge of space and time: a zone of not yet—not
> yet mapped, not yet regulated. It is a zone of unmapping: even
> in its planning, a frontier is imagined as unplanned. Frontiers
> aren't just discovered at the edge; they are projects in making
> geographical and temporal experience.
>
> —ANNA TSING, *Friction*, 32

EVERY MONDAY MORNING during the 2014 harvest season, CIMA held a team meeting. At 9:00 a.m. all the company employees—técnicos, processing-plant workers, even the secretary—would gather in a large room above CIMA's quinoa-processing plant to hear about the plan for the week and discuss pressing issues. After almost twenty years as an agricultural development NGO, CIMA had converted into a for-profit enterprise in 2009 to take advantage of rising prices. It quickly became one of the region's dominant quinoa-buying and -processing companies.

The meeting space had a distinct classroom-like feel. A dozen people sat at tables, facing the front of the room with notebooks and pens before them. Scribbled diagrams and anonymous calculations covered a large rolling whiteboard. Tall windows looked out at Salcedo, a quiet industrial area on the outskirts of the city of Puno. Salcedo had one paved road down the center, with the rest of the area served by dirt alleys snaking between cinder-block warehouses. As was typical for Puno, the room was about 55°F, and everyone was bundled up in coats and scarves. As we waited for the meeting to begin, a large thermos of hot water circulated around the room, and people took turns adding water to mugs of instant coffee or coca leaves they had procured from the break room.

When Emiliano walked in, small talk hushed, and it was clear the meeting was beginning. Emiliano became CIMA's CEO in 2009 when he took over from his father and reoriented CIMA around quinoa buying. He wore his typical black business suit, white-collared shirt, and gold chain necklace, a self-presentation that contrasted markedly from CIMA's employees, who wore jeans, down jackets, and hiking boots. After quick niceties, he wrote the word *zonification* on the whiteboard in all caps. Emiliano spoke with authority: "I need each of you to make a zonification plan," he instructed, looking at his team of six lead técnicos, who sat clustered in the front of the room. Técnicos served as the face of CIMA in the *campo* (countryside), which this time of year meant facilitating quinoa buys after the recent harvest and coordinating with farmers for the upcoming planting season: making plans about which seeds farmers should plant and training farmers in preparing their soil. This was a frenzied time of year for them.

It quickly became apparent that not everyone understood what Emiliano meant by zonification plan, so he clarified. He instructed técnicos to figure out exactly how much land each farmer they were working with could dedicate to quinoa and then to add this up to give him an aggregate total. In short, how much arable and semi-arable land was currently being planted with quinoa and how much land could be converted to quinoa during the next season? "I want us to have a clear plan for exactly what [variety] we will plant in each zone and exactly how much, and also where we will get the seeds," he continued.

Buying quinoa was a huge logistical undertaking that had only become more difficult during the boom. With demand surging, CIMA could barely keep up with incoming orders. It had come to Emiliano's attention that while CIMA had forged relationships with many farmers, it did not have reliable information about the farmer network and the quinoa available. Between the 2013 and 2014 harvests, CIMA had expanded quickly, adding three new técnicos in an effort to incorporate more farmers into its network and to meet the out-of-control demand. This added to the uncertainty, as not all the técnicos were true experts in their assigned zones. Each técnico was responsible for a different region within the Puno Department, and while seasoned técnicos might have rough estimations of each farmer's capacity, Emiliano needed the big picture. More precise documentation of the land the farmers managed would, in theory, allow him to make better business decisions. And ideally, such information could help him better align the unruly agricultural landscape with market demands.

The year 2014 marked the apex of the quinoa boom. While global demand had been rising quickly since 2008, prices almost doubled in a single

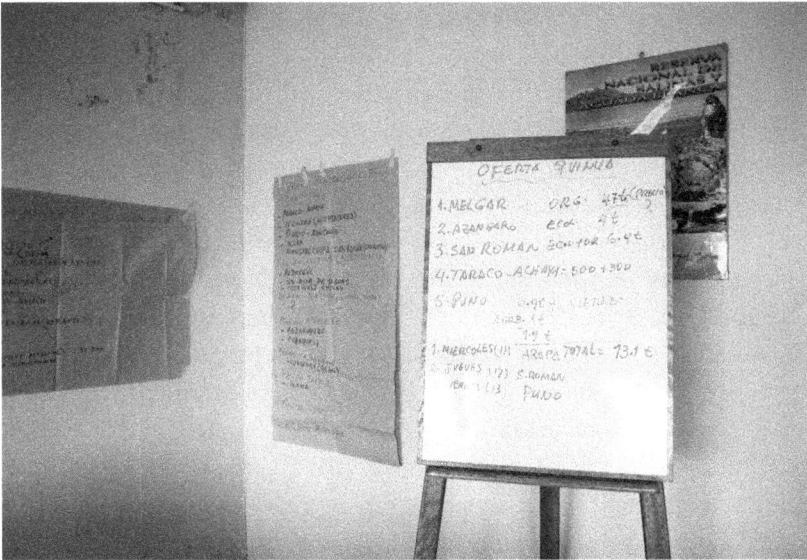

FIGURE 6. Rough drafts of CIMA's zonification plans in June 2014. Photo by author.

year between June 2013 and June 2014. Some of Puno's farmers received as much as US$4.71 for a kilogram of unprocessed quinoa, which would have sold for about US$1.50 in 2012 (see figure 17 in appendix). Established buyers along with an influx of newcomers scrambled to acquire a limited supply of quinoa. The bonanza was a time of excitement and dreams, but also one of anxiety and chaos. Established quinoa-buying and -processing businesses, like CIMA, were growing rapidly, with new clients reaching out each week in pursuit of high-quality processed quinoa. But the bonanza also generated new competition within the industry. Dozens of entrepreneurs from Lima flocked to the altiplano to take advantage of the high prices. Meanwhile, acopiadores, who had long undermined buyer-processors like CIMA, were working twice as hard to buy up quinoa. The number of intermediaries competing for quinoa mushroomed. Everyone wanted a larger piece of Puno's finite quinoa stock.

For farmers, quinoa's high price offered hope for a better future. Quinoa had long been primarily a poverty food, a cheap and nutritious staple that generated minimal, if any, profits for farmers.[1] In a context without other cash crops, the possibility of earning significant income from quinoa appeared truly momentous for the fifty-five thousand or so small-scale farmers in the Puno Region.[2] After decades of rural-urban migration, many hoped a lucrative export crop would provide a justification for younger generations to stay and work the land.³ Moreover, with a glut of buyers competing for the same quinoa, farmers found themselves with some bargaining power, many for the first time. But selling quinoa commercially required dramatic changes to how they grew the crop, including investing large amounts of time, energy, and resources not normally dedicated to quinoa and reconfiguring their farms spatially and ecologically to prioritize it.

Commodity frontiers are not discovered, they are created. Frontiers emerge from a way of seeing land and resources that foregrounds potential.⁴ The frontier gaze constructs land and resources ripe for extraction by erasing existing claims and devaluing existing social and ecological relations. Long imagined through metanarratives of civilizational progress, frontier spaces have been seen as transitional zones between civilization and barbarism, the liminal space between content and emptiness.⁵ Skyrocketing demand for quinoa signaled the beginning of a new era for agriculture in the altiplano. More than a bonanza, booming prices heralded a prosperous future for Puno's agricultural sector while also offering a long-awaited opportunity to "modernize" highland farming practices, an agricultural landscape long read as woefully unmodern and antiquated. Agricultural development organizations had been introducing new agricultural technologies and concepts from mainstream agronomy for decades, but farmers were often highly selective about which advice to take and which technologies to implement. Agribusiness people, policymakers, and representatives from international development agencies complained that highland farmers were stubborn and largely uninterested in outside advice. A strong price signal appeared to be just the incentive needed to motivate the "will to improve" among Puno's quinoa farmers.⁶ Discourses of modernity figured centrally in day-to-day industry practices. Surging demand for quinoa was not just a business opportunity; many saw it as a chance to remake Andean agriculture at large: to turn Puno's campesinos into quinoa *producers* and unproductive subsistence farms into productive quinoa export operations. The quinoa boom was made to fit into long-standing discourses about the region's "backwardness" because it offered a vision of modernity in the altiplano.

This chapter analyzes the creation of the quinoa commodity frontier at the height of the quinoa boom. It examines efforts to remake the social and ecological relationships constituting highland agriculture along with the social and ecological obstacles that frustrated this project. As the altiplano's first cash crop, the quinoa plants (and the people) needed to be disciplined in ways that facilitated quinoa production at scale and allowed the grain to flow seamlessly from farm fields into the gears of global capital. Producing quinoa and producing *commercial* quinoa were different tasks. Turning biodiverse altiplano farms into commercial quinoa production operations was a massive undertaking, one made urgent by the surging demand. Making what was long a regionally important staple into a globally circulating commodity required rapidly transforming the social and ecological relations underpinning quinoa. Facilitating quinoa's commercialization in turn necessitated a large-scale transformation of altiplano agricultural landscapes. Quinoa industry professionals, like Emiliano, sought to align agricultural landscapes with market demands and make them legible to the needs of capital. They needed to transform complex agroecologies into quinoa production systems . . . quickly.

On a practical level, aligning the agricultural landscape with quinoa export was a huge undertaking numerous actors carried out, albeit in a piecemeal and haphazard way. And while there were discrepancies between different industry actors' ideas about how to go about this process and there was no central coordination, there was a surprising alignment about what a "modern" agricultural landscape ought to look like. This transformation was both social and ecological, as were the roadblocks that prevented its complete achievement. While this project was commonly discussed as a technocratic one focused on implementing the right technologies and making discrete changes to production practices, it was also a political project that would reorient power dynamics and alter agricultural imaginaries. It was a struggle for control.

I track frontier dynamics primarily from the perspective of técnicos and management at CIMA, which was one of the most established quinoa-buying and -processing operations in Puno at the time. I spent much of the quinoa harvest season in 2014 (May and June) with CIMA management and técnicos as they scrambled to fill orders from a growing list of clients while making plans and projections for the coming season. In addition to conducting interviews with CIMA's executives and employees, I sat in on company meetings and joined the day-to-day work of buying quinoa. CIMA's chief goals at the time were expanding their farmer network while exerting more control over production practices. They wanted to grow their business by widening their "territory" and increasing the productivity of farmers already within their established network. Although CIMA had been involved in training farmers in quinoa production since the early 2000s, it sought to scale up these efforts in order to help enroll more farmers in commercial quinoa production. In addition to gaining access to larger amounts of quinoa, CIMA management wanted to exert more control over farming practices to ensure the quinoa it bought aligned with market needs and client specifications. CIMA and other businesses wanted control over what farmers planted, how they tended it, and whom they sold it to.

While a number of different industry actors shaped specific aspects of the transformation of quinoa from a local staple into an export crop—from the scientists discussed in chapter 1 to the chefs analyzed in chapter 2—it was the técnicos who carried out and negotiated much of the quotidian work of landscape transformation in Puno. Development agencies and quinoa buyer-processors, like CIMA, hired técnicos to interface with farmers. The técnicos' job frequently focused on delivering "expert knowledge" about agricultural production: educating farmers in proper production methods. But often their role was to translate between worlds. Técnicos, first and foremost, were cultural brokers. This chapter and the next highlight the key role these figures played in the transformation of altiplano socioecological landscapes.

I use the term *landscape* to explicitly entangle the social and the ecological. Making quinoa legible and appropriable required transforming both ecological and social worlds, which though always inseparable are often severed in academic work.[7] While agriculture is always an explicit social and ecological endeavor, landscape further gestures to the spatial character of this practice and the changes desired by quinoa industry professionals. Landscapes are lively, unfinished products always still in process. Yet the term landscape has also historically been used to imagine a large-scale, top-down "all-seeing positionally" mixed up in pursuits of control.[8] Both of these dimensions of landscape rub up against each other in quinoa's transformation: the desire for complete control of the landscape and the landscape's liveliness, its obstinate resistance against efforts to control it. Thinking with landscape should also remind us of the place-based understandings of personal and collective histories that a large landscape change project can imperil. In other words, the existing landscape is deeply meaningful to those who actively construct it and understand their own histories through it.[9]

PUTTING QUINOA PRODUCTION IN CONTEXT

It would be tempting to frame quinoa's commercialization as a shift from subsistence farming to commodity production: the "arrival" of capitalism at the rural Andean farm. Yet subsistence farming in the Andes is largely a myth, a misunderstanding of Andean agricultural livelihoods. The archaeological and historical record shows that extensive trade networks have long facilitated the exchange of Andean agricultural products.[10] For centuries, people in the Andes have practiced "vertical integration"; trading across altitudinal gradients allowed those at one elevation access to goods they otherwise could not procure.[11] Reciprocity-based economies focused on social reproduction and capitalist economies centered on accumulation have commingled here for centuries, with relations of reciprocity arguably becoming especially important in the context of exploitative capitalist political economy.[12] While almost all rural households in the altiplano save some agricultural production for home consumption, a "subsistence-based" farm is an exception rather than the norm in this context.

Instead, farmers juggle multiple market channels for their agricultural products along with various mostly short-term income opportunities off the farm. From a commercial agronomy perspective, this model appears woefully unproductive. Goods are not produced at scale, and farmers do not specialize in a particular market they could corner. The farms are "unproductive." But the very dynamics that make this system appear illogical in a classic agricultural capitalism mindset are also the strength of the system. According to Eric Wolf, this dual orientation—toward the household and the outside world—defines "peasant" logics.[13] This is a highly flexible strategy that allows farmers to adapt quickly to changing conditions, including a boom or bust. Many scholars today argue that peasant livelihoods are not holdovers from precapitalist times but instead a logical response to living at the margins of global capitalism, a rational strategy in particularly vulnerable economic contexts.[14] Yet Andeanist anthropologists have at times ignored the historical processes and power structures that shaped their field sites. In 1991 Orin Starn criticized fellow Andeanist anthropologists for selectively eliding evidence of social tensions, capitalist relations of production, and colonial power dynamics in their field sties in order to construct a "pure" society mostly unchanged since Inca times.[15]

Capitalism did take shape in an idiosyncratic way in the Andean altiplano. Anthropologists of capitalism have conceptualized capitalism as not a single monolithic entity but a set of relations that emerge in and articulate with specific local social, political, and ecological contexts.[16] Historian Nils Jacobsen argued that a "stunted" form of capitalism developed in the Peruvian altiplano, disfigured by the persistence of colonial dynamics that structured trade relations in Puno's countryside.[17] Not only did colonial categories of difference shape labor arrangements long after the formal end of colonialism, but various forms of unfree labor also defined capitalism in this region until quite recently.[18] The hacienda system—a semifeudal land tenure arrangement—dominated this region through much of the twentieth century. Landowners (*hacendados*) held large agricultural estates on which indigenous workers lived and labored in relations of debt peonage. The hacienda system was formally outlawed in Peru's 1969 Agrarian Reform, and the hacienda land was expropriated over the course of the 1970s.[19] Yet while the Agrarian Reform did dramatically reshape Peru's rural areas, it did not fully upend highly unequal relations of power. This history continues to shape the relations of power that undergird today's quinoa industry by delineating who has access to land, investment capital, and markets—much as the was the case over the previous five centuries.[20]

ENVISIONING AN AGRICULTURE
OF LEGIBILITY IN THE ALTIPLANO

By 2014 Emiliano had grown frustrated with the discordance between what the market needed, what farmers grew, and what his team could procure. He felt frustrated about the way CIMA had historically bought whatever quinoa was available rather than actively shaping the region's quinoa stocks to fit its needs. The boom brought higher stakes for his business and less wiggle room. He needed to know how much quinoa he could commit to selling, as contracts often specified multiple quinoa shipments over a prescribed amount of time. Emiliano, who had a master's degree in business administration, wanted to maximize: the boom provided an unparalleled opportunity to increase CIMA's revenues and grow its reputation in the eyes of national and international clients. But he needed to avoid overcommitting and fracturing delicate relationships with clients.

The discord between the agricultural landscape and market demands strained CIMA's business relationships. Sometimes farmers planted varieties CIMA could not buy. Other times they grew too much black quinoa when there was only demand for white. And often farmers were not using best practices that ensured the quinoa they grew met CIMA's specifications. Emiliano believed that zonification would help prevent some of these unforeseen obstacles and ensure that quinoa traveled more easily from farmer's fields into the flows of global capital. A better understanding of the available stocks would cut down on inefficiencies. Zonification was an explicit territorial project aimed at gaining a more precise understanding of the arrangement of plants on the landscape and their potential arrangement in order to facilitate their incorporation into markets.[21] Beyond simply making order out of chaos, it was part of the larger plan to reorganize Puno's agricultural landscape around quinoa production—a project CIMA was deeply invested in.

Seeking documentation and precise accounting of resources is a core aspect of frontier spaces. Mapping facilitates control, which is part of why it is central to colonial regimes, modern states, and development projects alike. Mapping inevitably simplifies, transforming a complex socioecological landscape into a set of discrete categories. Zonification helped construct quinoa as a unified resource, abstracted from existing social and ecological relations. Quinoa was collapsed into the categories relevant for export markets (white, red, and black), categories much less appropriate on farms where farmers selected from dozens of varieties with different characteristics. Zonification was about making resources legible to the gears of capital; establishing a sense of order from the perceived disorder of the quinoa frontier.

Puno's quinoa production landscape was about as far from an "agriculture of legibility" as it gets.[22] Peasant agriculture is especially notorious for its resistance to legibility projects.[23] The quinoa frontier was no exception. Puno's quinoa landscape is in some ways the opposite of a plantation model, in which a large farm produces a single product grown by laborers. The social landscape, with many smallholder farmers spread out across vast distances, each producing relatively little quinoa of varying quality, made buying and processing quinoa a complicated endeavor. In part because of this complexity, a defining feature of the quinoa industry is a prevalence of intermediaries and numerous market channels.[24] There is no single streamlined way that quinoa moves from farms to tables; instead there are many different potential routes depending on which intermediaries are involved, the social and physical location of the farmer, and the specific parameters of the quinoa in question. Emiliano and other industry actors who sought a more organized supply chain further argued that the chaos and multiplicity of middlemen worked to the detriment of farmers, allowing unscrupulous middlemen to take advantage of the fragmented knowledge farmers had about markets. The pursuit of legibility was not just about clarity; it was a struggle for control of the region's quinoa.

In *Seeing Like a State,* James Scott suggested that modern states employ a reductionist gaze in order to render the peoples and resources within their territory orderly and legible.[25] Through simplification, standardization, and classification, states attempt to order nature and society within their territory to better exert control over them. But this gaze facilitates more than state power in the abstract: it facilitates capitalist value making from the landscape.[26] Hence, this same sort of reductionist vision is essential in frontier zones, where resources and claims on them can be intractable. Scott used the example of the creation of modern forestry, which transforms complex ecosystems into abstracted agglomerations of single tree units that are easier to tabulate and administer. Socioecologies become singular quantifiable units of a resource. Altiplano agroecologies are translated into kilograms of quinoa. This is a way of seeing the landscape that facilitates extraction and management from afar. Making Puno's agricultural landscape legible was a necessary step in commercializing quinoa.

Zonification was not just about describing and reinterpreting; it was also one step in a larger project to reshape the agricultural landscape. The existing landscape reflected the logics of highland farmers, largely based on cultivating biodiverse farms and hedging bets in different markets. Emiliano's push for zonification entailed instructing técnicos to recommend specific quinoa varieties to farmers based on the specific agroecological zone where a farmer's fields were located *and* CIMA's buying ratio. He had analyzed current market demand patterns and decided that they needed to buy in a ratio of 80:10:10 (white:red:black) for the coming season: "We need to behave in accordance with the market, and this is what the market demands," he explained. While most exported quinoa was white, he was seeing interest in "tricolor" quinoa (*quinua mixto*), which required the right proportions of white, red, and black quinoa. Emiliano directed técnicos to notify farmers so they could plant for the next harvest season accordingly. Taming the frontier required creating conformity between market demands and the agricultural landscape such that the quinoa produced aligned seamlessly with the quinoa demanded.

But convincing farmers of Emiliano's planting ratio was another matter. Only two years earlier, in 2012, demand for red quinoa had skyrocketed. Quinoa buyers, including CIMA, struggled to find sufficient red quinoa. They urged farmers to plant red varieties for the following season, promising higher prices for red quinoa than for white and black. By the time harvest season arrived, demand for red quinoa had mysteriously plummeted.

International clients no longer wanted red quinoa, leaving farmers unable to sell their red quinoa or forcing them to accept very low prices. The fickle temporality of markets and the tempo of agricultural cycles were out of alignment, and this experience left farmers less willing to trust técnicos' suggested planting ratios.

While Emiliano wanted to commit to selling precise amounts of quinoa in twelve-month contracts, the altiplano's climate made that kind of consistency impossible. The liveliness of the ecological landscape obstructed such predictions. Buyers were scrambling in 2014 partly because it had been a low production year for farmers across the region. An early frost can generate huge losses in quinoa's final yields, and according to every farmer I spoke with about this, it was increasingly difficult to predict when the first frost might arrive. Speaking of "average" yields in this context is similarly challenging, as farmers and técnicos would often remind me. When I asked quinoa farmers and técnicos about average yields, most would hesitate and share that *fluctuation* is the norm, not the exception. Because of the altiplano's harsh climate, yields vary widely from year to year. The same producer might get 500 kg/ha one year and 1,000 kg/ha the next using the same quinoa varieties and the same production protocols. While these fluctuations occurred at the individual farmer level, often they were also regional in scale. Rain during the dry season was likely to cause mildew not for one farmer, but for many. These inevitable oscillations clash with contracts that assume consistent supply from month to month, year to year.

While quinoa was clearly being successfully brought into global commodity circuits, some aspects of quinoa's materiality and the larger landscape in which it was embedded prevented an agriculture of legibility. In recent years social scientists have challenged long-standing assumptions of agency as a distinctly human phenomenon. In the vast majority of social scientific studies, drama occurs among humans, while things classified as "environment" are relegated to the background setting. Social scientists increasingly emphasize the ways materiality matters to the way social phenomena play out. Within this larger questioning of deep-seated division between the "social" and the "natural," geographers in particular have highlighted the ways particular substances can "resist" commodification.[27] Though this literature tends to focus on new kinds of commodities, like privatized water and carbon offsets, the material substances that make up more typical commodities can also resist or obstruct easy commodification.[28] But the capitalism and nature literature tends to focus on developing general relationships between capitalism and nature, disregarding the cultural specificity of capitalist practices and understandings of nature.[29]

CIMA's técnicos were not unaware of the limits of the altiplano landscape in terms of productivity and sometimes felt compelled to educate Emiliano about these issues. Emiliano wanted access to more quinoa to grow his business and needed his técnicos to convince farmers to grow more quinoa. But técnicos tended to see their work as striking a delicate balance between promoting quinoa while ensuring farmers' production systems remained sustainable. Occasionally, individuals within CIMA would push back against the business mentality. When Emiliano brought up the need to make sure farmers were using "certified" commercial seeds at another team meeting in June 2014, Lucy, who ran the processing plant and assisted the técnicos, raised her hand to argue that farmers "always grow native varieties for security, and we should be supporting this." Another técnico, Julio, chimed in that she was right: they should not be recommending replacing all native varieties with commercial ones.

Rigoberto, Emiliano's father, also emphasized the need to "be responsible." Rigoberto was more of a rural development researcher and advocate than a businessman. While Emiliano regularly wore pressed suits and dress shoes to work, Rigoberto almost always had on a North Face fleece vest over a collared shirt and clean hiking boots; he was put together but ready for a trip to the campo. After working for various rural development projects in Puno in the late 1980s, Rigoberto and a colleague had launched CIMA as a nonprofit in the early 1990s with the goal of conducting research and securing development project funding that would improve the lives of Puno's agriculturalists. Many of the farmer relationships that benefited CIMA during the boom were actually formed years earlier when CIMA was a nonprofit. For Rigoberto, it was imperative that CIMA not just focus on the bottom line but also promote *sustainable* quinoa production. He had been one of the early advocates for quinoa's possibilities as a rural income generator in Puno, so he saw the boom as both a much-awaited opportunity and a worrisome situation.

A recently published study had found that in response to the high quinoa prices, many of Puno's farmers were shifting their crop rotations.[30] While farmers employed a range of rotations, the trend was toward more quinoa (sometimes up to four years consecutively in the same plot), less fallow time, and less emphasis on other crops such as potatoes, tubers, tarwi, alfalfa, or forage crops like oats and barley. While potato had historically served as the "lead crop," meaning the first crop after a fallow, some farmers were starting their rotations with quinoa after fallow seasons. Interested in what the mutual consecutive years of quinoa would mean for soil fertility, Rigoberto and some colleagues had been studying the crop rotations of farmers in CIMA's network. Rigoberto stood up to summarize the recent results of the soil fertility tests. It turned out that while producing quinoa in the same plot two years in a row was not a major problem for soil health, three successive years of quinoa in the same field was "very bad." They documented dramatic declines in soil health and consequently in yields during the third year. Rigoberto said he was planning on writing a "bulletin" about this to send to other quinoa industry professionals in the region through the region's Mesa Técnica de la Quinua, Puno's roundtable of individuals and entities involved in the quinoa industry.

Emiliano's pursuit of control over the territory in which his business operated clashed with the liveliness of the socioecological landscape and the chaos of the quinoa bonanza. While técnicos and those they worked for could dream up ways of rearranging farms to increase quinoa yields and streamline quinoa sales, these projects faced obstacles. Puno's social and ecological landscape was in some ways intractable, never fully compliant with the dreams of efficiency and order. Ecological imperatives, price volatility, the multiplicity of intermediaries, unclear rules, and weak social ties with producers further inhibited CIMA's pursuit of control and desire for predictability on the quinoa frontier.

TECHNICAL ASSISTANCE AND THE POLITICS OF KNOWLEDGE IN THE CAMPO

The context in which Puno's quinoa industry had begun to develop had changed drastically by 2014, leading industry professionals like Emiliano to reassess their goals and procedures. Training or "technical assistance" had long been a necessary component of CIMA's work and the success of other regional quinoa buyers. In order to sell commercial quinoa, CIMA needed to train farmers to produce it in ways that aligned with its parameters, and it needed farmers who felt compelled to sell to them. The trainings helped guarantee CIMA a supply of commercial grade quinoa. While CIMA's técnicos focused on buying quinoa during the harvest season, throughout much of the year they were teaching farmers how to convert their production systems to commercial quinoa operations. This was not the kind of thing that could be taught in a single hour or even a day. For this reason, CIMA's técnicos had identified farmers "with potential" over the years and worked with them to gradually reorient their farms to emphasize commercial quinoa. Trainings were usually small, conducted for individual producer associations. A training attendance might be a dozen farmers on a good day, meaning técnicos would travel from association to association doing the same training repeatedly. On top of that, técnicos would make supplementary visits to specific farmers to check on their progress or provide guidance on specific aspects of production.

Though CIMA was in the midst of the busy buying season, Emiliano was thinking about the future. For him, the existing model was proving woefully inefficient for the current situation. "We need to scale up our training efforts." Emiliano opened the following Monday meeting with a different directive. As CIMA's farmer network grew, the intimate trainings that had helped it cultivate relationships with farmers and farmer associations now felt burdensome and overly time intensive. While CIMA had a core group of farmers it had been working with for years, the newer farmers required extensive training. "We need to strengthen their knowledge," Emiliano continued. For him, scaling up trainings was the obvious way to do this. As soon as things "calmed down," he wanted técnicos to redirect their efforts to expanding their training program. He called on técnicos to start organizing massive trainings (*capacitaciones masivas*) at which hundreds of farmers could receive the same information at once.

This approach could help CIMA expand its farmer network and quickly transition farmers into *quinoa producers*. He envisioned creating demonstration parcels where CIMA could model best practices and experiment with new methods. This interest in massive trainings fit into Emiliano's broader reimagining of his own business and its relationship with farmers. "We're at a very important point right now because were asking big and important questions like what is the right crop rotation? What should buying quinoa look like?" he asked the meeting attendees rhetorically. While CIMA's interests were at the forefront for Emiliano, the massive trainings were part of a shared vision of the future of agriculture in the altiplano that transcended CIMA. He suggested collaborating with the Ministry of Agriculture and inviting producers from the Arequipa region, where farmers were replacing asparagus and bell peppers with quinoa, in his words "pioneering" a large-scale mechanized quinoa production model that Puno's farmers could learn from.

Existing trainings focused largely on imparting practical skills that would increase quinoa yields and make it more likely that a farmer's quinoa would meet CIMA's specifications. They encouraged a specific set of production practices, seeking to reshape how farmers interacted with the land. Common themes included how to properly compost, how to properly distribute seeds, how to properly process quinoa after harvest, and how to avoid losses when storing harvested quinoa. Those being trained had ample hands-on experience in quinoa production, and often those doing the training had little. Yet the técnicos were considered experts in commercial quinoa production, much of which applied ideas from mainstream agronomy to quinoa production. These trainings were moments when the hierarchy between the developers and those "being developed" was made evident.

Beyond training farmers in a discrete set of "best practices," the trainings also sought to instill a different way of seeing the farm, a more instrumental gaze focused on production of one particular element: a disembedding of quinoa from the larger system. "I want us all to be speaking the same language," Rigoberto told the técnicos as he explained his vision of the massive trainings. An overarching goal of technical assistance was to convince farmers to dedicate more time and energy to quinoa production. Altiplano farmers were expert risk managers, balancing the needs of multiple crop and livestock species while strategically juggling different market channels. In this strategy, dedicating too much time to one particular crop would not only be risky, it could foreclose other opportunities. But commercial quinoa required dedicating more time and energy to one crop.

A key aspect of all the basic training about commercial quinoa had to do with using furrows. Puno's farmers were accustomed to sowing quinoa seeds through dispersion: tossing handfuls of seeds into a field while walking through it in an orderly fashion. While this method used many extra seeds, once the plants had begun to grow, farmers would pull up the weak seedlings and let the strongest starts thrive. If a farmer had saved a sufficient supply of seeds from the previous harvest, the "waste" was no problem. This method took little time and energy. But técnicos encouraged farmers to use a more time-intensive method. The commercial seeds that CIMA recommended using had become exorbitantly expensive over the past year as more farmers took up commercial quinoa and only a small number produced commercial seeds. Digging furrows and individually sowing seeds in straight rows, as was taught in agronomy classrooms, would facilitate more attention to the plant during the growing season and presumably help retain soil

FIGURE 7. Técnico measuring a furrow width as two farmers watch. Photo by author.

moisture. Since the earliest manuals in commercial quinoa production were produced in the 1990s, the furrow has been central. Marcos, one of CIMA's técnicos, saw prompting this conceptual shift as a key challenge for técnicos: "You have to adapt [agronomy] to the producer's system, that is, how the producer thinks. So look, I toss my seeds out the traditional way and in just a short time my seeds are all sown. With furrows? No, that takes an entire day. The farmer isn't used to that—you have to explain the benefits of it and make it simple."

Promoting furrows was a practical matter. In theory, furrows could increase quinoa yields and facilitate farmers spending more time tending to quinoa. But promoting furrows was also part of a larger imaginative project that attempted to instill a new way of seeing the farm. Furrows, in their rigid geometry and clean lines, symbolized a more orderly and regimented farm. They drew from mainstream agronomy's efforts to rationalize farming through control and measurement.

While furrows were a ubiquitous recommendation, some técnicos saw trade-offs. Rodrigo, another técnico at CIMA, pointed out that dedicating more time to quinoa was ultimately a riskier strategy: "Generating that trust is in some sense about changing their way of thinking, their logic. But it's making it more risky too, because when you begin thinking like an entrepreneur, like a business, you have to take risks. They cannot think that everything is going to just come to them." No técnico recommended farmers convert their diverse farms into quinoa monocultures. But technical assistance was aimed at reimagining farms primarily as quinoa production operations with other supporting elements. Crop rotations and livestock became useful insofar as they supported the soil fertility needed to increase quinoa yields.

TÉCNICOS AND THE POLITICS OF TRANSLATION

Businesses like CIMA employed técnicos to carry out the work of transforming the social and ecological landscape. Sometimes the técnico's job was to deliver "expert knowledge" about agricultural production—educating farmers in "modern" production methods—in a top-down fashion in which they were positioned as the experts. But much of the time their role was to translate between worlds, making the needs of the business legible to farmers and farmers' realities and logics legible to their bosses. Técnicos, first and foremost, were cultural brokers. They played contradictory roles of translator, educator, mediator, and rule enforcer, moving between these roles in sometimes unpredictable ways. Research on development agents tends to highlight a strict hierarchy between the "developers" and those "being developed."[31] Yet the hierarchy that characterized relationships between técnicos and farmers was contingent, fraught, and questioned by técnicos and farmers alike.

Cultural broker figures are defined by their competencies in multiple worlds, divided loyalties, and complex allegiances.[32] They are go-betweens who mediate culturally distinct realities, often for the purpose of reducing conflict or producing a change in the quality of the relationship between them.[33] In his essay on culture brokers in colonial Mexico, Eric Wolf suggested they operate like a Janus, facing both directions while learning to cope with the tensions raised by conflicts of interests. Técnicos negotiated conflicting visions: that of their employers, who needed specific quantities of high-quality quinoa to complete orders and who had little interest in or patience for the idiosyncrasies of the campo, with that of the farmers, who had their own established way of farming and interacting with markets.

Like the scientists featured in chapter 1 and the chefs in chapter 2, intermediary figures like técnicos would not figure into a formal commodity chain or related global value chain approach to quinoa. But it became immediately clear to me when I began conducting fieldwork that they were indispensable to the articulation of the emergent global quinoa commodity chain. The chain metaphor centers actors who "transform" the commodity as it travels from producer to consumer, but in doing so neglects the many different figures mediating quinoa's value. Técnicos do not fit into schematic ideas of commodity chains but played essential roles in managing quinoa's value and articulating Puno's rural areas within larger circuits of exchange.[34]

Técnicos' patterned life histories suited them to this translational work. Most grew up physically and symbolically between the city and the campo. Some spent childhoods living in the cities of Puno or Juliaca while visiting family in the campo on the weekends, where they gained an appreciation for the unique challenges of rural life in the highlands. Others grew up in the campo but began attending an urban school at a young age, transitioning to the city while pursuing a degree from the local university in agronomy or agroindustry. As part of this movement, they had accrued the linguistic, cultural, and social capital necessary to navigate between these worlds with ease.

Victor, who began working at CIMA in the early 1990s, typifies this trajectory. Victor grew up in Juliaca with Quechua-speaking parents who had spent most of their lives in the campo and continued to maintain a *chacra*, or field, there on the weekends.[35] After studying agronomy at the National University of the Altiplano in Puno in the 1980s, Victor worked for a development project that required he live in an Aymara-speaking community for five years, an experience that shaped him profoundly: "The five years living in the campo had a big impact on me and still informs how I am in the campo: how I relate to people, how I see my work." Victor, like other técnicos, emphasized his empathy for farmers along with the importance of knowing the language for building trust. While he learned Quechua from his parents, he became fluent in Aymara. His trilingualism with Spanish, Aymara, and Quechua gave Victor facility in building trust with farmers.

Técnicos moved between the spaces of the city and the campo on a weekly or daily basis depending on the season. Most lived in the cities Puno or Juliaca in cities but spent much of their working lives with farmers. Some even rented rooms for the occasional overnight stay in the campo after a long workday. The campo is as much an imaginative space as it is a physical one, making the técnicos' journeys between these spaces complex. Country and city are loaded concepts in many contexts, as Raymond Williams has suggested: "On the country has gathered the idea of a natural way of life: of peace, innocence, and simple virtue. On the city has gathered the idea of an achieved centre: of learning, communication, light. Powerful hostile associations have also developed: on the city as a place of noise, worldliness and ambition; on the country as a place of backwardness, ignorance, limitation."[36]

But técnicos' local connotations brought specific baggage around race, culture, and "tradition" in the Andes.[37] As Sarah Radcliffe and Sallie West-wood have shown, racialized imaginative geographies continue to circulate widely in the Andes and to this day.[38] Urban areas of Peru's coast (Lima in particular) are coded as white, civilized, and modern, while rural areas (especially in the highlands or Amazonia) are read as darker, more Indian, and backward. And because regions are racialized in the Andes, they're also temporalized: the campo is at once stagnant, primitive, *and* the heart of "deep Peru," the key to national heritage.[39] The urban coast is at once a place of progress and a fall from grace. It's less authentically Peruvian.

Técnicos walked a fine line between valuing campo life on its own terms and their directive to change—to "develop"—the campo. Many shared with me their fascination with Andean agricultural systems, pointing out abandoned Incan terraces to me as we drove to visit farmers and explaining how some farmers decide when to sow their potatoes based on the blossoming of a particular wildflower. And yet despite this appreciation, their overarching mission was to overhaul this system. Técnicos emphasized the challenge of translating farmers' perspectives to their bosses. As Marcos explained, "We have to deal with people who work in an office, who have never farmed, many of them don't have any experience in the campo at all, and instead simply have an academic understanding of agriculture coming from the university. I'm not saying they're bad people, but they don't have any experience. . . . That's why I always end up fighting with my bosses." He stressed that textbook understandings of agriculture he had learned in college proved largely irrelevant in the Andean altiplano, and yet this was precisely the perspective his boss considered valid. As técnicos knew well, agronomic knowledge was political.[40] Their work was in part about navigating competing epistemologies. Though técnicos saw their role partially as one of defending the campo, it was not the farmers who paid their salaries and could fire them on a whim. And those to whom they answered wanted more than translation of the campo—they wanted its transformation.

Técnicos' authority was established through competing forms of legitimacy. To an extent, spending time in the campo legitimized a técnico in the eyes of their bosses. The most respected técnicos had spent considerable time *en campo*. And yet this badge of authority did not guarantee their ideas would be taken seriously. After explaining to me that he had spent his entire professional life "in the campo," Marcos lamented that those making decisions (referring to his bosses at development projects and processing businesses) did not understand or care to understand the vagaries of campo life: "Look, I see a need in the campo and I have to address it as such. There's no other way. But the majority [of the bosses] make decisions based on two or three documents they read on the Internet." He continued, "They don't listen to us técnicos. And I'm tired of this, I'm tired of saying 'no one will listen to me.' My bosses, they correct me, telling me to do this or not to do that. I've had to completely change how I operate to the point where I've felt awful because this is not the work I wanted to do." He went on: "As a friend once told me: 'One day we will have to make the decisions. That's the only way there will be real change.' People who have really spent time in the campo, who know the truth of it know what's needed." At the same time that they needed to communicate the needs of the campo, técnicos were limited by what their bosses were willing to accept. As cultural brokers, they were adept in navigating between worlds but were not considered complete authorities in either.

Interactions between técnicos and farmers were replete with hierarchies. Anthropologist Tania Li suggested that creating and maintaining clear divisions between the experts is essential to international development work: "[One must] confirm expertise and constitute the boundary between those who are positioned as trustees, with the capacity to diagnose deficiencies in others, and those who are subject to expert direction."[41] Técnicos had university degrees in agronomy and the trappings of the altiplano middle class: Columbia brand sweaters, clean hiking boots, and company-owned, late-model pickup trucks. These credentials and cultural capital comprised a competing form of legitimacy. While técnicos tended to emphasize their understanding of farmers, farmers occasionally reminded me and the técnicos themselves of the divide they saw between themselves and the técnicos, who had comfortable salaries and urban homes, luxuries farmers sometimes felt were undeserved, depending on the particular técnico in question. These dynamics were complex, especially when the fluidity of farmer/técnico categories is taken into account. Some técnicos grew up in the campo themselves, cultivated chacras, and had parents who were primarily agriculturalists. Some farmers also had professional careers unrelated to agriculture. There were not always clear categorical distinctions between farmers and técnicos.

While tensions between the "engineers," as farmers commonly called técnicos, and farmers occurred, farmers also acknowledged the help técnicos had provided them. Genaro, a farmer who had joined QCOOP in the early 2010s, recalled working with CIMA years earlier fondly: "They helped us form a producer association so we could improve our product—so we could increase our production. So, we expanded the agricultural frontier and CIMA came to train us, to orient us and teach us what a quality product should look like and how to produce better quinoa." When I spoke with him in 2016, he asked me to send his regards to one CIMA técnico in particular whom he had grown close to years before.

Implementing the market-oriented vision of quality quinoa was a year-round job. In the planting season, técnicos offered farmers "improved" seeds and trained them in proper furrowing. Over the course of the growing season, they would visit producer associations and provide advice about plant care and in many cases help farmers with organic certification documents. After the harvest they had to make sure farmers properly carried out winnowing and threshing, and they made visits to remind farmers of their commitment to selling to CIMA. This culminated in the postharvest buying season of May and June, when the quinoa *compras* took place.

"THEY'RE NOT FAITHFUL ANYMORE":
MAKING AN ORDERLY SOCIAL LANDSCAPE

At the team meeting the following Monday, Emiliano's tone was serious. Urging técnicos to send their calculations to him soon, he added that while they should be attending to their existing farmer network, the goal was expansion. "Where is the potential? Which zones can we expand into? Who has potential to become one of our producers? Honestly, what I'm not clear on is where we're working and where we're not," he chided. "What I want is by next week for you each to be able to tell me, 'based in my experience in my zone, I am working with this and that group of producers for this coming year and I see potential in this place and that place.'" CIMA had been slowly but surely cultivating relationships with more and more farmers over the years, but this effort took on new urgency in 2014 as clients wanted more quinoa at the same time as a new set of buyers were competing to buy up the region's quinoa stocks. Controlling more of the frontier meant forming relationships with more farmers and exacting more control over existing relationships. Yet this kind of clarity and control kept eluding Emiliano's grasp.

At the same time that CIMA's técnicos were under pressure to expand their farmer contacts, they were losing farmers whom they had been working with for years. CIMA understood the time they put into cultivating relationships with farmers as an investment. Building trust was not easy, CIMA management and técnicos reminded me time and again. Emiliano remarked to me in an interview that building these relationships had always been incredibly difficult (*muy duro*), yet it was also the crux of their business model.

With CIMA investing time and resources in training farmers over the course of the growing season, the implication was that farmers would sell their end product to the company. For many farmers, CIMA was paying their organic certification, a substantial investment in the farm. And often CIMA bought farmers seeds to encourage them to plant the varieties it sought. Instead of a contract, CIMA relied on this sort of informal quid pro quo and the assumed reciprocity it should generate: farmers would feel obligated to sell their quinoa to CIMA after CIMA had dedicated time and resources to them. This system had worked well in previous market conditions, when farmers would have had a hard time finding a buyer who would beat CIMA's prices. Plus, many farmers did feel a sense of obligation to CIMA for the help it offered. But the rapidly increasing prices of 2014 challenged this model. Indeed, all the time and energy CIMA's técnicos had put into equipping farmers to grow commercially proved convenient for the itinerant buyers who could profit from their efforts. A growing number of farmers were choosing not to sell their quinoa to CIMA, even after getting technical assistance and seeds from it. At the same time that CIMA's client list grew, more and more quinoa slipped from its grasp.

"They're not faithful anymore," Victor, CIMA's most senior técnico, told me one day as we sat together in the back seat of a pickup truck heading back to Puno after a long day of quinoa buys. Victor was pointing to a major issue for buyer-processors that arose with the entrance of new actors and the wild fluctuations in prices: the loyalty of farmers to particular buyers. The extreme escalation of prices in 2013 and 2014 made it more difficult for them to buy the amount of quinoa they needed to fulfill contracts. The changing prices produced what CIMA's management and técnicos understood as a crisis in farmer fealty. Most contracts with brokers (or importers for direct-export businesses, like QCOOP) include multiple evenly spaced shipments of quinoa, often on a monthly basis. A contract might stipulate 10 tons of quinoa per month for twelve months. The contract, signed at the beginning of this period, established the price at which the quinoa would be bought throughout the entire contract, based on the market price when the contract was signed.

The dramatic price fluctuations were partially to blame for this behavior. A contract signed in January 2014, when the average farm-gate price was US$2.86/kg, might be signed for US$3.14/kg (with 10% margins for CIMA, a standard rate for it). When the farm-gate price increased to US$3.60 by May, CIMA was in a difficult predicament: it would only be able to sell the quinoa it bought for US$3.14, but farmers knew they could get over US$3.60 if they sold to acopiadores or other businesses who could offer current market prices. Farmers had to choose whether to stay loyal to CIMA and accept a below-market rate or fracture their relationship with CIMA in order to take advantage of the high prices. Ensuring that the farmers CIMA's técnicos trained would in the end sell it their quinoa became increasingly difficult for CIMA as prices spiked. Much to CIMA's chagrin, a significant proportion of the farmers it worked with were choosing maximal profits over "loyalty." CIMA técnicos were showing up to buy the quinoa they thought they were owed and finding that it had already been sold to acopiadores or the growing number of new buyers from Lima flocking to the highlands. And while técnicos tried to remind farmers of the long-term investment CIMA had made in them, this approach proved futile with the surfeit of buyers—some of whom paid in cash on the spot and were less demanding than CIMA about quality.

Despite the obsessive calculation that characterizes frontier making, frontiers are spaces of incredible chaos. Emiliano was by no means an outlier in seeing the social dynamics as frustratingly messy and in need of better organization. Rigoberto, who had been a pioneer in quinoa's commercialization in Puno, told me that one of CIMA's primary challenges was "dealing with the disarray." Rigoberto and others who had helped launch the first efforts to commercialize quinoa in Puno in the 1990s saw their work in part as an effort to formalize the disorderly commercial relationships. Though Emiliano saw the problem as one that inhibited his business's success, Rigoberto and others in the industry argued that the chaos also works to the detriment of farmers who are taken advantage of regularly by intermediaries, especially the acopiadores. A 2011 report from Puno's regional government described the quinoa market as "disorganized," blaming many of the problems on the ruthless cunning and questionable ethics (the *viveza criolla*) of the acopiadores.[42] These informal buyers aggregated quinoa from different farmers. They bought quinoa in small quantities from individual farmers, and once they had a commercially significant volume, they then sold it to whomever would buy it. Acopiadores had historically helped transfer quinoa from farms to regional markets, yet during the quinoa boom these actors played a more complex role in shaping quinoa markets.

While loyalty between market actors is theoretically unimportant in a liberal conception of how markets work, issues of loyalty and disloyalty influenced the workings of power in the quinoa industry. Buyer-processors' insistence on farmer loyalty harkened back to the hacienda days when the loyalty of "peons" to a *hacendado* was required and legally enshrined through debt peonage. Historian Nils Jacobsen's analysis of wool markets in Puno suggested that these kinds of colonial power dynamics are built into the way commerce in this region works. In 2014 farmers were eschewing assumptions about the loyalty they supposedly owed others. They were making economically "rational" decisions, selling to the buyer offering the best price rather than to the buyer who expected their quinoa or who had bought it during previous seasons. But this was a problem for CIMA, which had constructed a business model based on a different set of assumptions about how farmers would behave. With increased competition, CIMA could no longer ensure the farmers it worked with would automatically sell to it. This insecurity brought CIMA's business model into question. How could it justify training farmers if some of these farmers might ultimately choose to sell their quinoa elsewhere? Técnicos were supposed to solve this issue. While technical assistance trainings often focused on discrete production practices, occasion-ally they involved teaching farmers business skills. Specifically, trainings cen-tered on "proper" commercial relationships, such as how to run a successful producer association, basic accounting, and how to prepare for a quinoa buy. And in 2014 Emiliano wanted these trainings to bring up the loyalty issue. Emiliano explained the need to make CIMA's expectations more explicit to farmers later in that meeting: "We need to have conversations with the farm-ers. We need a closeness [*una cercanía*]. There's really no guarantee that farm-ers will sell to us, so, we need to have dialogues with them."

Buyer-processors like CIMA saw themselves as working against unethi-cal dynamics. They saw themselves as the future of the industry. In contrast to the secretive and self-interested acopiadores, buyer-processors like CIMA offered a streamlined and ethical approach with the good of the farmers in mind. Emiliano and other buyer-processors I spoke to saw their work in part as an effort to modernize the chaotic quinoa industry. Buyer-processors had processing plants that could transform raw quinoa into a finished product. They could work directly with international clients. They bought quinoa from farmers organized into producer associations rather than individual producers, and sometimes they helped farmers form those very associations. That meant they could work with selected clients who needed high-quality quinoa, as they had some degree of control over the quinoa itself. They saw their work as a sort of service to the region. While they claimed acopiadores were harming farmers, undercutting them and offering no help in increasing their incomes, buyer-processors saw themselves as helping farmers improve their lives, offering rural development opportunities. They not only bought quinoa, they worked with farmers to transform their production techniques in order to, in theory, earn higher incomes.

Despite the complaints about the disorder, Puno's farmers were increas-ingly organized. In 2013, 20 percent of Puno's quinoa farmers were organized into producer associations or cooperatives, a number that would grow in the subsequent years.[43] During CIMA's NGO days, Rigoberto and his col-leagues had helped organize some of the first quinoa producer associations: groups of farmers who lived in the same region and worked together to re-direct their production systems toward quinoa export. Many industry actors argued that the associations empowered farmers, who could in theory bet-ter confront predatory intermediaries though sharing knowledge. But it was also practical for buyer-processors. With farmers spread out across vast dis-tances connected by dirt roads often laden with potholes, local associations made training farmers and buying from them more efficient. Creating producer associations helped CIMA grow its network of well-trained farmers that it could count on.

Some producer associations were attempting to form cooperatives in 2014. While there had long been only one quinoa cooperative in the region (QCOOP), a combination of quinoa's high price and development agencies interested in funding cooperatives led more groups to pursue this model. Yet cooperatives were still considered mostly an experiment that at the time many believed would not succeed in challenging the modus operandi. For CIMA, the interest in cooperatives, which would cut out buyer-processors and work directly with foreign clients, was a problem. It wanted farmers to be organized enough to facilitate training and buying, but not so organized that they could circumvent the local buyer-processors entirely.

Notably, the implied loyalty did not necessarily go both ways. With buying quinoa in Puno an increasingly complicated affair, Emilano began looking to buy quinoa from elsewhere. Due to quinoa's high price, large-scale commercial farmers in the Arequipa region were replacing cash crops like asparagus with quinoa cultivation. These farmers had experience in agroexport, and often these farms were run by agribusinessmen with a dramatically different kind of business ethic than Puno's farmers. Buying quinoa from Arequipa seemed refreshingly simple: a single farmer could guarantee a large amount, and there was no need for technical assistance. With markets for conventional (not organic certified) quinoa growing, Emiliano set his sights on expanding their operation outside Puno. He shared this news with his team at another Monday meeting in June 2014. "We're connecting with producers in Arequipa, in Tacna, but our relationships are not so close like they are in Puno." This being the case, he planned to buy from the dreaded acopiadores in Arequipa in the coming year and work on creating direct relationships with farmers in the future. Buying quinoa beyond Puno would supplement CIMA's quinoa from Puno during lean years and in theory help solve the problem of fluctuating yields and farmer disloyalty.

WE'VE ALWAYS PRODUCED ORGANICALLY

While increasing quinoa productivity and expanding CIMA's farmer network was at the forefront of técnicos' concerns, much of this had to happen within the confines of organic certification. Export demand for quinoa had largely been synonymous with *organic certified* quinoa before 2014.[44] While demand for conventional quinoa had grown, as Emiliano's interest in quinoa from Arequipa indicated, organic certified quinoa remained a priority. Expanding the quinoa frontier and making it legible to markets involved implementing the idiosyncratic organic certification bureaucracy. This meant training farmers in certification paperwork and convincing them it was worth their while.

I sat in on one of the organic certification trainings in the tiny town of Carillo. Twenty-five farmers—almost all women—gathered in a classroom owned by the municipality for the final workshop in a two-year-long series of trainings on commercial quinoa production, with an emphasis on organic production and "entrepreneurship." Edwin, who had been a técnico with CIMA but transferred to a new position with a development project, was leading the training. This particular project worked with a large number of farmers (over three hundred), some of whom had historically sold quinoa to CIMA, and many of whom were new to organic certification.

The workshop got off to a rough start. Edwin was clearly tired and annoyed by the low attendance at the final workshop, remarking that "maybe 1 percent of the total number of producers are here." A woman responded that many were in the field (*en chacra*), as that day was ideal for sowing seeds for the upcoming season. Changing topics and still evidently annoyed, Edwin declared that the day's theme was "traceability." He proceeded to divide the participants into five teams for an activity. Each team received a roll of clear tape along with five pieces of red printer paper with categories of the production process written on them (production, notebook, folder, initial storage, buying, processing, transport) and twenty five pieces of green paper with the names of different documents and tasks related to organic certification and documentation of farming practices more broadly (e.g., "photocopy of national personal identification," "list of certified producers," "history of the field," "polypropylene sacks"). Edwin instructed the farmers to tape the red papers on the wall in the correct order and then categorize all of the green pieces of paper below the red categories. The activity was a kind of quiz about which paperwork and which activities corresponded to which larger moment in the production process. The activity was quite difficult. After about half an hour of discussion among the groups and many green pieces of paper moving around numerous times, Rodrigo called the groups to attention.

He asked each group to present their schematic, noting in a disappointed tone that each group's diagram looked completely different. Not only did

FIGURE 8. Farmers participating in training about
organic certification procedures. Photo by author.

groups have green tasks and documents in different places, but they did not
all agree on the sequence of the production process. Should the notebook go
before production or after? Does the folder go before or after the notebook?
Edwin could not hide his frustration. "You're entrepreneurs [*empresarios*]
now," he chided. "You need to know this stuff. Today is our last workshop.
There's no more funds for this project so we can't help you with this anymore." Over the course of the workshop, he repeated the phrase "you're entrepreneurs now" multiple times, often while expressing frustration with
participants' misunderstandings of certification processes. His point was
that in order for farmers to successfully sell quinoa in the current context,
they needed to think like businesspeople. And business meant paperwork.

Organic certification required farmers to keep track of and document details related to their farm that without certification would have been unremarkable and absurd to track in a detailed way. The varying levels of literacy
among farmers made this even more difficult. Organic certification required
reading, writing, and a specialized knowledge of organic terminology and
processes. In some sense, adhering to organic production protocols was the
easy part. These bureaucratization practices privilege large producers, as the
burden of paperwork is high for small producers.[45] Beyond documents, several minute particulars had to be in order. The polypropylene sacks had to be
the correct color, and the farmers needed to learn to correctly differentiate

biotic from abiotic production factors to fill out documents properly. Técnicos struggled to get across the sheer number of tasks required of farmers seeking certification. One of the farmers stood up toward the end of the training to comment. Clearly frustrated with the amount of work they needed to put into documents to sell quinoa as organic, she declared, "Why is it so hard to sell quinoa these days?" Though it was not difficult in the sense of finding buyers, the organic certification process made what should be easy in a boom market—selling quinoa—burdensome.

And while paperwork may have been the heavy lifting with organic certification, técnicos also needed to help farmers increase their productivity without violating organic certification protocols. Técnicos were trained in "conventional" agronomy; however, many had become experts in organic production methods. One common recommendation was "biol," a natural fertilizer made by fermenting a selection of easily available products. I sat in on several biol trainings over the course of my fieldwork. The specific recipe varied, but the main components remained the same. Farmers were instructed to add specific quantities of cow manure, ash, milk, water, eggshells, and molasses to a large sealed barrel with a valve. This fermenter would, with time, create a rich fertilizer that would increase quinoa yields without resorting to chemical fertilizers that violate organic certification requirements. Yet making biol was labor intensive even if it was effective. Increasing productivity was a rather simple matter with chemical fertilizers, but a more complex process without them.

Many farmers remarked that producing organically was just producing in the traditional way: "without chemicals." A key difference, however, was that organic certification was costly and therefore did not make sense without higher yields than "traditional" methods allowed. Puno's Regional Agricultural Administration (Dirección Regional Agraria, DRA) estimated that the costs of producing a hectare of organic certified quinoa were about double those for conventional quinoa.[46]

As CIMA generally paid for its farmers' certifications (approximately $150 per farmer), it needed these farmers to dedicate substantial energy to ensuring they produced enough quinoa come harvest time. This required laborious practices: making biol, using natural pest deterrents, building scarecrows, and other measures that could improve fields. But the price premium for organic quinoa was shrinking. While organic certified quinoa historically had earned farmers 20–25 percent more than not certified, that figure was down to 7 percent in 2014.[47]

FIGURE 9. Farmer applying biol in a field of immature quinoa. Photo by author.

The organic certification process introduced yet another obstacle to the rapid expansion of the quinoa frontier. Certifying a plot takes three years. During the first two years, known as T1 and T2, certifiers verify that the land is not being cultivated with chemical pesticides or fertilizers, but no product sold from this land can carry the organic label. It is not until the third year that the land is declared free of chemical residues, and a farmer can sell their products as organic. "We've always produced organically," Yessica, a farmer with land in T1 remarked to me in frustration. Though she had not previously been formally certified, she said she had always grown quinoa without chemicals. But because organic certification entailed this multiyear wait, she would not receive the price premium this year. This lag time presented a challenge in the context of a sudden demand surge that the existing certified farmers could not meet. This further increased the pressure on técnicos to convince the existing certified farmers to take all measures to increase their yields, as they would need to wait for the pending group of farmers to meet the organic certification requirements.

While CIMA continued to prioritize organic quinoa in 2014, Emiliano was having second thoughts about the future. "It's very costly and it's a total headache," he told me one afternoon while giving me a ride into downtown Puno. He saw organic certification as adding risk for his business. The added cost of paying for certification meant that a "disloyal" farmer was doubly costly. He was considering stopping that aspect of the business to save himself the headaches.

The social landscape of quinoa production in Puno did not align easily with the organic certification bureaucracy or the intense pressures of the boom market conditions. While organic certification procedures are always in some ways adapted to the local context, the degree to which they can be integrated into existing social and ecological conditions is limited.[48] Organic certification assumes farmers are well versed in bureaucracy, can read and write well, and have the time to document their farming extensively. The high price, coupled with the multiyear lag time of organic certification, frustrated farmers, who felt they should be able to earn the organic premium immediately since they had "always produced quinoa organically." Though organic certification was pitched as a way to help small farmers who use the kinds of farming techniques Puno's farmers were accustomed to, it was evident to all that this model was a better fit for larger-scale farming enterprises.

CONCLUSION

Because quinoa was the first true cash crop in the Peruvian altiplano, reorienting the region's agriculture around commercial quinoa production was a massive undertaking. This was not simply a matter of replacing other crops with quinoa or planting more quinoa to meet the surging foreign demand. Instead, this project required a wholesale reimagining and remaking of the region's agroecologies and commercial relationships. This was not a highly coordinated top-down project. Instead, many individual and institutional actors (whose objectives at times aligned and at other times competed) carried this out in a piecemeal way. While this chapter explored the height of the boom from the perspective of buyer-processors and técnicos in particular, farmers, acopiadores, itinerant buyers from Lima, state actors, and development practitioners all played roles in this "modernization" effort. The perspective of CIMA's management and técnicos offers but one partial view of this conjuncture, yet their story makes evident the kinds of tensions, challenges, and dreams that defined that moment.

Reorienting agroecologies around quinoa export was in part about translating the landscape—that is, making it legible to export markets. Through zonification, CIMA management sought to quantify the chaotic socioecological landscape of quinoa production, converting this messy world into a clean figure in kilograms of quinoa. This was the frontier gaze in action: constructing potential, mapping resources, and erasing existing claims. CIMA wanted to use zonification not only to better apprehend the existing landscape insofar as it related to how much quinoa it could commit to selling, but also to exert influence over the landscape in a more strategic and precise way. Remaking this agroecology around quinoa production also required changing the ways farmers tended quinoa and convincing them to dedicate more time and energy to this particular crop relative to other aspects of their production systems. Técnicos were caught in the politics of knowledge: they needed farmers to respect them as authorities in quinoa agronomy. At the same time, técnicos acknowledged that farmers "knew best" in some ways. They had to translate back and forth between Emiliano's business mindset and the logics of the campo. But remaking the altiplano agriculture around commercial quinoa was more than transforming agroecologies and altering discrete production practices. CIMA management needed more orderly commercial relationships and needed to train farmers in the bureaucracy of organic certification. While CIMA attempted to expand its farmer network, it also faced a crisis of loyalty: farmers who had benefited from CIMA's training were choosing to sell their quinoa elsewhere in order to get the current market rate. CIMA needed to align the social landscape with it need for farmers to behave. The centrality of organic certification in quinoa export markets introduced yet another wrinkle in CIMA's efforts to expand its business and take advantage of the bonanza. The bureaucracy of organic certification was an awkward fit for the altiplano socioecological landscape and the boom moment—the time delay built into certification amid surging demand and because many farmers were not accustomed to or were, for reasons of literacy, handicapped by the rigorous documentation and paperwork protocols.

This chapter has explored the efforts to reimagine and remake the altiplano socioecological landscape to emphasize commercial quinoa production at the height of the boom. This process remains unfinished both because of the scale of the project and because the frenzied effort to remake the landscape was due in part to a price signal that changed. The next chapter also focuses on the boom moment, but zooms in on one particular aspect of this project, quality standards, and the role técnicos played in implementing them. Quality standards were both an effective and an imperfect tool for disciplining farmers' production practices. They provided an enforcement mechanism of sorts that helped ensure quinoa farmers adhered to the specific production protocols.

FOUR

Producing Good Quinoa

THE MORAL POLITICS
OF QUALITY STANDARDS

IT WAS MAY 2014—the peak of quinoa-buying season during the height of the boom—and CIMA had many outstanding orders. Despite boasting a large network of farmers with whom it had built relationships during its NGO days, CIMA was struggling to keep up with an influx of orders for both conventional and organic quinoa. I accompanied all six of CIMA's técnicos on a visit to Doña Maria's house one Saturday morning—the first stop in a long day of compras. The plan was to buy all of Doña Maria's quinoa harvest (about 1 ton) and pay her in cash on the spot. CIMA's técnicos were under pressure from management to buy more quinoa to satisfy new clients. The presence of itinerant buyers only intensified their stress. CIMA management, in turn, was behind on fulfillment of orders from new and established clients. Out of season frosts had produced small harvests that year at the same time that dozens of new buyers flocked to Puno, vying with CIMA for the limited supply of quinoa.

Doña Maria and her family were thrilled by the prospect of making PEN 12/kg (a little over US$4.00/kg) for the ton of quinoa they harvested that year, a sum they could have hardly imagined a year before when they began receiving training from CIMA to produce commercial quinoa. It would be the first time Doña Maria sold quinoa commercially—that is, to someone other than the informal merchants in the local town plaza. This was a rare opportunity to fulfill her dream for *algo más*, or "a little more."[1] Doña Maria was there, as were her husband who had come home from the mine for the week, their two children, and a grandchild. Everyone involved hoped this buy would go smoothly.

Samples of Doña Maria's quinoa had passed the preliminary quality exam just a week earlier. But before they could complete the compra, Lucy,

CIMA's quality control expert, still had to perform the sacred quality control ceremony to verify the quinoa's "goodness." Lucy took a small sample of the quinoa and measured it out to precisely 100 grams. She then pulled out a pair of tweezers from her backpack and began individually counting defective grains: those of contrasting color, called *puntos negros* (though they could be any color that contrasts with the color of the bulk of the quinoa), small grains (*menudos*), immature "green" grains, broken grains, germinated grains, and grains damaged in any other way. She completed the ritual of verification by writing down the quantities of each "irregularity" in a small notebook, using a small calculator to produce an overall figure representing this quinoa's quality. These imperfections were the commercial quinoa industry's highly moralized "matter out of place," the sorting of which at once served to differentiate good/bad quinoa *and* good/bad farmers.[2]

Soon after beginning the quality control assessment, Lucy put the rest of the team—who were packing Doña Maria's quinoa into polypropylene sacks—on pause. Less than an hour after arriving, we left without a single sack of quinoa. Doña Maria's quinoa had not passed CIMA's quality control analysis. Though there were moments when técnicos made exceptions to the rules, Lucy could not make one for Maria, whose quinoa contained far too many tiny and broken quinoa grains. Lucy attempted to console Doña Maria, explaining that she could still sell her quinoa in the town plaza for a lower price. But Doña Maria was upset, exclaiming, "The small grains and dark grains are good enough for me!"

Doña Maria and the rest of her family were disappointed, and in fact, once the call had been made, those of us in the trucks were instructed to load up quickly while Lucy explained the problem to Maria in more detail. Lucy consoled her, saying that CIMA would be back next year to buy quinoa and if she tended her quinoa a little more closely, she could surely make the US$4.81/kg she had dreamed of.

By harvest season the next year, quinoa's price had plummeted.

. . .

As demand (and prices) for quinoa skyrocketed in 2013 and 2014, industry actors scrambled to standardize Puno's quinoa. In order to circulate smoothly in global markets, quinoa needed to flow as one "golden stream."[3] Processors required quinoa that would behave predictably in their equipment from batch to batch. They needed to be able to mix together the quinoa from many farmers so it could flow through the processing plant as a single liquid grain. Actors farther down the commodity chain (brokers, exporters, importers, retailers) wanted assurance that quinoa they bought met agreed upon parameters. Yet as exports exploded and prices surged, quinoa remained heteroglot—variable from field to field, farm to farm, batch to batch, and region to region. The implementation of industry-wide quality standards was still in its infancy.

As a new global commodity, the ways quinoa would be defined, valued, and evaluated were unsettled questions when the boom hit, and little available quinoa conformed to the emerging expectations. Ideas about quality were not givens. The intensity and suddenness of the quinoa boom magnified conflicts regarding how to judge quinoa's quality while escalating the urgency with which farmers attempted to adhere to the emerging set of conventions. The quinoa boom brought the social and political work that standards do into sharp relief. Tensions around quinoa's quality represented broader struggles over who would control the quinoa industry, what good farming meant in this context, and the proper future of the so-called *grano de oro* (golden grain).

Quinoa's commercialization was hailed as an unprecedented opportunity for the inclusion of Andean *campesinos* who had previously been excluded from Peru's nontraditional agroexport boom and the country's "economic development" more broadly. Tracing the disciplinary work standards enacted shows a more complex and heterogenous story. The quinoa boom did not simply represent an opportunity for inclusion; it redefined the contours of inclusion and exclusion around a new set of axes. A farmer's ability to take advantage of the high prices caused by surging global demand depended on the ability to produce quinoa that conformed to the emergent idea of "good quinoa." But not every farmer had the same ability to produce what came to be known as quinoa *de calidad* ("quality quinoa").

While chapter 3 analyzed efforts to transform Puno's socioecological landscape to align with quinoa export, this chapter traces the politics animating the physical transformation of quinoa itself and the role quality standards played as disciplinary tools in the remaking of landscapes of quinoa production. Exploring the creation and enforcement of quality standards for quinoa demonstrates how standardization not only altered quinoa's physical form, it remade moral imaginaries and agricultural practices. Connecting standards literature to critical development studies, I argue that standards serve as highly effective tools to "render technical" political questions regarding the transformation of agroecosystems.[4] Framing "the problem" as farmers' inability or unwillingness to produce "high-quality" quinoa justified intervention. Similarly, defining existing production regimes as "traditional" and producing "substandard" "low-quality" quinoa made export appear as a self-evident means to progress. Standards helped depoliticize the transformation of agricultural systems toward export-oriented models, comprising an understudied aspect of what anthropologist James Ferguson called the "anti-politics machine."[5]

Social science research on the contestation of quality standards (i.e., before they are taken for granted) tends to focus on macroscale definitional disputes between national industries. Sociologist Amy Quark, for instance, followed the high-stakes standard making in the cotton industry, demonstrating how these processes can get caught up in larger geopolitical rivalries.[6] Another group of scholars situated quality standards within conventions theory, a broad body of work that seeks to understand the roles shared expectations of behavior and collective evaluative principles play in facilitating economic exchange. Scholars working within this framework have explored how ideas about quality are disseminated and enforced in global supply chains and when these processes succeed or fail.[7] This framework sees conventions (including but not limited to formal and informal quality standards) as tools to solve "coordination problems" or reduce "transaction costs" in global supply chains. Global supply chains, as this body of work makes clear, depend on integrating different expectations about quality and these quality conventions in turn impact the power dynamics of supply chains. Scholars working with convention theory have offered nuance to political economy–based understandings of global supply chains by highlighting the role norms and templates of behavior can play in generating power differentials, but this body of work tends to prioritize a more macroscale scope oriented toward generating typologies of global supply chains.

I join scholars working at a more minute scale to understand how quality standards shape the day-to-day practices and micropolitics that animate commodity chains.[8] Focusing on the ambiguities, ambivalences, and ethical tensions that arise in the translation of quinoa from a locally circulated good into an export commodity, this chapter shows how emergent ideas about quality generated new ideas about farmers: virtuous farmers produce virtuous quinoa, and vice versa. The intensity of the story that opened this chapter lies both in the collective disappointment about Doña Maria's quinoa failing the quality control test *and* in the way rejecting Maria's quinoa judged her worth as a farmer. Quality standards do not just render highly political questions *technical*, they render them *moral*: relating to ideas of right conduct. The production of quinoa that adheres to standards became both a technical problem and one that was seen as reflecting a farmer's proficiency and work ethic.[9] It was not just the standards' ability to render technical that made them effective; it was the moralizing inherent to standards that further lent them power.

Like the previous chapter, this chapter centers the work of técnicos. Though processors played an outsized role in creating the conventions around grain quality, técnicos carried out the day-to-day work of enacting and enforcing the standards. While standards may appear abstract and anonymous in this case, they frequently came into being in highly personal encounters between técnicos and farmers.

CONSTRUCTING QUALITY QUINOA

The question of quality was a key concern from the earliest efforts to imagine a "modern" quinoa industry in Peru. In the late 1970s the Inter-American Institute for Cooperation on Agriculture and the Simón Bolívar Fund partnered on a "diagnostic" study of Puno's quinoa industry to determine the challenges and opportunities in quinoa commercialization (referred to hereafter as the IICA study). A defining challenge, they concluded, was that the available quinoa in Puno was of decidedly poor quality. The problem was twofold: the quinoa they encountered was not uniform, and it had a preponderance of "impurities."[10]

It's true that quinoa was heterogenous, differing in size, shape, color, and more based on the variety a farmer cultivated. Yet quinoa's heterogeneity was not an error; it was a logical outcome of an agricultural system based in risk management. Quinoa's heterogeneity was embedded in existing seed saving, exchange, processing, and marketing systems.[11] The heteroglot end product the emergent industry found problematic was the result of generations of farmers selecting seeds to suit their own specific needs in terms of microclimate, pest threats, and taste preferences over the course of generations. Farmers across the Andes cultivate hundreds of varieties of quinoa, though it's difficult to say exactly how many.[12] In addition to having differences in color, taste, grain size, and culinary applications, quinoas differ in agronomic characteristics: some varieties survive untimely frosts and others

FIGURE 10. Display of approximately 380 quinoa germplasm accessions in Dr. Angel Mujica's office at the National University of the Altiplano (UNAP), representing dozens of varieties of quinoa. Photo by author.

prove hardy in the face of mildew. Hardy quinoas tend to produce small seeds with thick saponin layers, and high-yielding varieties tend to be weak in the face of frost. Because of these trade-offs, cultivating multiple varieties has long been vital to successful agriculture in the fickle altiplano climate. Indeed, Andean agriculture is based on strategically cultivating relationships between diverse crops and crop varieties to manage the challenges of the harsh highland climate and the dramatic microclimatic variations.[13] While farmers had developed these varieties through intentional selection over generations, quinoa's reproduction also eluded complete human control. Quinoa's propensity for cross-pollination, its sexual promiscuity, meant that quinoa was also always mixing on its own.[14] Even if a farmer grew only one variety, over the years this quinoa was likely to cross-pollinate with a neighbors' quinoa. Quinoa varieties, sometimes unintentionally, did not always stay stable from generation to generation.

In the existing agricultural imaginary, good farmers cultivated land in ways that aligned with Andean spiritual values.[15] Farming in the Andes is not simply an occupation, but a morally and spiritually powerful act that entails creating right relationships with what Marisol de la Cadena translates

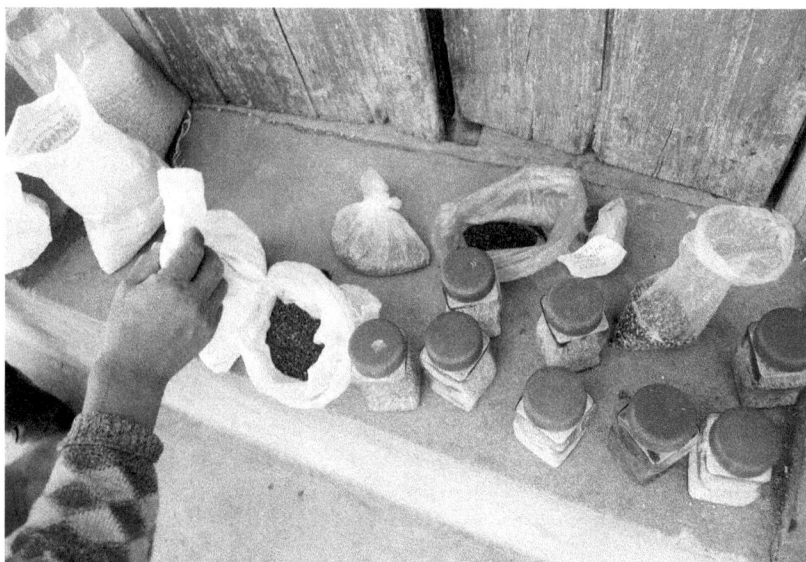

FIGURE 11. Farmer's collection of quinoa varieties. Photo by author.

as "earthbeings."[16] In this context, a virtuous farmer maintained relationships of reciprocity with various on-farm elements (soil, farm animals) and larger forces (wind, sun) and the powerful mountain spirits (*apus*).[17] A good farmer nurtured biodiversity and strategically cultivated relationships between different on-farm elements. This made decisions about crop rotations, seed varieties, and production practices morally fraught.

It's not that farmers and quinoa eaters didn't historically care about quality. Yet quality was not enforced through formally agreed upon parameters. Quality in this system was judged at the point of sale. Because quinoa constituted only one part of a complex crop rotation, quinoa harvests were small enough to process at home or at a part-time processing plant using "artisanal" techniques. Farmers generally sold by the sack to local merchants or sold it themselves in local markets, a dynamic that formed long-term social relationships between sellers and buyers. A 1977 study of quinoa market channels documented that most quinoa exchange took place via the *trueque*, a local custom wherein agriculturalists from distant communities exchange products. In fact, quinoa was the most prevalent product in the *trueque*, a dynamic reflecting the lack of formal market channels for quinoa at the time and quinoa's stigmatization outside rural communities.[18] Quality was managed at a more interpersonal level. A buyer felt assured of the product's quality because of accumulated trust with the merchant and the merchant's own need to maintain their reputation. There were some shared preferences; the IICA study noted that local consumers tended to prefer white quinoas over black and red ones. But this system allowed for multiple definitions of quality, such that a buyer could seek out quinoa that fit their own purposes.

What is the logical outcome of a genius agricultural strategy from one perspective is a problem of inconsistent product from another standpoint. Heterogeneity is a nuisance when viewed from a commodity logic of commensurability. The diversity of quinoa was a hindrance to the creation of formal market channels and the scaling up of the industry. Quinoa's materiality lent itself to sale by the sack and within a sack one could expect uniformity, but that sack's quinoa was likely distinct from a sack from another farmer. Because Puno's quinoa was not uniform, hypothetical buyers and processors trying to scale up their businesses could not mix quinoa from different farmers together into larger batches for processing. Different size grains require different processing equipment, such that mixing small grains and large grains together creates real logistic challenges to processing. Similarly, mixing quinoas with distinct levels of saponin would create inefficiencies, as some quinoa in the batch would require more "washing" than other quinoa. And buyers could not ensure the end product was uniform. Quinoa's socially produced material qualities—its heteroglot nature—prevented the scaling up of the industry.

Judgments of "poor quality" products resulting from "uneducated" farmers are common tropes in colonial export markets around the world. In 1940s Madagascar, the French colonial government justified a ban on smallholder vanilla production by saying that the farmers did not have the required skill to produce quality vanilla, a move that allowed for the concentration of plantation production systems.[19] Similarly, in late nineteenth-century Central America, banana industry leaders deemed bananas grown by small-scale producers low quality as part of an effort to justify the expansion of plantation banana production.[20] Sarah Besky's work on India's tea industry suggested that constructions of quality have served as tools in multiple colonial and postcolonial projects.[21] More recently, claims of poor quality product or production practices have legitimized outsider interventions in coffee and cacao production in the name of development.[22]

Framing existing agricultural practices and their resulting products as insufficient and "traditional" serves to justify intervention in the name of improvement. The identification of deficiencies and generation of prescriptions to remedy them lies at the heart of international development work.[23] Quality discourses in the quinoa industry were refracted through a developmentalist imaginary in which transforming quinoa and the associated agricultural systems to fit a particular concept of good quinoa was about modernizing the industry. These reports consider lack of training in "proper" agricultural practices and "modern" techniques as key culprits of this low-quality end product. The emergent development apparatus, the nascent businesses looking to process quinoa, and government officials in local agriculture agencies read good quality quinoa as modern: it was produced with a suite of modern technologies like certified seeds, clear delineation of fields, furrows, and mechanical threshing. Poor-quality quinoa was "traditional," a result of saved seeds, dispersion sowing, and use of the *chakitaqlla* (Andean foot plow) rather than a tractor. This rendering of traditional quinoa brought with it the symbolic baggage of Indianness in the Andes. Calling the quinoa someone produced "low quality" and imagining the practices that generated it as "traditional" temporalized farmers, locating most farmers in the region as outside of modernity.

Instead of many varieties adapted to the specific needs of unique microclimates, the "modern" quinoa industry that development actors, commercial actors, and agronomists envisioned would center around a handful of "improved" quinoas. But what would an improved quinoa look like? Mario Tapia, one of the first agronomists to build a career studying quinoa, outlined in a 1979 report on the status of Peru's quinoa industry the characteristics that he thought plant breeders ought to seek out. First off, the improved varieties should generate high yields, "similar to those of other countries with maize, sorghum, rice, and wheat." But in addition, these quinoas would need to be "free of saponin, generate high yields, a large grain, good culinary quality, [have] an erect staff with a defined panicle, [and be] resistant to diseases."[24] This concept of a single ideal quinoa was at odds with the existing agricultural system based in many varieties adapted to individual microclimates. The past was in seed saving and exchange among farmers—a system that produced diverse "rustic" quinoas, as the report referred to them. The future was in farmers purchasing a small number of improved varieties, bred for their commercially relevant characteristics and uniformity.

Because these super quinoas did not yet exist, the IICA study authors saw quality standards as a starting point for the industry. They suggested industry leaders create official quality parameters for quinoa that all actors across Peru's quinoa sector could recognize.[25] "Good quality quinoa is considered that which is uniform in color and size of grain, and that doesn't have any rubbish or rocks," declared the IICA study authors.[26] In 1982 a committee composed primarily of representatives from food processors and government entities published the first official state-sanctioned quinoa quality standards, known formally as "technical norms." These standards were a quantified and formalized version of the IICA authors' directive, legitimized by the state. The 1982 standards outlined three quality grades codified in terms of purity. They specified proportions of contrasting grains (3% maximum for grade 1); damaged grains (2% for grade 1); and other material such as sand, rocks, leaves, or dirt (1.5%), and they also specified the maximum humidity (14.5%).[27]

Standards are never neutral. While quality standards appear as objective metrics, standards are forms of moral, political, economic, and technical authority.[28] Middlemen and processors—people without intimate connection to on-farm realities of quinoa cultivation—dominated the committee that generated the 1982 standards. In fact, of the ten entities involved in producing this initial standard, only the Confederación Nacional Agraria represented the interests of farmers. Scholarship on standards makes clear that standards enact relations of power. Studies of the agroexport sector find that standardization projects tend to benefit larger producers.[29] Lois Stanford's study of the standardization of avocados in Mexico emphasized the ways the institutionalization of standards does not take place in a vacuum but within an existing set of power dynamics that shape the standards.[30] Sarah Besky found a related dynamic in the case of tea quality standards in India, suggesting that standards and the lexicon surrounding ideas of quality work to extend colonial norms of valuation and institutions (i.e., tea plantations and their associated institutional apparatuses) into contemporary capitalist circuits.[31]

Good quinoa, based on these standards, was uniform in color, something especially critical for middlemen. If accomplished, this uniformity would render quinoa produced on distant farms by different farmers interchangeable. William Cronon's work on wheat commodification in the nineteenth-century US Midwest demonstrated how the creation of quality standards transformed the unique wheat of individual farmers into one uniform "golden stream" disconnected from individual farmers and farms.[32] Creating standards allowed wheat to circulate over longer distances and in turn reworked industry power dynamics. Uniformity underpins the alienation the global markets depend on: it allows for the quinoa a farmer produces to be symbolically severed from the individual farmer at the point of sale and subsequently be mixed with quinoa from hundreds of other farmers. The creation of a rigid grading system for wheat articulated with other technological and conceptual changes: development of grain silos, changing property rights arrangements, and railroad transport. As was the case with wheat, the creation of quinoa quality standards was also meant to play an important role in a much broader overhaul of quinoa production and marketing.

Standards flatten difference, allowing equivalencies between grain produced by different farmers, and facilitating trade over long distances. And standards erase connections, obscuring how the quinoa was grown, by whom, and where. Obscuring links between specific workers and the products they make is necessary for the alienation the commodity form requires. Anna Tsing analyzed the sorting and resorting of matsutake mushrooms, arguing that assessment practices are crucial to erasing the social relations between producers and consumers and between people along commodity chains.[33] Sorting mushrooms from different mushroom collectors into classes erases connections. Yet studies that read quality standards exclusively through a lens of alienation tend to ignore the ways a standard's specifics matter. Sorting performs alienation, but the way something is sorted matters profoundly to who is included and who is excluded from an industry. Good quinoa in these standards had been substantially processed by farmers to remove debris. This meant more work for farmers and less for middlemen. It also had to have low humidity, which would allow the grain to be stored for a long time (even years) without deteriorating. By inscribing these ideas about good quinoa into a formal state-approved document, this particular vision of quality comes to be seen as neutral and authoritative.

It was not lost on the IICA study authors that standards might be primarily in the interest of middlemen. While the IICA study concluded that the current quinoa stock was of low quality and that quality standards would be necessary to modernize the industry, the authors also expressed concern about unintended consequences. Instituting standards might be premature, they suggested, given that "the consumer market for quinoa is not selective." Study authors worried not only that it was possible for the quality standards to generate higher costs for farmers and higher prices for consumers, but that "the benefits that would accrue from this process would likely be in hands of the intermediaries given the lack of rationality in quinoa commercialization."[34] While it was clear that a modern quinoa industry ought to involve standardization, the IICA study authors suggested that "we need to determine whether the current production structure is adaptable to quality standards and what the consequences would be for producers."

In practice, however, the 1982 standards had little tangible impact on the industry. Producing quality quinoa would involve educating farmers in a different agricultural production paradigm, yet little incentive existed for farmers to alter their agricultural practices without a price premium for quality quinoa. With few consumers willing to pay more for a "higher-quality" product, there was little incentive for farmers to adhere to the standards and in turn little incentive for middlemen to enforce them. These standards proved more aspirational than anything; they offered a vision of what quinoa *should* look like. Rigoberto, reflecting on this time, went so far as to tell me that these standards were "useless." Efforts to formalize quinoa production in the 1990s and early 2000s focused on reorienting production practices to reflect these standards without actually referring to or utilizing the official standard. While the qualities written into the initial 1982 standard (uniformity in color, lack of non-quinoa material, and low humidity) continued to form key elements in understandings of quinoa quality and formal codification of it, over the years other qualities have also come to matter. Grain size and saponin levels in particular took on more importance in the 1990s and 2000s. A 1997 quinoa production manual that CIMA published for farmers explained quality from its perspective: "The three most important factors for the quinoa consumer is the size of the grain, the purity, and the absence of saponin." The manual recommended best practices for managing impurities, classifying and separating different varieties, and managing the *puntos negros* or *ayaras* (wild quinoa) that could contaminate an otherwise pure white quinoa.

This dynamic would change dramatically when consumers in the United States and Europe developed a taste for quinoa. When demand for quinoa outside the Andes began rising in 2008–9, the effort to standardize the region's quinoa took on new urgency. In response to growing demand, the Ministry of Exterior Commerce created a working group to update the quinoa standards in order to "encourage quinoa's diffusion" and "facilitate internal and external commerce."[35] In 2009 the working group released a much more detailed set of standards than the 1982 ones. The new standards were more stringent with regard to purity. For instance, in the 1982 standards, Grade 1 allowed 3 percent contrasting grains. In the 2009 standards the maximum or Grade 1 was reduced to 1 percent. The 2009 standards also included new parameters such as microbiological characteristics, grain size, and maximum saponin content. But soon these standards were also seen as irrelevant and out of date. The quinoa standards working group was convened once again in 2013 to update the standards, with the increasing competition from neighboring countries in mind. The standards published in 2014 were even more stringent.

CONTRASTING GRAINS AND THE POLITICS
OF VARIETAL PURITY

> The price started to rise around 2008 or so and that's when the push to give technical assistance really started. The problem was the quinoa was low quality—it was mixed, no? The white had other colors in it—you know. But the real problem is that agronomists don't understand Andean agriculture.
>
> —JOSÉ, técnico

The meaning of quality is never self-evident, nor are a good's relevant qualities. A particular notion of quality must be constructed and rendered legitimate. For técnicos to train farmers to produce quinoa *de calidad*, they themselves needed to be taught what quality quinoa looked like and how to properly evaluate a batch of quinoa. At the beginning of the buying season in 2014, one of the weekly team meetings included a workshop to train CIMA's técnicos in differentiating good from bad quinoa. Lucy brought out a dozen Tupperware containers filled with quinoa samples labeled "pass" and "fail" for us to compare and handed out sheets with CIMA's quality standards and the sampling protocol. Each Tupperware container labeled "fail" held quinoa with a different "impurity," which Lucy held up and explained in detail, answering questions when the newer técnicos asked them. Discussing the different kinds of ugly quinoa (*quinua fea*), Lucy emphasized that all the técnicos needed to be able to analyze quinoa quality, as the team was increasingly splitting up to do multiple *compras* each day. "Just because the sample was clean doesn't mean the product they end up selling us will be. We need to be consistent about the quality analysis in the *campo* because it causes us headaches in the plant when a batch comes in that's low quality." Standard making requires qualification *and* moralization of the selected qualities. It is not just that grain size comes to matter. Large grain size is *good*. High saponin content is *bad*. Contrasting grains are *bad*. In constructing an ideal, standards moralize. Quinoa that doesn't pass the quality analysis is "ugly" and "dirty."

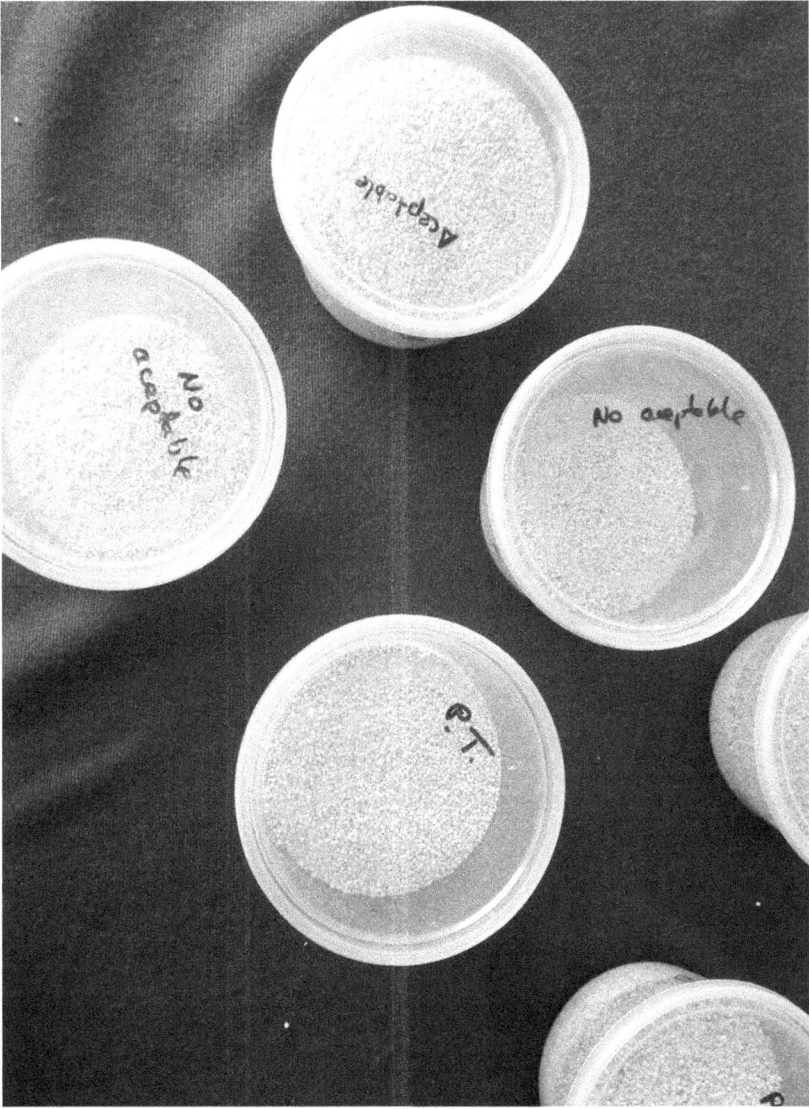

FIGURE 12. Plastic containers with acceptable and unacceptable quinoa, used in of CIMA's técnico training in 2014. Photo by author.

Having a preponderance of contrasting grains, colloquially called *puntos negros*, is one kind of impurity that differentiates good from bad quinoa. Naturally the wind will occasionally pick up quinoa pollen and blow it into an adjacent field, where it will pollinate another quinoa variety. Bees will also cross-pollinate quinoas. The combination of wind pollination and cross-pollination

FIGURE 13. CIMA's quinoa sample evaluation room, where samples of a farmer's quinoa are taken for quality inspection prior to buying the quinoa. Photo by author.

from pollinators means that most batches of white quinoa have some contrasting quinoa seeds speckled throughout. From a commercial perspective, even just a couple of these grains dramatically decreases the perceived quality of the quinoa. These contrasting grains contaminate quinoa's purity. Anthropologist Mary Douglas's *Purity and Danger* suggested that culturally specific concepts of pollution and contagion uphold moral values and social rules.[36] Classification as "matter out of place" not only revealed and helped enforce what good quinoa looked like from a commercial perspective, but also helped enforce a broader set of values about how a farmer should farm.

The main options a farmer had for reducing the contrasting grains in their quinoa was to plant fewer varieties in order to cut down on the chances of pollen from one variety coming into contact with another variety, to separate their fields with "natural barriers" like shrubs as a means of lowering the likelihood of cross-pollination, and to purchase seeds that had been tended with care to ensure "varietal purity." Many farmers employed a combination of these strategies, and técnicos spent considerable energy helping farmers implement these practices.

Rolando, a young farmer who was a member of QCOOP, explained the challenges of cross-pollination and biodiversity to me one day as he gave me a tour of his quinoa fields. Rolando began trying to make a name for himself as a "conservationist" farmer in 2014. This meant that in addition to growing what he called quality quinoa (*quinoa de calidad*) to sell to the cooperative, he also cultivated unique varieties that he could sell to researchers and universities in very small volumes (he sold by the capful, meaning one soda bottle cap of a variety) for high prices. He told me that he had grown fascinated with biodiversity as a child, and while all six of his siblings left the campo for jobs in cities across Peru, he always knew he wanted to stay and work the land. Rolando's diverse quinoa chacras were some of the most beautiful fields I had seen. At that moment, he was growing 120 different quinoa varieties, about half of which he sold to students and researchers at local universities working on quinoa research. The field had quinoas of many colors and heights, some with unique panicle shapes, and they were intercropped with *tarwi*, a local lupin species with bright indigo flowers that was in full bloom on this day. It was a sight to behold.

But Rolando needed to ensure that the varieties the researchers were interested in did not contaminate his "quality" quinoa. He separated his diverse quinoa plots from his commercial quinoa, cultivating them as far apart as possible. "The markets ask for high-quality quinoa and so I can't sell this [to the cooperative]," he explained, gesturing to a bright purple variety with spiraling panicles that towered beside us. "Cross-pollination used to be okay but not anymore. Now I keep them separate because you never know where a bee might be coming from." Rolando's separation of his diverse quinoa varieties from his commercial quinoa underscores how the vision of quality meant rearranging the spatiality of the farm. And while Rolando was able to find buyers for his diverse quinoas, the demand was low, such that it was not realistic for many more farmers to use this approach or else the price of the special varieties would drop further. The quality standards may have focused on the end product, but they enforced larger changes to the biological diversity and spatial arrangement of farms.

For his quality quinoa, Rolando purchased certified seeds from Peru's National Agricultural Innovation Institute (INIA) every few years. This was the best way to ensure the quinoa one grew was as pure as possible. INIA certified a number of seed producers (*semilleristas*) and sold their seeds. These farmers were supposed to take extra care to make sure that the quinoa they produced did not cross-pollinate in order to ensure the end result was a uniform variety. In other words, seed producers' job was to control the reproduction of quinoa seeds, not necessarily to produce better quinoas (that was the job of plant breeders) but to produce pure quinoas. While there were seed producers who were not certified through INIA, its certification program legitimized these seeds and worked as a stamp of official approval and authenticity. Certified seed producers could sell their quinoa as seed to INIA at a higher price because of this legitimacy, and INIA would in turn sell the seeds to other farmers.

Social theorist Michel Foucault developed the concept of biopower to point to the ways that modern states control their populations through assuming responsibility for the health, safety, and stability of citizen populations—that is, through exerting power over life itself. In *The Will to Knowledge*, Foucault described "a power that exerts a positive influence on life, that endeavours to administer, optimize, and multiply it, subjecting it to precise controls and comprehensive regulations."[37] While Foucault was referring to human life, science and technology studies scholars like Shiela Jasanoff have argued that this logic is extended into not only the lives of humans "but also the natural worlds with which humans live in close symbiosis," with seeds being an especially apt example.[38] Seed producers and the state entity that certified their seeds were instrumental actors in remaking quinoa populations. Through encouraging certain kinds of reproduction, the seed production program sought to shift the production systems toward a small number of more homogenous quinoas, making possible the uniform end product that buyers desired.

INIA began breeding "improved" quinoas in the 1980s, but there was negligible demand for these seeds for decades. By 2013 INIA offered thirteen official quinoa varieties, but only three were commonly used by Puno's farmers. Salcedo INIA was the most popular variety due to its high yields, large white seeds, and lack of saponin, but other INIA varieties, such as Negra Collana (the most recommended black quinoa), INIA 415—Pasankalla (the most recommended red quinoa), and with INIA 431—Altiplano and Kancolla (both white quinoas) were also commonly used. The degree to which INIA was actually improving quinoas was debated, and some técnicos and farmers considered INIA's seed program a sham. As one quinoa agronomist complained to me in 2016: "INIA claims these [varieties] like they invented them and that's just a lie. These are varieties the farmers have created and perfected and all INIA did is put their name on them and sell them for an up charge." But this opinion did not exactly contradict the goals of INIA's quinoa breeding program, as the director of the regional INIA office explained to me. Victor, who had worked at INIA for over a decade when I spoke to him in 2016, told me that the main goal of INIA's seed production program was to achieve varietal purity. In other words, this was less about genetic improvement and more about consistency and uniformity. He went on to explain to me the mismatch between farm diversity and varietal purity. "Achieving purity is actually very difficult," he explained. "Panicles cross with each other, and this is a huge problem. So, what we do is we work to get pure varieties because in campo they are crossing with each other."

Purchasing seeds is a rather strange practice. Taking a Marxian perspective, saving seeds from year to year means that farmers control their own means of (re)production. As geographer Ralph Jack Kloppenburg's analysis of the development and dissemination of hybrid corn in the US made clear, turning seeds into a commodity that farmers buy is challenging because plants naturally produce their own means of reproduction (seeds) from season to season. Plant biology frustrates the commodification of seeds.[39] Historically, farmers in the region saved a small amount of their quinoa harvest to use as seed for the following year and also acquired new varieties through informal exchanges with other farmers.[40] But the degree of uniformity that the standards required meant that a growing number of farmers began buying certified seeds. Técnicos recommended buying new certified seeds at least every few years, as even the certified seeds would "degrade" (cross-pollinate) after a couple of seasons. As noted in the previous chapter, sometimes buyers would even cover the cost of the seeds to increase the likelihood that the end product was to their liking.

But a seed shortage developed in 2014, complicating the shift toward certified seeds. The price of INIA's seeds became astronomical. In one of the June 2014 team meetings at CIMA, Emiliano brought up "the seed scarcity problem." He had been planning to require farmers to use INIA seeds for the upcoming season, some of which CIMA would buy. But just the day before he had changed his mind. He complained that certified seeds would cost too much (over PEN 350 per hectare for CIMA or the farmer), and it was a risky investment: "The certified seeds are a big investment and there's a lot of risk for us. The producers might not even sell to us in the end." Instead, he wanted his técnicos to work on acquiring quality seeds that were not INIA certified and therefore cheaper. He instructed técnicos to identify farmers in their zones who might be willing to become seed producers for the next season.

The imperative of uniformity that quality standards codified made contrasting grains appear as a problem rather than an inevitable outcome of a biodiverse agroecological system and the specific characteristics of quinoa's reproductive anatomy. While the quality standards did not indicate how quinoa should be produced and instead focused on the end product, ensuring quinoa had few contrasting grains required farmers to alter the layout of their farms to create separation between quinoas and, at least in some years, to purchase seeds specially tended to ensure their purity.

MERMA AND THE WORK ETHIC OF QUALITY

Merma, which translates as waste or scraps, also figured centrally into the quality equation for buyer-processors. Merma includes all the extraneous material that was mixed in with quinoa after harvest but that needed to be removed through processing: chaff, tiny sticks, pieces of leaves, and pebbles along with broken, discolored, or immature quinoa grains. When técnicos bought quinoa from a farmer (processors called this the "raw material"), a portion of the weight of what they bought would be discarded during processing. But some quinoa contained more merma than other quinoa. And more merma meant more work for processors and a lower return on the quinoa they bought. If a buyer-processor bought quinoa with 10 percent merma for the same price as a batch with 15 percent merma, the processor was making less money on the higher merma batch. The closer a farmer's quinoa aligned with the quality standards that the final product needed to align with, the less product they would pay the farmer for only to have to discard it. For buyers, processors, and other intermediaries, good-quality quinoa then had little merma. Technically, the specific parameters for the "raw material" they purchased were up to buyers, as the quality standards specified characteristics of the final product.[41] Buyers would decide exactly how much merma they could accept. So while all the buyers I spoke with referenced the technical norms for their end product, and técnicos often referred to it in conversations with farmers, what they could accept depended on their own calculations about the nature of their processing plant, the needs of their clients, and how much work they reasonably could require of farmers before the farmers would choose to sell elsewhere.

Johny, who worked in QCOOP's processing plant, explained the merma issue to me in terms of good and bad farmers: "So a good farmer probably will sell a product that, after all processing is done, leaves about 10% merma—stuff we can't sell. But with a farmer who does poor work—who's not a good worker—we have to discard 15-20%. We can't pay a farmer well who doesn't do good post-harvest work. Our costs are directly related to the quality of the product the farmer gives us." Reducing merma was about reducing costs, and the more postharvesting work the técnicos could foist on farmers, the better for buyer-processors. By moralizing the issue—making it about being a good farmer—Johny obscured the politics at play. The standards rendered quality moral, and they rendered it technical. Johny was far from alone in framing merma through the lens of work ethic. Guillermo, a Lima-based buyer-processor, made clear that he saw merma as a reflection of the effort a farmer put into their quinoa. "Basically, there are farmers who do a good job and farmers who don't," he told me in a 2016 interview. "The farmers who do good work will always give the buyer a reasonably good product, the best product the farmer can offer. They work hard during post-harvest. At the same time, there are farmers who don't put in the same effort, and who offer a lesser product." Hard-working farmers produce good-quality quinoa, and those whose quinoa does not meet expectations have been lazy.

It's true that producing quinoa that aligned with the standards was time intensive for farmers. Quinoa quality standards were actively remaking expectations about labor along the supply chain. In addition to using a seed variety that fit buyers' needs (large seeds, varietal purity, minimal saponin), reducing merma required farmers to take special care during the growing season. Preparing the soil diligently would reduce the likelihood of broken grains, using products like biol would help increase the likelihood that grains would reach their full size potential, and close monitoring of any pest issues would further decrease the chances of damaged grains. Beyond this extra work during the growing season, reducing merma entailed rigorous postharvest processing. Some farmers threshed quinoa manually, hitting quinoa panicles against the ground on a tarp to separate the grains from the panicle, and then followed this with winnowing the grain using the wind. Midsize quinoa farmers generally rented mechanized threshers (which would also winnow) from the local municipality or the regional agriculture office to make this process go faster, though this equipment varied in quality and also came with the risk of generating broken grains. These machines were scarce and especially hard to come by during the boom, and renting them was not cheap. Técnicos would often find machinery that they would transport to the farmers, who would pay for the rental. But the postharvest

FIGURE 14. QCOOP's técnicos threshing dried quinoa panicles with a motorized thresher. Photo by author.

activities required to produce quinoa that complied with buyers' needs was labor intensive whether or not a farmer employed traditional techniques or rented a mechanized thresher. Both of these strategies required soliciting help from extended family or neighbors (though it was faster than doing it by hand, operating a mechanized thresher required at least three people).

While the dominant discourse around merma put the responsibility for quality on the farmers, implying that not passing the quality standards meant that a farmer had been lazy or uncommitted, a merma politics also had to do with the plant technology a buyer had access to. In June 2015 CIMA had just completed construction on a new processing plant. As competition between quinoa processors ramped up during the quinoa boom, processing plants became company secrets. State-of-the-art technology could assure prospective clients of a high-quality product, thereby winning processors lucrative contracts. Yet processing-plant technology was not yet standardized in 2014. Different plants had different machines and techniques; there were no companies completely dedicated to quinoa-processing machinery at the time. Quinoa-processing equipment was made on an ad hoc basis and often involved adapting machinery intended for rice or other grains. A new plant brought much speculation among industry actors. What machinery was being installed, and who was making it? Would this new technology out-compete other plants in the region? I felt lucky then, when Fabio, CIMA's processing-plant manager, offered to walk me through the plant one afternoon. Before entering the plant, we enveloped our shoes with medical grade coverings and donned white plastic coats and shop glasses to prevent us from tracking dirt into that plant and also to keep us from leaving the plant covered in quinoa dust. Metal tubes connected large stainless steel machines and vats that reached to the ceiling, filling the warehouse-like space.

Fabio was most excited to show me the new optical sensor. Other plants in the region used optical sensors that operated in black/white, which could individually remove nonwhite quinoa from a batch of white quinoa, for instance. Yet this sensor "saw in color," Fabio boasted, differentiating red and black quinoa that their competitors' scanners would have lumped together as dark. So not only could this machine pick black quinoas out of a white batch, it could also individually select black quinoas out of a batch of red. This was important, Fabio remarked, as the market "asked for" red quinoa in some years. The 2014 technical norm for quinoa defined 0.5 percent contrasting grains as the upper limit for the end product. This meant that processors needed the end product they sold to have fewer than one contrasting grain in every one hundred grains of quinoa. CIMA's new optical sensor allowed them more flexibility with regard to the contrasting grains in quinoa they bought. Because this state-of-the-art machine could pick out contrasting grains better than CIMA's previous sensor, it could accept quinoa from farmers with higher levels of contrasting grains than it had done in the past. Lucy explained this to me one day as we sat beside each other in the backseat of a pickup truck on the way to a buy. She declared that she would always rather have too many *puntos negros* than too many small grains (*menudos*), since the new sensor could remove the contrasting grains. "There's less waste with the puntos negros," she said, explaining that she had some wiggle room with the contrasting grains: she could accept 1.1–1.5 percent based on her assessment of other quality factors, but above 1.5 percent never passed.

As Becky Mansfield's work on the construction of quality in the imitation crab industry has made evident, quality is not simply a social construction with material effects. Instead, ideas about quality result from "complex interactions between natural inputs and their environments, production techniques and technologies, and foods and their uses."[42] The commercial vision of quality quinoa was not simply about alienation and power; it was also rooted in practical concerns related to existing processing technology. Different processors had different parameters for the "raw material" they bought from farmers, based in part on the markets they aimed for and also the processing-plant equipment they had.

The discourse around merma suggested that farmer work ethic was a primary factor that drove the end product quality. Hard-working farmers who implemented the best practices técnicos taught them would produce good quinoa, and lazy farmers generally did not put in the effort and energy to generate quinoa that complied with the buyers' needs. Yet diligence was only one factor that influenced the characteristics of a farmer's quinoa.

GEOGRAPHIES OF INCLUSION/EXCLUSION

The dominant vision of quality presented practical problems for farmers. The meritocratic discourse espoused that producing quality quinoa was about hard work and willingness to experiment with different practices. And certainly, producing quinoa that met quality standards required a massive amount of work, especially during the postharvest processing activities. Yet every farmer did not have the same ability to produce quality quinoa. The quinoa quality standards generated a politics of inclusion and exclusion that mapped onto a number of factors beyond an individual farmer's diligence, such as geography, access to capital, and ability to harness family labor. These dynamics all factored into whether or not a farmer was able to produce quality quinoa and take advantage of the high prices during the quinoa boom.

Even farmers who desperately wanted to participate in markets and were willing to put in extra labor, participate in trainings, and work closely with técnicos could not always produce quality quinoa. In May 2014, Marcos brought me along to visit a farming community in a region farther from Lake Titicaca and higher in altitude, almost five thousand meters above sea level. Marcos had been working in quinoa commercialization for several years at other agencies but had recently been hired at CIMA as part of its effort to expand into new territory and integrate more farmers into its buying networks. His job was to locate farmers who were well positioned to produce quality quinoa in this new "zone" where CIMA did not have a network. He was supposed to find farmers who had decent amounts of land

and who were willing to put in the work. The farmers in this region had not participated in formal quinoa markets before or produced quinoa in compliance with CIMA's quality parameters, making Marcos's work here more difficult and potentially more rewarding. If their quinoa was deemed good enough, this would be a major success in his tenure at CIMA. Marcos was proud of the work he and these farmers had put in over the past few months, repeating on various occasions how diligent and smart (*listos*) they were. He emphasized how he had grown close to these farmers and enjoyed working with them, claiming that they really wanted to sell their quinoa and were willing to put in extra effort to increase the quality of their product so it could meet CIMA's standards.

Almost two hours after leaving Puno, we finally reached the house of Don Roberto, the president of the local farmers' association. We were there to pick up samples to bring back to the plant for analysis and to check on the plants that still hadn't been harvested. As we walked through an unharvested field, Marcos told me that the plants were not looking good, despite all the hard work. The climate in Moqsa was more of an obstacle than Marcos had hoped. Farmers with land close to the lake benefited from an ideal altitude for quinoa and "lake effect": humidity sheltered these areas from the harshest frosts and the most extreme heat. But Moqsa was over fifty miles from Lake Titicaca and considerably higher in elevation, making freezes more frequent and intense. "Here in Moqsa, it's difficult because the producers can't comply with the parameters. The higher altitude means smaller grains and they have to plant native varieties rather than the commercial ones. They plant *mestizo, misti, kancolla, rosado taraco*, and some others—varieties we [CIMA] don't really want to buy. They grow very little *Salcedo INIA* here because it really doesn't do well [here]. But they want to sell their quinoa and many of the farmers planted large parcels this year [in anticipation]."

Marcos openly worried that he had convinced farmers to invest in quinoa production but that, ultimately, they might not be able to get the prices he promised. The native varieties that did well in this region also tended to produce small grains (undesirable for CIMA) and to have high saponin levels (also undesirable). Moreover, even if farmers planted large-grained or sweet varieties, environmental factors (low temperatures lead to smaller grain size irrespective of variety) and studies show that more arid conditions lead varieties with low saponin to develop a thicker saponin layer. Because the area was at such a high altitude, growing quinoa that conformed to the standards was more difficult, and maybe even impossible. "What's the future of this zone? I don't know—it's not producing good enough quinoa [right now]. And the management doesn't support me—they need to be patient for this zone to develop and they're not. This kind of change doesn't happen overnight. We need to find varieties that are better adapted and that produce good quality, and we don't have that."

Marcos thought that it would take another year or two of hard work and experimentation to get quinoa in this region to conform to the standards. It was doable in time he thought, but he doubted that his boss at CIMA would allow him to keep working in the region if this harvest was not up to snuff. And he was upset that the business he worked for was thinking in the short term. In his mind, as much as CIMA talked about caring for the farmers' well-being, it only wanted to work with farmers who could quickly be made to meet its standards.

When I saw Marcos again in 2016, he had been let go from CIMA. I brought up Moqsa and asked how everything had ended up. It had turned out poorly, and Marcos was clearly still upset about it. After all the time and energy the farmers and Marcos had put in, CIMA did not buy their quinoa because it did not meet the company's parameters for grain size. "All their quinoa was rejected. Literally, all of it." he said. "I had one farmer who produced 20 tons of quinoa—that's a massive amount of quinoa. All of it was rejected." The region's microclimate made producing quinoa that conformed to CIMA's standards incredibly difficult. The issue was that 20–30 percent of the quinoa produced in Moqsa was too small. Only specific, very hardy varieties of quinoa could grow in this region, and the hardier varieties tended to produce small grains. For Marcos, the problem was not the quinoa's quality. Instead, he thought that the priorities of buyers like CIMA were out of alignment. He insisted that the quinoa was marketable but that CIMA's management was not interested in doing the work to make it so. He was especially frustrated with the processing-plant manager who had been adamant that CIMA could not buy the quinoa from Moqsa. Marcos argued that the small quinoa could be turned into quinoa flour or quinoa flakes, but the manager "didn't want to put time into that." He complained that what was perfectly good, albeit small, quinoa was "just merma" for CIMA. In the end, he said the farmers he had worked with sold their quinoa in the plaza little by little for a low price.

And while Marcos was convinced that with time the farmers could generate quality quinoa, CIMA's management was not willing to take that gamble. It needed good quinoa, and fast. CIMA's management was not "patient" enough to put in the years needed to generate a "good product" in the northern region, according to Marcos. The entire area was deemed unsuitable for commercial quinoa production, and CIMA stopped investing its time, funds, and energy there at the end of 2015. CIMA's casting off of the entire northern zone after this single harvest shows how the quality standards generated exclusions. Some farmers had an easier time meeting standards than others, with geography being a key factor.

While the quinoa boom was constantly framed as an incredible opportunity for inclusion that promised income opportunities for farmers long cast aside by markets and modernity, only some farmers could actually produce the kind of quinoa the markets demanded. Even those willing to made radical adjustments to how they farmed were not guaranteed the export market price if they could not meet the protocols. Farmers like Doña Maria and those of Moqsa were excluded from the rewards of the quinoa boom. The standards not only generated exclusions, they rendered these exclusions technical. They made the exclusions appear inevitable and without a single source of blame. Técnicos were following bosses' orders, buyers needed quinoa that processors could process without added fees, and "the market" demanded homogeneity.

CONCLUSION

The homogenous white quinoa consumers are accustomed to is by no means "natural," and instead requires investments in social, political, and material work. The quinoa boom depended on the rapid but piecemeal implementation of a standardization apparatus that attempted to physically transform quinoa from a heteroglot agricultural product into a uniform commodity. Quality standards collapsed difference to render quinoas from different farmers and distant regions commensurable, ensuring that quinoa would flow smoothly through the networks of global capital and enabling its global circulation.

The implementation of these standards enforced one particular vision of quality across a heterogenous landscape. Quality standards rendered technical dramatic shifts in agricultural practices and local livelihoods. In paying attention to the implementation standards, we learn how new agricultural imaginaries and agricultural practices were enforced during the quinoa boom. Standards involved highly moralized sorting: sorting good grains from bad ones and hardworking farmers from unmotivated ones. Standards by definition include and exclude; quinoa quality standards defined who had the opportunity to reap the benefits of quinoa's windfall prices and who did not. Quality was often framed through a meritocratic lens through which hard work generated "good" quinoa. And indeed, quinoa processors used standards to shift more processing labor onto farmers. Yet a number of factors from geographical location to access to capital shaped the contours of inclusion/exclusion, with willingness to invest more time in quinoa as only one of the factors at play.

The quality standards not only remade ideas about good/bad quinoa, they reshaped ideas about good/bad farmers and good/bad farming. In order to participate in quinoa exporting, farmers needed to conform to these ideals and adopt associated concepts and practices. In other words, the standards not only physically transformed quinoa's own materiality, they enforced the remaking of agricultural landscapes along with their associated practices and ideological underpinnings. The moralizing and disciplinary work standards do articulates with local context in ways that matter. These standards took on local meanings: quinoa that passed the stringent quality standards and the farmers who produced it were considered modern, while quinoa that failed the test was considered traditional, a category that was further mapped onto the farmer who produced it and the methods they employed.

Quinoa's commercialization was pitched as an opportunity for "inclusion," based on a shift away from the modernization paradigm in agricultural development centered on "commodity crops" like wheat and rice. Yet these quality standards reinforced existing inclusions and exclusions while generating new ones, benefiting some farmers and not others, while requiring major changes to production practices. Analyzing the inclusion/exclusion work standards enact in the context of the "revalorization" of a marginalized food brings into question the "development" and decolonial potentials of these sorts of projects. The quality standards that facilitate the expansion of quinoa markets also devalue local knowledge and farming practices while excluding many farmers from participating in markets.

Standards proved effective disciplinary mechanisms when the price was high. Farmers had the incentive to implement new farming practices and take on the extra labor involved in producing quality quinoa. Yet when prices dropped, it made little sense to farmers to invest in improved seeds and to do extra processing tasks. It would become harder for buyers to find farmers willing to put in the extra time, money, and effort when the prices plummeted. The work of técnicos became even more fraught. The disciplinary power of quality standards fluctuated alongside markets; their implementation was not a linear progression from contested to hegemonic. Instead, the market influenced how well the standards worked.

PART THREE

Bust

FIVE

———————

Disarticulations

UNEVEN RISKS AND FRAGILE RELATIONS
IN THE QUINOA BUST

WHEN I RETURNED TO PUNO in October 2016 after more than a year away, my first stop was CIMA's office. After the requisite two days of rest to adjust my body to the altitude, I took the ten-minute combi-ride from downtown Puno along the lake to the outskirts of town.[1] After so long away, the blue lake sparkled even brighter than I remembered, and I was struck by the steep rock formations that mark the edge of the Salcedo District. After reaching Salcedo, I wove my way on foot through the dirt alleys until I reached the concrete fortification that surrounded CIMA's office and processing plant. I rang the buzzer and waited, noticing the eerie silence of the place. Though it was a Monday morning, which had historically been a busy office day at CIMA, the parking spaces out front were empty. I couldn't hear voices or the hum of machinery. After I had waited a couple of minutes, CIMA's secretary arrived to open the gate. Shirley was always warm and welcoming, though I could tell that she was surprised to see me. After we caught up, she asked who I was there to visit, noting that she was the only person in the office. I checked my phone and saw a new text message from Rigoberto letting me know he was running behind and would be at CIMA soon. Shirley set me up in the conference room, and I perused the collection of texts in the built-in bookshelves.

When Rigoberto finally arrived, he got right to the heart of the matter. "Look, the reality is that things have changed," he said. In 2014 and 2015 CIMA had been a rapidly growing business. As chapters 3 and 4 described, CIMA management had been hiring more employees, securing larger contracts, and working to expand their farmer network. Those days were over. Quinoa's price had plummeted 40 percent between September 2014 and August 2015, and it kept tumbling in 2016 (see figure 17 in appendix).[2]

Rigoberto shared that in early 2016 he and Emiliano had made the decision to dramatically scale back operations. They laid off half of their lead técnicos, reducing a team of six to a team of three. And they sold their fleet of pickup trucks, leaving the remaining técnicos to use public transportation to visit farmers. The trucks had been critical to CIMA's expansion, as they enabled técnicos to reach more and more farmers in the expansive and rugged altiplano geography. But fuel was a major cost that no longer appeared worth it. This meant that técnicos could visit farmers far less frequently, as getting to the remote areas where many farmers live took much longer by combi. "Relationships with farmers are difficult now—more difficult than before," he said. The disappointment was evident on Rigoberto's face as he explained that a growing number of farmers felt that "CIMA and others" were taking advantage of them, that is, not paying them a fair price. "There's a clear tension now," he added. CIMA, which had long been held up as a model of successful farmer relationships and ethical conduct, was struggling to maintain the trust of farmers in their network. Rigoberto had put years of work into cultivating trust with farmers and building a reputation for CIMA, work he had started two decades earlier, long before the boom. This made the dynamic especially upsetting for him. "[The farmers] think the [buying] businesses are the enemy," he lamented, frustration evident on his face.

By 2016 the quinoa boom had indisputably busted in Puno. The quinoa bust was, in some ways, quite predictable. Booms and busts are commonplace in a global economic system established on prospecting, uncertain gambles, and resource exhaustion. Today's interconnected economy runs on boom-bust cycles, a drama built into the very structure of global capitalism.[3] Fluctuation, not stability, is the norm. In a country with a history defined by mineral extraction for more than four centuries, everyone knew that booms were fleeting. No one I spoke with in Peru's quinoa industry had expected the windfall prices to last forever. But the bust hit sooner and more dramatically than anyone, me included, had imagined. This chapter charts the complicated fallout from the price collapse in Puno, especially the unraveling of industry relationships and the associated sets of informal expectations and norms that had held them together. Quinoa's shifting production geography between 2014 and 2016 incorporated new regions and new producers into quinoa's global circuits. In Puno this period was characterized by exclusion and disconnection. This chapter is about the rupturing relationships within Puno's quinoa industry and, on a larger scale, the struggle to keep Puno's industry relevant in increasingly competitive global quinoa markets.

According to the *Oxford English Dictionary*, the term *bust* can refer to "a period of economic difficulty," but also the breaking or splintering of something. The quinoa bust was both of these things for Puno's quinoa industry actors: a sudden shift from temporary economic prosperity and possibility to a politics of scarcity *and* a splintering of the ad hoc relations that had come to hold together the quinoa industry in Puno, albeit in a loose and highly uneven way. Research on global commodity chains has by and large focused on incorporation, that is, the formation of trade relationships that facilitate the movement of commodities from producers to distant consumers. The commodity chain metaphor directs attention to connection and in doing so limits our understanding of the ways global production networks do not just reflect but actively reproduce uneven geographies.[4] This chapter shifts the focus to disconnection and expulsion, looking at how certain actors were expelled from global commodity circuits or struggled to remain connected.[5]

This chapter transitions from an ethnography of an export boom to what James Ferguson called an ethnography of decline.[6] Like Ferguson's study of the Zambian Copperbelt, I am interested in the lived experiences of the bust as both an economic phenomenon and an affective one. The sense of disappointment was palpable among farmers, buyer-processors, técnicos, and other industry actors, many of whom had seen their dreams of a better future collapse along with prices. Quinoa-related businesses were closing, farmers were refusing to sell quinoa in hopes of getting better prices down the line, and some técnicos were having trouble finding work. The linear vision that industry leaders like Emiliano had promoted, whereby Puno's quinoa industry was slowly but surely on its way to becoming orderly, efficient, and modern, now felt lofty and unrealistic. While we tend to think of booms and busts as financial phenomena, they are also deeply emotional experiences.[7] The quinoa bust was both an economic and affective event for those in Puno's quinoa industry that played out in myriad ways, sometimes dramatic and at other times mundane and quotidian. While frustrations with the way industry operated were common during the boom times, many industry actors had felt that with effort these problems could be at least partly overcome. The bust crushed this sense of guarded optimism. It gave way to a general feeling of discontent and despair as an industry that many had worked so hard to get on its feet crumbled around them.

Chapters 3 and 4 tracked the delicate and uneven interpersonal relationships that held together the nascent quinoa export industry in Puno during the boom. These relationships were always already more than just "trade relations."[8] They were laden with power asymmetries, disparate and sometimes racialized expectations, and legacies of colonialism, and were haunted by the recent memory of terror from the country's decade-long civil war. But they were also sometimes more than just trade relations in the sense that often these professional relationships had become friendships or other kinds of not easily categorized, meaningful relationships. Many of these connections, already delicate, began to splinter in the wake of the price collapse. The tenuous bonds and fragile interdependencies that comprised the emergent commercial quinoa industry in Puno were fracturing. Quinoa's expansion into new production zones generated a contraction of social relations among Puno's industry actors.

The unraveling altered dynamics of power in the industry and laid bare the uneven distribution of risk and opportunity that quinoa exporting had generated. The stakes were different for farmers, técnicos, buying and processing businesses, and exporters. And within those categories, there were wide disparities in the risks individuals and groups had taken on. In addition to the rupturing of relationships, the bust generated a new set of winners and losers. The price fall reshaped the stakes for all industry actors, albeit in markedly different ways. While generally the price fall foreclosed opportunities, for a select few the bust generated new opportunities. The chapter charts a range of reactions to, experiences of, and strategies around quinoa's price fall, without presuming to tell "the whole story" of the quinoa bust.

Practically speaking, the bust created problems for my own relationships. The generosity of CIMA management and employees had made possible my participant observation during 2014 and 2015. They had saved me a seat in the pickup truck whenever possible, allowing me to tag along on trips to the campo. But there were no more pickup trucks at CIMA. Their técnicos now left for farmer visits directly from their own homes, before sunrise. Rigoberto and Emiliano let me know that they wanted to support my research in any way they could but that they could not add more to the técnicos' plates. Their three técnicos were already spread thin, and coordinating with me would increase their workload. From 2016 through 2018 I stayed in touch with CIMA management and employees, but I had to turn elsewhere for participant observation of the rapidly changing industry. In 2018 CIMA closed permanently, attesting to the dramatic changes in risks and opportunities.

The chapter's ethnography reflects the shifts my own social network had undergone since the boom. While I do draw on interviews with CIMA management and técnicos, and CIMA's story informs this chapter, new research relationships allowed me to offer a broader view of the fallout of the bust. In 2016 I built connections with individuals and institutions with whom I had initiated relationships during earlier research trips. I got to know managers of other buyer-processors, formed relationships with leaders of development projects, and worked with employees of various state entities related to agriculture (Peru's National Institute for Agrarian Innovation and the Regional Agricultural Administration [Dirección Regional Agraria]), and some of CIMA's former técnicos invited me to tag along on the new work they had found. I spent considerable time working with QCOOP, the major quinoa cooperative in the region, forming relationships with their team of técnicos, managers, elected officials, and cooperative members (farmers), who generously welcomed me into their work lives and allowed me to attend meetings and other events.

Toggling between the ultimate drivers of the quinoa bust, stories about these drivers, the practical fallout for Puno's industry actors, and their affective experiences of this moment, I tap the power of ethnography to connect macroscale forces and the contours of daily life. The first part of the chapter traces quinoa's shifting production geography: quinoa's transformation from a mostly endemic Andean crop into a bona fide global commodity not exclusively tied to the Andes. Next I follow how the price fall reshaped the social and economic worlds of different quinoa industry actors as the power dynamics, opportunities, and stakes shifted. While the price fall led some to leave the industry altogether, the realignment of industry relationships meant that those who continued with quinoa would do so in a radically different environment.

CHANGING PRODUCTION GEOGRAPHIES

Ten months prior to her appearance before the quinoa producers of Calaya in 2013 described in the book's introduction, First Lady Nadine Heredia had sown the symbolic "first quinoa" seed in Lambayeque, a region far from Puno that lies along Peru's northern coast. Surrounded by Ministry of Agriculture officials donning costume Inca regalia, Heredia sprinkled a handful of seeds across the ground in front of a photographer. A crowd of locals who

FIGURE 15. First Lady Nadine Heredia participating in photo op as part of the launch of the Pro Quinoa Program in Lambayeque, Peru. *Source:* Presidencia Perú's Flikr / Creative Commons BY-NC-SA 2.0.

had gathered to watch erupted in applause. Given the region's lack of quinoa production (historically or at that time), Lambayeque was seemingly a strange place to reenact the ceremonial sowing of the year's first quinoa seed, which legend has it the Inca supreme leader himself did each year to mark the beginning of a new agricultural cycle.[9] Known for its production of rice, peppers, cotton, grapes, and avocados, the Lambayeque Department did not produce any quinoa whatsoever in 2013. It was also odd to hold this event in early July, more than three months before quinoa seeds were customarily sown. Yet because of the northern coast's year-round warmth, seeds could be planted year-round, making quinoa's traditional agricultural cycle irrelevant here. Further, from the perspective of Peru's Ministry of Agriculture, the July date made sense because the event had been conceptualized as a celebration of the launch of a new program that promoted quinoa production along the coast (again, an area of Peru that historically had not grown quinoa). Heredia's sowing of the seeds was meant to signify the beginning of a new era for Peruvian quinoa.

Peru's Ministry of Agriculture had established the Proquinua Program in 2012 in an effort to expand quinoa production into new regions of Peru and build the country's quinoa exports. Officials promoted quinoa as a lucrative crop with high profit margins but also as a less water-intensive alternative to rice in a region facing ever more frequent droughts and inconsistent irrigation flows. Proquinua would offer certified seeds, technical assistance, and other services to incentivize large-scale agricultural producers along Peru's coast to replace rice with quinoa. According to reports, the US$43 million investment would cover 60–70 percent of production costs for Lambayeque's farmers and provide them with contracts guaranteeing the sale of their harvest. The Proquinua Program sought to turn an Andean peasant crop into a coastal agroexport.[10]

The Proquinua Program imagined a different future for quinoa in Peru, one in which production was not tied to the altiplano and all the complications of climate, storage, transportation, history, and culture that highland agriculture entails. This project was one piece of a larger public and private effort to encourage farmers outside quinoa's historic territory of the high Andes to convert existing agricultural fields to quinoa production. Policymakers envisioned quinoa within the country's broader portfolio of high-value export crops currently produced along the temperate coast in large-scale capital-intensive farms, including asparagus, artichokes, and paprika. The coast's temperate climate, expansive flat fields, large irrigation systems, and cheap wage labor would help produce quinoa efficiently and at scale.

This vision extended beyond quinoa. As the minister of agriculture at the time, Juan Manuel Benites, explained during the official program launch, Proquinua was part of the state's broader effort to develop commercial production of various highland crops along Peru's coast, which had long been dominated by large-scale, export-oriented agricultural operations: "We are confident in the success of the Proquinua and confident that this experience will be vital for replicating this model with other profitable crops and in particular other Andean grains, such as tarwi, kiwicha, and kañiwa."[11] Proquinua was, as Benites made explicit, a pilot project for a larger dream in which unique Andean crops would gain international acclaim and in turn develop global markets as consumer "superfoods." In fact, two years later Peru's Ministry of Exterior Commerce would launch the Superfoods Peru campaign at product expos around the world in an attempt to recast Peru as the "land of superfoods." But making this dream a reality was not just about drumming up interest among foreign businesspeople and wealthy, health-conscious consumers. It entailed extracting Andean crops from complex highland agroecologies and inserting them into large-scale mechanized production systems along Peru's coasts.

This effort was, at the start, a massive success. Entrepreneurial farmers across Peru's well-irrigated, temperate coast took up quinoa with abandon. It is difficult to exaggerate the intensity of the growth of coastal quinoa production. While the coastal areas of the Arequipa Department produced fewer than 500 tons of quinoa in 2008, fewer than 2,000 in 2012, and 5,300 tons in 2013, this figure rose to 33,200 tons in 2014. That same year, national production more than doubled, increasing from 52,129 tons in 2013 to 114,725 tons a year later, almost exclusively as a result of the sudden uptake of quinoa in the coastal departments of Arequipa, Lambayeque, La Libertad, Tacna, Lima, and Ica.[12] In 2014 Peru's total production (and exports) surpassed that of Bolivia, historically the global leader in quinoa production (see figure 19 in appendix).

The rapid development of coastal quinoa production dramatically remade the country's quinoa production geography. Puno had consistently dominated quinoa production, traditionally producing about 80 percent of Peru's quinoa throughout the twentieth century and up until the boom. As recently as 2012, Puno had produced 82 percent of the nation's quinoa, and it was still responsible for 79.5 percent in 2013.[13] The highlands as a whole had produced over 96 percent of the nation's production in 2012. Quinoa cultivated along Peru's coast grew so rapidly that by 2014, Puno accounted for just 35 percent of national production, despite record outputs in Puno that year. (See www.emmamcdonell.com/quinoa-boom-bust-maps for time-series maps of quinoa's changing production geography within Peru.)

Puno's long-standing and uncontested title as Peru's quinoa heartland was suddenly under threat. Not only had many coastal farmers integrated quinoa into their production systems, but their yields far surpassed what highland farmers could ever hope for. This was a matter of climate, geography, and infrastructure. The coast's year-round warmth and predictable weather allowed multiple harvests each year. In part due to the coastal producers' ability to harvest three times per year, annual yields averaged 5,000 kg/ha along the coast, with some farmers reporting 8,000 kg/ha annually.[14] In contrast, in Puno, 1,000 kg/ha annually is considered a successful year.[15] The economic and political geography played a role too. The large, chemical-intensive production systems along Peru's coasts had the advantage of irrigation infrastructure (unlike the almost entirely rain-fed altiplano farms) and favorable government policies along with access to investment capital. Coastal farmers tended to be seasoned businesspeople, and quinoa was just another opportunity. The coastal quinoa production system was radically simplified compared to Andean quinoa production systems. The complex intercropping and crop rotations that define Andean agriculture were not part of these new quinoa farms. Instead, quinoa was treated like any other export crop, fitting the grain into a plantation logic of substitutability, efficiency, and economies of scale.[16]

Global demand for quinoa grew about 40 percent in 2014. Yet Peru's production increase was so intense that it outpaced the rising demand, generating a production glut and corresponding price fall (see figure 17 in appendix). Quinoa's price began tumbling toward the end of 2014. The price at port (FOB Callao) peaked in early 2014 at US$6.27/kg. By the end of the 2015 harvest season, the price at port was US$4.01/kg. In early 2016 it had fallen to US$2.50/kg, where it would remain for the following two years.[17] The "farm-gate" price followed a similar trajectory.[18] While Puno's farmers earned US$3.60/kg on average and up to US$4.30/kg in 2014, this figure fell 60 percent by 2016.[19]

In other parts of the world, 2015 did not seem remotely like a quinoa *bust*. At the same time that prices were falling in Puno, in the United States quinoa was transitioning from a high-end fashion food to a mainstream staple. That year, Costco began selling 3 lb. bags, and General Mills launched Cheerios Ancient Grains, featuring quinoa, spelt, and kamut. Meanwhile, demand for quinoa was growing quickly among wealthy health-conscious eaters in Western Europe, India, and China. But not all this quinoa originated in the Andes.

Cultivation along Peru's coast was just the beginning of the grain's expansion. Although quinoa production trials had taken place outside South America for decades, commercial quinoa production had remained exclusive to the Andes. The quinoa boom transformed this dynamic. The number of countries growing the crop increased rapidly, from eight in 1980, to forty in 2010, to seventy-five in 2014.[20] Twenty more countries reported sowing quinoa for the first time by 2015. By 2018, 120 countries had some degree of quinoa production.[21] While most of these countries were not cultivating quinoa at commercially significant levels, the United States, Canada, China, Spain, and France developed considerable commercial production during this period, such that non-Andean countries began to play a role in global quinoa markets (see figure 19 in appendix). Long inextricable from the Andean highlands, quinoa appeared to be in the process of becoming another "placeless" commodity.[22]

Terms like *boom* and *bust* serve as shorthand for a range of circumstances. A boom might mean growing demand for a good, growing price for a good, or in the case of minerals, a sudden find of a large resource deposit. Often, a boom entails some combination of those factors. A bust could refer to a drop in demand, falling prices, or the sudden exhaustion of a resource. In quinoa's case, demand was still growing when prices fell, meaning that the quinoa bust did not register for the vast majority of quinoa consumers across the world. Calling this moment a "bust" is context specific. Quinoa's very success globally led to the contraction of Puno's quinoa industry in 2015–17. The bust in Puno was the quinoa boom in Saskatchewan, Canada, where farmers were taking up quinoa production as an alternative to conventional cereal crops. In a single season, Puno went from being one of two global production hubs (along with Oruru, Bolivia) to being outcompeted by industrial-scale farmers along Peru's coast who had no experience with the crop.

This transformation was not simply a result of the inevitable pursuit of what economists call "economies of scale," a natural tendency for larger-scale operations to outcompete smaller-scale ones and a corresponding push toward growing the scale of production. Quinoa's global expansion resulted from orchestrated scientific collaborations around quinoa germplasm that were generating quinoas that could be produced at different latitudes.[23] As chapter 1 explored, an international network of quinoa researcher-promoters developed over the course of the twentieth century, a network that disseminated quinoa seeds and knowledge about quinoa production beyond the Andes. The UN IYQ played a key role in encouraging quinoa production outside the Andes and influenced governmental agencies and agribusiness companies to invest in quinoa production elsewhere.

NEW CALCULATIONS ON THE FARM: SHRINKING MARGINS AND PERISHABILITY POLITICS

In 2016 a growing number of farmers refused to sell their quinoa. Instead, many chose to save their harvest for a later date when, hopefully, they could earn the price they felt they deserved. Quinoa's materiality shaped the ways industry relations disintegrated during the bust. As a dried grain, quinoa could remain intact for up to four years if stored carefully. While there was always some risk that rats or mold could destroy stored quinoa, many farmers had carefully crafted their storerooms to mitigate those risks, something técnicos had advised them to do. The situation for Puno's quinoa farmers differed markedly from those faced by producers of perishables like fresh fruits or dairy, who are generally forced to accept the current price because of the time-sensitive nature of their goods.[24] Quinoa's materiality combined with the altiplano's arid climate gave farmers some very limited leverage, or at least some choice, about when they sold their quinoa.

I helped Edith, a farmer who primarily sold to QCOOP, harvest quinoa on a sunny day in May 2017. As we took a break under a small patch of shade to sip soda, we chatted about her plans for the quinoa we were harvesting. Her harvest from 2016 was still sitting in sacks in her storage room, as she had refused to sell it despite pleas from QCOOP's management. Between selling cow's milk and wages from her husband's taxi, she and her husband had been able to cover their family's expenses over the last year and could wait on selling the quinoa for more favorable market circumstances. At present, she complained that it was not worth it to sell. The amount of work she put into ensuring her quinoa passed the demanding quality criteria and complying with organic certification did not make sense given the price that the cooperative was offering at the time (PEN 4.70/kg or about US$1.50/kg), the same price as a year before. She might sell a little quinoa if she needed money, but she planned to try to hold out for a higher price.

Not every farmer had the means to stow away quinoa. Though a number of farmers I spoke with in 2016 and 2017 had saved their quinoa for months, at some point many needed cash and reluctantly sold their quinoa for less than what they thought it was worth. Liliana was a young farmer who lived with her new husband on her parents' farm and was also a cooperative member. She had stored quinoa for as long as she could in 2016, but by the end of the year the favorable prices she had hoped for had still not arrived. She had to sell her quinoa for the disappointing price. "I can't afford to [store quinoa] anymore," she told me. "The rich farmers can afford to still keep stocks and wait for higher prices, but I can't do that. I [won't be able to] take advantage of good markets because I need the money from quinoa, even when the price is still low." She was frustrated that she did not have this possibility, which meant she would just have to sell her quinoa for the going market price.

This issue of stockpiling quinoa revealed latent tensions among farmers. While some farmers could attempt to take advantage of market changes, saving up years of quinoa and selling when the price was high, farmers who were more reliant on income from quinoa were at the whims of markets. While the low prices were not good for farmers as a group, some farmers fared better than others after the price fall. Farmers with large stocks and enough money to get by without selling could hold off on selling their quinoa, while others could not. Similarly, farmers with multiple other income streams—jobs in Juliaca, large cattle herds for milk, or family members who worked in nearby mines—could adapt to the low prices more readily than those who had become more dependent on income from quinoa. Yet a second windfall never arrived, and the better off farmers who could wait until 2018 to sell still only earned marginally higher prices.

Saving quinoa was not a new practice. "Having quinoa stored away is like having money in the bank," Alex, a QCOOP técnico, told me when we discussed the issue of farmers "refusing" to sell quinoa. Quinoa, like other nonperishable agricultural products, could function like a store of value among highland agriculturalists, one that often stored value better than the official national currency.[25] But what had been a routine and unremarkable practice historically was now a problem for private quinoa buyers and for the cooperative. Farmers had been willing to sell all their quinoa at once when prices were sky high, but with prices low, they were in no rush. Buyers had largely not figured into their calculations the potential for farmers to refuse to sell. Buyers and the cooperative had contracts that often spanned twelve months, meaning they were frustrated by farmers' tactics.

The fact that the cooperative was offering the same price as a year before surprised and frustrated Edith and Liliana. They knew many other farmers were also withholding their quinoa from the cooperative in hopes of not just waiting for a better price but forcing the cooperative to offer a higher price. But this tactic did not appear to be working. Some farmers told me they suspected the cooperative management had been secretly buying from outside the cooperative to comply with contracts and avoid needing to raise the price paid to cooperative farmers, but no one had proof. Yet these accusations attest to the way relationships between farmers and the cooperative that many had been proud of were withering as some farmers began to question the model in its entirety. And while the cooperative model was distinct from the models CIMA and other private buyer-processors used, a similar dynamic of frustration and distrust was emerging in the wake of the price fall.

By the end of 2016 the falling prices were leading many farmers to reevaluate the place of quinoa in their production systems. While some farmers had been stockpiling quinoa, when it was time to sow quinoa for the 2017 harvest, there was still no indication of a rising price. After years of técnicos encouraging them to invest more time and energy in quinoa, farmers were questioning whether it made sense anymore. Investing in quinoa had been a risk that paid off during the boom but increasingly appeared to be a poor bet. Producing commercial quinoa that met export quality criteria and complied with organic quality standards was much more work than just growing quinoa for one's family or for local markets. The question for farmers in Puno was not whether to produce any quinoa, but how much quinoa to grow and whether to continue to put in the extra time and energy required to produce quality quinoa.

The calculation was in part about the drudgery of commercial quinoa production. This dynamic was not unlike what agricultural economist Alexander Chayanov found when he studied the economic logics of Russian peasants in the early twentieth century.[26] He argued that they were not making decisions about their farming based on a profit calculation of the sort that the business might make and instead sought balance between rewards and the drudgery of work.[27] Given that the harvest season is already incredibly busy and tiring for farmers, the toil of taking extra steps after harvest to comply with stringent quality criteria only made sense when rewards were high. Quinoa had historically been a low-labor input product for Andean farmers, especially when compared to the time and energy milk or wool production required. Yet the extra work that producing export quinoa entailed previously had been justified by a high price. But with small margins, the work was not worth it for many. While many farmers I spoke with sowed the same amount of quinoa in 2017 as in 2015 and 2016, some were no longer willing to deal with the extra hurdles (quality criteria) export markets required given the small margins. Some chose to sell quinoa to acopiadores, who accepted the "lower quality" quinoa and also paid a lower price. Still others had scaled back their quinoa production and adjusted their income strategies based on quinoa's price.

Living at the margins of the global periphery had led Andean farmers to develop highly flexible economic lives. Because of the multiple income streams from farm products and off-farm incomes, along with basic food needs generally being met from their own farms, many farmers were able to adjust their portfolios to some extent to attempt to take advantage of the boom conditions. Among farmers, there was considerable disparity in who could leverage the high prices during the boom, as well as disparity in who was most affected by the bust. After the bust, many were able to be-grudgingly pivot away from quinoa as well, taking on more work in the city, for instance, or dedicating more energy to expanding their cattle herds. This did not mean removing quinoa from the production system but dedicating less energy to the crop. While farmers had taken on some risk in dedicating energy to quinoa, they had also designed their economic lives to weather the sort of uncertainty of the quinoa bust.

RISING TENSIONS

The bust complicated the business of buying and processing quinoa for Puno's established buyer-processors, cooperative management, and the téc-nicos who worked for these entities. Farmers' efforts to save their harvest rather than sell it frustrated buyers and the técnicos who facilitated quinoa buys. Even though the price was low, CIMA and QCOOP and other qui-noa businesses still needed quinoa to fulfill their contracts. Francisco, one of CIMA's remaining técnicos, suggested that the farmers had come to expect too much for their quinoa. "The margins don't make sense like they used to but there are still margins. It's a business of cents," he told me, suggesting that farmers' expectations had become inflated during the boom. He went on to compare the prices CIMA offered with the prices farmers might receive "in the plaza" to make the point that while the price difference might seem small, the cents quickly added up to dollars.

Management and employees who had been with CIMA since before the boom felt a sense of loss over the breakdown of relationships with farmers that they had maintained during the past two decades. While the business model for CIMA and other established highland buyer-processors had fo-cused on building strong connections to local producers, these relationships deteriorated rapidly with the price fall, laying bare the fragility of the bonds between técnicos and farmers. When I spoke with Francisco in early 2017, he told me that just a few days before he had been presenting to a group of farmers when an angry farmer stood up and publicly accused CIMA of cheating them. The farmer said that she had heard that quinoa was selling for $15/kg in the United States and that the only way it made sense for them to get so little was if CIMA was paying farmers far below what they de-served and pocketing the difference. These kinds of public accusations had become commonplace during técnicos' interactions with farmers, a marker of the frustration farmers increasingly felt and the difficult position técnicos found themselves in as go-betweens.

QCOOP faced a similar set of issues. Quinoa was "escaping" as farmers sought out better deals outside the cooperative or refused to sell as they awaited higher prices. This made it difficult for the cooperative to complete orders on time. Linda, a farmer who was also an elected cooperative official, explained the issue to me in 2017 as we sat together on a combi ride into Juliaca. "Product is still escaping. An intermediary might pay you 60 soles [PEN per arroba] and the cooperative might pay 62. But why would I bring my quinoa to the cooperative if they can reject it for poor quality while the intermediary will take it *merma* and all for 60?"[28] The issue of "loyalty" that arose during the boom only became more difficult amid the desperation brought about by the bust. Técnicos tended to see farmers' refusal to sell their quinoa as shortsighted because of the way it undermined the cooperative and the local buyer-processors. Various técnicos emphasized to me that farmers did not see the long-term implications of selling outside the business and cooperatives that had "treated them well." If these businesses folded, farmers would be left with a much less charitable set of buyers, the acopiadores.

The frustration cut both ways. Farmers who sold to private buyer-processors were accusing businesses like CIMA of cheating them, and farmers in the cooperative were denouncing cooperative management of corruption and lack of transparency. They too had become suspicious after hearing of the high prices quinoa earned abroad and the low prices they were being offered. This was leading some farmers to turn away from the cooperative that many had worked so hard to build. Tensions were high as farmers accused elected officials and cooperative técnicos of corrupt practices— stealing from the cooperative and engaging in shady buying practices. The last three cooperative managers had been fired for various kinds of shady dealings and the low prices farmers were receiving made them even more suspicious of cooperative management. "Are they for the cooperative or for their own enrichment?" Rolando, a farmer who had helped form the cooperative and who still sold to them, asked me, shrugging. He continued, "It's fine to pay the manager a good salary but only if there are results." The price fall was fracturing the relationships that had loosely held together Puno's fledgling quinoa export industry.

While buyers complained that farmers' fears that they were being taken advantage of were exaggerated or misguided, farmers had plenty of examples to support their anxieties. One such example was the infamous Soler Foundation, a story that many farmers referenced when sharing their fears about the intentions of "the businesses" or the cooperative. Soler had shown up in Puno in 2013 to buy large amounts of quinoa from farmers across the region. Unlike CIMA or QCOOP, they did not have an existing farmer network and tried to build one on the fly. Much to the chagrin of the existing buyer-processors, Soler was indiscriminate about whom it bought quinoa from. It bought from hundreds of farmers who were not in existing networks and, promising a higher price than CIMA or QCOOP, Soler also bought quinoa from farmers who had been working with CIMA or the cooperative. It bought all this quinoa on credit, promising to return with cash once it had sold the quinoa. Soler foundation never returned; it folded, and these farmers never saw their money.

RISK AND OPPORTUNITY
FOR BUYERS AND PROCESSORS

By 2017 the main altiplano-based buyer-processors were already closing their doors or discussing shutting down as imminent. "You barely make any money processing quinoa," Mario lamented as we spoke in his office in Juliaca in early 2017. Mario had been in the quinoa-processing business since 2010. His Juliaca-based processing plant was small at first, processing a maximum of 5 tons/day. But he began developing processing equipment himself, and by 2013 his plant could process 1.5 tons/hour. In 2013, with prices skyrocketing, he expanded his business to focus on certified organic quinoa. He hired a team of técnicos and paid for farmers' organic certifications, following a business model similar to CIMA's. But this model proved less feasible during the height of the boom and even more so when the price collapsed. Farmers, Mario complained, routinely sold to "whomever they wanted," even after Mario's company had paid for their certification. In 2015 Mario had contracted to sell 1,000 tons of organic-certified quinoa, but he ended up with only 400 tons. This had broken his trust in farmers while also fracturing his business's relationships with brokers. He claimed that their refusal to remain loyal in the changing market conditions "came down to a lack of respect" among farmers. He said that his processing business became more about "giving back" than making money as time went on, and his margins dwindled. The fact that Mario and other altiplano-based buyer-processors felt they were helping farmers—often framing their work as a sort of social service—intensified the frustration. Mario felt farmers owed him respect in the form of loyalty, and he ultimately depended on this loyalty. After lapsing on his contracts with brokers in 2015, he said he felt he had little choice but to completely reimagine the business. Mario blamed farmer conduct for his business's collapse. He shook his head, telling me that when the price collapsed, some of these same farmers came back to him wanting to sell their quinoa to him for the original price. In early 2016 Mario deemed working with farmers' associations too complicated, referring to it as "a headache." He laid off the técnico team and shuttered his organic quinoa-processing business.

As an entrepreneur with some funds to invest, Mario was quick to find new ways to adapt to the changing market context. He had started manufacturing quinoa-processing equipment for his own processing plant but found that he could sell this equipment for a sizable profit to others starting quinoa-processing plants. Because the scale of quinoa markets had grown so quickly, few companies manufactured quinoa-specific processing machinery, and processing machinery was still largely made ad hoc. Many plants used manually retrofitted rice-processing machinery, with varying success. Large agroexporters along Peru's coast were building massive quinoa-processing plants that would dwarf any of the altiplano-based plants, and they needed high-quality processing machinery. While Mario had begun selling quinoa-processing equipment before the bust—operating a side-by-side quinoa buying-processing operation and a processing machinery plant, in 2016 he pivoted his business to exclusively focus on manufacturing specialized quinoa-processing machinery. He told me he was making good money selling this equipment as many new businesses wanted to process quinoa, and very few companies produced these machines. While business had slowed down since the price fall, he said his manufacturing business was still doing well and was increasingly getting international orders, most recently from Spain, Chile, and Turkey.

Mario's shift from processor to processing equipment manufacturer illustrates the dynamism among this group of middlemen, many of whom were reorganizing their businesses or turning away from quinoa altogether in 2016 and 2017. But it also underscores the shifting geography of quinoa processing. The altiplano's processors now competed with larger and better-financed plants in Lima and Arequipa, many of which had state-of-the-art technology and served large agroexport companies. Some of these same companies that historically had contracted with Puno's buyer-processors had decided to vertically integrate as global quinoa demand grew. In Arequipa, for instance, there had been no quinoa-processing facilities outside the highlands before 2012. By 2015 there were four. Mario complained that in the highlands the mentality was that you use equipment until it no longer functions, whereas on the coast, businesses were constantly trying to update their technology. The altiplano's buyer-processors, many of whom saw themselves as largely responsible for making the quinoa boom possible, were losing ground to large agroexporters along Peru's coast, who boasted robust international connections and investment capital, and for whom quinoa was one part of a portfolio of products. Once again, altiplano's buyer-processors felt, coastal elites were benefiting from their hard work. Entrenched power asymmetries were undermining the potential for a sustainable altiplano-based quinoa industry.

Puno's buyer-processors tended to blame their changing lot on the farmers' refusal to sell their quinoa, along with the ways acopiadores and new itinerant buyers, many of whom had contracted with processing plants and exporters in Lima or Arequipa, undermined their business models. This frustration mapped onto historical dynamics within Peru that saw wealth concentrated in the coastal cities even if resources (minerals, quinoa) were not. The consternation over "unscrupulous" coastal businesspeople was then a familiar frustration. It resonated with long-standing sociopolitical divisions and fit into existing narratives.

But these new buyer-processors based outside Puno were not all having an easy time. I met Manuel, an agribusinessman based in Arequipa's agricultural heartland of Majes, while he was visiting Puno in early 2017. He picked me up in his decade-old Mercedes Benz SUV, a marker of status that made him stand out in Puno but also an indication of an earlier time when his financial conditions were better. He was visiting Puno to try to find a buyer for his now defunct processing plant in Arequipa. Manuel was more of an agribusinessman than a farmer. After earning a bachelor's degree from Lima's agricultural university in the 1980s, he had pursued a master's in agribusiness at University of California, Davis, before returning to Arequipa to develop his various agricultural business ventures. He had invested in numerous products over the years. Disappointed but unfazed by quinoa's bust, he said that for him and for other farmers in Majes, booms and busts were just part of business.

Back in 2012, when quinoa prices were rising every week, he had invested in building the first quinoa-processing plant in Arequipa, outfitting it with state-of-the-art technology. He had converted some of his own fields to quinoa and began talking to his neighbors about doing the same. Within a year his processing plant was rented out every day to process his quinoa and that of his neighbors. Business was good. He even began his own quinoa-buying venture in 2014 to supplement the income from selling the quinoa he grew and the processing-plant rent. But his fortune changed when the price began to fall. He was having trouble finding farmers who would sell for the price he offered, and in 2015 the demand for renting his plant fell as Arequipa's farmers turned away from quinoa with the price fall. He ended up renting the plant to a large agroexport company based in northern Peru in 2015, but it terminated the rental agreement in early 2016. By early 2017 he had an empty processing plant that was gathering dust. When I met him, he had just filed for the Peruvian equivalent of Chapter 11 bankruptcy.

In general, the quinoa bust's implications for Peruvian actors could be summarized as foreclosed opportunities. But this stood in marked contrast to the opportunity outside business interests saw. As existing industry relationships crumbled in Puno and businesses closed their doors, a Singapore-based multinational agroexport enterprise saw an opening. One man's bust is another's golden opportunity. Olam Group, a company with operations in sixty countries that boasts a $47 billion revenue stream, broke into the quinoa business in Peru in early 2017. Among the world's largest suppliers of cacao, coffee, cotton, and rice, Olam possessed ample funds to invest in its new quinoa operation. First, the company bought out one of the major coastal processing plants along with all that company's personnel. Olam began building up a network of farmers in Puno, offering a higher price than existing buyers to win over farmers.

Alejandro, who had worked as a técnico for the company Olam bought, was tasked with acquiring quinoa for Olam. He said that because he had been working in different capacities with quinoa farmers in the region for over a decade, farmers trusted him. It helped that Olam was offering a higher price than other companies, something Alejandro could not explain. He was buying from all over—from existing businesses, directly from producer associations, and from individual producers who were not organized into producer associations. While other buyer-processors tended to see Olam as a threat and a scavenger, benefiting from their work, Alejandro criticized the business practices of the existing buyers: "Competition between the companies is really ugly these days."

From the perspective of those Puno farmers, Olam had appeared suddenly. No one had heard of the company at the end of 2016. But by June

2017 farmers, técnicos, and other industry actors in Puno were constantly speculating about how Olam's presence would impact the industry. "Their goal is clear. They want to monopolize quinoa," Linda, a farmer and elected secretary for QCOOP, told me. She explained that Olam was buying from the cooperative and also from the cooperative's competition (other Puno-based buyer-processors, other farmer organizations). It was buying all the quinoa it could. "They are going to destroy the intermediaries. It might seem like a good thing right now, but what intentions will they have in the future when they control the industry? If they monopolize everything, they will pay farmers whatever they want" warned Linda. In 2022 Olam had become Peru's second largest quinoa exporter, overtaking major Peruvian agro-expoeters including Globenatural and Colorexa.[29]

While all industry actors complained about the way the industry was currently organized—many calling it disorganized and chaotic—no farmer, técnico, state actor, or entrepreneur I spoke with saw Olam's arrival as a positive development. Tensions were high between farmers, buyers, and técnicos, but the sudden appearance of a large outside company was not seen as a solution to industry woes. If anything, many expressed concerns that this change would exacerbate the collapse of the dream of a prosperous quinoa industry in Puno.

REPUTATION, RISK, AND OPPORTUNITY FOR TÉCNICOS

The bust meant the closure of buyer-processing businesses and scaling back of others alongside a dramatic reduction in international development funding for quinoa-related projects. The quinoa boom had created many técnico positions in Puno. But in 2016 and 2017 técnicos were being laid off. While quinoa-related businesses and projects had been hiring for years on end, many were now letting employees go. Técnicos were a dynamic group who tended to change jobs and organizations frequently. Their skillset was easily transferable between private, nonprofit, and public sectors, as between 2010 and 2015 there was growing demand for people who could effectively articulate between farmers and quinoa-related businesses and state-led and international development-funded projects, such that new opportunities would arise frequently. Some of this had to do with the nature of development funding, which generally financed two- to three-year projects. But the steady rise in quinoa-related técnico positions that began in 2008 was quickly reversing. Not only were buyer-processors closing, but international development agencies no longer saw quinoa in the same light. When quinoa's price was rising, a surfeit of international development agencies had launched quinoa-related projects, mostly related to training farmers in commercial quinoa production and organic certification. Quinoa export, as was outlined in chapter 1, was imagined as an unparalleled poverty alleviation tool in the Andean highlands. But when quinoa's price fell, the case to be made for quinoa as a poverty alleviation tool was harder to make. Many of these development projects did not have their funding renewed, and in general it became much more challenging to find developing agency funding for quinoa. The contraction that the quinoa bust generated led many técnicos to seek out different kinds of work or to leave the region.

While técnicos were generally professionally agile and accustomed to making frequent job changes, they too had taken on personal risks as representatives of businesses and development projects in the campo. While some were able to leverage their reputations with farmers into new opportunities during the bust, others found themselves with tarnished reputations that limited their professional options.

The trajectory of Carlos, whom I met while he was a técnico at QCOOP, illuminates the ways técnicos' personal reputations among farmers mattered to their professional trajectories. A young técnico, Carlos had been hired by Soler Foundation before he even graduated from college to build farmer relationships across Puno and to buy as much quinoa as possible. Carlos and Soler's broader team of técnicos were able to buy quinoa from hundreds of farmers in the region in 2013, offering higher prices than more established buyers like CIMA or QCOOP and accepting slightly lower-quality quinoa. At the time Carlos thought he was doing good work, helping farmers fully take advantage of the windfall prices. So when Soler suddenly folded and management stopped returning phone calls, Carlos was aghast and disgusted.

His reputation was severely tarnished through his association with Soler: "I was the face of the organization in the campo," he told me. While Carlos had no part in the decisions of his superiors, whom he called criminals, farmers directed their frustration at him. After all, it was Carlos who convinced them to sell their quinoa on credit and Carlos who picked up the quinoa. Carlos said that not only did these farmers lose trust in Carlos, many had shared their distrust with friends and family, and his reputation was tarnished beyond just those who were caught up with Soler.

After the Soler debacle, Carlos briefly worked at CIMA, though he found the reputation he had gained in the campo made him less effective in this position. QCOOP hired him in 2015 to lead a project funded by the National Agricultural Innovation Program that would offer biodigesters to cooperative members for a much-reduced cost. These devices break down organic material in a sealed tank (*anaerobically*). While this process is slower than (*aerobic*) compost, if done properly, the gases produced are stored and can be used for cooking. Biodigesters were pitched as a solution to multiple problems for highland farmers. In theory, they would put household food waste to use in restoring soil fertility while also providing a source of cooking gas that could help transition rural households away from the smoke-based biomass cooking that public health experts warned was causing unsafe household air pollution levels.[30] Carlos spent months trying to convince QCOOP's farmers of the utility of the biodigesters. While the project funded Carlos's position, farmers themselves had to buy the biodigesters, albeit at a reduced price. Carlos told me that from the beginning he had been skeptical of the cost quote the biodigester company had provided, which seemed low to him, but he was reassured that the biodigesters were high quality. When the biodigesters finally arrived, it was clear that they did not function as described and were poorly constructed. Yet there was nothing to be done as they could not be returned. The farmers who invested in these devices were disappointed, and once again, Carlos was the face of the project. He lost the respect of the cooperative's farmers and felt disillusioned with técnico work. His positions at Soler and QCOOP had ended poorly, with him taking the hit for decisions made by those far above him in the pay scale. In early 2018 he decided to cut his losses and move to Arequipa to start fresh. He felt burned by agricultural development work in Puno and felt that these marks against his reputation undermined his ability to be an effective técnico in the region. At the same time, there were fewer and fewer técnico positions in Puno as quinoa-related projects completed and generally did not receive further funding cycles. After taking a few months off work, Carlos ended up working a couple of short-term positions in Arequipa and then gaining a consulting position for Wildlife Conservation Society, a move that he hoped was a route out of técnico work.

The expansion of quinoa's commercial production geography outside of the Andean highlands and the corresponding price fall introduced myriad challenges for Puno's fledgling commercial quinoa industry. The plummeting price revealed the disparate stakes of quinoa commercialization for farmers, buyer-processors, and técnicos. It revealed the risks industry actors had taken and the ways the particularity of individuals' positions influenced who was most vulnerable to the shocks of the market. While the impacts of the bust on farmers, buyer-processors, and técnicos were patterned, a number of factors shaped individuals' experiences and their degree of vulnerability.

By 2018 all four of the main Puno-based buyer-processors, including CIMA, had closed down or were taking "breaks" of undetermined length. Some of these buyer-processors were able to pivot their operations in light of changing industry dynamics, and others were stuck with large loans and few ideas regarding how to pay them off. QCOOP was still operational, though plagued with large unpaid debts and strained relationships with its members and clients. The low farm-gate prices frustrated Puno's farmers, which few felt justified the work they had put into producing quinoa of commercial quality. Many farmers were reconsidering the role of quinoa in their production systems and adjusting their economic lives in light of the low prices. Técnicos, long central figures in the articulation of Puno's quinoa industry, were losing their jobs as Puno's quinoa market contracted. Accustomed to frequent job changes because of short development project funding timelines and the fickleness of markets for agricultural products, técnicos by and large could adjust. Many found work in other agricultural sectors, and some pursued jobs outside Puno, though many reported a real sense of loss at leaving the quinoa sector that had brought them a real sense of hope and possibility. While for most local actors the bust revealed the risks they had taken on, the price fall also generated opportunities, especially for entities based beyond Puno. The closure of Puno-based buyers and processors created an opening for the expansion of Olam, a Singapore-based multinational agricultural commodities company, to launch a quinoa operation in the Peruvian highlands. The bust was not only about plummeting prices; it also marked dramatic shifts in industry power dynamics.

The price fall generated tensions and fractures in the relationships that had loosely held together Puno's fledgling quinoa export industry. While the bust was an economic experience, it also spawned affective experiences, largely of loss and frustration. The price fall shifted the interests of different actors in ways that strained existing trade relationships. Many of the institutional relationships and sets of expectations that had been formed during boom times could not withstand the challenges the price fall created. The existing set of fragile relationships sustaining the industry began to break down as low prices tested their durability.

The deterioration of industry relationships would intensify with the contamination scandals that erupted alongside the price fall. These twin struggles—the price fall and the contamination scandals—would define 2016 and 2017 agricultural cycles and collectively unravel Puno's quinoa industry. This unraveling is the subject of the next chapter, which traces the centrality of trust in trade relationships and ways the inevitably fragmented nature of market knowledge transformed into insurmountable uncertainty and suspicion.

SIX

Fragmented Knowledge and Intractable Residues in the Quinoa Supply Chain

> Look, quinoa production along the coast was not well thought
> out or really analyzed at all. People just saw skyrocketing prices
> and planted quinoa in lieu of onions or asparagus or rice or
> whatever.
>
> —MARTIN, Lima-based agricultural product exporter

IN APRIL 2014—when quinoa prices were at an all-time high—a container of Peruvian quinoa was denied entry into the United States after officials from the US Food and Drug Administration (FDA) detected agricultural chemicals that the US Environmental Protection Agency (EPA) had not approved for use on quinoa. The container in question was sent on a three-week return journey back to the Port of Callao, Peru's largest port, just north of Lima. A few weeks later, US officials rejected another container of Peruvian quinoa after it too was found to have traces of pesticides exceeding the EPA's maximum residue levels (MRLs). By the end of 2014, US ports had rejected over a dozen shipments of Peruvian quinoa, totaling just over 1 percent of the total quinoa Peru exported to the United States that year.[1] At the same time that quinoa's price was plummeting in 2015, news of contaminated quinoa and rejected shipments brought yet another crisis to Peru's now struggling quinoa industry.

The immediate economic impact of the rejected containers was significant for the exporters whose shipments had been rejected. A container, which holds 20 tons of quinoa, would have contained about US$135,000 worth of quinoa. The cost of moving the container itself was around US$3,000 at the time. Yet a returned container is not just a problem because of the bottom line. On the industry level, the rejections generated new anxieties about chemical residues that in turn unraveled industry relationships and the assumptions that held them together. A rejected container can tarnish the reputations of export businesses, of buyers, of producer associations, and even of entire producer regions, generating tension and distrust that reverberate across the supply chain. US importers have contractual obligations with US wholesalers, who in turn have contracts with retailers and product manufacturers. These contracts delineate an amount of quinoa, the specifications of the quinoa (color, size, etc.), and a delivery date, among other things. When a container is rejected at a US port, the shipment delivery date is suddenly delayed for at least a month, leaving the importer, wholesaler, and retailer with logistical problems and fractured business relationships.

Initially, exporters explained the issue as one of import bureaucracy that could be resolved through negotiations between Peru's government and importing countries. Because quinoa was a relatively new global commodity, importing countries like the United States had not approved many chemicals for use on the grain. Many of the same agricultural chemicals that caused importing countries to reject quinoa shipments were acceptable on wheat or asparagus. Further complicating matters, some of these rejected shipments included certified organic quinoa, which should have been held to an even higher standard than "conventional" quinoa in terms of chemical application. The detection of unapproved chemicals on organic certified quinoa made clear that the issue transcended bureaucratic fine print. Finding pesticides and fungicides, some considered highly toxic, on organic certified quinoa undermined the legitimacy of the organic certification apparatus writ large. Organic certification's system of checks should have guaranteed a product without these kinds of agricultural chemicals, spurring an outright crisis of trust in Peru's quinoa industry as a whole and the organic quinoa sector in particular. While the chemical traces generated a crisis of reputation for Peruvian quinoa at large, Puno's industry actors would disproportionately feel the impact given the region's concentration of organic certified quinoa farmers and the lack of alternative export crops for farmers to turn to.

As containers of rejected quinoa piled up in Peruvian ports at the end of 2014, the entire industry hoped this was an isolated problem that could be resolved quickly. But the issue proved messier than anyone initially imagined. Even as industry actors and industry groups took steps to remedy the issue, US ports returned nine more containers to Peru in 2015.[2] In 2015 the FDA's Pesticide Residue Monitoring Program flagged quinoa as an import that "may require special attention."[3] A study commissioned by Peru's Ministry of Agriculture would find over twenty different agricultural chemicals on its samples from Peru's quinoa supply, including carbofuran, which the EPA banned in 2009; atrazine, which is banned in the European Union

(EU) and the United States restricts the use of; and chlorpyrifos, which the EPA would ban in 2021 because of the "unacceptable" health risk the chemical poses. While the United States had been Peru's primary quinoa buyer since the earliest days of quinoa export (65% of Peru's total quinoa exports in 2012 and just over half in 2014), the amount exported to the United States declined about 20 percent between 2015 and 2016. The reputation of Peruvian quinoa among importers and wholesalers in Peru's largest quinoa market suffered. Foreign buyers began seeking out Bolivian quinoa, which came to be perceived as a less risky investment. In fact, Bolivian quinoa sold for more than Peruvian quinoa in 2015.[4]

Between 2015 and 2017 the traces of invisible chemicals and the crisis of reputation they generated unmade some industry relationships and reworked others. This chapter focuses on the social and political effects of the uncertainty the contamination issues brought about and the ways efforts to remedy the situation shaped industry relationships. Supply chain actors inevitably possess fragmented knowledge about the larger global supply chain they are involved in, given the length and complexity of these chains.[5] This partial or imperfect knowledge commonly includes information about the product (e.g., its origins, its characteristics), broader market trends (e.g., price changes), extraneous factors like weather events, or even the structure of the supply chain itself (e.g., market segmentation, end consumers). Operating successfully in a sprawling global supply chain is in large part about managing the uncertainties derived from this situated and highly partial knowledge one has about the larger supply chain. The possibility of pesticide residues and their potential to lead to rejected shipments introduced yet another layer of uncertainty that would create doubt and frustration. Suspicion reverberated along the different trade relationships, magnifying tensions, fracturing trust, and occasionally helping build new alliances.

First, I trace the complex and shifting blame narratives industry actors told about the contaminated quinoa. The distrust rumors generated did not originate in the contamination scandals. Instead, the scandals exacerbated existing tensions and long-standing dynamics of distrust. The rumors revealed ambivalent alliances and fissures between different groups of actors along the chain and the assumptions different groups make about one another. The quinoa export industry was formed in the backdrop of the highly uneven social and racial politics characterizing the Andean highlands. Mainstream understandings of global supply chains tend to envision individual supply chain actors as self-interested, making decisions based on the (admittedly imperfect) information they have access to. This chapter emphasizes how this fragmented knowledge can take shape in narrative form and the ways fear, anxiety, and rumor can inflect "market behavior."

In Puno, where a growing number of quinoa farmers were producing certified organic quinoa, the scandals undermined the legitimacy of the organic certification apparatus. The scandals at once generated new forms of distrust alongside new forms of credibility. The second part of the chapter examines how the loss of trust in organic certification processes helped make the chemical analysis the arbiter of quinoa's purity. Chemical analyses of quinoa batches—a practice only introduced to the industry in 2015 in the wake of the rejected containers—became standard protocol, a development that some argued, ironically, allowed for more rather than less fraud. Calls for increased "traceability" did not restore trust but further entrenched inequalities and redirected risk in the commodity chain. The chemical analysis, I argue, was not a neutral technology that increased transparency but instead could be used to shift and manipulate risks.

The anxiety about contamination compounded existing industry struggles, articulating with and intensifying the tensions the price fall generated. Though the chapters on the price fall and the chemical residue issues are sequential, these were concurrent phenomena. Prior to the contamination scandals, Puno's industry leaders felt confident that the superior quality of quinoa produced in the Andean highlands and its perceived purity would ensure a future for Peruvian quinoa even amid the rise of new quinoa industries across the world. Prior to the scandals, a common sentiment was that while farmers outside the Andes could produce quinoa, they could not do it organically. Thus, the erosion of trust in organic certification and the perceived purity of Puno's quinoa heightened fears about the growing competition from new quinoa farmers along Peru's coast and abroad.

This chapter also grapples with the limits of ethnographic ways of knowing. My own knowledge of the supply chain was also fragmented, shaped by the actors I had access to and the sort of information these people were willing (and unwilling) to share with me. What do we do with the phenomena our research methods don't offer access to? How do we deal with uncertainty and unknowability in our findings? Whose stories do we trust when our interlocutors' tales don't align? In commodity chain studies, what do we do when we can't fully "follow the thing" or accurately trace the assemblage with confidence? While anthropologists have spent a lot of time talking about the politics of knowledge, we have said less about unknowledge and unknowability in our findings—what we and/or those we work with can't figure out or are uncertain about and choose not to disclose. With the contamination scandals, I could not precisely verify how exactly toxins made their way into the quinoa supply and who was at fault. Stories conflicted, hard facts were hard to come by, and those I spoke with pointed fingers in multiple directions. I wasn't alone in desperately wanting but being unable to fully trace the contaminated quinoa. Many farmers, buyers, processors, and exporters struggled to understand sources of contamination. In this context, ethnography does not offer access to exactly what happened and instead helps us see the social work that unknowns and uncertainty can do.

CONFLICTING TALES OF BLAME

Contamination would not have been so detrimental if the source of the problem had been evident. The issue presumably could have been resolved quickly if there was a discrete and known source. As chapter 3 outlined, blending quinoa from many individual farmers and multiple farmer associations is necessary for processing quinoa at scale, for transforming sacks of quinoa into a liquid global commodity. Many products that circulate in our economy have serial numbers that effectively allow them to be traced back to a single factory or farm, but a grain like quinoa functions more like a liquid, undermining "traceability" efforts. And given the small scale of the farms in Puno and the small amounts of quinoa most farmers sold at once, quinoa from many different farmers was processed together in a single batch. Mixing quinoa alienated quinoa from individual farmers and therefore made tracing contamination back to a single farm practically impossible. The flip side of the mixing that rendered quinoa uniform was that no one could trace the chemicals with precision.

The intractability of the toxins in quinoa generated massive uncertainty—a void that was filled with rumor. Contradictory tales of blame emerged about how quinoa came to test positive for high levels of chemical pesticides. There was no incontrovertible evidence indicating which story was right and which was wrong. "The truth" was to some extent beside the point. Rumors themselves did social and political work in this context. Rumors often create or solidify alliances, marking distinctions between and Us and Them.[6] Tales about quinoa contamination at times reinforced existing solidarities but at other times upended them, generating multidirectional suspicion between and among groups of industry actors. The stories of blame eroded the nascent trust that held industry relationships together and degraded the social capital the boom years had begun to build up at a time when collaboration was more necessary than ever before.

At the outset, several exporters suggested the problem was not about excessive use of agrochemicals and instead was a problem of import bureaucracy and producers' lack of knowledge about pesticide regulations. Because quinoa was a relatively new import commodity, many importing countries' environmental regulatory bodies (e.g., US EPA, EU's DG SANCO) had approved very few chemicals for use on quinoa. Many common agricultural chemicals that were permitted on established agricultural commodities would lead to a rejected container if residues were found on quinoa. This meant that, as one exporter told me, even conventional quinoa effectively had to be organic in terms of the chemicals used on it when exporting quinoa to the United States or Europe. Starting in December 2014, Peru's Ministry of Agriculture began discussions with the FDA and EPA to fast-track the approval of more chemicals for use on quinoa. At the same time, it began lobbying for Codex Alimentarius, the FAO's set of international standards for agricultural commodities, to include quinoa in the cereals category, which would permit quinoa farmers to apply the same MRLs as applied to cereal crops like wheat. By the beginning of 2016, the EPA had approved the use of three more chemicals that could be permitted on quinoa.[7] After further negotiations between the ministry and the EPA, quinoa was officially included in the EPA's cereals category later that year.[8] While import bureaucracy contributed to the container rejections, the question of how chemical residues were making their way into the quinoa supply remained pressing, especially given the delay between the initial container rejections and the approval of new chemicals.

The dominant blame narrative pointed to coastal quinoa producers as the source of contamination. The logic was that the coastal quinoa producers were large-scale agribusinesses accustomed to using chemical fertilizers and pesticides, unlike highland farmers. Moreover, the Peruvian coast's warm, insect and fungi-friendly climate would have made producing quinoa without significant amounts of chemical pesticides and fungicides challenging. It seemed obvious to many that the source of the rejected containers was coastal quinoa producers. Proponents of this version of events suggested that the coastal producers had used chemicals indiscriminately on quinoa, not paying attention to which chemicals had been approved by importing countries. Even an official press release from Peru's Ministry of Agriculture blamed the "excessive use of chemical pesticides" and "inadequate management of [quinoa] in some coastal valleys" for the rejected containers.[9] This narrative gained traction in Peruvian media reports about the rejected containers. In an April 2015 interview in *Gestión*, one of Peru's main business news outlets, Luz Gómez, a prominent quinoa agronomist, blamed coastal producers: "The poor management of quinoa leads to pests and the coastal farmer is accustomed to controlling pests with fungicides and pesticides, without knowing which products to apply. This has contaminated the quinoa and now our quinoa stock has chemicals."[10] Pío Choque, president of the National Association of Quinoa Producers, echoed this blame narrative in a 2015 article in *El Correo* in which he called out coastal producers for "tarnishing the credibility of Andean quinoa."[11] And indeed, studies of quinoa production in coastal regions confirmed that coastal quinoa farmers did face major pest issues during the 2014 and 2015 seasons and at least in some cases used pesticides excessively, applying more than the recommended doses, closer to harvest dates than recommended, and used chemicals that were not permitted by some importing countries.[12]

For many in Puno's quinoa industry, this version of events was common sense. This story fit into a real and imagined geography of Peru, manifesting assumptions about coastal and highlands farmers. In particular, it affirmed existing ideas about indigenous peoples and their relationships with nature. Quinoa's purity was tied up in ideas about the purity of indigenous farmers. Coastal producers were assumed to be profit motivated, using chemicals indiscriminately out of carelessness and greed. Andean farmers, in this story, were morally pure and committed to "traditional" agricultural practices that worked in harmony with nature. Puno had long been considered quinoa's heartland, where Peru's most authentic and "natural" quinoa originated. Andean production "is ecological and organic" one newspaper article declared with confidence.[13] The flip side of Puno's ostracization as a "traditional" and culturally "backward" region was a perception that the region and the people who live there embodied authentic indigeneity and an associated harmonious relationship with nature. It was inconceivable that the contaminated quinoa originated in the altiplano.

At the same time, this tale of blame generated a sense of righteousness and solidarity among Puno's industry actors. "[The coastal producers] are disgracing the reputation of Peruvian quinoa. They're ruining it for all of us," exclaimed Rigoberto when I asked for his take on the contamination scandals in 2015, echoing a sentiment expressed to me on a number of occasions by actors aligned with Puno's quinoa industry. The idea that new quinoa producers along Peru's coast had undermined the credibility of all Peruvian quinoa reinforced a common enemy for Puno's quinoa industry actors, the coastal farmers, who were already demonized for the price fall.

Some buyers and exporters began refusing to buy coastal quinoa in light of this narrative. Alberto, who ran the "superfoods division" for a major Peruvian food conglomerate, picked me up one afternoon in 2017 in his late model BMW SUV for a lunch interview in Lima. After a decade working for an agrochemicals company, in 2015 he was hired to launch a quinoa buying and export operation for this company. While quinoa was still his main focus, he was now also in charge of the purchasing and exporting of kañiwa, chia, amaranth, and maca. As we sat in traffic on our way through the bustling commercial center of the Miraflores neighborhood, he explained how the perception of coastal quinoa as contaminated affected his buying operation. Like many companies just getting into quinoa business during the boom, his operation had bought coastal quinoa for a short time. Coastal quinoa was attractive for someone like Alberto because of the efficiency. It proved simpler logistically to buy coastal quinoa than highland quinoa, as he did not need a team of técnicos to interact with dozens of small farmers. He could buy substantial quantities from a single producer. But when I spoke with him in 2017, he made clear that he would not buy coastal quinoa again: "We only buy from the highlands now: Puno, Ayacucho, Huancayo. We bought from the coast one year and it was a problem so nowadays we just buy from the Andean highlands. It guarantees us a better product—less contaminated, fewer pesticides. It saves us time and money." Given the prominence of this story of blame, buying quinoa from the highlands seemed like an obvious way to reduce one's likelihood of buying quinoa with chemical residues.

Yet in 2016 a growing number of industry actors acknowledged that this narrative did not capture the entire story. Though many industry actors in Puno maintained a public script blaming the coast for the chemical residue issues, in private, a growing number began to acknowledge a more complex situation. Quinoa originating in the highlands, some of which was certified organic, was also testing positive for unapproved chemicals.[14] In response to the crisis, Peru's Ministry of Agriculture had monitored samples of quinoa shipments from different regions of the country between September and December 2014, trying to specify where the rejected quinoa originated. At the national level, 64 percent of the quinoa samples they tested did not comply with MRLs established by the EPA, the EU, or Codex Alimentarius.[15]

Almost half of the "nonconforming" samples originated in highland regions, and 40 percent of Puno's samples did not conform, though comparatively, none of the samples from La Libertad, Piura y Arequipa (primarily coastal regions) passed.[16] The report cast doubt on the dominant blame narrative, in which coastal producers recklessly applied chemicals to their quinoa while "traditional" highland farmers only knew how to farm in their "ancestral" ways. Instead, it appeared that the application of chemical fertilizers and pesticides was more widespread, a revelation that threw the assumed purity of highland quinoa (and of highland farmers) into question.

I spoke about this issue with Paolo one morning in 2017. Like Rigoberto, Paolo had been in the quinoa industry before it was really an industry. Starting in the early 1990s, he had worked for a Puno-based NGO with various interests, including malnutrition, and through that work began helping organize quinoa farmers into associations and offering technical assistance. After he left the NGO, Paolo opened a quinoa buying and processing company, building a major processing plant and building on the work he had done for the nonprofit. His company would become one of the main quinoa buying and processing operations in the Puno region.

"We've lost our reputation. No one has trust in Puno's quinoa anymore," Paolo told me as we sipped Nescafé in his office outside Juliaca one morning in 2017. While initially the contamination scandals had been viewed as a coastal problem, it was increasingly clear that buying quinoa in the highlands did not guarantee a chemical-free product. Because of the way quinoa's purity was entangled with the perceived purity of Andean campesinos, mounting evidence that quinoa originating in the highlands also had chemical residues proved disproportionately scandalous, a dynamic familiar to indigenous peoples the world round who must perform indigeneity according to Western expectations of authenticity or risk losing all legitimacy.[17] The potential involvement of "traditional" farmers in the chemical-laden quinoa heightened the scandal's intensity.

The Ministry of Agriculture's report confirmed what some industry middlemen, like Paolo, had already been dealing with privately. With quinoa shipments from all over the country testing positive for unapproved chemical pesticides and fungicides, Puno's industry actors began asking more questions and leveling blame in new directions. These dynamics threatened the sense of unity the story of bad coastal actors had allowed. Rumors swirled, and alternative blame narratives developed. Some industry actors insisted the nonconforming quinoa could not have been produced in Puno, suggesting that Puno's farmers only knew how to farm "traditionally." Proponents of this narrative suggested that unscrupulous middlemen were trafficking quinoa produced along the coast into Puno and selling it as highland quinoa. They argued that a sort of commodity washing scheme had emerged in which middlemen sought to transform the marked coastal quinoa into pure highland quinoa. As a growing number of buyers considered the coastal quinoa undesirable, moving coastal quinoa the to the highlands and selling it as highland quinoa could have in theory increased the likelihood of finding a buyer. This version of events reinforced ideas about the moral purity of indigenous farmers and reinforced the moral integrity of Puno's industry while leveling blame outward, toward the anonymous coastal middlemen figures moving quinoa in shady ways.

Part of the logic of this narrative had to do with the rejected containers. Wilberto, a newer técnico for QCOOP, for instance, was suspicious that the rejected quinoa had made its way back into the national quinoa stocks through the underground economy: "All that quinoa produced with massive quantities of pesticides in the last year or two? No one really knows where it went after the rejections. I don't think there's any export market that will accept it. They say a lot of it is being sold to Peruvian consumers, but the exporters might be mixing it into the exports." Though tracing the ultimate destination of the rejected quinoa was not possible, later studies have revealed that the quinoa available to Peruvian consumers frequently has high levels of pesticide residues, exceeding MRLs for various export markets.[18]

While this story of trafficked quinoa circulated widely among Puno's industry actors, there was little definitive evidence for how quinoa from Puno was testing positive for agricultural chemicals, and thus alternative explanations emerged. Some farmers suggested that the established buyer-processors and exporters were orchestrating the movement of quinoa, mixing high-quality organic certified quinoa from Puno with cheap quinoa bought from the coast to increase their margins. This tale of blame was most popular with farmers, many of whom had grown to distrust the buyer-processors and perceived them as taking advantage of farmers. Yet some buyer-processors and exporters themselves subscribed to this version of events. Amid the uncertainty, buyer-processors and exporters had begun to distrust their competitors, suggesting that the movement of quinoa was not being done by shady coastal entrepreneurs but by Puno's own buyer-processors cutting corners. On various occasions, exporters and buyer-processors shared rumors with me about which buyers-processors were mixing highland and coastal quinoa.

Another theory was that Puno's farmers themselves were buying coastal quinoa from the underground economy. I heard uncorroborated tales of pickup trucks showing up in farming communities with cheap quinoa that farmers could buy and upsell. As has been documented by previous studies, a secretive informal network of acopiadores operates in the quinoa industry, making this conspiratorial tale seem plausible to some. Some buyers told me that farmers who had certified two hectares were selling 6 tons of quinoa, an impossibility without quinoa cultivated outside those two hectares. And finally, some industry actors conceded that some of Puno's farmers were probably applying unapproved chemicals themselves. Proponents of this story, who included buyer-processors, farmers, and técnicos, said that the assumption that Puno's farmers would never use chemical pesticides and fungicides was false. Though the highlands had fewer pests, farmers still faced insect and fungal outbreaks. Paolo, for instance, suggested that the larger contamination issues were creating a race to the bottom. He proposed that Puno's farmers were increasing their pesticide use since the scandals had erupted: the problem was getting worse. "If you are producing honestly, without chemicals, you're doing way more work. And you see your neighbor who is just applying some chemicals rather than going through the whole process of making biol or applying manure and you think 'why should I be doing all this extra work when they pay him the same amount?'" This tale folded into the moralization of quinoa production methods discussed in chapter 4, emphasizing a distinction between good farmers and bad ones.

While some individuals primarily subscribed to one of these narratives and saw one group of actors as primarily to blame, most industry actors I spoke with suggested that more than one of these versions of events had some truth behind it. Others claimed the truth was a mix of all of these dynamics—and therefore that no one could be trusted. The source of the problem did not actually matter in some sense, as the result of this degree of uncertainty and suspicion was a general erosion of trust between and among all groups of actors in the chain.

REVERBERATING DISTRUST

The conflicting tales of blame generated distrust between and among groups of actors that in turn reverberated through the supply chain. For quinoa buyers and processors, the contamination issue had introduced an additional logistical burden into an already complicated buying process. The longer the contamination remained an issue, the more strained business relations became, both with clients abroad and with farmers. Buyers were frustrated with farmers on multiple levels: as the previous chapter indicated, the lower prices led some farmers to save quinoa rather than sell it, and even when buyers were able to acquire the amount of quinoa they needed, in the end, the batch could have chemical residues. Mario explained his frustration: "The quinoa I buy could be contaminated and I won't know until after I bought it." While buyers could make judgments about which farmers appeared trustworthy, in the end they could not verify the quinoa they bought did not have pesticide residues until after they bought it. With the low prices, buyers were both struggling to acquire the amount of quinoa they had contracted for and worrying about whether that quinoa would meet their needs. "That's the risk I run as a business," Mario concluded.

Buyers and processors were quite aware that the trust problems with farmers went both ways, something that made doing business in those uncertain times difficult. As the previous section and previous chapter outlined, Puno's farmers speculated that the buyers were taking advantage of them, paying them low prices and mixing their quinoa with coastal quinoa to increase their margins. As we sat in his office on the outskirts of Juliaca one afternoon in March 2017, Mario lowered his voice to admit that he had been buying almost all of his quinoa lately at the border with Bolivia: "We've been going to [the Desaguadero border crossing] to buy Bolivian quinoa, maybe 90 percent of the quinoa we bought last year was from Bolivia." After laying off his team of técnicos after the price drop, he changed his strategy to a simpler one with a different set of risks: buying the Bolivian "seconds" while refocusing his business around manufacturing quinoa equipment. He made clear that he was not proud of this, but that it was necessary to keep his quinoa buying business afloat and to complete the contracts he'd signed. It was not possible, he emphasized, to complete the contracts without the Bolivian contraband quinoa. In these uncertain times, buying from the border and subsequently testing it for chemicals seemed more certain than investing in organic certification and teams of técnicos in Puno. He went on: "The advantage is that Bolivian quinoa is bigger than Peru's and it has fewer impurities. So, you might get 88 good kilos for every 100 kilos you buy, whereas in Puno it's closer to 80. And this is the rejected quinoa in Bolivia—that's how big the size difference is." Mario said he knew other businesses were doing the same thing, but no one would admit it. "No one knows how much comes across the border, but I'd estimate that last year maybe 20,000 tons came from Bolivia to Puno. Lots of businesses are doing it. I might be the only person who's honest with you about it, but I know because I've seen some of my colleagues [at the border] on Sundays, and there's no other reason to make that trip. Everyone's doing this, they're just not talking about it." While I could not verify Mario's accusations about industry colleagues, contraband quinoa is big business. A 2012 study estimated almost a quarter of Peru's total quinoa "production" was actually grown in Bolivia, before being smuggled into and commercialized in Peru.[19] A 2010 study found that about 50 percent of Bolivia's total quinoa production was sold as contraband to Peruvian buyers.[20]

Mario maneuvered through different market channels, taking advantage of market segmentation to manage some of the risks potential chemical residues generated. If the quinoa he bought tested positive for agrochemicals that would prevent export, he could sell it to Peruvian companies who sold to domestic consumers or sell it to exporters who had clients in less selective international markets such as India. The EU allowed more chemicals than the United States, so depending on which chemicals the quinoa tested positive for, export to the EU could be an option. If the quinoa had chemicals that were permitted in conventional quinoa by importing countries, he would sell to exporters as conventional quinoa. If the analysis came back clean, he said some buyers would sell this quinoa as organic, bending the rules as it did not come from certified farmers. "It might have some cypermethrin on it, but you can't take samples when you're buying at the border so if it tests positive, we just sell it to exporters as conventional for a lower price."

While Mario had adapted his business model to the changing conditions, not all businesses could use market segmentation to their advantage. QCOOP's clients, for instance, bought exclusively certified organic quinoa, making any unapproved chemical residues especially devastating for them. As a cooperative, they could not justify buying quinoa from the Bolivian border as Mario had, as they were committed to buying exclusively from cooperative members. QCOOP lost two major clients during 2016 and 2017 because of contamination issues and corresponding delayed shipments. One of these clients, an organic and fair-trade buyer based in France, scheduled a phone call with the management in January 2017 to discuss the issues. Julio, the cooperative's manager at the time, tried to explain why their shipments had been chronically late in the past few months, but the buyer representative interrupted him to make clear that he did not want to hear excuses or details: "It's very very important that you comply with the contract in terms of volume, timing, and price. We too have to comply with our contracts with retailers and when you don't comply it causes problems for us with our relationships with the supermarkets." He went on to address the issue of contamination head on. Though QCOOP's shipments to this particular company had not yet tested positive for chemicals, he was aware of this issue: "Look, many of our competitors have given up the quinoa business because of this problem of contamination. We need very strong vigilance with the chemicals, and we will have to stop buying from you if there's a problem." The fractured reputation of Peruvian quinoa made relationships with international buyers, who could buy their quinoa elsewhere, delicate.

A week after that phone call, one of QCOOP's shipments tested positive for chemicals after it had arrived in European ports. Rumors began to swirl about who might be contaminating the cooperative's quinoa. Some farmers speculated that QCOOP's management was buying cheap quinoa from the coast and selling it with fair trade and organic certification to remedy the cooperative's financial problems and struggles to acquire enough quinoa from their members. This, some suggested, could explain why despite farmers withholding quinoa from the cooperative, the price hadn't risen. No one had proof, but with tensions between cooperative members and management flaring, some farmers felt this was a reasonable assumption.

Some farmers thought that fellow cooperative members had indeed been the source of the chemical residues. As Mario's comments about other buyers reveal, the contamination crisis sowed distrust not just between different groups of actors but among those in the same group. While the tales of blame had initially reinforced solidarities, as the scandals persisted, a growing number of industry actors felt they could not trust anybody. Farmers, whose power was in large part dependent upon the strength of their organizations and in some sense their mutual trust, increasingly felt distrustful of each other.

As I helped Román, a QCOOP member, move his sheep out to pasture one afternoon, he shared his perspective. Román, who was running for elected position in the cooperative because of his frustration with the situation, told me he felt he could no longer trust neighbors he had known his entire life. He had become especially suspicious of a couple of farmers who consistently had high quinoa yields:

> So for instance, my neighbor, Don Lolin, over there. He doesn't raise a single sheep. He has a couple cows, but I've never seen him put even a little manure

in his fields. Not once. I'm here, putting all kinds of manure on my fields but still he gets his potatoes before everyone else, and his quinoa grows bigger. And I've been thinking, how does he do it? So, one of the times the guys who operate the tractor come to my place and I asked them: "When do you visit Don Lolin? When do you apply the fertilizer for him?" And they told me "We go at night, don't you know?" And I said: "Ah so you just apply the manure or what?" And they laughed in my face. And I realized this has to be the case. And this is why there's distrust—it's because of this deception. And the same thing is going on with Don Guillermo and the rest of them who are all about productivity. What we need is to follow up, to monitor.

The specter of contamination was stoking latent tensions among farmers— those considered most "successful" like Don Lolin were also the subject of scrutiny in the wake of the contamination issues. "Trust," Román continued, "is the real issue here."

Other farmers told me that they doubted farmers in their associations were using pesticides—often repeating the idea that "we only produce traditionally here." Erma rejected the idea that farmers in her producer association were applying pesticides but speculated that her neighbors might be buying quinoa from itinerant merchants who came to rural communities in Puno with cheap coastal quinoa. She told me a rumor she'd heard about this trafficked quinoa: "I heard there was a lady with a truck full of quinoa just the other day looking for someone to buy it. They said she was selling it real cheap. No one knows for sure where it's from, but it must be from the coast." This movement and exchange of quinoa was not technically illicit; it was deceitful to pass it off as one's own quinoa harvest. And purchasing quinoa and reselling it as one's own was certainly barred in organic certification protocols. Yet moving, circulating, and being exchanged is exactly what commodities are meant to do.

Farmers relied on other members of their producer associations adhering to the rules, which for many producer associations in Puno, and all associations within QCOOP, now meant organic certification. Mixing, again, complicated matters. If one farmer used pesticides and it contaminated the batch, the entire association could lose a trade relationship. Yet there was no way to locate the offending individual, as quinoa from many farmers was combined upon purchase. While selling a single homogenous commodity of quinoa mixed from various farmers is necessary for it to work as a global commodity, this mixing makes tracing contamination back to a single farmer practically impossible.

"The truth," Román told me, "is that these people are selfish. They are try-ing to make a few extra dollars for themselves but they're going to ruin the credibility of the whole association. They're ruining it for everyone." This sentiment, that a few bad apples were ruining the reputation of a producer association's quinoa, of a cooperative's quinoa, of a buyer-processor's quinoa, of Puno's quinoa, or of Peru's quinoa, was common. Farmers I spoke with emphasized that it was really just a few people doing this and that most of them were producing according to the rules. "We're really just screwing over ourselves with the contaminated quinoa," concluded Román.

DELEGITIMIZED DOCUMENTS

"Documents are the place where abstracted representations meet actual, messy contexts, inciting confusion and competing interpretations."[21] When Wilberto and I crested the hill beside Doña Felicita's house one morning in February 2017, it was clear she had been expecting him but was surprised to see me on the back of the motorbike. Felicita and I, who only knew each other casually at the time from cooperative events, exchanged pleasantries, and after a short conversation about the hailstorm the day before, Wilberto pulled a clipboard and folder with Felicita's first and last name out of his backpack. The folder contained a stack of papers he needed filled out in the next few minutes as part of the organic certification process for Felici-ta's farm. First he handed a pen to Doña Felicita, who could not read, and opened an ink pad. She dutifully signed and fingerprinted all ten papers. She did not ask what they contained, and Wilbert did not explain. It was clearly a ritual they both had grown accustomed to.

Wilberto then proceeded to ask some questions about Doña Felicita's farm—how many animals she had, how many children, the biggest chal-lenge they faced in production—adding the answers to the already signed papers. Doña Felicita then walked us to her five quinoa fields so Wilberto could measure them. As he walked the perimeters, Doña Felicita and I chat-ted. She laughed as she told me that she didn't understand what the técnicos were doing. "But it's fine, it's routine," she added. "They do this every year now." She knew this process was related to ensuring her quinoa was clean, free of chemicals, but the process itself was mystifying. Wilberto returned to sketch a map of the fields with their dimensions and then asked to see her folder (known as "the folder"). Each time a farmer with organic certification completes a task related to quinoa production, they are supposed to record it in their folder, creating an archive of the dates various activities—planting, applying manure—are carried out and the quantities of all "inputs" (fertilizers, etc.). Felicita went into her house to find the folder and brought it out for Wilberto to evaluate. The pages were blank. Thankfully, Wilberto was not too upset. He reminded her she needed to keep better track of the dates and quantities of inputs and that her son (who could read and write) should help her fill out the folder in real time. He asked her the dates and quantities—something that clearly overwhelmed her given that some of these activities had happened five months earlier—and marked down her responses, though he knew these were vague estimations. Wilberto handed the folder back. We moved on to the next farm, repeating the same basic routine throughout the day with farmers who had kept up with their folders to varying degrees. Wilberto would visit nine more farmers that day, and by the end of the week, QCOOP's técnicos would collectively have finished the paperwork for almost six hundred farmers.

· · ·

Since 2012 organic certification had expanded dramatically in Puno's quinoa industry. Certified organic quinoa sells for a premium over uncertified quinoa, offering farmers higher prices. Given that existing quinoa production practices among Puno's farmers did not rely extensively on agrochemical inputs, organic certification appeared to be an obvious opportunity for farmers and the region's industry that would formally certify farmers as organic who were already producing in ways that would comply with certification standards. Moreover, for many in Puno's quinoa industry, organic certification was an important strategy to keep the region's quinoa relevant in a more competitive global market. The logic was that while the coast and regions with more temperate climates could outcompete on yields, these other regions could not produce quinoa without substantial agrochemical use. Expanding organic certification offered an opportunity to clearly differentiate highland quinoa from what was increasingly called commodity quinoa (*quinua commodity*), referring to quinoa produced without added value mechanisms like organic certification. As international development agency funding flooded Puno during the quinoa boom, the vast majority of the development projects focused at least in part on expanding organic certification among Puno's quinoa producers.

In 2013 more than 30 percent of the quinoa exported from Peru was certified organic. In Puno, being a "serious" commercial producer meant having organic certification.

Labeling schemes for food products proliferated in the 2010s. While organic and fair-trade certifications have existed since the 1990s, a dizzying array of ecolabels certify the qualities of a growing number of food products. Organic, Fair-trade, Rainforest Alliance, Non-GMO Project, and the Marine Stewardship Council's certifications focus on different qualities, but all use a complex set of standards, inspection procedures, and audits to verify specific qualities that are not otherwise detectable to consumers. These certifications center around the production of documents and the performance of filling them out. Organic certification in particular is based on a complex set of documents and documentation procedures, something common among transparency projects of all sorts.[22] We can read these efforts as attempts to transfer techniques of surveillance developed for the factory to the weakly surveilled agrarian sector.[23] The system is "doubly weak," geographer Tad Mutersbaugh has argued, because "it combines difficult-to-surveil agricultural fields" with a reliance on the third-party certifiers, who make occasional field visits to determine whether organic qualities are truly embedded in the commodity.[24] These agents must ascertain whether the documents the farm provides are reliable. Yet as Shaila Galvin found in her research on organic certification in Uttarakhand, India, organic certifiers often rely on a judgment of character to determine the veracity of the document's claims.[25] Técnicos were not certifiers and instead were tasked with helping quinoa farmers comply with certification procedures, training them in paperwork protocols as much as production protocols.

Anthropologists have pointed to the performative nature of bureaucracy in general and documents in particular.[26] In the quinoa industry, it was not simply a question of whether documents were performative (everyone knew they were) but of the complex gradations of performativity and the workarounds actors create to adapt complex social and agricultural realities to a bureaucratic system like organic certification. On one level, Wilberto's work helping Doña Felicita fill out her documents was necessary. It was a practical response to her illiteracy and the need for these documents to have specific elements copleted by certain dates rather than an attempt to cover up unscrupulous behavior. But it was not the kind of procedure that was technically permitted. It was a workaround that helped adapt the certification apparatus to the realities of rural life in Puno.

Puno's industry actors could agree that underlying the growing sense of distrust among Puno's actors was not only suspicion of each other but the failure of the organic certification system to guarantee a product free of chemicals. Although the certification process in theory should ensure that a product is produced within organic certification guidelines—without anything on the long list of prohibited chemicals—it became clear that the functioning of the system relied on the honesty of various actors involved.[27] In the case of quinoa, the purity of the product was guaranteed in part through organic certification and in part through a pervasive idea that highland farmers were too traditional—and too poor—to use chemicals in their production systems. The system depended on trust and honesty. While the documents were supposed to ensure trust, when it became clear that the information contained in these documents was not always accurate (though it was unclear which documents were inaccurate), the legitimacy of all documents came into question.

Organic certification is based on what we might call a representational view of documents—that they reflect some sort of reality, an external truth. But what happens when the documenting, the process of creating documents is done in such a way that it generates documents with information, but not necessarily truthful information? The documents themselves do not "contain" the truth—but they come to circulate as objects of information, whose value depends on their reflection of some truth. And what if the documents had represented the reality they claimed to, only to be moved or used for different purposes? These questions weighed heavily on quinoa industry actors during from 2015 to 2017.

Prior to the contamination scandals, no one in Puno's quinoa industry would have said that the certification documents reflected reality with precision. Everyone knew these documents were performances necessary to acquire the end product of certification and that the details—the dates, the quantities of manure—were fudged. These were approximations serving as a means to an end. There was trust that the parts that mattered were true— the nonuse of chemicals, the source of the quinoa. It became clear in 2015 and 2016, however, that the certification documents were not always reflecting the reality they claimed to. Industry actors struggled to figure out which documents were truthful and which were not. The existence of inaccurate documents and the inability to differentiate the accurate from the inaccurate led to the delegitimization of the system as a whole.

Some industry actors blamed rushed procedures or shoddy work at the moment of document creation (especially at the farm). The workarounds and adaptations that had become standard practice in recent years were coming back to haunt the industry. Julio, who had worked for several development projects related to quinoa development, told me that he felt that the organic certification model in its entirety was not trustworthy: "You need to note that the certifiers are private businesses. The buyer usually pays them, or the exporter pays, or sometimes a [development] project. You find a group of farmers and certify them." He emphasized that the certifiers had a bottom line, and the more farmers they certified, the more money they made. Because the certifiers were private businesses, their interest was ultimately profits, something Julio suggested led to rushed certification. The assumption that Puno's indigenous farmers didn't use chemicals, he argued, meant that the certifiers were likely to do minimal inspections there in particular. "A state agency is supposed to supervise the certifiers but they have other more urgent work," said Julio. "There are plenty of rules and regulations," he added, "but in reality, they don't spend a lot of time on enforcing them."

While Julio thought that rushed procedures were the primary issue, he acknowledged that intentional fraud could also be at play. Many industry actors felt that the way certification documents circulated after their generation was a much larger issue than the creation of untruths in the original documents. Documents are produced at the farm—documenting the kinds of inputs used along with other sorts of activities. But these documents circulate; copies are made for buyers, and sometimes buyers store the documents if they help pay for the farmer's certification. Copies are made again as buyer-processors make sales to exporters, who need verification of the product's organic-ness. In this movement of the documents, some actors suspected there could be manipulation.

Julio suspected that some buyers and exporters fabricated documents or manipulated the certification process in different ways. "There are many tricks," he explained, describing buyers bringing the certifiers to three specific farms that are really producing organically and having them walk from farm to farm so they're too tired to visit more farmers. This dynamic was questionable to me, given the interest buyers had in not finding chemical residues on the quinoa of the farmers they certified, but it speaks to the multidirectional distrust that characterized this moment. Farmers, técnicos, and exporters alike told me stories of buyers certifying a small number of farmers while buying much more quinoa from elsewhere and selling it as if the certified farmers had produced it. Many actors in Puno said Lima's buyer-processors were most guilty of this: "They go up to Puno, they certify thirty farmers, and then they process and export 300 tons of quinoa (more than these farmers could produce) and sell it with those papers as proof of its certification," explained Gustavo, a técnico, in exasperation. "It's just one big mess at this point." Some buyers leveled similar blame story at farmers, claiming that certified organic farmers were selling the quinoa of other family members who did not have certification because of the premium price they would earn. "Look, if a farmer has two hectares certified and they sell 4 tons of quinoa, there's obviously something strange going on. But we have no good way to monitor this," Gustavo, a Puno-based buyer-processor, told me. Buyer-processors said certification agents should be limiting the amount of quinoa a particular farmer could sell in a given year based on the number of hectares sown, but that was not yet a standard procedure.

It was not possible for me to verify these rumors or the scale of these sorts of dynamics. Ethnographically, the circulation of such stories underscored the growing sense that the whole organic certification apparatus was irredeemably corrupt. Not only had industry actors lost trust in each other, they'd lost trust in the organic certification system as a whole. Documents that comprised certification were no longer assumed to represent the reality they claimed to. Certification had always involved workarounds and adaptations—rushed inspections, filling out folders after the fact—and yet the larger system had remained intact. The contamination scandals undermined the legitimacy of the entire apparatus, revealing how profoundly it had depended on honesty.

EL ANÁLISIS MANDA

> The dream is to have a device that immediately tests the quinoa for chemicals—like what they have for milk. There's a little tool that you can carry around with you and insert into any size milk sample and it immediately gives you an adulteration reading. So you can tell if the milk you're about to buy is contaminated—be it one liter or 100 liters. That's what we need for quinoa.... It would restore trust.
>
> —MARIO, buyer-processor and processing-plant
> equipment manufacturer

If industry actors trusted neither each other nor the organic certification documents, who or what could be trusted? "Now, the analysis is all that matters," Paolo told me in an interview. "For us, it's much better to sell after we've done an analysis because if the batch is free of pesticides, we have the possibility of selling it for a higher price since it's theoretically organic. But if there's pesticides or other chemicals, then we cannot sell it as organic." One of the key shifts in the industry after the contamination scandals and corresponding delegitimization of organic certification was the rise of the chemical analysis as the final arbiter of quinoa's purity. As organic certification documents came to be seen as unreliable and performative, buyers and exporters put their faith in the chemical analysis. It became standard protocol for buyers, processors, and exporters to send quinoa samples to laboratories for testing either before buying quinoa or before selling their product.

Alberto, the Lima-based exporter discussed earlier in the chapter, explained to me how testing had been integrated into his business model to protect himself from risk. He would not buy a batch of quinoa until after a sample had passed a chemical analysis:

> Let's say you're from Puno. You're selling quinoa and you're a member of a farmer association. No, you're the president of the association. So, I come to you and say "I'd like to buy your quinoa. I want one container of quinoa, but I need to analyze it first." So I get a sample of your association's quinoa and I send it to the lab. So, it takes seven days to do this. If the test comes back negative—I buy your quinoa. But if it comes back positive for chemicals, I don't buy your quinoa. I have to keep searching for quinoa. And I need to do this same process again with the analysis and the seven days. On the coast it's less likely you're going to find quinoa that passes so you could waste months doing that and on the coast the farmer makes you sign a contract before you do the analysis.

While a degree of distrust and suspicion had characterized relationships between quinoa farmers and buyers since the beginning of the industry, the breakdown of trust was evident in the dramatic expansion of quinoa analyses. No one's word was accepted at face value anymore.

One of the main conclusions of geographer Julie Guthman's study of organic certification in California was that the focus on inputs rather than process is a major reason organic certification does not deliver the transformative potential many in the organic movement thought it would.[28] Focusing the certification process on inputs, she argued, ultimately paved the way for the growth of large-scale mechanized organic production sometimes called "industrial organic" in the late 1980s and 1990s. While the organic movement started with a radical countercultural vision of promoting small-scale alternative farming techniques, ultimately, organic farming "replicated what it set out to oppose" as organic farmers became subject to the same imperatives of intensification and extensification that the movement was formed to oppose.

This focus on inputs can undermine the system in another way, as illustrated by Peru's quinoa bust. Because the certification process ultimately seeks to ensure a final product without traces of chemicals, when buyers realized they could not put trust in the certification documents, the chemical analysis came to replace the quinoa certification documents as the meaningful representation of quinoa's purity. Industry actors came to see "clean" quinoa as organic such that the organic certification bureaucracy (e.g., the production folder, all the procedures and paperwork over the course of the growing season) lost its meaning beyond its necessity in gaining final approval for a batch's sale. It was the analysis that ensured a product's organic quality rather than the organic certification bureaucracy, which notably did not include any tests. Ironically, this opened the door to fraud in another way as some buyers admitted to selling uncertified but chemical-free quinoa as organic.

The chemical analysis was not a neutral technology. The chemical analysis meant that those who could afford it could significantly reduce the risk that they would buy or sell quinoa with residues, or if they did buy quinoa with chemical residues, they could send that quinoa through market channels that allowed it. This was an effort to shift risk back onto the farmers. Yet only some actors had the means to use this tool. At $200 per analysis, farmers and farmer associations could not afford to test their own quinoa; even if they did, it would not offer useful information about how the quinoa was contaminated. Instead, the chemical analyses were useful for actors farther down the chain—processors, exporters, importers—in cutting down their risks. The chemical analyses directed blame back up the chain but could never specify a source.

The chemical analysis offered a limited but useful access to "the truth" in terms of the qualities of the product. Buyers could feel more secure that the batches they shipped were unlikely to contain chemicals, but the tests were not foolproof. Testing a small sample of a large container meant that even after a negative chemical analysis, there was a possibility that down the line another test would reveal otherwise. Testing a sample was ultimately very different than testing all the quinoa. While a chemical analysis provided some assurance, it was not a guarantee that none of the quinoa in a shipment would have chemical residues. Ultimately, the chemical analysis itself was simply a document as well. It could be moved, manipulated, fabricated. While a growing number of industry actors paid for these analyses, they did not restore trust. Audit procedures are generally framed as neutral tools to increase transparency, yet it was clear that the chemical analysis was about shifting risk.

The meanings made possible by documents are not merely representational, but aesthetic, indexical, and material as well.[29] The chemical analysis, like certification documents, was a performance necessary for buyers and exporters to undertake, even if it, like certification, was not a guarantee. Documents are supposed to contain information, to reflect a reality; however, they are always encountered by particular people in particular contexts, making their interpretation inseparable from the contingencies of the encounter.

The utility of a test result was limited again by the discrepancy between the sample and the batch. If a sample came back as positive for unapproved chemicals, there was no way to identify the culprit with precision given the amount of mixing of quinoa from different sources. Mario explained: "There's no way to know which farmer contaminated my quinoa. The chemical analyses are expensive, about US$200, so I can't test every farmer's quinoa. I wait until I have about 30 tons to do the analysis. So, I buy 100 kg from one producer, 50 kg from another and all this quinoa is mixing together and in the end I might have the quinoa of one hundred producers in this one batch. There's just no way to trace the chemicals to one farmer."

This situation was frustrating for farmers too. Farmers did not have the means to test their quinoa, and their personal reputations were mixed in with the quinoa from other farmers. A buyer could end a trade relationship with an entire producer association if a chemical analysis came back positive, even if only one farmer had contributed quinoa with residues.

The response to contamination crises in food supply chains is the development of more complex bureaucracies. Geographer Susanne Freidberg's work is instructive here.[30] She tracked the aftermath of the 2004 food scares in Britain (hoof-and-mouth disease and mad cow disease, among others), finding that damaged trust in food supply chains and among the British public led to the construction of a complex set of standards and audits, an "audit culture." The increasing importance of standards and audits in commodity chains is often justified to ensure trust. While audit procedures are a common response to lack of trust in institutions, the audit can never entirely fill that lack.[31] Sometimes these procedures can even sow more distrust.

"The two defining issues in Puno's quinoa industry right now are traceability and quality," Julio told me over tea one evening in 2017 in a Starbucks in one of Lima's wealthy neighborhoods. Alongside the increased use of chemical analyses came a growing discussion of the importance of traceability and surveillance. *Traceability* refers to the ability to trace a product back to its origins, such that any sort of contaminant encountered toward the consumer end of the chain can be traced all the way back to an individual location—a business or a farm. Traceability in industrial food systems is much easier to facilitate than in food systems characterized by many small farmers, as is the case with quinoa. Quinoa's materiality—as a grain that is combined before or during processing—made imagining a traceability system difficult. Currently there were lots of documents, but the documents could not actually connect residues to a single source in a reliable way.

Julio had been working in different aspects of Peru's agriculture industry his entire working life: he briefly exported quinoa to Japan in the 1990s, worked at the Ministry of Agriculture and Irrigation in various capacities, and most recently was working as a consultant. During 2015–17, the International Trade Center contracted him to work on a two-year project focusing on organic quinoa production in Puno and Ayacucho. We met a little less than a year after the project wrapped up, when he had moved on to different work. The formal themes of the project echoed the goals of every quinoa development project I encountered in Puno: organic certification, increasing productivity, increasing incomes, increasing consumption, improving relations between actors in the value chain, improving the management of cooperatives and associations, and traceability. But Julio told me that in reality the focus was on increasing productivity and trying to create a traceability system to resolve the ongoing contamination issues.

Julio was tasked with developing a traceability system for quinoa, something he emphasized was a tall order: "Organic production needs some sort of traceability infrastructure. The whole system is fucked right now. It's especially hard to install traceability with so many small producers. It's one thing to build a traceability system with three big farms and another with thousands of small ones." He pointed out that this problem was not unique to quinoa and was increasingly an issue in organic production of lots of products. In 2014 he had gone to Germany for the BioFach Expo, the world's largest trade fair for organic food and agriculture. There, he found several businesses had emerged that were selling traceability systems. These high-tech traceability apparatuses used georeferencing, apps, and QR codes to track products across sprawling global supply chains. Farmers are required, in an app, to enter information into the system, in Julio's words "so that what you say exists really does." The basic idea was that at any point in the commodity chain, if contamination of any kind is detected, one should be able to trace this quinoa back to its source. Someone should be blamed and held accountable for "irregularities." But even with these state-of-the-art systems, he said, "you just keep cutting down on the likelihood of cheating. In the end people will do what they want to do. There are no guarantees."

The development project he was working on didn't have funds to pay for one of the expensive systems on display at BioFach, and instead he was tasked with developing a traceability system suited to quinoa. The project lasted only two years, and during that two years he was able to produce a "diagnostic," basically a set of plans for how producer communities could manage a traceability system. But a diagnostic, he emphasized, is not implementation, and there were never funds available to put this plan into action. "All of this costs, of course," he said, looking deflated. It had been over a year since the project wrapped up, and to his knowledge no one had attempted to fund the system he had designed.

Like all social relationships, ongoing business relationships are built on a sense of trust. But increasingly these relationships eroded as trust was placed in the chemical analyses. The sense of trust that undergirded organic certification no longer existed. As trust broke down, so did trade relationships. While many actors put hope in technical solutions—more precise chemical analyses, an airtight traceability system—the rise of the chemical analysis did not solve the problem but instead redirected risk onto farmers. While the chemical analysis was meant to replace the lost trust, it couldn't restore it. And in the end, the chemical analysis was just a document that could be manipulated too.

CONCLUSION

In the wake of the price fall, small amounts of chemical residues set off major changes in Peru's quinoa industry that reverberated across industry relationships. These intractable and invisible chemical compounds exacerbated the uncertainty that already pervaded Puno's quinoa industry. The fragmented and partial nature of knowledge along the chain became a pressing dilemma in day-to-day life for industry actors. Rumors about the source of the chemical residues upended trade relationships, and attempts to wrangle the uncertainty remade industry practices. Distrust and suspicion rippled throughout the supply chain.

Anthropologists have shown how all kinds of exchange systems—not only ones we would term capitalism—depend on "entrustment," diverse kinds of obligations and expectations embedded in exchange relations. The inherent uncertainties and risks of marketing agricultural commodities (weather, pests, glutted markets) make trust particularly critical in these industries.[32] Indeed, much of the work that goes into maintaining global supply chains is about building and maintaining trust across difference—between actors with different and sometimes competing interests and distinct social positions and backgrounds. During the chemical residue scandals this trust fell apart, and the measures to restore trust proved ineffective. Not only did industry actors lose trust in each other, many lost trust in the organic certification apparatus, which could no longer guarantee "clean" quinoa. Instead, the chemical analysis came to replace existing loyalties and obligations. The chemical analysis, however, was not a neutral technology that simply increased transparency. It could be used to redirect risk and could be manipulated to allow some middlemen to use market segmentation to their advantage.

Puno's quinoa industry faced a crisis of reputation. As the chemical residue issues persisted, a growing number of industry actors sought out ways to repair this region's reputation. Many feared that Andean quinoa would become synonymous with the so-called commodity quinoa as the rejected containers had marked Peruvian quinoa as inferior to Bolivian quinoa in the eyes of foreign clients. The unruly contaminants threated to expel the Puno Region from its central position in global quinoa markets. The next chapter explores the efforts to restore the reputation of Puno's quinoa and differentiate it from other sources of Peruvian quinoa.

SEVEN

(Re)building Reputation

ORIGIN-BASED LABELS AND THE
ELUSIVE PROMISE OF DIFFERENTIATION

ON A SATURDAY MORNING in November 2016, I joined a group of quinoa processors, development practitioners, and the president of a producer association—nine people in total—in the temporary offices of a Swiss development project to discuss what some saw as the best way to ensure a future for Puno's quinoa industry. "What we are going to do is differentiate Puno's quinoa. We're going to make sure consumers know that *Quinoa Aynok'a* is the highest quality quinoa. But if this is going to work, we must design these rules carefully," declared Nancy, a consultant that Peru's Ministry of Agriculture had hired to help develop a collective brand for Puno's quinoa. Nancy had flown to Puno from Lima for a mere twenty-four hours to present information on the status of the collective brand project (*marca colectiva*; hereafter the marca) and guide the members of the collective brand in developing rules to govern it.

"As you're all aware, the stakes are high. You all know that better than me," she continued, clicking from the title slide of her PowerPoint presentation. "Quinoa Aynok'a: Ancestral Quinoa of the Altiplano" read the slide in large black text beside an image of the logo that a graphic designer had developed for the brand. Nancy had helped design a number of collective brands all over Peru, and Puno's quinoa was just her latest project. It was clear that much of this presentation was a standard spiel she gave groups designing collective brands, and that she had not studied the particularities of the quinoa situation, something those present pointed out throughout the presentation.

For the entirety of the morning and into the early afternoon, Nancy detailed the drafts of the use regulations (*el reglamento de uso*) and the procedure rules (*el reglamento interno*) that she had created, the two documents that, once completed, would govern the marca. The plan was for her to hand off these drafts to the marca members, who would debate the details and formalize the marca in the next couple of months.

. . .

Amid volatile market conditions—falling prices, rapid expansion of quinoa production into new regions with higher yields, and the reputational crisis for Puno's quinoa set off by pesticide residues—rethinking how Puno's quinoa industry could compete in global markets took on urgency. The industry's vision of quinoa development had long centered on logics of efficiency, technification, and modernization. As chapter 3 showed, a huge amount of institutional and material work had gone into making Puno's quinoa equivalent to quinoa produced across the world. But in the wake of the bust, industry actors began talking about how they could make Puno's quinoa distinct. Increasingly, industry actors began envisioning a different kind of future—one in which the authenticity of Puno's quinoa was the region's competitive advantage. The basic logic was that in an increasingly competitive global quinoa market, the only way Puno's quinoa industry could continue to compete was by distinguishing quinoa produced there as uniquely traditional, authentic, and natural.

With farmers along Peru's coast reporting annual yields over five times the yields common in Puno and rumors circling that US agribusinesses were developing massive, mechanized quinoa plantations, a growing number of industry actors concluded that Puno's commercial quinoa industry would never be able to compete with emerging quinoa production in areas with temperate climates and capital to invest. As prices continued to fall, distinguishing Puno's quinoa from non-altiplano and internationally grown quinoa based on quality and purity came to be seen by some as the only viable option for ensuring a future for the region's commercial quinoa industry. In 2015 a handful of industry leaders began collaborating to generate a collective brand, with the goal of marketing Puno's quinoa as distinctive from and superior to what was increasingly referred to by Puno's industry actors as commodity quinoa. This effort sought to create a unique high-end quinoa that was separate from the placeless commodity quinoa that flooded supermarket shelves. Quinoa Aynok'a would not just be quinoa; it would be quinoa produced by "traditional people" using "traditional methods" in its ancestral homeland.

This chapter explores the effort to legally and symbolically differentiate Puno's quinoa from other quinoa through a collective brand. The marca was a response to issues outlined in the previous two chapters: falling prices, growing competition, and the tarnished reputation of Puno's quinoa. Actors accustomed to competing came together to collaborate in an effort to repair the reputation of Puno's quinoa and to seek out higher prices compared to "quinua commodity." The chapter focuses on the conflicts animating the development of Quinoa Aynok'a, specifically with regard to the creation of rules and a governance apparatus for this new product. The creation of these kinds of origin-based labels is motivated by not simply an economic logic but also a moral one.[1] The idea was that creating a brand could offer a price premium for the region's quinoa, while highlighting that Puno's quinoa deserved recognition for its unique purity. Puno was quinoa's ancestral homeland and hence deserved special status. A brand would define and bureaucratize this purity. This moral component would also complicate the process, though, as debates about details of policies were also subject to moral positions about whom the marca ought to benefit and what kinds of rules were just.

This project has thus far proven unsuccessful. No quinoa has been sold under the marca, and by 2018 most members of the marca themselves called the project a failure. While most work, anthropological and otherwise, on origin-based labels focuses on success stories—place-based products that make it to market—this chapter explores failure. Because of the emphasis on already existing products, we know little about the challenges that go into creating a place-based product in the first place. Products with origin-based labels must be symbolically and materially created: people need to define them (what exactly differentiates champagne from sparkling wine, for instance?), build reputations around them that lead consumers to seek them out, and construct collectively run institutions to manage these reputations. There must be rules for maintaining the consistency of the product and sanctions for producers who disobey these guidelines or cut corners. There need to be ways to prevent dupes and adulteration that ensure only those who produce the good properly can sell their product with the specific name. While consumers may assume that these sorts of products already exist in mostly finished form and the origin-based labels act as a formal stamp of approval, in many cases the creation of these connections between taste and place is more intentional and experimental.[2] Even the definitions of products like champagne, which we may think of as existing in their current form for centuries and long before any formal intellectual property protection, were actually the results of heated debate and conflict.[3]

Industry actors wanted to distinguish the marca's quinoa based on its "naturalness," "indigeneity," and "authenticity"—characteristics that producers outside the Andes, it seemed at the time, could not compete on—but struggled to figure out how this was practically feasible for them. During 2016 and 2017 I followed the marca project carefully, attending the monthly meetings of marca membership and conducting individual interviews with members and other involved parties, such as hired consultants and individuals who sought entry into the marca rule-making process. This chapter draws on observations from the formal marca meetings and the many conversations outside of the meetings that were just as critical to understanding the challenges marca members faced. Tracing this rule-making process ethnographically provides insight into dynamics that a more macroscale policy analysis would miss. Subtle social dynamics of distrust, competing interests, and fluctuating interest in the project undermined the marca members' ability to agree upon rules and complete the marca.

In recent years, demand for products linked to particular places and peoples has grown dramatically. While discriminating culinary connoisseurs have long paid premiums for *scotch* whisky and sparkling wine produced in Champagne, France, supermarket shelves now offer a growing array of single-origin coffees, heritage foods, and disappearing delicacies as a growing number of consumers seek out culinary traditions linked to real or imagined landscapes. Well-to-do consumers prize goods with "authentic" and "exotic" origins rooted in place.[4] While European agricultural industries have used origin-based labels to protect regional agricultural industries since the early twentieth century, the place-based product is increasingly going global. The so-called quality turn has led to a growing number of collectivities that produce unique agri-food products to pursue distant consumers through promoting and formalizing their products' connection to place. Ideally, origin-based labeling can help small-scale producers of a good to unify, build a collective reputation for their product, and build a niche for their product based on its quality and connection to place. International development organizations now promote these tools as rural development strategies to help marginalized populations better confront competitive global markets. But as this chapter shows, creating an origin-based label is not easy and in some cases is not possible.

Creating Quinoa Aynok'a and any origin-based label requires collaboration among individuals and entities accustomed to competing with each

FIGURE 16. Display of products with Quinoa Aynok'a label at the 2017 Quinoa Congress in Puno, Peru, as part of promotion of the collective brand effort. Photo by author.

other. It is a collective action problem that requires balancing the needs of the group with individual interests. This chapter conceptualizes collective reputation as a common-pool resource that is subject to similar management principles as other more classic common-pool resources, like forests or fisheries. I join other scholars who have begun to think about reputation as a collectively managed resource that all members of a defined community can use in prescribed ways (i.e., a commons). Unlike public goods, the characteristics of common-pool resources make it difficult (but not impossible) to exclude beneficiaries from obtaining benefits from use. Common-pool resources can also be depleted through overuse or mismanagement (they are "rivalrous and semi-excludable" in policy jargon).[5] While reputation may not be depleted in the same way a forest or fishery might be depleted, it can be damaged if users do not utilize or maintain it properly.[6] This chapter adds materiality to this discussion, emphasizing that managing a product's reputation is not only a symbolic issue but a material problem.[7] The questions that marca members struggled with had to do less with governing the symbolic dimensions of the product and more with standardizing and controlling quinoa's materiality. A commons framework helps us think about the ways those involved in origin-based label schemes must balance private interests and shared responsibility.

PLACE-BASED FOODS AS DEVELOPMENT TOOLS

In recent years, place-based products have captured the attention of consumers and scholars alike. And wealthy consumers increasingly seek out authenticity and exotic foods.[8] The archetypical "placeless" commodity is now the foil of the "place-full" commodity—those goods explicitly linked to a place and/or a people. Mezcal, rooibos tea, and marcona almonds are just a few examples of products marketed for their unique relationship to a place and that now have complex institutions governing their production and marketing.[9] Connections between products and places are increasingly protected through different kinds of collective trademarks. Several legal formations, including geographic indications, appellations of origin, and collective brands, have been developed to protect products with intimate links to places and peoples.[10] Speaking to their growing prominence, these tools and the rigor of protections for them have become the subject of high-profile disputes at the World Trade Organization.[11] These products include well-known goods with long histories in global markets like champagne, tequila, and Darjeeling tea. Increasingly, producers of products with less clout in global consumer markets are employing these tools in pursuit of recognition and market expansion.

While commonly imagined as a kind of response to the "industrial" food system and the decontextualization of agricultural products, the degree to which these place-based products truly resist the capitalistic impulse to homogenize and disconnect producers and consumers is up for debate.[12] Geographers Ian Cook and Philip Crang have argued that while purportedly connecting producers and consumers, place-based products can actually produce a double commodity fetish "that on the one hand limits consumers' knowledge about the spatially distanciated systems of provision through which food commodities come to us; but, on the other hand, and at the same time, also puts an increased emphasis on geographical knowledges about those widely sourced food commodities."[13] Origin labels "re-enchant" food commodities for consumers, differentiating them from the homogenous standardized products, but do not fundamentally challenge the workings of the global food system or connect producers to consumers in a meaningful way.[14] Other scholars understand the increasing popularity of these products as less about resistance to an industry food system and more about the changing relationships between social distinction and food. Sociologists Josée Johnston and Shyon Baumann, for instance, have argued that the desire for products linked to specific places and histories is less about resisting an industrial food system and more about the pursuit of distinction through the cultural capital that comes with knowledge about the origins of exotic food products.[15] While some scholars see potential for empowering marginalized populations, some anthropologists argue that these sorts of intellectual property mechanisms can also be an imposition—a Western invention intended for the protection of inventions by individuals that works awkwardly when attempting to protect more nebulous collective traditions.[16]

As markets for gourmet goods intimately connected to particular geographies grow, development institutions are increasingly promoting the development of place-based products as a rural development strategy.[17] There are two parts to the logic underlying the proposal that place-based products can serve as an effective rural development tool. The first is that marginalized populations often produce unique products that wealthy consumers would value for their rarity and connection to place, yet they are not marketed to these audiences or made legible to them. The second idea is that marginalized populations often cannot compete successfully in markets with goods from other producers. Differentiating their product from the standard commodity (e.g., Puno's quinoa versus quinoa) effectively takes them out of the general market and creates a product with "added value," ideally selling for a premium in comparison to the standard commodity. Studies of this phenomenon in Europe, where there are many protected products and where these products tend to have strong legal protections, show that origin-linked registration increases the price of the final product between 20 and 50 percent.[18] Several development institutions, most prominently Biodiversity International and FAO, now promote these tools for agricultural producers in the Global South. Policymaking institutions have published a handful of reports that emphasize the value of these sorts of tools for rural development for marginalized communities generally and indigenous peoples specifically.[19]

Unfortunately, development reports and academic literature on origin-based labels are biased toward success cases. This emphasis on success stories undermines understandings of when and where these tools can be effective and what effective might even mean. The promotion of these tools without a rigorous understanding of the factors that predict success has led some scholars to even suggest institutions promoting these tools may be leading developing countries to "chase an elusive dream."[20]

In addition to focusing on success stories, existing scholarship is dominated by studies of products originating in Europe, where legally recognized origin-based labels have a long history, have ample state support, and tend to be recognized and valued highly by consumers. Anthropological and sociological work on the politics of place-based products has begun expanding this research beyond the Global North, though this literature is in its infancy. These studies outside the Global North tend to focus on products that already have reputations, such as tequila, rooibos tea, and Darjeeling tea.[21] They have provided insight into how global political economy shapes these projects. As the construction of place-based products is increasingly promoted as a rural development tool, we must better understand the challenges communities face in developing this category of commodities and the ways dynamics of inclusion and exclusion figure into the institutional development process.

A number of works have analyzed the lore and storytelling needed to "invent" links between places and products.[22] These studies reveal how producers of place-based products often must play into consumer desires for "preindustrial" times when connections between consumers and producers were supposedly intimate and personal, and also must conform to stereotypes about what producers should look and act like.[23] Many products registered for circulation in these alternative agrifood networks originate in rural regions perceived as backward or anti-modern.[24] Yet these very qualities can allow producers to circumvent mass commodity markets and "use their traditions to exploit growing niche markets."[25] Anthropological work has shown how the efforts to draw new borders around places of production vis-à-vis marks of origin can generate new cultural identities and invite new forms of producer subjectivity and consumer identification.[26] While this focus on the ways place-based products can mobilize and remake identities helps us to think about how power and representation figure in, the institutional dimensions are often considered secondary in ethnographic literature.

Another group of works has shifted the analytical locus from the invention of tradition and identity politics to the practical dimensions of managing these goods, asking how these intangible connections between product, place, and taste are governed and bureaucratized. This group of studies examines how local products are transformed into globally legible commodities through the formation of institutions centered around the ownership and management of collective reputation. A handful of scholars have started thinking about place-based products within a commons framework. These scholars have conceptualized collective reputation as a resource that all members of a defined community can use in prescribed ways (i.e., a commons) and also have the shared responsibility to maintain. Unlike public goods, like fresh air or a park, the characteristics of common-pool resources make it difficult (but not impossible) to exclude beneficiaries from obtaining benefits from use. The second defining feature of common-pool resources is their capacity to be depleted through overuse or mismanagement (they are "rivalrous and semi-excludable").[27] While reputation may not be depleted in the same way as a forest or fishery, it can be damaged if users do not utilize or maintain it properly.[28] This framework focuses attention on the rules that ultimately define and govern the commodity. The commons analogy helps us think about how the reputation can be harmed by a small number of users not following rules and how it is not easy to exclude unauthorized agents from utilizing said reputation.

These works are inspired by Elinor Ostrom's classic book on common-pool resources.[29] Ostrom's Nobel prize–winning study analyzed the successful management of common-pool resources around the world, drawing on numerous case studies to identify a common set of principles that predicted success. She found eight clear trends that she called the "design principles" for common-pool resource management:

1. Define clear group boundaries.
2. Match rules governing use of common goods to local needs and conditions.
3. Ensure that those affected by the rules can participate in modifying the rules.
4. Make sure the rule-making rights of community members are respected by outside authorities.
5. Develop a system, carried out by community members, for monitoring members' behavior.
6. Use graduated sanctions for rule violators.
7. Provide accessible, low-cost means for dispute resolution.
8. Build responsibility for governing the common resource in nested tiers from the lowest level up to the entire interconnected system.

Ostrom studied existing governance institutions, especially ones that had endured the test of time and proven themselves effective in the long run. But Quinoa Aynok'a still didn't have a governance institution in 2016; instead, individuals were in the process of developing rules. Rather than focusing on the management of the commons, this chapter explores an attempt to create a common-pool resource. The goal is not to apply the design principles to point out what caused the marca to fail, but instead to explain why contextual factors made following these principles especially challenging for this group.

THE BEGINNINGS OF THE MARCA

[A collective brand] is one of the best tools to support rural development in excluded populations, through the enhancement of their customs and traditional products.

—*Guide to Collective Brands* pamphlet, Agro Rural,
UNIDO, INDECOPI, 2015

The concept of a collective brand for Puno's quinoa was born at the height of the boom. In 2013 Peru's Ministry of Exterior Commerce and Tourism sent a consultant to one of the meetings of Puno's Mesa Técnica de la Quinua (hereafter the Mesa) to propose that the members create a brand for the region's quinoa. This proposal was part of a broader nationwide initiative to develop collective brands as a development strategy.[30] A year earlier, the Peruvian government had begun officially promoting collective brands. The Ministry of Agriculture's Agro Rural program began partnering with the state's Intellectual Property Institute (INDECOPI) to promote the construction of collective brands. After five pilot projects in 2012 had generated collective brands for a group of honey producers and native potato producers, among others, Agro Rural was looking to expand into new products, and quinoa appeared as an obvious opportunity.

But with prices high, there was little incentive among Puno's industry actors to develop a collective brand for quinoa at the time. Mesa members were busy expanding their businesses, growing their producer associations, and working on increasing productivity of their farms. Everyone was making money—so what was the upside to this brand? There was little motivation for a collaborative project with little clear benefit at a time when everyone involved in the Mesa was so busy. Industry actors I spoke with interpreted this initial proposal as an imposition by Peru's central government, which did not understand or care to understand the needs of the region. Peru's quinoa industry was clamoring for more technical and financial support from the Ministry of Agriculture, but no one had requested help in forming a collective brand. The nail in the coffin was the proposed logo, which reinforced the perception of the proposal as an imposition from Lima. Agro Rural's consultant hired a graphic designer to create a logo for Puno's quinoa, which featured a woman wearing a pollera and a large, brimmed hat, the kind of hat women wore in the Cajamarca region in northern Peru, not Puno. This image did not symbolize Puno in the eyes of puneños and could represent Puno only to the untrained eye of the limeño consultant who lumped highlanders into one symbolic category. The initial marca conversation stagnated almost immediately.

In the wake of the bust, the value of differentiation became evident to some industry actors in Puno. A growing number of industry actors saw distinguishing Puno's quinoa as the only way the industry could survive the mounting challenges the industry faced. Possibilities for differentiating Puno's quinoa came up at Mesa meetings, including creating a denomination of origin and pushing further expansion of organic certification, but the collective brand model quickly came to be seen as the most practical option.[31] While a denomination of origin requires verification that a good's qualities arise from its unique connection to a particular region through academic studies and extensive engagement with international bodies like the World Intellectual Property Organization, the collective brand does not require scientific proof of the distinction from related products based on geography. Instead, in the case of a collective brand, a group of people develop a brand that is or is not linked to a particular place and construct rules regarding who can use the brand and how. In the case of Quinoa Aynok'a, there was consensus that the rules would stipulate that no one producing quinoa outside the boundaries of the Puno Department of Peru could use the name. I was initially puzzled about why those involved in the marca had decided to pursue a collective brand rather than a geographic indication, which in my mind was more legible internationally. Indeed, Peru had acquired a denomination of origin for Pisco decades before.[32] The answer was unanimous among marca members. A geographic indication was too complicated: "Perhaps in the future we'll get a geographic indication. In fact, we've been talking about it, but the marca is a simpler process so we're starting with that. And you see how complicated this already is? There's no way in this complicated mess of a situation we could secure that. But the marca—I still have some hope," Paolo, who was one of the original members of the marca, told me after a marca meeting in 2016. The need to show indisputable proof of the difference between quinoa produced within Puno and outside it was daunting, not to mention probably expensive, making a marca a more feasible option.

And while many actors involved in the industry claimed that there were clear differences between Puno's quinoa and other quinoa, there was no consensus about what those differences were. A growing number of farmers, buyers, and even some Peruvian consumers without a stake in the industry—even those unaware of the marca project—came to have an opinion on what made Puno's quinoa different. Some people told me Puno's quinoa tasted better than other quinoa; others said it was more nutritionally dense. As the previous chapter outlined, some emphasized its lack of chemicals and claimed that quinoa could not be produced organically outside the highlands. There was no consensus among farmers or other industry actors about how or why Puno's quinoa differed. Given Puno was Peru's undisputed quinoa production hub for so long, it would have been surprising to find a developed consensus about the superiority of the region's quinoa before the sudden competition brought on by the boom. Instead, I found an emerging discourse that Puno's quinoa was distinct but little agreement about how. While no one brought this to my attention unprompted before the bust, the idea that it was different became a major topic of discussion after the price fall and corresponding expansion of quinoa production into new areas.

In 2015 the Mesa's president got back in touch with Agro Rural's program on collective brands to seek support for starting anew, and the Mesa formed a committee on the marca to push forward the project. The Mesa was an open body that was intended to represent the needs of the industry as a whole and provide a forum for discussing and resolving industry level issues. The committee received funds from Agro Rural (part of the Ministry of Agriculture) and the Ministry of Exterior Commerce and Tourism to hire a consultant and a graphic designer to help design the rules for the collective brand and the logo and packaging. While the original intention was to build a brand that would help secure a future for the region's quinoa industry, it quickly became clear that the project would need to be more exclusive. The marca project officially broke off from the Mesa when it was clear that the next step in securing the collective brand was to form a legal organization that could own brand rights. Legally speaking, they had no choice. In addition, on a practical level it seemed obvious that a small, dedicated group could move forward with the project more quickly than a large, open, unwieldy group.

It was at this moment that a clear exclusionary move was initiated: the Mesa committee meetings, which had been technically open to the public, became closed affairs. This group started meeting in a small room above Paolo's processing plant on a roughly monthly basis. A rather idiosyncratic group of six representatives—three owners of processing plants who also bought quinoa, one representative of a cooperative of quinoa producers, one representative of a small cooperative of quinoa producers who primarily produced quinoa seeds, and one representative of a producer association that produced mainly seeds—worked with Agro Rural consultants to form a legal entity that would own the rights to the brand. This entity would be called the Association for Ecological Andean Grain Agroindustrials (Asociación de Agroindustriales Ecológicos de Granos Andinos). In the beginning, membership was open—anyone could be part of this process—but once the business formalized in early 2016, only these initial members could participate in the rule-making process. The organization chose the name Quinoa Aynok'a based on the recommendation of a consultant who saw the word as easily pronounceable in many languages, and because it refers to a specific agricultural rotation system employed in some parts of the altiplano.[33] They trademarked the name; thus the six members would collectively own rights to the use of the name and logo and have the right to exclude others from doing so.

Puno's industry was not alone in turning toward differentiation during the quinoa bust. In fact, Puno's marca was competing against several other efforts to link quinoa to place. At the time, Bolivia's quinoa industry was seeking out a geographic indication for Quinoa Real, the exceptionally large quinoa produced in Southern Altiplano. In addition, a Cuzqueño agronomist and French geographer who had also been one of the key promotors of quinoa's global expansion had been attempting to spearhead a pan-Andean collective brand that would include Peru, Bolivia, Argentina, Ecuador, and Chile.[34] Producers in the Lambayeque Department of Peru, who had only started producing quinoa during the boom, were launching a collective brand project. And farmers in Los Lipez, Bolivia, had secured a geographic indication in 2005, though a 2011 study found that these producers only sold a small amount of the quinoa through this channel and had seen little benefit from their special designation.[35] Meanwhile, French farmers who had recently taken up quinoa production were looking to secure a collective brand for their quinoa, marketing their product to French consumers as "local" and leveraging the media coverage that portrayed the quinoa boom as harming Andean farmers to make their case.

The initial challenge of *defining* Quinoa Aynok'a proved conflictive. All marca members agreed that the brand should only include quinoa produced within the administrative borders of the Puno Department, a department comprising sixty-seven thousand square kilometers and that contains the entirety of Peru's portion of the Andean altiplano. All parties also agreed that the product would need to be certified organic—not only to differentiate it from the quinoa produced along Peru's coast but more broadly because the group saw production without agrochemicals as Puno's competitive advantage. The idea was that while other areas might very well take up quinoa production and be able to produce the grain cheaper, because quinoa was native to the Andean highlands, not only was its most natural and authentic form from the Andes, but the altiplano's uniquely harsh and arid climate meant that few pests threatened quinoa. While marca members agreed on these general contours, deciding which characteristics ought to be institutionalized and how this would be enforced proved challenging from the start.

All common-pool resources require definition. For an archetypal common-pool resource, like a forest, this might entail delimiting a territory and defining what kinds of species and ages of trees can be harvested and are therefore part of the resource. In the case of place-based products, the resource at hand is less straightforward in the early stages of the creation of the commons. While a forest or the fishery ostensibly already "exists" in a tangible way, there was no existing definition for Quinoa Aynok'a—only a rather vague sense that Puno's quinoa differed from other quinoa. Quinoa Aynok'a needed to be materially and symbolically delimited. In order to collectively manage a good and its reputation, first the good and a reputation need to be constructed in a clear and precise way. Popular understandings of place-based products tend to imagine already existing products with clear definitions that simply require protection and promotion. This perception is reinforced by the ways many of these products are marketed, which often suggest that they are the result of ancient traditions and have existed since time immemorial. This way of framing these products views the label as a tool to rescue the product from obscurity. For instance, Slow Food, an international organization focused on protecting "endangered" foods in part through origin-focused labeling, invokes a language of extinction and disappearance.[36] Yet as was clear in the case of Quinua Aynok'a, these sorts of labels also encourage further differentiation rather than simply protecting already existing distinctions.[37] Quinoa Aynok'a did not exist as a symbolically and materially distinguished commodity that needed protection; the possibility of protection generated its creation. Even in the case of products that existed to some extent symbolically and materially prior to acquiring a label, the existence of these labels and their promise incentivizes groups to further differentiate and agree to firmer definitions for their products than existed prior to the creation of the label. These definitions ensure a level of internal consistency.

"The key to differentiating our quinoa, in my opinion, is standardizing it. And that's a major undertaking," explained Mario at a meeting of marca members in October 2016. From his perspective, the marca members ought to focus on creating a tangible material distinction between the quinoa they sold and other quinoa. The best way to go about this, he suggested, was to select a particular quinoa variety. "We need to pick one variety and stick with it. Or perhaps one white variety, one red one, and one black one. But if this is going to work, we have to have complete consistency, or consumers aren't going to see this as a higher value product than standard quinoa or standard organic quinoa." After the meeting, he gave me a ride to a bus stop in Juliaca and reiterated that he thought that the only way this would work was through a more thorough material differentiation of the product: "To differentiate we need to standardize." Paolo thought along similar lines. Labeling was not enough in his estimation to create a product with lasting value in the eyes of consumers, and selecting a specific quinoa variety could help ensure consistency. He told me that exporters he worked with increasingly wanted single varieties: "We're mixing all these varieties into a category we call "white," but they cook differently, they even look different. Gastronomically it's a problem, and it's a clear place for us to differentiate our quinoa in the markets—by having total consistency in the variety." Mario and Paolo were a small but vocal minority within the marca members who thought that in order to better differentiate the product from other quinoa and ensure it was homogenous, they needed to select a single variety of quinoa. The mixture of varieties in the three market categories of white, black, and red, in their minds, went against the pursuit of purity that was tied up in their ideas about quality. Paradoxically, standardization is central to differentiation. Like other commodities, a collectively managed commodity must itself be uniform. These standards must differentiate their product from related products (i.e., standard quinoa) in such a way that consumers perceive a notable distinction. But standardization in the case of collectively managed goods is more complex than is the case for commodities without these sorts of management institutions. Diverse groups accustomed to competing with each other must agree upon standards they can all follow.

Other marca members disagreed, seeing this plan as a logistical nightmare. While selecting a single variety sounded in theory like a good way to differentiate the marca's quinoa, in practice this appeared unfeasible and difficult to enforce for a group with minimal resources and busy schedules. Who, for instance, would verify the variety? They emphasized that it would be incredibly difficult to monitor and administer this. Moreover, efforts to increase the production of the improved varieties had been going on for years, but many farmers still chose to cultivate native varieties or a mixture of varieties, something discussed at length in chapter 4. Ensuring that all farmers were selling the same quinoa variety to the marca would entail major investments in monitoring the sales. If there was not a price premium for farmers, it was unlikely many would put in the extra effort. At the same time, this model would generate exclusions. Salcedo INIA, the variety Paolo proposed as the white variety the marca should define itself around, produced large, white grains with little saponin, making it preferable for processors. But this variety was vulnerable to pests and inclement weather. As chapter 4 discussed, farmers in some zones could not grow it due to its vulnerabilities. Even those who lived in regions where it could be grown noted its poor production in years with less clement climate. Noting the mounting pressures various industry actors faced, other marca members thought that keeping things simple, not prescribing the use of limited quinoa varieties, would make it more likely the marca could succeed, even if it meant the end product was not so different from other certified organic quinoa.

Some marca members worried that selecting a single variety could create major costs for marca members with little reward. Inevitably, this process entails intentionally or unintentionally excluding those who cannot meet the standards. As the previous chapter explored, during the bust in particular, buyer processors juggled multiple market channels, selling to different clients and maintaining some stake in domestic markets as well. Marca members envisioned Quinoa Aynok'a as only one new market channel that would hopefully offer a premium, as opposed to a wholesale shift from selling quinoa to selling Quinua Aynok'a. Gustavo, one of the marca members, explained to me: "For instance, I might sell 20 percent of my quinoa as Quinoa Aynok'a one year but 80 percent might be sold to regular brokers or exporters. My idea is not that we all [of a] sudden sell all our quinoa through the marca but instead that it's another market channel for us and perhaps there's a price premium involved. I need this built in flexibility." For Gustavo, putting all this extra effort into selecting a single variety for the marca promised little payoff.

The marca members were desperately trying to create rules that suited local needs and conditions, as Ostrom's work would recommend. But they struggled to figure out how to apply an instrument based on creating consistency for a crop with as much intraspecies diversity as quinoa. Likewise, the social complexity of the industry and the multiple market channels that characterized selling quinoa erected more obstacles. While they were committed to creating rules that responded to "local" needs, again and again, marca members had to return to the touchy question of *whose needs exactly*. By the end of 2017, there was no clear consensus about whether or not to select specific varieties of quinoa for the marca. Because the current marca president and secretary were not in favor of selecting a single variety, most members thought that their vision would win out. Quinoa Aynok'a would not be radically different in a material sense; it would be organic certified quinoa produced within the contours of the Puno region by producer associations and/or processing companies and buyers who had paid the marca user fees. Thus the label itself, highlighting Puno as the location of origin rather than the qualities of the grain produced, would be used to differentiate Quinoa Aynok'a from other quinoa.

THE POLITICS OF EXCLUSION

At the Agro Rural consultant's presentation described at the opening of this chapter, nine people were present, as well as me and the consultant. Yet only two of these people were marca members. Instead, the room was filled primarily with interested parties—business owners who wanted to use the marca and técnicos who wanted to be able to explain to the farmers they worked with how they could access the marca. Rigoberto from CIMA was there, as were various técnicos sent to represent other organizations. When the marca broke off from the Mesa to form a legal entity in 2015, only the six individuals—each of whom represented an institution—wanted in. At that time, while the value of differentiating Puno's quinoa was a recurring topic of conversation, not everyone felt that a collective brand was the best avenue to pursue that end. For many, joining the marca appeared like a lot of additional work with no clear payoff. But as quinoa's price remained stubbornly low and the crisis of reputation for Puno's quinoa persisted, a growing number of quinoa industry actors who had not been interested in the marca in 2015 began to see it as a potential solution that could save Puno's struggling quinoa industry or at least benefit their own interests.

In 2017 marca members faced mounting pressure from other industry actors to complete the process and to make clear who could participate and how. Could a producer association join? Or would processing plants be the "users"? What about buyers who rented processing plants from others? What would the fee structure look like, and what other requirements would users need to comply with before they could join? Though the six founding members had the power to design the rules that would govern the marca, the ultimate goal when they embarked on this project on 2015 was to allow other "users" to utilize the marca to sell their quinoa. In other words, these six members might govern the marca, but in the end there should be clear mechanisms for industry actors to use the brand. Yet amid this growing sense of urgency, the founding members were struggling to agree on the terms by which different individuals and entities could actually use the marca.

Defining policies about marca users entailed drawing lines of inclusion and exclusion. As Ostrom's principles underscore, exclusion (i.e., "defining group boundaries") is critical. These conversations ultimately centered around whom the marca ought to benefit. Was the marca about saving Puno's quinoa industry and restoring the reputation of the region's quinoa, or was this a project to create another market channel only a few entities had access to? The basic idea at the outset was that a formal procedure would need to be implemented to certify marca users. A cooperative or producer association or processing plant could use the marca if it complied with all the rules (as the certification procedure would indicate) and paid a fee. But the logistics of how this would work in practice were up for debate, and over time marca members began to see a focus on processing plants as the "users" as most feasible.

The question of which processing plants could participate proved controversial. Marca members agreed that only certain processing plants could be certified by the marca, and all quinoa sold under the marca would need to pass through those specific plants. While buyer-processors both bought quinoa and processed the quinoa they bought in their plants, they also rented out their plants on an hourly basis to other groups who needed their quinoa processed, which raised the question (that was never settled) about how buyers who used certified plants would be classified. Initially, the idea had been to only certify processing plants owned by the founding marca members to simplify the process of monitoring the quinoa produced under the marca. But processing-plant owners who were not members were complaining in public forums like the Mesa about this exclusion. Marca members were accused of attempting to acquire monopoly power in the industry by using the marca as a tool to benefit themselves rather than as a means of uplifting a struggling industry. The marca members who owned processing plants denied this, arguing that the exclusion of other processing plants was about ensuring quality. They explained that they could not trust processing-plant owners outside the marca to rigorously implement the marca rules and to uphold the necessary high standards.

But the issue of inclusion and exclusion was about more than whom this could benefit. It also, as Ostrom's work suggests, would be one of legitimacy. Marca members needed to toe a fine line between creating buy-in and a sense that the broader industry had a stake in the marca, while also drawing clear and pragmatic lines around who could use the marca and how. While they had to create an exclusive group in order to secure the right legal status, this had also left the vast majority of industry actors excluded and unrepresented in the rule-making process, which was a problem for generating buy-in. They needed industry actors, or at least those who could affect Quinoa Aynok'a's reputation, to feel a sense of responsibility for maintaining it.

This issue also came to a head with farmer participation. When it became known that neither individual farmers nor producer associations could directly participate in the marca, there was notable discontent. By 2017 word of the in-process marca had reached many farmers across the region, and many hoped that the marca would help them earn higher prices for their quinoa. At a Mesa meeting that year, farmers came specifically to complain that the marca was "for the businesses" only. Not only did processing-plant owners and buyers who were not founding marca members come to see the marca as an attempt by a few business owners to take control of the industry, but a growing number of vocal farmers also increasingly saw things this way. Marca members, who felt they had good intentions and that they were spending lots of their free time on something that might not in the end benefit them, were upset to hear these accusations. In the marca meeting following that Mesa meeting, Alan, who was usually quiet at these meetings, declared: "It's not for the businesses or the cooperatives, it's for the whole region of Puno." Paolo agreed, lamenting that the farmers did not participate in the marca process and claiming that they had been invited long before. "The issue is the high expectations. People have false expectations that the marca is going to solve their problems immediately and it cannot work like that." While all members claimed that their primary goal was to help the farmers, working through the details of the regulations time and again forced them to make calls on who would be included in the marca and who could benefit. Members increasingly did not feel confident that they could promise any premium to farmers at the outset or even in the long run, given the complexity of quinoa's market channels. Lara, who represented QCOOP, brought this up at multiple meetings. If the entities that sold through the marca used multiple market channels, meaning only a small portion of the quinoa they sold would carry the Quinoa Aynok'a stamp, how exactly would they keep track of whether the marca quinoa was consistently selling for more and which farmers' quinoa actually was sold through the marca? The flexibility of business models during the bust meant that neither buyers nor the cooperative wanted to make firm calls on where a certain farmer's quinoa would end up and how much of their quinoa they could sell through the marca. It seemed to her like "a lot of accounting" and ultimately a headache. While issues of pragmatism almost always justified the tendency toward making the marca a more exclusive apparatus that could benefit a few processing-plant owners, the resultant framework was unlikely to generate dramatic changes for others. At the same time, marca members feared that since they weren't being offered clear benefits, farmers might not feel compelled to comply with production guidelines and therefore could undermine the marca.

The debate about processing plants folded into a discussion about fee structure. In June 2017 the marca secured funds to pay another consultant part time to organize their paperwork. The time-consuming nature of the bureaucratic elements of the project was preventing the formalization of the marca. Marca members did not have the time to figure out the necessary legal paperwork, and with the Agro Rural consultant's contract completed at the end of 2016, they had no one to help with this. A Swiss NGO that already had a quinoa project offered funds to pay someone to figure out the legal paperwork and to help get the marca development process moving faster. It hired Juan José, who had been working on quinoa in various capacities since the late 1980s and had most recently been working with the NGO on quality standards, as discussed in chapter 3.

In August 2017, Juan José presented the work he had done over the past month, bringing to the fore the question of the fee structure. The fee structure model the Agro Rural consultant had proposed was based on the number of producers an entity represents. Juan José passed around a printout with a chart of each organization currently in the marca and the number of farmers each claimed to represent. These numbers, which everyone present said were inaccurate estimations they had included in formal documents from a year prior, nonetheless brought up questions about how these different organizations might quantify the number of farmers they actually "represented." While it was evident that the cooperatives and producer associations did represent farmers, the processing-plant owners could not, in any convincing way, represent farmers, and the number of farmers they bought quinoa from fluctuated from year to year, sometimes dramatically. For the sake of discussion, Juan José felt that the number each entity claimed to buy from, whether cooperative or buyer, was relevant. The numbers were as follows: 15, 20, 10, 10, 22, and 500. Everyone knew these numbers were meaningless and had just been used to keep paperwork simple. Juan José explained his concerns: "The issue is that we've been assuming that organizations are going to pay based on the number of farmers they have or represent. But if QCOOP has 500 farmers, and actually I know they have more like 600, what happens if they do not sell quinoa from all their farmers with the marca? They have various markets and some buyers likely do not care to buy the quinoa with the marca. So, do they need to pay so much more than other organizations?" If surviving in the volatile market conditions that characterized the quinoa industry at the time meant being nimble, juggling different market channels, marca members would not want to create a fee structure that would undermine this. Yet at the same time, some pointed out that it would be unfair for a small organization to pay the same membership fee as an organization that would sell twenty times the quantity of quinoa. Juan José suggested that the fee structure could somehow focus on individual shipments and how many farmers' quinoa was in a particular shipment. This could prevent organizations that utilized multiple channels, and only sold some of their quinoa with the marca logo, from being at a disadvantage.

But the trust issue again surfaced in debates about the fee structure. Juan José continued: "And how will we make sure this is an honest number—that a group does not underestimate the number of farmers' quinoa sold under the marca? And who will decide whose quinoa enters the marca?" If the marca could not trust businesses to honestly report how many farmers' quinoa was included in a marca shipment or how many farmers they worked with regularly, the fee structure would not work.

INSUFFICIENT FUNDS

Most importantly, the fee structure needed to provide the marca with enough money to run effectively. The marca needed high enough fees to cover its operating costs, though marca members still did not have a clear idea of the actual operating costs because so many questions that would impact this were still up for debate. This created a catch-22: given that the marca was in its infancy and could not guarantee users a price premium or even a clear new market channel, the fees could not be very high or else no one would agree to pay them. Marca members were caught between the significant operating costs that creating and maintaining a high-quality collective brand would require and that fact that potential users would not be willing to pay without a guarantee of the benefits.

Paolo could not contain his frustration about this at a meeting in March 2017. "It's been over a year since we made this official and we don't have a single sol in the bank. Not one. We paid a lawyer and a couple of consultants and now we're without funds." Marca members were facing pressure to complete the governance regulations as more of Puno's industry actors were clamoring for a marca. Yet the marca had no revenue, and institutions that might provide financial support were less generous than members had hoped. This meant members themselves were pressuring each other to come up with financing to get the marca running. Even the marca members were losing faith that the marca could succeed. Putting up finds for the marca looked risky for them, not to mention the fact that the entities the members represented were struggling during the chaos of the bust. Paolo continued, "No one is willing to offer up their own funds, so we're stuck looking for groups to contribute. AgroRural isn't interested anymore, and we've spoken with the NGOs and they don't have funds for us either. None of this can go forward until we find money to hire an administrator and I don't see that happening soon." While Agro Rural had provided funds to cover consultant fees and a small allotment for marca members to travel to regional product expos to market the marca, those funds had long since dried up. In addition, members unanimously thought that the trips to expos had been a waste of time and money, as they had been marketing a product that did not yet exist. But these were the stipulations of the Agro Rural financing, which had a standardized list of items money could be spent on (marking materials, travel to expos, and the Agro Rural's consulting hours). The Swiss development project had pitched in to hire a second consultant, but again, this funding was just enough to cover Juan José's monthlong effort to get paperwork in order.

To move forward, members would have to figure out a revenue strategy to cover operational costs. Yet contamination issues and pervasive distrust meant that marca members felt the operation costs would need to include rigorous monitoring of quality. "We need an administrator—someone to run the marca. And we need them to have their own team of field techs. We can't trust the employees of each business to supervise. We can't trust anyone. But we don't have funds for this." For Mario, this was the core dilemma the marca members faced. The lack of an operating budget made the possibility of hiring an administrator unlikely. While it was becoming clear that facilitating the marca would be expensive—salaries for an administrator and técnicos were not cheap—it appeared increasingly difficult to find funds. The two main development projects working on quinoa in the region were ending in 2017 and 2018 respectively, and it was unclear whether new projects would begin. After the price fall, the frenzied enthusiasm for the potential of quinoa export as a development tool had waned, and the standard two- to three-year timeline for development projects meant that many projects initiated during the boom were coming to a close. Even if new projects did begin and were willing to offer support, relying on development projects, with their short timelines, was unreliable and only offered a temporary solution to the lack of operating capital.

FLUCTUATING INTEREST

As was evident at Nancy's presentation, where only two of the nine people present were marca members, the fluctuating level of interest among members created a major obstacle to making progress. In general, marca meetings were not a priority for members, who all had other "day jobs" and responsibilities they needed to prioritize. This was a side project, and other, more pressing tasks often took precedent. Participating in the marca was turning out to be a more substantial commitment than most members had envisioned at the outset. Meetings routinely lasted over two hours, and many members had a significant commute from the city of Puno to Juliaca (one hour) or to/from various places in the campo. Last-minute cancellations were common, and some members did not bother to explain their absence.

By mid-2017 a growing lack of conviction that the marca would ever come to fruition made it even more difficult for members to find motivation to attend meetings. There was no guarantee that all this work would pay off in any quantifiable way. Attempting to justify to his colleagues why he had missed multiple meetings in a row, Alan said, "Working at this rhythm, I don't see the marca as something worthwhile for my business. We've analyzed and we don't see a benefit. Maybe in the long run there is a benefit, but the medium term, no. The market is too unstable. When the price goes down everyone wants a marca and when the price goes up no one cares about it. I'm just being honest." Because he was technically a member of the marca, his vote was important, and decisions could not be made without a majority of members present at the meetings. This made his absence consequential beyond his voice not being heard in meetings. Without a quorum of members, votes could not be taken, and so many meetings ended with little progress, in part because of low attendance. This issue of motivation was a defining obstacle for marca members, but something we hear little about in the literature on place-based products, in part because of the bias toward products that already are at some level successful.

Members' changing job titles and shifting priorities contributed to the variable motivations. With the dramatic changes the quinoa markets had undergone, most members had altered their business models, switched positions, or rethought their strategies since the start of the marca in 2015. For some, this meant they no longer had much at stake with the marca. Mario was a quinoa buyer-processor when he joined the marca in 2015, but as discussed in chapter 5, he had since pivoted toward manufacturing quinoa machinery. Though he still did some quinoa buying and selling, this was only a small part of his livelihood by 2017, leaving him with little to gain from the marca. He continued contributing to the marca meetings because he thought the marca would be good for the industry at large—he said it was a way for him to give back—but his attendance was sporadic.

This issue came up with those representing quinoa cooperatives as well because interest in the marca could change quickly following elections within an organization. Lara had been secretary of QCOOP when the marca effort was initiated and in this capacity joined the marca to represent the interests of the cooperative. She believed in the potential of the marca for the region's quinoa industry and attended most meetings. But at the end of 2016 a new cooperative president was elected. The new president saw the marca as a waste of time and wanted the cooperative to focus on building its own reputation rather than collectively building the region's reputation. QCOOP was well known to international buyers as the oldest and largest quinoa cooperative in Peru, and discussions had been going on within cooperative management for years about building a cooperative-specific brand. The cooperative had even paid a graphic designer to create packaging for its quinoa years earlier, but the project never came to fruition because of the complexity of dealing with retailers and the lack of interest among buyers for using their packaging.

Lara continued to attend marca meetings even without the support of the cooperative president because she felt a sense of duty to see this through. But when it came time to gather the official paperwork verifying that each member represented a particular entity, the cooperative president refused to sign documents deeming Lara as a representative of QCOOP. This issue stalled the legal paperwork necessary to make the marca official for over a year. When the presidency changed once again in late 2017 and a president who did support the marca was voted in, Lara was able to get this documentation. But by then marca members had grown weary of the process and were doubting whether the marca might ever be completed.

As Alan's justification for missing meetings suggested, interest to some extent mapped onto whether an individual saw an advantage for their organization. Gustavo, who was the president of a quinoa seed cooperative, also struggled with this. When the possibility of the marca only using certain seeds was on the table, it seemed possible that his seed cooperative could be a major beneficiary of the marca, potentially the preferred seed supplier. But in time even those who had been vocally supportive of specifying a seed variety were losing hope that that level of control made practical sense. By the middle of 2017 Gustavo had stopped attending meetings.

Overcoming the collective action problem at the heart of building a common reputation necessitated marca members committing to the marca project and seeing it through. Even the legal apparatus of collective brands required was based in that stability—the entities governing the marca would need to remain stable. Yet the changing market conditions and dramatic changes in the quinoa industry that made the marca look promising were also the source of professional instability that sometimes undermined marca members' commitment to the project. Adding to this issue was the constant and pervasive distrust that the pesticide residue issues analyzed in the previous chapter had exacerbated.

PURITY, TRUST, CONTAINMENT

"We need to have the contamination issue totally under control before the marca goes public. There's no way around that," Paolo declared to the group in the first minutes of a meeting in early 2017. As everyone in the room knew, the risk of contamination was still present. Buyer-processors complained that they were still receiving contaminated quinoa from farmers, and a QCOOP shipment had just been sent back even after going through the chemical analysis protocol. The pesticide residue problems analyzed in the previous chapter and the distrust they fueled complicated the marca project. The dominant pesticide residue story outlined in the previous chapter, which blamed coastal producers for growing and selling quinoa with pesticide residues, was used to make the case for the unique purity of highland quinoa. But with quinoa from Puno also testing positive for chemical residues, differentiating Puno's quinoa as pure, natural, and authentic became a messy pursuit.

The fact that quinoa supposedly produced in Puno was still occasionally showing up positive for chemicals made marca members anxious. "It would be an absolute disaster if we went through all this work to create the marca, which is totally based around a superior reputation, and then quinoa sold with our label was found to contain chemicals. It would ruin all our work. It would ruin everything," Lara told me after the meeting, echoing a sentiment all members expressed at different moments. If the point of a consumer buying this Quinoa Aynok'a was a guarantee of purity and naturalness, marca members had to make sure there was no possibility quinoa with residues could be sold with their logo.

Distrust sowed by the contamination scandals hamstrung the effort to collaborate. The founding marca members no longer had faith in each other's integrity, especially when it came to following rules. This was not simply about trusting the moral compass of different marca members but having confidence that members would perform due diligence when it came to guaranteeing a product without chemical residues. "I know that I'm doing good, honest work. I know that I would take the time to make sure the product I sell under the marca is the highest quality, but how can I be sure [others are] doing the same? I don't have trust in the other members right now. How could I?" As Paolo's statement makes clear, as the contamination issues persisted, marca members struggled to trust one another to do honest work or always put forth the highest quality product. And if the core marca members did not have faith in each other, how could they trust the future users of the marca who would not have invested all the time and energy they had and in theory might feel they had little to lose?

This lack of trust undermined members' faith in the entire project and led them to question whether all the effort was worth it. Mario echoed this sentiment when I spoke to him in his office one afternoon before a marca meeting: "Look, businesspeople are not honest. We're not. I know for a fact that other marca members are buying from acopiadores and selling their product as organic. There's just not honesty in the chain. You know how we work—everyone says that they're transparent and honest, but the facts don't back this up." Mutual distrust was preventing members from putting in the effort required to design the marca institutional apparatus. The less trust they had in their colleagues, the less hope they had for the future success of the marca, and the less incentive they had to show up to the long meetings, many of which ended with little progress made, precisely because of the low attendance.

Not only did members fear that once the marca was completed other members would not take the necessary precautions to meet the superior quality promised by the marca, but the lack of trust among members also made them question the intentions of other members during the rule-making process. While the basis of the marca was ostensibly the collective interest of Puno's quinoa industry writ large, a sort of social project for the good of all, the personal interests of each member came through in conversations outside the meetings and in stances members took regarding marca governance. Each member claimed that they personally had the interests of the industry—often "the producers"—in mind; some accused others of having less pure intentions. When the presidency of the marca changed in 2018, this issue of intentions intensified. "He's a businessman. He doesn't care about public good. He's looking for resources for himself and that's clear to everyone," Juan José told me after he completed his consultancy for the marca. It was clear that Alan was elected not because people wanted him in charge but because no one else was willing to put in the time. This was one of the core dilemmas of building a collective reputation for Quinoa Aynok'a: in order to put effort into the development of a collective brand or other reputation tool, members needed to trust each other enough to assume that others would follow the rules they were designing. Without this basic level of trust, developing and collectively managing a product would be exceedingly difficult.

The proposed remedy for the lack of trust was surveillance. By early 2017 members unanimously agreed that the marca would need additional surveillance beyond organic certification. The initial solution to the lack of trust was to develop a rigorous traceability system, something that would ideally allow members to sidestep this issue of trust and force good behavior. Creating a surveillance apparatus was easier said than done. The members got in touch with Julio, the consultant who had been working on designing a traceability system for organic-certified quinoa, mentioned in the previous chapter. The basic design Julio proposed was to have QR labels on each sack of quinoa that would in turn be linked to quinoa as it moved between hands. The marca, rather than just individual business owners, would store this information, and thus the marca could conceivably trace quinoa close to its origins. Yet the necessity of mixing quinoa during processing and the cost of the analysis prevented any precise tracking back to an individual farmer. Instead, as before, quinoa could be traced back to a group of producers, whoever's quinoa had been in a batch, which could be over a hundred farmers. The difference was that the marca would store the tracing information rather than individual buyers. In some sense, the QR system would not allow for blaming specific farmers, but it would allow for blame to be leveled at specific businesses or users of the marca. So, if a shipment of marca quinoa was rejected, blame could be directed at a specific processor, buyer, or producer association.

The problem was that marca members did not trust users to actually implement the QR codes with honesty. Paolo explained this during a marca meeting: "We cannot trust the employees of each business to do the monitoring work. Even if I did trust the owners of the businesses and presidents of the cooperatives—which I don't—it's their employees who would go to the campo and run the traceability system. They would be the ones monitoring the farmers, but they are under the command of their boss and then it also brings up the question of who monitors the businesses." Marca members agreed that an unbiased, disinterested party would need to do the monitoring. Paolo continued: "We need an outside manager—someone unaffiliated with any marca member—to supervise and manage the marca. And we can't just put our trust in anyone because you know how us Peruvians are."

Until the end of 2016 the conversation around surveillance had focused on monitoring the farmers. Yet in early 2017, with growing distrust among all industry actors, marca members increasingly emphasized the need for surveillance of the businesses, too. This tension between self-surveillance and surveillance of farmers came up repeatedly in meetings. Those members who were farmers themselves—the representatives from the two cooperatives—felt that the system should focus on making sure the businesses involved were following the rules and leave farmer monitoring to the cooperatives and producer associations. Although owners of processing plants acknowledged that businesses needed some degree of monitoring, they tended to see farmer surveillance as the primary goal of traceability, making the proposed QR system woefully insufficient. With distrust reverberating along the chain, the politics of marca surveillance—who would be surveilled, who would do the surveilling—was unresolved at the end of 2017.

CONCLUSION

"The marca is paralyzed; it's been abandoned," Mario lamented matter-of-factly when I returned to Puno in late 2018. "When Paolo was secretary and basically leading the marca, we were progressing some, but ever since . . . there's been no leadership, no meetings." By September 2018, just over three years since the project began, there was a consensus that the project had failed, barring an influx of financial support that no one held out much hope for. While marca members' hope was waning when I left Peru in September 2017, a year later the marca's failure appeared to be an accepted fact. I met up with Lara a few days later at a café in downtown Juliaca: "For me, Alan killed it," she declared. "He didn't have any true interest in the marca—as a businessman he had other priorities and interests. We haven't met in three or four months now, and even at the last meeting we got nothing done. We haven't progressed one bit since you were here [referring to September 2017]." While Lara had lost faith in the marca, she still held out hope that one day Puno would have a collective brand: "Creating a collective brand is not easy. This has been very, very difficult. But I hope that one day we start again and that the marca is then run by producers rather than business-people. For me, that's one of the big problems here. That mostly business-men were trying to run it."

In an increasingly crowded global quinoa market where Puno's industry competed with new quinoa producers across the world, differentiation appeared as an obvious and promising strategy. The coastal farms in balmy Lambayeque, where farmers could harvest twice per year, would always boast higher yields. Large-scale farmers in Saskatchewan, Canada, or Lima-based agroexport conglomerates had more access to investment capital and technology. The marca project sought to leverage Puno's primary competitive advantage, the authenticity of this quinoa. At the outset of the project, a number of industry actors had held out hope that the marca would be able to revitalize the possibilities of a prosperous quinoa industry in Puno, one in which farmers would be paid a fair price, local buyers and processors would do well, and técnicos would have plenty of rewarding work. Yet legally and symbolically distinguishing Puno's quinoa based on its Andean origins and superior quality proved arduous and, ultimately, untenable. Tracing the attempt to develop a collective brand for Puno's quinoa ethnographically reveals how subtle social dynamics can undermine this process. Distrust among marca members—not only sowed by contamination scandals but also resulting from highly asymmetrical relations of power—undermined the project. While in theory a strong monitoring system could have helped create trust in the marca, marca members struggled to figure out how to fund a monitoring apparatus, especially before they could reasonably guarantee users a price premium or significant new market channel. At the same time, power disparities in the industry not only created tension during the rule-making process but also led members to struggle to secure buy-in from the larger industry. Meanwhile, the inconsistent levels of commitment among marca members, whose faith in the process constantly wavered, compromised the group's collective action. An era ended when the marca members abandoned Quinoa Aynok'a in 2018. The future many industry actors had imagined for quinoa export from Puno had not materialized. Prices were too low, countless trade relationships were broken, and development agencies were moving their funding elsewhere. The promised rewards of differentiation proved elusive.

Conclusion

WHEN I RETURNED TO PUNO in late 2018, the dynamics described in the final three chapters of this book had consolidated. Puno's quinoa industry barely resembled the one I had begun studying in 2013. I met Paolo one afternoon at his processing plant in the outskirts of Juliaca. After an employee escorted me through the small steel door built into the concrete block fortification enclosing the plant, I was asked to wait for Paolo in his office while he drove across town for our meeting. As was typical, Paolo was running behind schedule. I busied myself admiring his quinoa product display, which I'd never previously had a chance to take in despite visiting Paolo's plant on a number of occasions for marca meetings and interviews. A glass display shelf featured a curated and carefully arranged collection of quinoa granolas, quinoa chips, and snack bars. Having been in the quinoa business over two decades—before there really was a "quinoa business"—Paolo had carefully tracked quinoa's transformation from a local staple into a globally circulated commodity. He was among a small group of people in Puno who decades prior had envisioned a bright future for quinoa, not just as a poverty food but as an export good that could alleviate that very poverty. Surely, I marveled, watching a steady stream of new quinoa products enter supermarket shelves must have been exciting, like watching a dream slowly but surely come true.

When Paolo finally arrived, he sat down behind his desk and let out a long sigh. He was having a difficult week, he told me. He had just decided that, for the time being, he would shut down his business. "There's plenty of demand, but the market is far too unstable." He had chosen to not renew the organic certification for his processing plant, as it was too costly to cover if he was not consistently selling (organic) quinoa. "I'm not going to be in the market. I'll re-evaluate in May of next year but if it's not better by then, I will close the business for good." Whispers of a coming price rise had made the decision clear. He explained to me that if the prices really did rise, it would be a major problem for someone like him. He didn't have the funds to pay producers if they entered another boom. And, he added, "there's just no way for me to compete with a multinational corporation like Olam."

Paolo was not alone in arriving at this conclusion. CIMA had shuttered its quinoa-buying and -processing business months earlier. Sierra Exportadora, one of the larger quinoa processors that worked in and beyond Puno, had sold its processing facilities to Olam. QCOOP remained open, though some of the elected cooperative officials questioned how long they could survive with their current model. The price for quinoa was inching up, offering hope for farmers and anxiety for midsize buyers who had previously driven the quinoa export market in Puno.

Quinoa's rise to global stardom was supposed to bring lasting modernity to rural areas in the Andes. It was pitched as a different kind of development, not the sort that ravaged local landscapes and forced dramatic cultural changes. Instead, it was based in an ecologically sustainable and culturally sensitive development that leveraged local cultural traditions and helped sustain existing social and ecological relationships.[1] It was supposed to offer lucrative but *sustainable* income opportunities outside the mining sector that would attract youth back to rural towns and increase the quality of life of farmers.

The concern with sustainability, which conjures images of stability and stasis, is at odds with a global economy based on fluctuation, one that lurches from crisis to crisis. Quinoa's enrollment in global commodity circuits subjected it, and those involved in its marketing, to the whims of global capital. Like markets for coffee, cacao, and other globally traded agricultural goods, dramatic price fluctuations for this grain are likely to become the norm rather than the exception. Quinoa had become yet another tropical commodity subject to the vulnerabilities of global markets.

While this book's title refers to the quinoa bust, it's likely that this book traced the first quinoa boom and bust, potentially the first of many. In some sense, this was a story about the hope and disappointment of capitalism in the global periphery. Opportunity, potential, and dreams thrive in boom times. All booms bust. Potential and uncertainty are two sides of the same coin. The crash perpetually looms on the horizon—it is not a question of if, but when. The collective dreams quinoa helped crystallize were linear in nature, as most dreams of development are: onward and upward toward a better future. Progress. The linear narratives of quinoa's rise ("revalorization," "commercialization," "transformation") did not factor in a bust. The bust laid bare the false premises of these tales of potential.

The quinoa boom had generated an incredible sense of hope among a diverse set of actors. Hope for sustainable income opportunities for agriculturalists in the high Andes. Hope that the massive inequalities between Peru's rural and urban areas, the highlands and the coast, could be reduced. Hope for a reversal of decades of rural-to-urban migration that had decimated agricultural communities in the highlands. And hope that indigenous Peruvians would be treated with respect and their cultural practices would be properly valued. These kinds of aspirations helped motivate the formation of a powerful social-technical network around quinoa. As chapter 1 showed, the sense of possibility different scientific and development actors saw in quinoa helped catapult it to miracle crop status. Yet the spectacle of the miracle crop obscured discrepancies between ideas about what exactly quinoa's potential was, concealing contradictions that would become all too evident during the boom and bust. Quinoa's repackaging—its transformation from Indian food to Peruvian food—also was motivated by hope for a better future, one in which Peruvians of all classes would include quinoa in their diets and have a sense of Peruvian-ness, while doing the same for those who had long grown and eaten the grain. Yet the enduring structures of race and power in Peru meant that influencers like the well-known chefs discussed in chapter 2 had to whiten quinoa to make it palatable to more Peruvians, that is, to distance it from its tinge of Indianness. Though the boom was a time of hope, as chapters 3 and 4 demonstrated, this was simultaneously an anxiety-ridden time for many in the industry. Agricultural production systems in Puno had developed under a previous set of logics that made reorienting them around quinoa export more than a simple matter of commodity substitution. Técnicos, in particular, played a central role in rapidly remaking farming practices and agroecologies, as well as the very logics and moral economies underpinning them. The bust laid bare the uneven social dynamics shaping industry relationships, deepening tensions. Industry actors scrambled to make ends meet in dynamic sets of circumstances. The sense of control that actors like Emiliano sought during the boom unraveled when pesticide residues sent tensions and mistrust rippling through the commodity chain. Differentiation provided a glimmer of hope amid the bust—a way to restore the dream of quinoa in Puno through distinguishing the region's quinoa based on its purity and authenticity. This dream too proved elusive.

By the conclusion of my field research in 2018, it was clear that the quinoa boom had left a sea of broken promises in its wake. The monetary benefits the quinoa boom brought to farmers proved fleeting. Many farmers had never gotten the chance to benefit from export markets because of the rapidly changing geographies of production. Farmers who did manage to sell quinoa for export for several years were seeing low prices. The effort required of them to produce commercial quinoa made less and less sense. Puno's buyer-processors who had played a key role in constructing a quinoa export industry had closed their doors, replaced by a multinational corporation with the capital to weather the storms of a fully globalized commodity and flexible acopidaores who obeyed a different set of rules that did not include loyalty as even a transient consideration. Quinoa's ascent to the dinner tables of the Peruvian middle classes had not equalized or improved, in any calculable way, the perceptions of indigenous Peruvians or remedied the uneven and racially defined power structures shaping society.

The longitudinal story this book tells provides a very different portrait than a snapshot from 2014 or 2015 or 2016 would suggest. The winners and losers shifted over the course of the boom and bust as risks and opportunities changed. Collaborations formed, and relationships ruptured. This study attests to the importance of sticking around long enough to watch dynamics play out. The aftermath of the boom is perhaps more critical to understand than the boom itself. Seeing the ruins of capitalism is at least as important as tracking the euphoria. Analyzing the bust revealed unintended consequences not yet visible during the frenzied bonanza.[2]

The quinoa case offers a cautionary tale for efforts to commercialize local crops in the name of sustainable development. Wealthy consumers increasingly prize novel agricultural goods with "stories behind them," a dynamic that has helped propel a number of little-known crops to the Global North's supermarket shelves.[3] Teff and fonio—both African grains—are recent additions that now sit on the shelves of upscale markets in the United States and Europe.[4] Entrepreneurs hawk a host of potential superfoods each year at product expos such as Natural Foods West in hopes of launching "the next quinoa." Entrepreneurs, development institutions, and NGOs collectively tout the win-win of commercializing local staples: local food systems remain intact while income is generated for marginalized producers. The local culture is preserved alongside the ecosystem, everybody gets fed, and everyone gets paid. Yet the story of quinoa casts doubts on this dream, and perhaps especially on its sustainability. The win-win was temporary, the miracle crop a mirage.

Quinoa's "success" abroad generated unintended consequences. Success, we must ask, for whom? For how long? Defined how? As the quinoa case shows, there are no guarantees that those who *should* benefit from these sorts of initiatives will benefit, let alone benefit for an extended period. Quinoa's rapid shift from a regional industry into a national and global one highlights the likelihood that those who initially farmed the crop will not be able to dominate markets once the product is "successful." The quinoa example suggests that the emancipatory potential of "revalorizing" local crops is limited. Efforts to "revalorize" crops that have come to be racialized and denigrated through the long-term symbolic domination wrought by European colonialism and its aftermath are often justified through claims of decolonization.

Quinoa's commercialization was supposed to challenge, or at least put a dent in, age-old power structures. At the outset, quinoa seemed positioned to remake the asymmetrical relationships that have directed connections between Puno's rural farmers and the middlemen who buy their produce. Quinoa farmers produced a suddenly valuable crop that would presumably offer them leverage in trade relationships where historically they had little. In turn, some saw the potential of an Andean cash crop to reverse extractive relationships between Peru's wealthy coast and poor highlands. A homegrown industry that Puneños ran would fly in the face of long-term trends: foreign or Lima-based extractive companies taking resources and leaving destruction in their wake. Quinoa seemed to promise a new future for Puno. Quinoa could not, however, transform the position of Puno's quinoa industry within global or national political economies. The commercialization and export of quinoa overall reinforced existing dynamics rather than posing a true challenge to them.

ACKNOWLEDGMENTS

This book would never have come to fruition without the generosity of many colleagues, mentors, friends, and institutions. I was fortunate to receive funding for my field research from the Fulbright Program, the Andrew W. Mellon Foundation, and the Tinker Foundation. Multiple entities at Indiana University provided financial support for my fieldwork, including the College of Arts and Sciences, the Office of Sustainability, the Office of Vice President for International Affairs, and the Sustainable Food Systems Working Group. This field research would not have been nearly as productive without the support of multiple Foreign Language and Areas Studies (FLAS) grants from the US Department of Education for training in Quechua. I'm very thankful for the fiscal support and intellectual community the Ostrom Workshop provided during my time at Indiana University. After I completed my fieldwork, fellowships from the Native American and Indigenous Studies Program and the College of Arts and Sciences at Indiana University allowed me to focus on analysis and writing. A Ruth S. Holmberg Award for Faculty Excellence from the University of Tennessee at Chattanooga offered me a course release that enabled the final phase of book revisions.

Though my name is on the cover of the book, this book is the result of thinking with others. Any great insights from this book are thanks to the excellent feedback I received over the years, the questions the feedback raised, and the resulting dialogues. I owe a great debt of gratitude to my dissertation research committee members for their guidance, constructive criticism, and encouragement throughout this process. In addition, I'm thankful to Lissa Caldwell and Andrew Mathews for opening my eyes to the field of anthropology as an undergraduate and encouraging me to continue my studies. I am grateful to have had the opportunity to participate in several symposia and writing communities that shaped this book for the better. Feedback from colleagues at the Seeds, Science, and Indigenous Food Sovereignty Workshop at Carnegie Mellon University and the Political Agronomy Symposium at the University of Lausanne helped me hone chapter 4. I am especially grateful for the constructive criticism I received from Florence Bétrisey, Valérie Boisvert, Xan Chacko, Sheila Rao, John Soluri, James Sumberg, Matthew Turesky, and Karl Zimmerer at these events. I received excellent feedback on drafts of chapter 1 at the Critical Approaches to Superfoods Workshop at Indiana University, the Revisiting the Historical Connections between Agriculture, Nutrition, and Development Symposium at the University of Basel, and the Threatened, Forgotten and Lost Foods Symposium at the Université Bordeaux Montaigne. Thanks especially to Julie Guthman, Sarah Ives, Hannah LeBlanc, and Emily Reisman for their incisive comments. I'm grateful to the members of the Latin American History Writing Group at Indiana University for welcoming me in and for the rigorous feedback on early drafts of chapters 2 and 3. Special thanks to Edward Brudney, Sarah Foss, Denisha Jashari, Christopher Jillson, and Amanda Waterhouse. I am thankful to the Women and Non-Binary Faculty Writing Group members at University of Tennessee Chattanooga who encouraged me through the final phase of revisions.

I'm grateful to all those who have taken the time to give feedback on my chapter drafts and push my ideas forward over the years. Thank you Sarah Besky, Joseph Bristley, Eduardo Brondizio, Leigh Bush, Jessica Cattelino, Rodrigo Chocano, Daniela Dietz, Peter Finke, Bradley Jones, Shaila Galvin, María Elena García, Ilana Gershon, Shane Greene, Werner Hertzog, Amanda Hilton, Rebecca Lave, Fabiana Li, Stephen Macekura, Carey McCormarck, Andrew Ofstehage, Laura Ogden, Sarah Osterhoudt, Javier Puente, Andrea Rissing, and Gretchen Sneegas. Conversations with Alipio Canahua, Gisela Cánepa, Manuel Glave, Corinna Howland, María Mayer-Scurrah, Ana María Pino, and Paige West helped shape the direction of this project. I'm especially grateful to Lisa Markowitz and Ted Fischer for their constructive feedback on the entire manuscript.

I gave lectures on sections of this book at the University of Zurich, Washington University, St. Louis, and University of Edinburgh and am grateful for the comments, emails, and encouragement that I received from audience members. Some sections of chapter 1 appeared in *Critical Approaches to Superfoods* (2020) in "Imagined Futures for a Neglected and Under-utilized Crop: Quinoa's Unrealized Development Potential as a Boundary Object," and an earlier version of chapter 4 was published in *Agriculture and Human Values* (2023) as "Rendering Quality Technical: Modern Quinoa, Modern Farmers, and the Moral Politics of Quality Standards."

I'm grateful to Kate Marshall at UC Press for taking a risk on an early-career scholar and to both Kate and Chad Attenborough for helping shepherd this book through publication. Jordan Blekking and Tamara van der Does put together sharp maps and charts for me on a short timeline. I appreciate the care with which Sharon Langworthy copyedited this text.

None of this would have been possible without the immense magnanimity, kindness, and patience of my colleagues in Peru's quinoa industry. I owe a great debt of gratitude to all those who shared their lives with me. For the sake of preserving their anonymity, only first names appear here. I'm especially grateful to Ángel, Aristides, Bernardo, Carlos, Edith, Edualdo, Edwin, Elva, Enrique, Ermelinda, Eusebio, Eva, Fabio, Fernando, Giovanna, Guino, Jorge, José, José Luis, Juan José, Kennedy, Lola, Lucio, Lucy, Manuel, Moisés, Nelly, Pancho, Pedro, Percy, Rene, Roberto, Rolando, Roger, Rufo, Vicente, Salustiano, and Susana. Thank you Geny and Camucha for your warmth and hospitality.

While professional relationships made this book possible, I would not have found the willpower to finish this book without other kinds of support. I'm especially grateful to Jordan, Leslie, and Tamara for the friendship, laughter, and moral support during grad school and beyond. Thank you, Judy, for keeping my feet warm and encouraging me to get out for walks during long days of writing. Thank you, Mom, for your keen editorial eye, your interest in my work, and for visiting me in Peru. Thank you, Margot, for giving me a good reason to stop procrastinating and for sleeping through the night during the final revisions phase.

Words can't possibly do justice to the immense gratitude I have for Eddie. I'm grateful for the unconditional support, encouragement, and regular attempts to convince me that "it is better than I think." I'm grateful for your brilliant editing, visits to Puno, and your commitment to prioritizing both our careers equally along with the sacrifices that has entailed. And thank you for taking the lead on parenting during the final phase of book writing.

Though the heart of this book has been a joint effort, flaws and oversights are all mine. Those whom I owe thanks to but have neglected to mention in my haste, please accept my apologies.

Quinoa Production, Export, and Price Charts

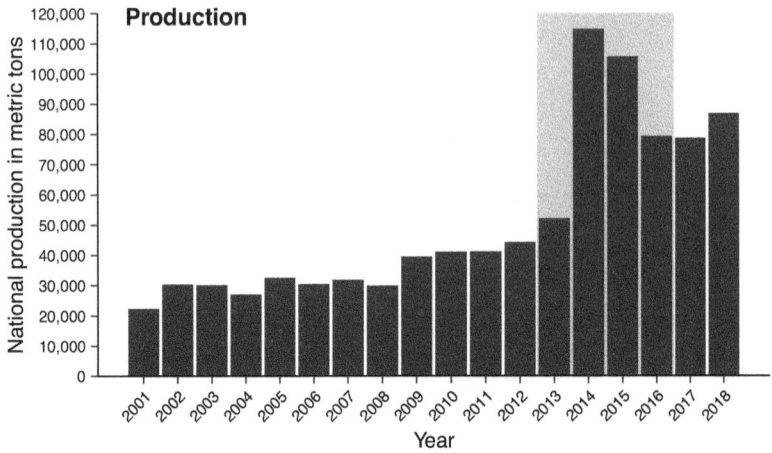

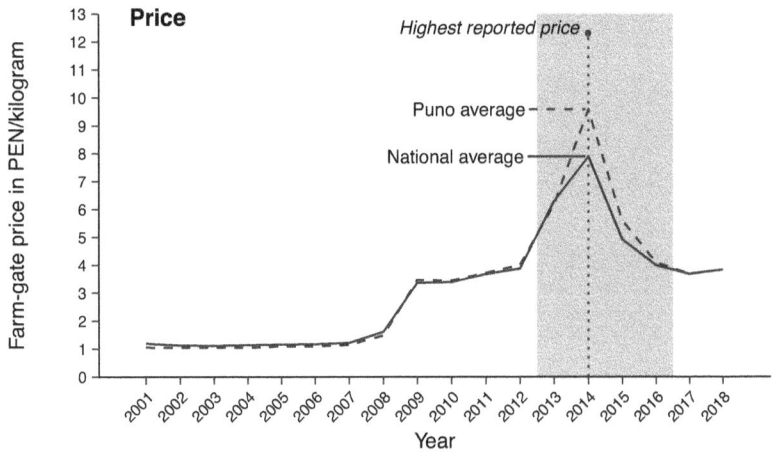

FIGURE 17. Quinoa production and price in Peru, 2001–2018. Farm-gate price refers to price paid to farmers for unprocessed quinoa. Averages are calculated over the entire year and, for national values, across regions. Quinoa's farm-gate price peaked in 2014, the same year Peru more than doubled its total quinoa production volume. *Sources:* FAO, *FAOSTAT Statistical Database* ([Rome]: FAO, 1997–) and Ministerio de Agricultura, *Quinua peruana: Situación actual y perspectivas en el mercado nacional e internacional al 2015* (Lima: Ministerio de Agricultura/Dirección de Políticas Agrarias/Dirección de Estudios Económicos e Informacion Agraria, 2015).

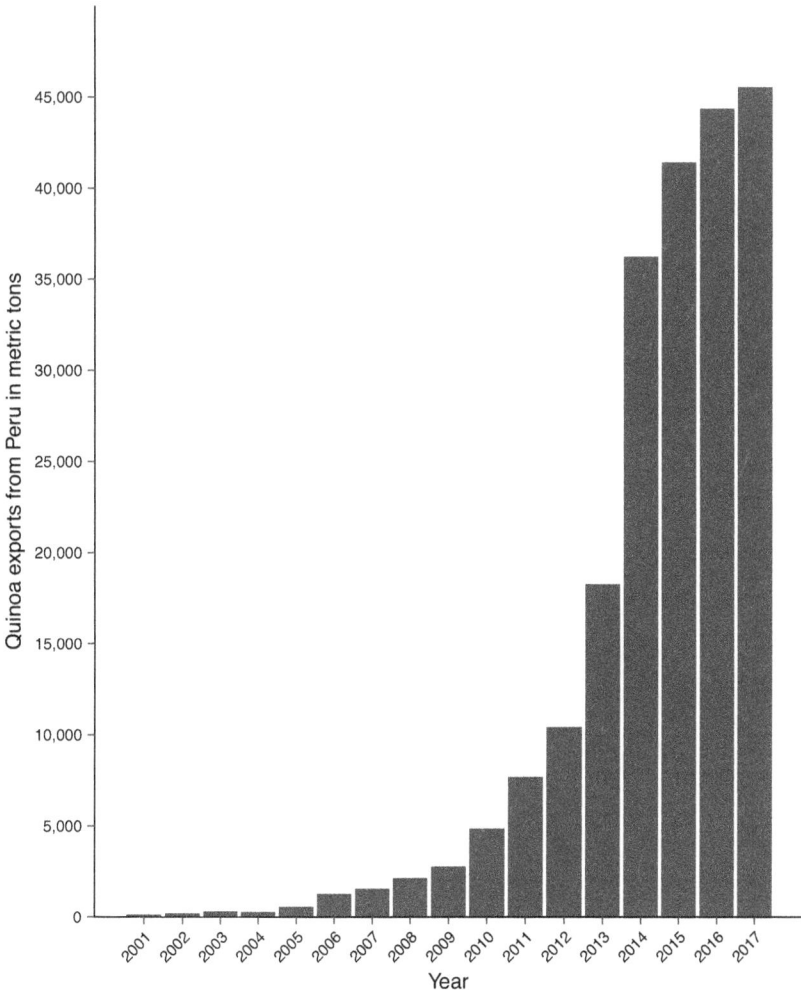

FIGURE 18. Quinoa Exports from Peru, 2001–2017. Peru only exported a small amount of quinoa before 2012, when exports began to skyrocket.[1]

by Volume

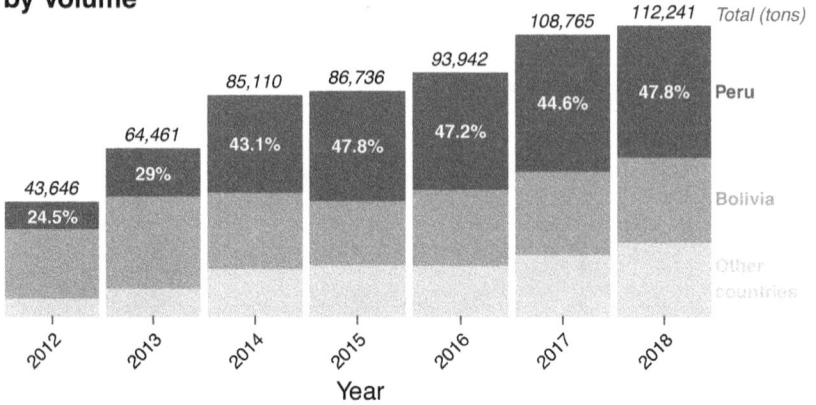

by Value

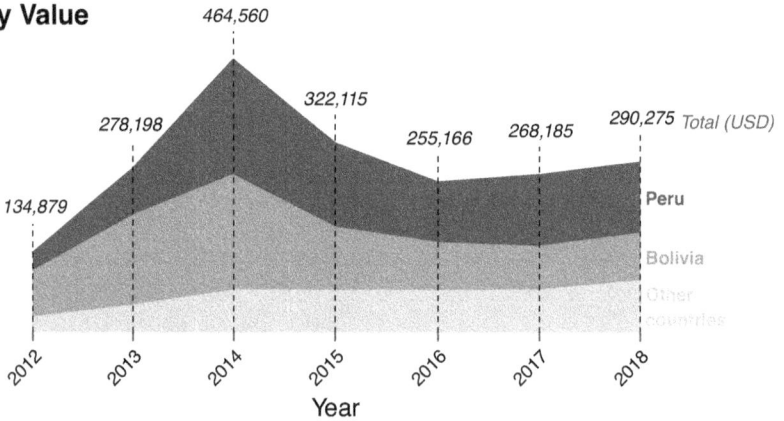

FIGURE 19. Aggregated quinoa exports, 2012–2018. Country-wise 2012 export data by volume estimated by UNSD. Bolivia and Peru are the main quinoa-exporting countries, though their proportion of the global quinoa trade shrank as other countries developed quinoa industries between 2012 and 2018. Beginning in 2014, Peru overtook Bolivia as the world's chief quinoa-exporting country. *Source:* International Trade Centre, "Product 100850: Quinoa "Cheonopium Quinoa," *Trade Statistics*, 2023, https://intracen.org/resources/data -and-analysis/trade-statistics#export-of-goods.

NOTES

INTRODUCTION

1. Although Peru's Ministry of Agriculture has changed names various times, for simplicity's sake I refer to it at the Ministry of Agriculture throughout.

2. Calaya and most other place-names below the level of the region are toponyms.

3. On the self-presentation of Peruvian politicians and symbols of indigeneity, see Vich, "Magical, Mystical"; and Vich, "29 de julio."

4. A *pollera* is the wide wool skirt considered traditional for Andean women. While it is daily dress for many women in Andean countries, city folk and politicians may occasionally wear polleras as costumes. For an in-depth discussion of the complex symbolic politics of dressing *de pollera*, see Weismantel, *Cholas and Pishtacos*.

5. Tsing, *Realm of Diamond Queen*.

6. All translations were done by the author. As interviews were carried out in Spanish, interview quotes are also translated by the author.

7. Instituto Nacional de Estadística e Informática, *Perú*.

8. Instituto Peruano de Economía, "Puno"; and Instituto Nacional de Estadística e Informática, *Puno*.

9. On agrarian change and industrialization, see Berndt, "Uneven Development"; and Watts, "Agrarian Question in Africa."

10. An estimated twenty-one thousand informal gold miners reside in Puno, making it the heart of informal gold mining in the country. Medina, *Formalización*. On Juliaca's contraband economy, see Ødegaard, "Border Multiplicities."

11. On the ways North American demand for year-round fresh produce reshaped export agriculture in Latin America, see Thrupp, *Bittersweet Harvests*; and Tinsman, *Buying into the Regime*.

12. Though alpaca fiber export did boom a couple of times during the twentieth century. See Orlove, *Alpacas, Sheep, and Men*; and Jacobsen, *Mirages of Transition*.

13. On the relationship between quinoa export and migration in Bolivia, see Kerssen, "Food Sovereignty."

14. Ferguson, *Expectations of Modernity*.

15. Indigenous identity is complex in Peru, owing to the legacies of colonialism, leftist movements in the mid-twentieth century that promoted class-based *campesino* identity, indigeneity's affiliation with the heavy symbolic baggage of the term *indio*, and a push for farmers to identify as producers. I have chosen to retain the term *Indian food* to capture the racist underpinnings of the concept and because it was used by my interlocutors. See Gelles, "Indigenous Identity"; García, *Making Indigenous Citizens*; and Cadena, *Indigenous Mestizos*. On the concept's complexity more generally, see Li, "Indigenous Identity in Indonesia."

16. Hirsch, *Acts of Growth*; and García, *Gastropolitics*.

17. López-Canales, "Peru on a Plate"; McDonell, "Creating the Culinary Frontier"; and Matta, "Valuing Native Eating."

18. Dove, "Agronomy of Memory."

19. Scott, *Seeing Like a State*.

20. Guthman, "Good Story Behind It."

21. Literary scholar Zilkia Janer has pointed out that cuisines currently being incorporated in the global culinary scene are still measured against French cuisine. Janer, "(In)Edible Nature."

22. Philosopher Lisa Heldke has argued that these shifting relationships between taste and class identity drive the growth of culinary tourism motivated by "an expedition in the unknown, a pursuit of the strange." Heldke, *Exotic Appetites*, xv.

23. Johnston and Baumann, *Foodies*.

24. McDonell, "Despensa Nacional."

25. *Lepidium meyenii, Chenopodium pallidicaule*, and *Physalis peruviana*, respectively.

26. The list of crops that fall into this category and that are receiving attention from development agencies is long. It includes fonio, moringa, amaranth, lúcuma, rooibos, and açaí. See Biodiversity International, "Species List"; and Biodiversity International, "Neglected No More."

27. While ecological "work" may seem like a misnomer, I intentionally invoke a growing number of anthropologists who understand labor as a collective ecological act. Besky and Blanchette, *How Nature Works*.

28. Tsing, *Friction*.

29. Berlant, *Cruel Optimism*, 23.

30. All of which are in the amaranth family.

31. Parry, "Staff of Life," 16.

32. Domestication takes place over centuries, but archaeologists have found evidence of humans eating a wilder version of quinoa eight thousand years ago. See Bruno and Whitehead, "Chenopodium Cultivation"; and Dillehay et al., "Preceramic Adoption."

33. Hence the other major quinoa growing region beside the Bolivia Uyuni Salt Desert.

34. *Oxalis tuberosa, Ullucus tuberosa, Chenopodium pallidicaule,* and *Lupinis mutabilis,* respectively. Some farmers also include alfalfa, which provides fodder and fixes nitrogen, or barley as fodder.

35. Ulloa and Juan, *Relación histórica,* 290.

36. The only other plant-based "perfect proteins" are buckwheat, hempseed, blue-green algae, and soybeans.

37. Also see McDonell and Wilk, *Critical Approaches to Superfoods*; and McDonell, "Miracle Foods."

38. Haushofer, *Wonder Foods.*

39. Kimura, *Hidden Hunger.*

40. The "region" is the largest geographical unit in Peru; similar to a state or province in many countries. Puno is also the name of a city, which is the capital of the Puno region, the Puno province, and the Puno district. In the text, I use the term to refer to the region and indicate when I refer to the city of Puno specifically.

41. Official quinoa production figures exist only since the mid-twentieth century. While Peru and Bolivia jockey for the title of chief quinoa producer on the global level, Peru has consistently overtaken Bolivia since 2014, making Puno the world's quinoa production hub.

42. Gade, "Carl Troll."

43. Winterhalder, Marsen, and Thomas, "Dung as Essential Resource," 89.

44. *Limeñizada* refers to the social, cultural, and political dominance of Lima, Peru's coastal capital city.

45. Renique, "Otra cara."

46. The inextricable ties between ideas about indigeneity and the concept of the Indian in Peru make for a complex identity politics. Many people who would by outsider standards be considered indigenous do not identify as such. See García, *Making Indigenous Citizens.*

47. Pratt, *Imperial Eyes*; and Zimmerer, "Vertical Environments."

48. Radcliffe and Westwood, *Remaking the Nation,* 109–12.

49. Greene, "Entre Lo Indio," 446.

50. *Limeño* refers to a person from Lima, Peru's coastal capital city. On the term's entanglement with race, see Cadena, *Indigenous Mestizos,* 11.

51. *Puneño* refers to a native of the Puno region.

52. Mariátegui, *Siete ensayos.*

53. Mariátegui, *Siete ensayos,* 1.

54. This approach is inspired by the regional political ecology framework. See Blaikie and Brookfield, *Land Degradation and Society"*

55. "Field technician" is the closest English translation. I've chosen to retain the Spanish term to emphasize that this is an established and legible job category in this context.

56. *Farm-gate price* refers to the price farmers receive. Throughout the book, *price* refers to farm-gate price unless otherwise indicated. Prices are converted from new Peruvian sol (PEN) into US dollars. Conversions are approximate because of

changing exchange rates and inflation. Exchange rate is calculated for a specific year mentioned or an average exchange rate when there is a span of years discussed.

57. *Poverty foods* are foods linked to poor people. While claiming these foods are consumed out of necessity would be an overstatement, their low price makes them accessible to those with few economic resources, and they are often calorically dense. While poverty foods in the United States are often considered "junk food"—part of a much broader conversation about class dynamics and food—quinoa was an incredibly nutritious poverty food. This is closely connected to but not the same as *hunger food*. See Van Esterik, "Hunger Foods."

58. The regional average in 2014 was US$3.17/kg for conventional (nonorganic) quinoa, though I saw offers reach PEN 12.30 or about US$4.37/kg, as was also reported by the Ministry of Agriculture. These figures are in 2014 exchange rates. Ministerio de Agricultura, *Quinua Peruana*.

59. Ministerio de Agricultura, *Análisis económico*.

60. Ministerio de Agricultura, *La quinua*.

61. Lane, *Potosí*; and Moore, "Amsterdam Standing on Norway."

62. Gootenberg, *Between Silver and Guano*.

63. Orlove, *Alpacas, Sheep, and Men*; and Jacobsen, *Mirages of Transition*.

64. Bebbington, "New Extraction"; and Li, *Unearthing Conflict*.

65. These are contrasted with the "traditional" Latin American agricultural exports like coffee, bananas, and sugarcane. Thrupp, *Bittersweet Harvests*.

66. This metaphor comes from Galeano, *Las venas abiertas de América Latina*.

67. On the ways crop booms can generate aspirations, see Münster, "'Ginger Is a Gamble.'"

68. Other scholars thinking about booms as affective experience include Hirsch, *Acts of Growth*; and Osterhoudt, "'Nobody Wants to Kill.'"

69. Bellemare, Fajardo-Gonzalez, and Gitter, "Foods and Fads."

70. Li, *Land's End*.

71. Ferguson, *Expectations of Modernity*.

72. Roseberry, Gudmundson, and Samper Kutschbach, *Coffee, Society, and Power*; Thrupp, *Bittersweet Harvests*; Li, *Land's End*; Soluri, *Banana Cultures*; Dove, *Banana Tree*; Tilghman, "Matoy Jirofo, Masaka Lavany"; Münster, "'Ginger Is a Gamble'"; Neimark et al., "'Civilized Commodity'"; and Hall, "Streets Paved with Prawns."

73. Notable exceptions include Walsh, "After the Rush"; Münster, "'Ginger Is a Gamble'"; and Ferguson, *Expectations of Modernity*.

74. The assemblage concept frames the social realm as "materially heterogeneous, practice-based, emergent and processual," and is helpful for cross-scalar thinking. McFarlane, "Translocal Assemblages," 561.

75. Hopkins and Wallerstein, "Patterns of Development."

76. Hopkins and Wallerstein, "Commodity Chains," 159.

77. Gereffi and Korzeniewicz, *Commodity Chains*.

78. Bair, "Global Capitalism."

79. Gereffi, Humphrey, and Sturgeon, "Global Value Chains."

80. Bair and Werner, "Uneven Geographies."

81. Bair, "Global Capitalism," 168.

82. Bair, "Global Capitalism," 167.

83. Faier, "Fungi, Trees, People"; Tsing, "Sorting Out Commodities"; and Freidburg, *French Beans*.

84. Osterhoudt et al., "Chains of Meaning."

85. Tsing, *Friction*, 1.

86. Other studies have also commented on the complexity of quinoa circulation patterns in the high Andes. See IICA, *Producción de quinua*; Ofstehage, "Gift of the Middleman"; and Mercado and Ubillus, "Characterization of Producers."

87. *Acopiador* translates roughly as "collector." These actors gather quinoa from various farmers and market stalls and sell the bulk quinoa at a markup.

88. IICA, *Producción de quinua*.

89. Bair and Werner, "Uneven Geographies."

90. Mintz, *Sweetness and Power*.

CHAPTER 1. REIMAGINING THE FUTURE OF A NEGLECTED CROP

1. Albes, "Quinoa," 51.

2. Albes, "Quinoa," 61.

3. Albes's denigration of the indigenous agricultural system exposes his ignorance. He declared that there had not been "any attempt at seed selection," a comment heedless of the deliberate processes that made possible the existence of many quinoa varieties.

4. See also Turetsky, "Quinoa"; and Hester, "Save the Fleet."

5. Albes, "Quinoa," 61.

6. Brown and Michael, "Sociology of Expectations."

7. McDonell, "Miracle Crop."

8. Guthman, *Problem with Solutions*.

9. Ferguson, *Anti-Politics Machine*; Li, *Will to Improve*; Kimura, *Hidden Hunger*; and Rao and Huggins, "Sweet 'Success.'"

10. McDonell, "Miracle Foods."

11. LeBlanc, "What Makes Food Super?"

12. LeBlanc, "What Makes Food Super?"; Guthman, *Problem with Solutions*; and Haushofer, *Wonder Foods*.

13. The Pan American Union (Organization of American States after 1948) published one of the most important outlets for commercial information about Latin America at the time. The article likely introduced numerous major businesspeople and diplomats to the grain. See D'Armond Marchant, "Pan American Union."

14. On the centrality of sociopolitical networks and charismatic nutrients, see Kimura, *Hidden Hunger*.

15. Star and Griesemer, "Institutional Ecology," 408.

16. Earle, *Body of the Conquistador*; Pilcher, *Tamales*; and Fu, *Other Milk*.

17. Haushofer, *Wonder Foods*.

18. Bracker, "Latin Nations."

19. Viñas et al., "Valor Alimenticio."

20. White et al., "Nutritive Values."

21. Alcázar, "Monografía de la quinua," 366.

22. Pilcher, *Tamales*; Earle, *Body of the Conquistador*.

23. Laudan, *Cuisine and Empire*.

24. DuPuis, *Nature's Perfect Food*; and Haushofer, *Wonder Foods*.

25. There is no single monolithic "Western diet," but here I use the phrase to refer to a wheat-and dairy-heavy diet that came to be seen as distinctly Western.

26. Collazos, "Dieta del indio," 343.

27. Collazos, "Dieta del indio," 345.

28. Convención de Quenopodiáceas. Chenopod refers to the Chenopodium or goosefoot genus. The conference was named in this way to include some discussion of the closely related Andean grain, *kañiwa*.

29. *Anales* (1968).

30. Mozaffarian, Rosenberg, and Uauy, "Modern Nutrition Science."

31. Alvistur, White, and Collazos, "Valor biológico."

32. Eiselen, "Quinoa."

33. Kloppenburg, *First the Seed*; and Baranski, *Globalization of Wheat*.

34. While this volume uses the terms *underexploited* or *neglected* species, as this discourse expanded, these crops would become known by several names, including minor crops, new crops, forgotten crops, and orphan crops.

35. NRC, *Underexploited Tropical Plants*, 1.

36. NRC, *Underexploited Tropical Plants*, 1.

37. NRC, *Underexploited Tropical Plants*, v.

38. Other species in the volume included amaranth, teff, winged beans, and acacia.

39. NRC, *Underexploited Tropical Plants*, 1.

40. NRC, *Underexploited Tropical Plants*, 2.

41. NRC, *Underexploited Tropical Plants*, 1.

42. NRC, *Underexploited Tropical Plants*, 3.

43. Notably, this mission parallels that of anthropology as originally conceived to save endangered cultures and languages from disappearing, sometimes called the "salvage anthropology" era.

44. The fantasy of finding a species that can solve development problems overlaps with the bioprospecting discourse that emerged in the 1990s, which also relied on the construction of potential and extinction panics. See Hayden, *When Nature Goes Public*; Greene, "Shaman's Needle."

45. NRC, *Underexploited Tropical Plants*, 2.

46. NRC, *Underexploited Tropical Plants*, 2, 22.

47. NRC, *Lost Crops*, v.

48. Robinson, "Amaranth, Quinoa."

49. The ICUC and the Global Facilitation Unit for Underutilised Species combined to become Crops for the Future in 2009.

50. Tally, "New Crops Symposium."

51. Tapia, *Cultivos andinos.*

52. Stevens, "Rediscovering the Lost Crop."

53. "Paraguay Gains on Malnutrition," *New York Times*; and Bracker, "Latin Nations."

54. Bracker, "Latin Nations."

55. Escobar, *Encountering Development.*

56. I use *problematize* in the sense developed by Li, *Will to Improve.* On the "discovery" of malnutrition, see Worboys, "Colonial Malnutrition."

57. Viñas et al., "Valor Alimenticio," 18.

58. Weber, "Inca's Answer."

59. Some scholars argue that the construction of dependence was intentional. Escobar, *Encountering Development.*

60. Ministerio de Agricultura, *Aspectos económicos.*

61. Salvatierra, "Reducir el precio."

62. NRC, *Lost Crops*, 12.

63. Ferroni, "Food Habits"; Arévalo and Portocarrero, "Priorización y desarollo"; and Cusack, "Quinoa."

64. Blythman, "Unpalatable Truth"; Romero, "Quinoa's Quandary"; and Thier, "Cursed Crop."

65. McDonell, "Nutrition Politics"; Bellemare, Fajardo-Gonzalez, and Gitter, "Foods and Fads"; and Gamboa et al., "Price Volatility."

66. Alcázar, "Monografía," 358.

67. Alcázar, "Monografía," 369.

68. "Charming Botanical Strangers," *New York Times.*

69. Elmer, "Quinua"; Bazile, Jacobsen, and Verniau, "Global Expansion of Quinoa."

70. Elmer, "Quinua," 23.

71. *Anales*, 2nd ed., 8.

72. *Anales*, 2nd ed.,7.

73. Bazile, Jacobsen, and Verniau, "Global Expansion of Quinoa."

74. Mujica et al., *Resultados.*

75. Alandia et al., "Global Expansion."

76. Schlick and Bubenhein, "Quinoa."

77. Jacobsen, "Worldwide Potential"; and Zurita-Silva et al., "Breeding Quinoa."

78. Zhang, "Quinoa Genome."

79. Jarvis et al., "Genome," 307.

80. Shiva, *Monocultures of the Mind*; and Kloppenburg, *First the Seed.*

81. Bracker, "Latin Nations."

82. Bracker, "Latin Nations."

83. Brush, "Andean Potato Agriculture."

84. A shift away from thinking about "jobs" to "income-generating activities" in global development institutions also made this vision of quinoa's future compelling in the 1980s. See Benanav, "Origins of Informality."

85. Egoávil, Reinoso, and Torres, "Costos y canales"; Ramos, Reinoso, and Torres, *Estudio de factibilidad*; and Instituto Interamericano de Cooperación para la Agricultura, *Curso de quinua*.

86. Mayer, *Ugly Stories*.

87. Seligmann, *Quinoa*.

88. Peru's Truth and Reconciliation Commission found that indigenous communities were targets of the violence, and 75 percent of those killed were first-language Quechua speakers. Amnesty International, Peru, *Truth and Reconciliation*.

89. Berson, "Quinoa Hack"; and Thier, "Cursed Crop."

90. Cusack, "Quinoa," 31.

91. Schaffer, "Quinoa Evangelist."

92. Berson, "Quinoa Hack."

93. Cusack, "Quinoa," 31.

94. On the politics of climate change "adaptation," see Orlove, "Adaptation."

95. Padulosi et al., "Underutilized Species"; Ruiz et al., "Quinoa Biodiversity"; Bazile, Jacobsen, and Verniau, "Global Expansion of Quinoa"; and FAO, *Quinoa*.

96. Bazile, "Quinoa."

97. Zhu, "Can Quinoa Help Us."

98. Notably, some projects, such as a partnership between Biodiversity International and the International Fund for Agricultural Development, launched in 2011 (called IFAD-Neglected and Underutilized Species), framed quinoa's value in terms of climate change adaptation but had a regional focus on Andean production of quinoa.

99. Deelder, "Quinoa"; and Rao, "Quinoa." On the development of the idea of "climate smart agriculture," see Lipper and Zilberman, "Climate Smart Agriculture."

100. Jovanovic, Stikic, and Jacobsen, "Climate Change."

101. SWUP-MED is an acronym for sustainable water use securing food production in dry areas of the Mediterranean region.

102. International Development Research Centre, *Scaling up Quinoa*.

103. Zurita Silva et al., "Drought Responses."

104. Ruiz et al., "Quinoa Biodiversity."

105. Maliro et al., *Prospects in Africa*, xi.

106. In biodiversity competitions, farmers who specialize in selecting varieties and "conservationist" farmers who cultivate many varieties compete for the best variety and/or the most varieties. On IYQ programming, see FAO, "Master Plan."

107. FAO and Biodiversity International, *Concept Note*.

108. FAO, "IYQ Objectives."

109. FAO, *Master Plan for IYQ*.

110. FAO, "IYQ Objectives."

111. Star, "Not a Boundary Object."

112. FAO, "Launch of IYQ."

113. On the politics of quinoa germplasm as property, see Li, "Politics of Seeds." For analyses of struggles over seeds and ownership see Demeulenaere, "Ontology of Seeds"; and Montenegro de Wit, "Stealing into the Wild."

114. Food and Agriculture Organization, "Graziano Da Silva."

CHAPTER 2. WHITENING A *COMIDA DE INDIOS*

1. Both Malabar and Ámaz closed permanently in 2020.

2. Kiwicha (*Amaranthus caudatus*) is the most important Andean amaranth species.

3. Hayden, *When Nature Goes Public.*

4. Greene, "Shaman's Needle."

5. Dove, "Agronomy of Memory."

6. Guanábana is the fruit of the *Annona muricata* tree, which tastes similar to pineapple but has a banana-like texture. Pasankalla is a specific variety of quinoa known for its auburn color.

7. Ministerio de Agricultura, *Quinua peruana* ; and Higuchi et al., "Ethnic Identity."

8. Morales and Higuchi, "Who Is Eating Quinoa?"; and Higuchi et al., "Ethnic Identity."

9. Banco Central de Reserva del Perú, "Circular."

10. On the effort that goes into maintaining the symbolic power of "national foods," see Wilk, *Home Cooking.*

11. Also see Matta, "Unveiling the Neoliberal Taste"; García, "Taste of Conquest"; and López-Canales, "Peru on a Plate."

12. On the curious mixture of capitalist zeal and "inclusion" politics, see García, "Taste of Conquest."

13. Ministerio de Agricultura, *Quinua Peruana.*

14. INDECOPI, *Productos Banderos.*

15. Bourdieu, *Distinction.*

16. Bourdieu, *Distinction,* 7.

17. Veblen, *Leisure Class*; and Simmel, "Fashion."

18. Wilk, "Loving People."

19. Some have suggested that this is a simple matter of cultural appropriation. The morally laden concept of cultural appropriation is prevalent in media accounts but undertheorized in academic literature, and I have found it to be not especially helpful in analyzing the complex relationships between social hierarchy and food at play here. See Rogers, "Cultural Exchange to Transculturation."

20. Ho, "#FoodGentrification and Culinary Rebranding."

21. O'Hagan, "Celebrity Greens."

22. Brondizio, "Staple to Fashion Food."

23. Mishan, Heal, and Bourne, "Humble Beginnings."

24. Bétrisey and Boisvert, "Amaranth's 'Rediscovery' in Mexico"; and Price, Cruz-Garcia, and Narchi, "Foods of Oppression."

25. Quijano and Ennis, "Coloniality."

26. Calvo and Rueda Esquibel, *Decolonize Your Diet.*

27. Finnis, *Reimagining Marginalized Foods.*

28. While journalistic accounts of Andean quinoa farmers starving in the face of high quinoa prices are overblown, quinoa's high price in 2013 and 2014 temporarily prevented Peru's urban poor from accessing quinoa, a longtime dietary staple.

29. But see also Cooper, "No 'Food Gentrification.'"

30. Hobart, "'Queer-Looking Compound.'"

31. Matta, "Valuing Native Eating."

32. See also Julia Sarreal's analysis of yerba mate in Argentina and Seth Garfield's study of guaraná in Brazil. Sarreal, *Yerba Mate*; and Garfield, *Guaraná.*

33. For a comparative case on the reinvention of "heritage grains" in the Carolina Lowcountry, see Jones, "Producing Heritage."

34. Fischer and Benson, *Broccoli and Desire*; and Lyon, "Just Java."

35. Arguedas, "Análisis de genio popular," 73.

36. Arguedas, "Análisis de genio popular," 74.

37. Price, Cruz-Garcia, and Narchi, "Foods of Oppression."

38. Wilk, "Loving People."

39. Finnis, *Reimagining Marginalized Foods.*

40. Mendelson, *Chow Chop Suey.*

41. Dietler, "Culinary Encounters."

42. Earle, *Body of the Conquistador.*

43. In addition to foods, bodily comportment and practices like chewing coca leaves took on related symbolic dimensions. See Allen, *Hold Life Has*; and Cadena, *Indigenous Mestizos.*

44. While quinoa overall did fit into a category of foods understood as Indian foods, the ways these foods map onto social identities is not straightforward and was likely context dependent. See Orlove, "Down to Earth."

45. Markowitz argued that alpaca meat came to be associated with disease and Indianness during the colonial period. Discourses of race invoked hygiene such that Indianness was seen as contagious. Markowitz, "Highland Haute Cuisine." García, "Taste of Conquest"; Weismantel, *Food, Gender, and Poverty*; and Weismantel, *Cholas and Pishtacos.*

46. Manrique, *La piel.*

47. Gotkowitz, *Histories of Race.*

48. With Peru's independence, national identity came to be imagined through the concept of *mestizaje* (which translates roughly as "racial mixing"): a blend of Spanish and indigenous heritage (but especially Incan elements).

49. Wade, *Race and Ethnicity*; Cadena, *Indigenous Mestizos*; Weismantel, *Cholas and Pishtacos*; Manrique, *La piel*; and Vich, "Dinámicas de racismo."

50. Lauer, *La cocina francesca*; and Lauer and Lauer, *La revolución gastronómica peruana*.

51. See Hanna Garth's concept of a "decent meal," which emphasizes this importance of culturally specific ideas about a proper meal and how this relates to ideal womanhood. See Garth, *Food in Cuba*.

52. Ayala Macedo, "Consumption of Quinoa in Peru"; Smith and Trivelli, *El Consumo Urbano*; and Solorio and Revilla, *Alimentación andina*.

53. Gascón, "De la quinua al arroz"; Orlove, "Stability and Change"; and Weismantel, *Food, Gender, and Poverty*.

54. This correlates with the way María Elena García found Quechua speakers in the Cusco region navigated speaking Quechua. See García, *Making Indigenous Citizens*.

55. Carreño, "Places Are Kin."

56. Seligmann, *Quinoa*.

57. Quijano and Ennis, "Coloniality of Power," 533.

58. Matta, "República gastronómica."

59. Schaffer, "Quinoa Evangelist."

60. Schaffer, "Quinoa Evangelist."

61. Fabricant, "Andean Legacy."

62. Belasco, *Appetite for Change*.

63. Ancient Harvest, "US Quinoa."

64. West, *Imagined Primitive*.

65. Also see Cánepa, "Los antropólogos."

66. Loyer and Knight, "'Inca Superfood.'"

67. Fabricant, "Andean Legacy."

68. Wood, *Supergrain*.

69. Fabricant, "America Embraces."

70. Jordan, "Heirloom Tomato."

71. Guthman, "Fast Food/Organic Food."

72. Mintz, *Sweetness and Power*.

73. Ancient Harvest, "US Quinoa."

74. Trapp, "You-Will-Kill-Me-Beans"; and Wilk, *Home Cooking*.

75. Johnston and Baumann, "Culinary Other"; and Molz, "Eating Difference."

76. Ives, *Steeped in Heritage*.

77. West, *Imagined Primitive*.

78. Neophiles seek out new foods, while neophobes are those who avoid novel tastes.

79. Orlove, *Allure of the Foreign*; and Vich, "Dinámicas de racismo."

80. "Cuzqueña Quinua Commercial."

81. See also Cox Hall, "Cooking Up Heritage."

82. Cánepa, "Los antropólogos," 31.

83. Fan, "Can Ideas about Food."

84. Janer, "(In)Edible Nature," 385.

85. Palomino Gonzales, "Gourmetización"; and Palomino Gonzales, "Quinua gourmet."

86. Fuentes, "Gastón Acurio."

87. López-Canales, "Peru on a Plate"; McDonell, "Culinary Frontier"; and García, "Devouring the Nation."

88. "Entrevista con Diego Muñoz," *La Vanguardia*.

89. Morán, "Gastón Acurio."

90. García, "Devouring the Nation"; and McDonell, "Culinary Frontier."

91. On the meanings of value, see Graeber, *Theory of Value*.

92. On the complexity of markets and race, see Weismantel, *Cholas and Pishtacos*; and Seligmann, "To Be In Between."

93. Here I invoke de la Cadena's discussion of the racialized concept of *gente decente* in Peru. Cadena, *Indigenous Mestizos*.

94. Jordan, "Heirloom Tomato."

95. Méndez, "Incas Sí, Indios No."

96. Earle, *Return of the Native*; and Flores Galindo, *Buscando un inca*.

97. Vich, "Magical, Mystical"; Cadena, *Indigenous Mestizos*; and Molinié, "Resurrection of the Inca."

98. Cadena, *Indigenous Mestizos*.

99. Earle, *Return of the Native*; and Flores Galindo, *Buscando un inca*.

100. Greene, "Entre Lo Indio."

101. Greene, "Todos Somos Iguales," 289.

102. Alcalde, "Between Incas and Indians."

103. Kimura, *Hidden Hunger*.

104. McDonell and Wilk, *Critical Approaches to Superfoods*.

105. Scrinis, "On the Ideology of Nutritionism."

106. Hayes-Conroy et al., "Doing Nutrition Differently"; and Mudry et al., "Other Ways of Knowing."

107. Conrad and Zuckerman, *Countering White Supremacy*.

CHAPTER 3. THE QUINOA FRONTIER

1. On the complexity of the concept of profit for agriculturalists in the Andean highlands, see Mayer and Glave, "Alguito." Studies from the 1990s found that Puno's quinoa farmers typically saved 65 percent of their quinoa production for home consumption. By 2014 that figure among quinoa farmers in Puno was estimated at between 5 and 22 percent. Solorio and Revilla, *Alimentación andina*; and IICA, *Producción de quinua*.

2. INEI, *Censo nacional agropecuario*. While farmers here do generally sell farm products, there is not a single lucrative crop, and incomes from selling farm products are small. According to Fairlie Reinoso, in 2012 there were about ten thousand quinoa farmers organized into 130 producer associations. Fairlie Reinoso, *Cadena exportadora*.

3. Urrutia and Trivelli, "Migración y la agricultura."

4. Li, "What Is Land?"

5. Turner, *Frontier in American History.*

6. Li, *Will to Improve.*

7. Willow et al., "Contested Landscape."

8. Bender and Winer, *Contested Landscapes*, 3; and Rissing and Jones, "Landscapes of Value."

9. Basso, *Wisdom Sits in Places.*

10. Mayer, *Articulated Peasant.*

11. Murra, " El 'control vertical.'"

12. Guillet, "Reciprocal Labor."

13. Wolf, "Aspects."

14. Popkin, *Rational Peasant.*

15. Starn, "Missing the Revolution."

16. Tsing, *Friction.*

17. Jacobsen, *Mirages of Transition.*

18. Renique, *Batalla por Puno.*

19. On the complicated outcomes of Peru's Agrarian Reform and its aftermath, see Mayer, *Ugly Stories*; and Cotlear, *Desarollo campesino.*

20. Seligmann, *Quinoa.*

21. On territoriality and plants, see Besky and Padwe, "Territory."

22. Scott, *Seeing Like a State.*

23. Dove, *Banana Tree.*

24. Egoávil, Reinoso, and Torres, "Costos y canales"; IICA, *Producción de quinua*; and Mercado and Ubillus, "Characterization of Producers."

25. Scott, *Seeing Like a State.*

26. Rissing and Jones, "Landscapes of Value."

27. Murdoch, "Inhuman"; Whatmore, *Hybrid Geographies*; and Bakker and Bridge, "Material Worlds?"

28. Bakker, "Neoliberalizing Nature?"

29. Faier, "Fungi, Trees, People."

30. Soto et al., "Sistemas de rotación."

31. Ferguson, *The Anti-Politics Machine*; Li, *Will to Improve*; Grillo and Stirrat, *Discourses of Development*; and Lewis and Mosse, *Development Brokers.*

32. Wolf, "Aspects of Group Relations."

33. Miklavcic and LeBlanc, "Culture Brokers."

34. This dynamic relates to the hybrid countryside and the global countryside concepts, see Murdoch, "Co-Constructing the Countryside"; and Woods, "Global Countryside."

35. While "agricultural field" is the closest translation, the chacra is a space that people nurture and that nurtures people in return, a space of mutual care and becoming. Apffel-Marglin, *Subversive Spiritualities.*

36. Williams, *Country and City*, 1.

37. Gandolfo, *City at Its Limits*; and Weismantel, *Cholas and Pishtacos.*

38. Radcliffe, Westwood, and Westwood, *Remaking the Nation*, 109–12.

39. These conceptual categories shift with scale and articulate with Peru's spatialized racial hierarchy, such that someone from Lima would likely consider someone from Juliaca to have rural origins.

40. Sumberg, *Agronomy for Development*.

41. Li, *Will to Improve*, 6.

42. Marca Vilca et al., *Comportamiento*, 54.

43. Soto et al., "Sistemas de rotación."

44. Prior to 2014, approximately 60 percent of Peruvian quinoa was organic and 40 percent conventional. Ministerio de Agricultura, *Quinua Peruana*.

45. Gómez Tovar et al., "Certified Organic."

46. Fairlie Reinoso, *Cadena Exportadora*.

47. Fairlie Reinoso, *Cadena Exportadora*; and Mesa de Trabajo de la Quinua, Puno, *Plan Operativo*.

48. Mutersbaugh, "Serve and Certify"; and Galvin, *Becoming Organic*.

CHAPTER 4. PRODUCING GOOD QUINOA

1. Edward Fischer and Peter Benson examine the complex desires for *algo más* that motivate Guatemalan broccoli farmers to produce for export. Fischer and Benson, *Broccoli and Desire*.

2. Douglas, *Purity and Danger*.

3. The "golden stream" metaphor comes from geographer William Cronon's analysis of the nineteenth-century commodification of wheat in the Midwest. Cronon, *Nature's Metropolis*.

4. Li, *Will to Improve*.

5. Ferguson, *Anti-Politics Machine*.

6. Quark, *Global Rivalries*.

7. Ponte, "Bans, Tests, and Alchemy"; and Ponte and Gibbon, "Quality Standards."

8. For another ethnography of quality, see Besky, *Tasting Qualities*.

9. The moral dimension of these standards did not simply inhere in the standards themselves. Nor was moralization exclusively evident in their enforcement. The line between standards being moralizing versus standards coming to take moral meaning in their enforcement is nuanced and often blurry.

10. Egoávil, Reinoso, and Torres, "Costos y canales."

11. Zimmerer, *Changing Fortunes*; and Skarbø, "Lost Crop."

12. Estimates of how many varieties of quinoa exist vary widely because of the difficulties of defining a "variety" and also because quinoa's high cross-pollination rates lead to more variation and change over time. Tapia, *Quinua y kañiwa*.

13. Flores-Ochoa, *Pastores de puna*; and Mayer, *Articulated Peasant*.

14. Studies show that quinoa cross-pollination rates can reach 17 percent. Wheat, in comparison, which is mostly self-pollinated, has a rate of less than 1 percent. Gomez-Pando, Aguilar-Castellanos, and Ibañez-Tremolada, "Quinoa Breeding."

15. Apffel-Marglin, *Subversive Spiritualities*.
16. Cadena, *Earth Beings*.
17. Flores Ochoa, "Enqa."
18. While *trueque* translates as barter, this elides some nuance. Trueque is a complex, ritualized exchange that does not conform to a standard definition of barter. See Ferraro, "Trueque." See also Egoávil, "Comercialización de la quinua."
19. Osterhoudt, *Vanilla Landscapes*.
20. Soluri, *Banana Cultures*.
21. Besky, *Tasting Qualities*.
22. Fischer and Victor, "High-End Coffee."
23. Li, *Will to Improve*.
24. Tapia, *Quinua y kañiwa*, 65.
25. This directive dovetailed with a national effort to achieve product standardization. In 1972 President Juan Velasco Alvarado's administration launched the Institute of Technology Research and Technical Norms to generate closer relationships between science, technology, and industry. Agricultural product standardization was a key element of their work and Velasco's vision of a modern Peru.
26. Egoávil, Reinoso, and Torres, "Costos y canales."
27. ITINTEC, *Norma técnica peruana*.
28. Busch, *Standards*.
29. Daviron and Ponte, *Coffee Paradox*; and Jacques et al., *Tropical Food Chains*.
30. Stanford, "Constructing 'Quality.'"
31. Besky, *Tasting Qualities*.
32. Cronon, *Nature's Metropolis*.
33. Tsing, "Sorting Out Commodities."
34. Egoávil, Reinoso, and Torres, "Costos y canales," 29.
35. Soto Mendizábal, Valdivia Fernández, and Solano Oré, *Normas técnicas*.
36. Douglas, *Purity and Danger*.
37. Foucault, *Will to Knowledge*, 137.
38. Jasanoff, "Biotechnology and Empire," 283.
39. Kloppenburg, *First the Seed*.
40. Zimmerer, *Changing Fortunes*.
41. I put "raw material" in scare quotes because while from a buyer-processor point of view the quinoa they buy from a farmer is raw material, this quinoa has already undergone considerable processing, and this framing devalues the work of farmers.
42. Mansfield, "Spatializing Globalization," 9.

CHAPTER 5. DISARTICULATIONS

1. While often referred to as public transportation, the "combi" system of passenger vans in the Peruvian altiplano is composed of many private companies that run specific routes.
2. Kobayashi and Beillard, *Price Fluctuation*.

3. Moore, "Transcending the Metabolic Rift."

4. Bair and Werner, "Uneven Geographies," 996.

5. Bair and Werner, "Uneven Geographies."

6. Ferguson, *Expectations of Modernity*.

7. Osterhoudt, "'Nobody Wants to Kill.'"

8. Freidburg, *French Beans*.

9. This fits into a much longer pattern of Peruvian politicians appropriating Inca imagery in their pursuit of legitimacy. See Vich, "Magical, Mystical"; and Greene, "Getting over the Andes."

10. Agro Rural, "Programa Proquinua."

11. Agro Rural, "Programa Proquinua."

12. Ministerio de Agricultura, *Quinua peruana*; and Ministerio de Agricultura, *Análisis económico*.

13. INEI, *Censo nacional agropecuario*.

14. Gómez-Pando et al., "Contexto del cultivo"; and Nolte, *Quinoa Outlook*.

15. Ministerio de Agricultura, "Quinua."

16. Haraway, "Capitalocene."

17. Ministerio de Agricultura, "Análisis económico."

18. The price paid to farmers.

19. Ministerio de Agricultura, *La quinua*.

20. Bazile, Jacobsen, and Verniau, "Global Expansion of Quinoa."

21. Alandia et al., "Global Expansion."

22. Morgan, Marsden, and Murdoch, *Worlds of Food*.

23. Li, "Politics of Seeds."

24. On perishability politics, see Besky, *Tasting Qualities*; Brondizio, *Amazonian Caboclo*; and Freidberg, *Fresh*.

25. Mayer and Glave, "Alguito." Many farmers still recalled the annual 7.600 percent inflation rate in Peru in 1990, when currency had been an especially poor store of value.

26. The term peasant is considered pejorative in some contexts. In the peasant studies literature developed especially in the *Journal of Peasant Studies*, the term is meant to be analytical and to position rural smallholders within a capitalism world system.

27. Chayanov, *Peasant Economy*.

28. An *arroba* is a common unit of measurement for buying and selling quinoa in the Andes; it measures 11.5kg.

29. Pantaleón et al., "Dinámica de la producción."

30. Johnston Taylor, "Cooking for a Cleaner Environment."

CHAPTER 6. FRAGMENTED KNOWLEDGE AND
INTRACTABLE RESIDUES IN THE QUINOA SUPPLY CHAIN

1. Nolte, *Quinoa Outlook*; Ministerio de Agricultura, "MINAGRI y FDA"; El Comercio, "Algunos envíos"; and FDA, "Import Refusals Database."

2. FDA, "Import Refusals Database."

3. FDA, *Pesticide Residue Monitoring Program*.

4. Barrenechea Cabrera, *Resultados*; and Ministerio de Agricultura, *Quinua Peruana*.

5. Derks, Turner, and Thúy Hạnh, "Bastard Spice."

6. Paz, "Chisme and Rumor."

7. Gestión, "EE.UU. permitirá"; and Gestión, "Senasa gestiona."

8. Cillóniz, "MINAGRI mejora condiciones."

9. Ministerio de Agricultura, "MINAGRI y FDA."

10. Gestión, "Quinua peruana."

11. Ayma, "Estados Unidos."

12. Soto et al., "Sistemas de rotación"; and Latorre Farfán, "Quinoa Cultivation."

13. Ayma, "Estados Unidos."

14. Meaning unapproved by the EPA and/or the EU.

15. Nonconforming in this study meant the sample did not pass one or more of the standards set by those three entities.

16. Barrenechea Cabrera, *Resultados*.

17. Conklin, "Body Paint"; and Muehlmann, "Real Indians."

18. Higuchi et al., "Banned Pesticides."

19. IICA, *Producción de quinua*.

20. Y apura Balboa, "Caracterización del contrabando."

21. Hetherington, *Guerrilla Auditors*, 8.

22. Hetherington, *Guerrilla Auditors*.

23. Mutersbaugh, "Serve and Certify"; and Gómez Tovar et al., "Certified Organic."

24. Mutersbaugh, "Serve and Certify," 537.

25. Galvin, *Becoming Organic*.

26. Mathews, "Scandals, Audits, and Fictions."

27. Shaila Galvin also found this dynamic. Galvin, "Farming of Trust."

28. Guthman, *Agrarian Dreams*.

29. Riles, *Documents*; Hetherington, *Guerrilla Auditors*; and Bear, "Antinomies of Audit."

30. Freidburg, *French Beans*.

31. Power, *Audit Society*; and Strathern, *Audit Cultures*.

32. Freidburg, *French Beans*.

CHAPTER 7. (RE)BUILDING REPUTATION

1. Paxson, "Locating Value."

2. Trubek, *Taste of Place*.

3. Guy, *When Champagne Became French*.

4. Johnston and Baumann, *Foodies*.

5. Ostrom, *Governing the Commons*.

6. Megyesi and Mike, "Organising Collective Reputation."

7. Nonini, "Global Idea of 'Commons'"; Colloredo-Mansfeld, "Community Commodities"; Ofstehage, "Nusta Juira's Gift"; Megyesi and Mike, "Organising Collective Reputation"; Aragon, "Where Commons Meet Commerce"; and King, Lenox, and Barnett, "Reputation Commons Problem."

8. Johnston and Baumann, *Foodies*.

9. I am focusing on agricultural products, but handicrafts and pottery are also often marketed for their relationship to a place or people. See Chan, "Competitive Tradition."

10. There's a fascinating literature on geographic indications and related phenomena. For a complex discussion of the distinctions between different kinds of protections and the global-level institutions and treaties governing them, see Parasecoli, *Where It Comes From*; Mitchell and Terry, "Contesting Pisco"; and Trubek, *Taste of Place*.

11. Kerr, "Good Port."

12. Barham, "Translating Terroir."

13. Crang and Cook, "World on a Plate," 132.

14. See also Goodman, "Quality 'Turn.'"

15. Johnston and Baumann, *Foodies*.

16. Coombe and Aylwin, "Bordering Diversity and Desire."

17. Barham and Sylvander, *Labels of Origin*; and Dogan and Gokovali, "Geographical Indications."

18. Vandecandelaere, Teyssier, et al., *Strengthening Sustainable Food Systems*; and Vandecandelaere, Arfini, et al., *Linking People*.

19. For instance, see FAO, *Labelling and Certification Schemes*.

20. Kerr, "Good Port," 8.

21. Bowen, *Divided Spirits*; Bowen and Zapata, "Geographical Indications"; Besky, *Darjeeling Distinction*; and Ives, *Steeped in Heritage*.

22. Hobsbawm and Ranger, *Invention of Tradition*.

23. Terrio, *French Chocolate*; and Guy, *When Champagne Became French*.

24. Bryant and Goodman, "Consuming Narratives."

25. Parrott, Wilson, and Murdoch, "Spatializing Quality"; and Coombe and Aylwin, "Bordering Diversity and Desire."

26. Coombe and Aylwin, "Bordering Diversity and Desire"; and Trubek, *Taste of Place*.

27. Ostrom, *Governing the Commons*.

28. Megyesi and Mike, "Organising Collective Reputation"; and King, Lenox, and Barnett, "Reputation Commons."

29. Ostrom, *Governing the Commons*.

30. Agro Rural, "Marcas colectivas."

31. These other proposals did not disappear. Part of the reason the initial group involved in the marca was so small was that many actors initially thought organic certification would be enough for differentiation (the contamination scandals that eroded confidence in organic certification had not yet taken place), and some actors

thought that the long-term goal would need to be a denomination of origin, once the marca was secured.

32. Mitchell and Terry, "Contesting Pisco."
33. On the aynok'a system, see Urdanivia, "Andean Quinoa."
34. Personal communication with Didier Bazile, 2019.
35. Ofstehage, "Nusta Juira's Gift."
36. Slow Food USA, "Ark of Taste"; and Slow Food International, "Good Practices."
37. Trubek, *Taste of Place.*

CONCLUSION

1. Hirsch, *Acts of Growth.*
2. Tsing, *Mushroom.*
3. Guthman, "Good Story Behind It."
4. Andreotti et al, "Neglected Species."

APPENDIX

1. SUNAT, *Estadísticas de Comercio Exterior* (Superintendencia Nacional de Aduanas y Administración Tributaria, 2020). www.sunat.gob.pe/estad-comExt /modelo_web/web_estadistica.htm; FAO, *FAOSTAT Statistical Database* ([Rome]: FAO, 1997–); and IICA, *El mercado y la producción de quinua en el Perú* (Lima: Instituto Interamericano de Cooperación para la Agricultura, 2015).

BIBLIOGRAPHY

Agro Rural. "Marcas colectivas para el desarrollo del agro." Lima: Ministerio de Desarollo Agrario y Riego, September 24, 2013. www.agrorural.gob.pe/marcas -colectivas-para-el-desarrollo-del-agro/.

———. "Minagri presentó Programa Proquinua para impulsar la reconversión productiva del agro." Noticias. Lima: Ministerio de Desarrollo Agrario y Riego, July 10, 2014. www.agrorural.gob.pe/minagri-presento-programa-proquinua-para -impulsar-la-reconversion-productiva-del-agro/.

Alandia, G., J. P. Rodriguez, S. E. Jacobsen, D. Bazile, and B. Condori. "Global Expansion of Quinoa and Challenges for the Andean Region." *Global Food Security* 26 (September 1, 2020): 100429.

Albes, Edward. "Quinoa: A South American Cereal." *Bulletin of the Pan American Union* 47, no. 1 (1918): 51–61.

Alcalde, Cristina. "Between Incas and Indians: Inca Kola and the Construction of a Peruvian-Global Modernity." *Journal of Consumer Culture* 9, no. 1 (2009): 31–54.

Alcázar, Jorge. "Monografía de la quinua." *Boletín del Instituto Internacional Americano de Protección a la Infancia* 22, no. 3 (1948): 357–69.

Allen, Catherine. *The Hold Life Has: Coca and Cultural Identity in an Andean Community*. Washington, DC: Smithsonian Institution Press, 2002.

Alvistur, Enrique J., Philip White, and Carlos Collazos. "El valor biológico de la quinua." *Sociedad Química del Perú* 19 (1953): 197–209.

Amnesty International, Peru. *The Truth and Reconciliation Commission: A First Step Towards a Country without Justice*. August 26, 2004. www.amnesty.org/en /documents/amr46/003/2004/en/.

Anales de la Convención Internacional de Quenopodiáceas. Puno, Peru: n.p., 1968.

Anales de la Convención Internacional de Quenopodiáceas. 2nd ed. Potosí, Bolivia: n.p., 1976.

Ancient Harvest. "US Quinoa." 2022. https://ancientharvest.com/quinoa/us -quinoa/.

Andreotti, Federico, Didier Bazile, Cristina Biaggi, Daniel Callo-Concha, Julie Jacquet, Omarsherif M. Jemal, Oliver I. King, C. Mbosso, Stefano Padulosi, Erika N.

Speelman, and Meine van Noordwijk. "When Neglected Species Gain Global Interest: Lessons Learned from Quinoa's Boom and Bust for Teff and Minor Millet." *Global Food Security* 32 (March 1, 2022): 100613.

Apffel-Marglin, Frédérique. *Subversive Spiritualities: How Rituals Enact the World.* New York: Oxford University Press, 2012.

Aragon, Lorraine V. "Where Commons Meet Commerce: Circulation and Sequestration Strategies in Indonesian Arts Economies." *Anthropology of Work Review* 32, no. 2 (2011): 63–76.

Arévalo, Adolfo, and Javier Portocarrero. "Priorización y desarollo del sector agrario en el Perú." Lima: Fundación Friedrich Ebert, 1986.

Arguedas, José Maria. "Análisis de un genio popular: Violeta Parra." *Revista de Educación* 13 (1968): 66–76.

———. "Llamado a algunos doctores." *El Comercia*, July 10, 1966.

Ayala Macedo, Guido. "Consumption of Quinoa in Peru." *Food Reviews International* 19, nos. 1–2 (January 5, 2003): 221–27.

Ayma, Diego. "Estados Unidos devuelve 200 toneladas de quinua peruana." *El Correo*, August 30, 2015, sec. https://diariocorreo.pe/economia/estados-unidos-devuelve-200-toneladas-de-quinua-peruana-613876/.

Bair, Jennifer. "Global Capitalism and Commodity Chains: Looking Back, Going Forward." *Competition & Change*, June 1, 2005, 153–80.

Bair, Jennifer, and Marion Werner. "Commodity Chains and the Uneven Geographies of Global Capitalism: A Disarticulations Perspective." *Environment and Planning A: Economy and Space* 43, no. 5 (May 1, 2011): 988–97.

Bakker, Karen. "Neoliberalizing Nature? Market Environmentalism in Water Supply in England and Wales." *Annals of the Association of American Geographers* 93, no. 5 (2005): 542–65.

Bakker, Karen, and Gavin Bridge. "Material Worlds? Resource Geographies and the 'Matter of Nature.'" *Progress in Human Geography* 30, no. 1 (2006): 5–27.

Banco Central de Reserva del Perú. "Circular." Serie Numismática Recursos Naturales del Perú. Banco Central de Reserva del Perú, 2013. https://www.bcrp.gob.pe/billetes-y-monedas/monedas-de-coleccion/serie-numismatica-recursos-naturales-del-peru.html.

Baranski, Marci. *The Globalization of Wheat: A Critical History of the Green Revolution*. Pittsburgh: University of Pittsburgh Press, 2022.

Barham, Elizabeth. "Translating Terroir: The Global Challenge of French AOC Labeling for Rural Development." *Journal of Rural Studies* 19 (2003): 127–38.

Barham, Elizabeth, and Bertil Sylvander. *Labels of Origin for Food: Local Development, Global Recognition*. Cambridge, MA: CAB International, 2011.

Barrenechea Cabrera, Jorge. *Resultados del monitoreo de contaminantes en la quinua*. Lima: SENASA, 2016.

Basso, Keith. *Wisdom Sits in Places*. Albuquerque: University of New Mexico Press, 1996.

Bazile, D., S. E. Jacobsen, and A. Verniau. "The Global Expansion of Quinoa: Trends and Limits." *Frontiers in Plant Science* 7 (2016): 622.

Bazile, Didier. "Quinoa: A Model Crop for Tomorrow's Agriculture." In *Biology and Biotechnology of Quinoa: Super Grain for Food Security*, edited by Ajit Varma, 397–417. Singapore: Springer, 2021.

Bear, Laura. "The Antinomies of Audit: Opacity, Instability and Charisma in the Economic Governance of a Hooghly Shipyard." *Economy and Society* 42, no. 3 (August 1, 2013): 375–97.

Bebbington, Anthony. "The New Extraction: Rewriting the Political Ecology of the Andes?" *NACLA Report on the Americas* (September/October 2009): 12–20.

Belasco, Warren J. *Appetite for Change: How the Counterculture Took on the Food Industry*. New York: Pantheon, 1989.

Bellemare, Marc F., Johanna Fajardo-Gonzalez, and Seth R. Gitter. "Foods and Fads: The Welfare Impacts of Rising Quinoa Prices in Peru." *World Development* 112 (December 1, 2018): 163–79.

Benanav, Aaron. "The Origins of Informality: The ILO at the Limit of the Concept of Unemployment." *Journal of Global History* 14, no. 1 (2019): 107–25.

Bender, Barbara, and Margot Winer, eds. *Contested Landscapes: Movement, Exile, and Place*. New York: Routledge, 2020.

Berlant, Lauren. *Cruel Optimism*. Durham, NC: Duke University Press, 2011.

Berndt, Christian. "Uneven Development, Commodity Chains and the Agrarian Question." *Progress in Human Geography* (March 2018): 1–14.

Berson, Joshua. "The Quinoa Hack." *New Left Review* 85 (2014): 117–32.

Besky, Sarah. *The Darjeeling Distinction: Labor and Justice on Fair-Trade Tea Plantations in India*. Oakland: University of California Press, 2014.

———. *Tasting Qualities: The Past and Future of Tea*. Oakland: University of California Press, 2020.

Besky, Sarah, and Alex Blanchette. *How Nature Works: Rethinking Labor on a Troubled Planet*. Albuquerque: University of New Mexico Press, 2019.

Besky, Sarah, and Jonathan Padwe. "Placing Plants in Territory." *Environment and Society* 7 (2016): 9–28.

Bétrisey, Florence, and Valerie Boisvert. "Amaranth's 'Rediscovery' in Mexico: A Path Toward Decolonization of Food?" In *Critical Approaches to Superfoods*, edited by Emma McDonell and Richard Wilk, 169–86. London: Bloomsbury, 2020.

Biodiversity International. "Neglected No More." Awareness and Policy Briefs, 2007. https://alliancebioversityciat.org/publications-data/neglected-no-more-achievements-ifad-nus-project-2001-2005framework-its-follow.

———. "Species List." Neglected and Underutilized Species Community, 2018. www.nuscommunity.org/nus/neglected-underutilized-species/species-list/.

Blaikie, Piers, and Harold Brookfield. *Land Degradation and Society*. London: Methuen, 1987.

Blythman, Joanna. "Can Vegans Stomach the Unpalatable Truth about Quinoa?" *Guardian*, January 16, 2013. theguardian.com/commentisfree/2013/jan/16/vegans-stomach-unpalatable-truth-quinoa.

Bourdieu, Pierre. *Distinction: A Social Critique of the Judgment of Taste*. Cambridge, MA: Harvard University Press, 1984.

Bowen, Sarah. *Divided Spirits: Tequila, Mezcal, and the Politics of Production*. Oakland: University of California Press, 2015.

Bowen, Sarah, and Ana Valenzuela Zapata. "Geographical Indications, Terroir, and Socioeconomic and Ecological Sustainability: The Case of Tequila." *Journal of Rural Studies* 25 (2009): 108–19.

Bracker, Milton. "Latin Nations See New Food in Quinoa." *New York Times*, July 27, 1948.

Brondizio, E. S. "From Staple to Fashion Food: Shifting Cycles and Shifting Opportunities in the Development of the Acai Palm Fruit Economy in the Amazon Estuary." In *Working Forest in the Neotropics*, edited by D. J. Zarin, J. R. R. Alavalapati, F. E. Putz, and M. Schmink. New York: Columbia University Press, 2004.

Brondizio, Eduardo. *Amazonian Caboclo and the Acai Palm: Forest Farmers in the Global Market*. New York: New York Botanical Garden Press, 2008.

Brown, N., and M. Michael. "A Sociology of Expectations: Retrospecting Prospects and Prospecting Retrospects." *Technology Analysis & Strategic Management* 15, no. 1 (2003): 3–18.

Bruno, Maria C., and William T. Whitehead. "Chenopodium Cultivation and Formative Period Agriculture at Chiripa, Bolivia." *Latin American Antiquity* 14, no. 3 (September 2003): 339–55.

Brush, Stephen. "Ethnoecology, Biodiversity, and Modernization in Andean Potato Agriculture." *Journal of Ethnobiology* 12, no. 2 (1992): 161–85.

Bryant, Raymond L., and Michael K. Goodman. "Consuming Narratives: The Political Ecology of 'Alternative' Consumption." *Transactions of the Institute of British Geographers* 29, no. 3 (2004): 344–66.

Busch, Lawrence. *Standards: Recipes for Reality*. Cambridge, MA: MIT Press, 2013.

Cadena, Marisol de la. *Earth Beings: Ecologies of Practice across Andean Worlds*. Durham, NC: Duke University Press, 2015.

———. *Indigenous Mestizos: The Politics of Race and Culture in Cuzco, Peru, 1919–1991*. Durham, NC: Duke University Press, 2000.

Calvo, Luz, and Catriona Rueda Esquibel. *Decolonize Your Diet: Plant-Based Mexican-American Recipes for Health and Healing*. Vancouver, BC: Arsenal Pulp Press, 2015.

Cánepa, Gisela K. "Los antropólogos y los sucesos de Ilave." *Quehacer* 148 (May–June 2004): 26–31.

Carreño, Guillermo Salas. "Places Are Kin: Food, Cohabitation, and Sociality in the Southern Peruvian Andes." *Anthropological Quarterly* 89, no. 3 (2016): 813–40.

Cerveza Cusqueña. "Cusqueña Quinua Commercial." Advertisement for Cusqueña Quinua. Posted on July 30, 2015. YouTube video. www.youtube.com/watch?v=4sEdQfKIGFw&t=1s.

Chan, Anita Say. "Competitive Tradition: Intellectual Property and New Millennial Craft." *Anthropology of Work Review* 32, no. 2 (2011): 90–102.

Chayanov, A.V. *The Theory of Peasant Economy*. Madison: University of Wisconsin Press, 1966.

Cillóniz, Bruno. "MINAGRI mejora condiciones para ingreso de quinua peruana a EE.UU." AgroForum, April 15, 2015. www.agroforum.pe/agro-noticias/minagri -mejora-condiciones-ingreso-de-quinua-peruana-a-ee-uu-7194/.

Collazos, Carlos. "La dieta del indio." *Archivos Venezolanos de Nutrición* 5 (1954): 343–46.

Colloredo-Mansfeld, Rudi. "Work, Cultural Resources, and Community Commodities in the Global Economy." *Anthropology of Work Review* 32, no. 2 (September 1, 2011): 51–62.

Conklin, Beth. "Body Paint, Feathers, and VCRs: Aesthetics and Authenticity in Amazonian Activism." *American Ethnologist* 24, no. 4 (1997): 711–37.

Conrad, Alison, and Jennifer Zuckerman. *Identifying and Countering White Supremacy Culture in Food Systems.* Durham, NC: Duke Sanford World Food Policy Center, 2020.

Coombe, Rosemary J., and Nicole Aylwin. "Bordering Diversity and Desire: Using Intellectual Property to Mark Place-Based Products." *Environment and Planning A* 43, no. 9 (September 1, 2011): 2027–42.

Cooper, Ryan. "Sorry, There's No Such Thing as 'Food Gentrification.'" *Week*, January 10, 2015, sec. Opinion. https://theweek.com/articles/447513/sorry-theres-no -such-thing-food-gentrification.

Cotlear, Daniel. *Desarollo campesino en los Andes.* Lima: Instituto de Estudios Peruanos, 1989.

Cox Hall, Amy. "Cooking Up Heritage: Culinary Adventures of Peru's Past." *Bulletin of Spanish Studies* 97, no. 4 (April 20, 2020): 593–613.

Crang, Philip, and Ian Cook. "The World on a Plate: Culinary Culture, Displacement and Geographical Knowledge." *Journal of Material Culture* 1, no. 2 (1996): 131–53.

Cronon, William. *Nature's Metropolis: Chicago and the Great West.* New York: W. W. Norton, 1991.

Cusack, David. "Quinoa: Grain of the Incas." *Ecologist* 14, no. 1 (1984): 21–23.

D'Armond Marchant, Annie. "The Bulletin of the Pan American Union, 1893–1943." *Bulletin of the Pan American Union* 77 (1943): 564–73.

Daviron, Benoit, and Stefano Ponte. *The Coffee Paradox: Global Markets, Commodity Trade and the Elusive Promise of Development.* New York: Zed Books, 2005.

Deelder, Merel. "Quinoa: A Climate Proof Food." Food Unfolded, May 8, 2021. www.foodunfolded.com/article/quinoa-a-climate-proof-food.

Demeulenaere, Elise. "A Political Ontology of Seeds: The Transformative Frictions of a Farmers' Movement in Europe." *Focaal*, no. 69 (2014): 45–61.

Derks, Annuska, Sarah Turner, and Ngô Thúy Hạnh. "Bastard Spice or Champagne of Cinnamon? Conflicting Value Creations along Cinnamon Commodity Chains in Northern Vietnam." *Development and Change* 51, no. 3 (2020): 895–920.

Dietler, Michael. "Culinary Encounters: Food, Identity, and Colonialism." In *The Archaeology of Food and Identity*, edited by Katheryn C. Twiss, 218–42. Center for Archaeological Investigations, Occasional Paper No. 34. Carbondale: Southern Illinois University, 2006.

Dillehay, Tom D., Jack Rossen, Thomas C. Andres, and David E. Williams. "Preceramic Adoption of Peanut, Squash, and Cotton in Northern Peru." *Science* 316, no. 5833 (June 29, 2007): 1890–93.

Dogan, Bilge, and Ummuhan Gokovali. "Geographical Indications: The Aspects of Rural Development and Marketing through the Traditional Products." *Procedia: Social and Behavioral Sciences* 62 (2012): 761–65.

Douglas, Mary. *Purity and Danger: An Analysis of Concepts of Pollution and Taboo.* New York: Routledge, 2003.

Dove, Michael R. "The Agronomy of Memory and the Memory of Agronomy: Ritual Conservation of Archaic Cultigens in Contemporary Farming Systems." In *Ethnoecology: Situated Knowledge/Located Lives,* edited by Virginia D. Nazarea, 45–70. Tucson: University of Arizona Press, 1999.

———. *The Banana Tree at the Gate: A History of Marginal Peoples and Global Markets in Borneo.* New Haven, CT: Yale University Press, 2011.

DuPuis, E. Melanie. *Nature's Perfect Food: How Milk Became America's Drink.* New York: New York University Press, 2002.

Earle, Rebecca. *The Body of the Conquistador: Food, Race and the Colonial Experience in Spanish America, 1492–1700.* Cambridge: Cambridge University Press, 2012.

———. *The Return of the Native: Indians and Myth-Making in Spanish America, 1810–1930.* Durham, NC: Duke University Press, 2007.

Egoávil, Mario, Jorge Reinoso, and Hugo A. Torres. "Análisis de los costos y canales de comercialización de la quinua." Fomento de la producción agroindustrial de quinua en el Departamento de Puno. Lima: Fondo Simón Bolívar, Ministerio de Agricultura y Alimentación, Instituto Interamericano de Ciencias Agrícolas, Universidad Nacional Técnica del Altiplano, 1979.

———. "Comercialización de la quinua en el altiplano peruano." Seminario de Historia Rural Andina. Lima: Universidad Nacional Mayor de San Marcos, 1983.

Eiselen, Elizabeth. "Quinoa: A Potentially Important Food Crop of the Andes." *Journal of Geography* 55, no. 7 (1956): 330–33.

El Comercio. "Algunos envíos de quinua peruana fueron rechazados en EE.UU.," December 17, 2014. https://elcomercio.pe/economia/peru/envios-quinua-peruana-rechazados-ee-uu-181901-noticia/.

Elmer, L. A. "Quinua (Chenopodium Quinoa)." *East African Agricultural Journal* 8, no. 1 (July 1, 1942): 21–23.

Escobar, Arturo. *Encountering Development: The Making and Unmaking of the Third World.* Princeton, NJ: Princeton University Press, 1995.

Fabricant, Florence. "America Embraces Its Native Foods." *New York Times,* November 16, 1994, sec. C.

———. "Quinoa, Andean Legacy, Arrives." *New York Times,* February 12, 1986, sec. C.

Faier, Lieba. "Fungi, Trees, People, Nematodes, Beetles, and Weather: Ecologies of Vulnerability and Ecologies of Negotiation in Matsutake Commodity Exchange." *Environment and Planning A: Economy and Space* 43, no. 5 (May 1, 2011): 1079–97.

Fairlie Reinoso, Alan. *Cadena exportadora y políticas de gestión ambiental de la quinua en el Perú*. Crecimiento verde e inclusivo. Ayacucho: Red LATN, 2015.

———. *La quinua en el Perú: Cadena exportadora y políticas de gestión ambiental*. Lima: Pontificia Universidad Católica del Perú. Instituto de Ciencias de la Naturaleza, Territorio y Energías Renovables, 2016.

Fan, Judith E. "Can Ideas about Food Inspire Real Social Change? The Case of Peruvian Gastronomy." *Gastronomica* 13, no. 2 (2013): 29–40.

FAO. *FAOSTAT Statistical Database*. [Rome]: FAO, 1997–.

———. "International Year of Quinoa Objectives." UN Food and Agriculture Organization, 2013. www.fao.org/quinoa-2013/iyq/objectives/.

———. *Labelling and Certification Schemes for Indigenous Peoples' Foods—Generating Income While Protecting and Promoting Indigenous Peoples' Values*. Rome: United Nations Food and Agriculture Organization, Alliance of Biodiversity, International Center for Tropical Agriculture, 2022.

———. "Launch of the International Year of Quinoa." *FAO News*, February 20, 2013. www.fao.org/quinoa-2013/press-room/news/detail/en/.

———. *Master Plan for the International Year of Quinoa: A Future Sown Thousands of Years Ago*. Rome: FAO, 2013.

———. *Quinoa: An Ancient Crop to Contribute to World Food Security*. UN Food and Agriculture Organization, Regional Office for Latin America and the Caribbean, July 2011.

FAO and Biodiversity International. *Concept Note—Celebrating the International Year of Quinoa: A Future Sown Thousands of Years Ago*. UN Food and Agriculture Organization/Biodiversity International, June 2012.

FDA. "Import Refusals Database." United States Food and Drug Administration, 2016. www.accessdata.fda.gov/scripts/importrefusals.

———. *Pesticide Residue Monitoring Program Fiscal Year 2015 Pesticide Report*. United States Food and Drug Administration, 2015. www.fda.gov/food/foodborneillness contaminants/pesticides/default.htm.

Ferguson, James. *The Anti-Politics Machine: Development, Depoliticization, and Bureaucratic Power in Lesotho*. New York: Cambridge University Press, 1990.

———. *Expectations of Modernity: Myths and Meanings of Urban Life on the Zambian Copperbelt*. Berkeley: University of California Press, 1999.

Ferraro, Emilia. "Trueque: An Ethnographic Account of Barter, Trade and Money in Andean Ecuador." *Journal of Latin American and Caribbean Anthropology* 16, no. 1 (2011): 168–84.

Ferroni, M. A. "Food Habits and the Apparent Nature and Extent of Dietary Nutritional Deficiencies in the Peruvian Andes." *Archivos Latino-Americanos de Nutrición* 32 (1982): 850–66.

Finnis, Elizabeth, ed. *Reimagining Marginalized Foods: Global Processes, Local Places*. Tucson: University of Arizona Press, 2012.

Fischer, Edward F., and Peter Benson. *Broccoli and Desire: Global Connections and Maya Struggles in Postwar Guatemala*. Stanford, CA: Stanford University Press, 2006.

Fischer, Edward F., and Bart Victor. "High-End Coffee and Smallholding Growers in Guatemala." *Latin American Research Review* 49, no. 1 (2014): 155–77.

Flores Galindo, Alberto. *Buscando un inca: Identidad y utopía en los andes*. Lima: Editorial Horizonte, 1988.

Flores Ochoa, Jorge. "Enqa, Enqaychu illa y Khuya Rumi: Aspectos mágico-religiosos entre pastores." *Journal de la société des américanistes* 63, no. 1 (1974): 245–62.

——, ed. *Pastores de puna: Uywamichiq punarunakuna*. Lima: Instituto de Estudios Peruanos, 1977.

Food and Agriculture Organization of the United Nations. "Graziano Da Silva: FAO destaca logros en Año Internacional de la Quinua." Posted December 17, 2013. YouTube video. www.youtube.com/watch?v=geiTlXWCyzM.

Foucault, Michel. *The Will to Knowledge*. Vol. 1, *The History of Sexuality*. London: Allen Lane, 1976.

Freidburg, Susanne. *French Beans and Food Scares: Culture and Commerce in an Anxious Age*. New York: Oxford University Press, 2004.

——. *Fresh: A Perishable History*. Cambridge, MA: Harvard University Press, 2010.

Fu, Jia-Chen. *The Other Milk: Reinventing Soy in Republican China*. Seattle: University of Washington Press, 2018.

Fuentes, Carmen. "Gastón Acurio: Perú es la nueva despensa europea." *ABC Español*, January 20, 2007. www.abc.es/hemeroteca/historico-20-01-2007/abc/Sabados/gaston-acurio-peru-es-la-nueva-despensa-europea_1631017185790.html.

Gade, Daniel. "Carl Troll on Nature and Culture in the Andes." *Erdkunde* 50, no. 4 (1996): 301–16.

Galeano, Eduardo. *Las venas abiertas de América Latina*. Mexico City: Siglo XXI Editores, 1971.

Galvin, Shaila Seshia. *Becoming Organic: Nature and Agriculture in the Indian Himalaya*. New Haven, CT: Yale University Press, 2021.

——. "The Farming of Trust: Organic Certification and the Limits of Transparency in Uttarakhand, India." *American Ethnologist* 45, no. 4 (2018): 495–507.

Gamboa, Cindybell, Monica Schuster, Eddie Schrevens, Miet Maertens, Cindybell Gamboa, Monica Schuster, Eddie Schrevens, and Miet Maertens. "Price Volatility and Quinoa Consumption among Smallholder Producers in the Andes." *Scientia Agropecuaria* 11, no. 1 (January 2020): 113–25.

Gandolfo, Daniella. *The City at Its Limits: Taboo, Transgression, and Urban Renewal in Lima*. Chicago: University of Chicago Press, 2009.

García, María Elena. "Devouring the Nation: Gastronomy and the Settler-Colonial Sublime in Peru." *Latin American and Caribbean Ethnic Studies* 17 (2020): 99–126.

——. *Gastropolitics and the Specter of Race: Stories of Capital, Culture, and Coloniality in Peru*. Oakland: University of California Press, 2021.

——. *Making Indigenous Citizens: Identities, Education, and Multicultural Development in Peru*. Stanford, CA: Stanford University Press, 2005

——. "The Taste of Conquest: Colonialism, Cosmopolitics, and the Dark Side of Peru's Gastronomic Boom." *Journal of Latin American and Caribbean Studies* 18, no. 3 (2013): 505–24.

Garfield, Seth. *Guaraná: How Brazil Embraced the World's Most Caffeine-Rich Plant.* Chapel Hill: University of North Carolina Press, 2023.

Garth, Hanna. *Food in Cuba: The Pursuit of a Decent Meal.* Stanford, CA: Stanford University Press, 2020.

Gascón, J. "De la quinua al arroz: Cambios en los patrones alimenticios de la sociedad andina." *Debate Agrario: Análisis y Alternativas* 27 (1998): 59–98.

Gelles, Paul. "Andean Culture, Indigenous Identity, and the State of Peru." In *The Politics of Ethnicity: Indigenous Peoples and Latin American States,* edited by David Maybury-Lewis, 239–66. Cambridge, MA: David Rockefeller Center Series on Latin American Studies, Harvard University, 2002.

Gereffi, Gary, John Humphrey, and Timothy Sturgeon. "The Governance of Global Value Chains." *Review of International Political Economy* 12, no. 1 (2005): 78–104.

Gereffi, Gary, and Miguel Korzeniewicz. *Commodity Chains and Global Capitalism.* London: Bloomsbury, 1993.

Gestión. "EE.UU. permitirá el ingreso de quinua peruana tratada con fungicidas." December 24, 2015. https://gestion.pe/economia/ee-uu-permitira-ingreso-quinua -peruana-tratada-fungicidas-107819-noticia/.

———. "Quinua peruana baja de precio por malas prácticas de agricultores de la costa." April 6, 2015. https://gestion.pe/economia/quinua-peruana-baja-precio -malas-practicas-agricultores-costa-91601.

———. "Senasa gestiona la aprobación de nuevas tolerancias de plaguicidas para cultivos de kiwicha, cañigua y quinua." March 19, 2016. https://gestion.pe/economia /senasa-gestiona-aprobacion-nuevas-tolerancias-plaguicidas-cultivos-kiwicha -canigua-quinua-114750-noticia/.

Gómez Tovar, Laura, Lauren Martin, Manuel Angel Gómez Cruz, and Tad Mutersbaugh. "Certified Organic Agriculture in Mexico: Market Connections and Certification Practices in Large and Small Producers." In "Certifying Rural Spaces: Quality-Certified Products and Rural Governance, special issue, *Journal of Rural Studies* 21, no. 4 (October 1, 2005): 461–74.

Gómez-Pando, Luz, Ángel Mujica, E. Chura, A. Canahua, A. Perez, A. Tejada, A. Villantoy, M. Pocco, V. Gonzales, S. Marca, and W. Ccoñas. "Contexto del cultivo en su área originaria: Perú." In *Estado del Arte de la Quinua en el Mundo en 2013,* edited by Didier Bazile, 450–61. Santiago de Chile and Montpelier: FAO and CIRAD, 2014.

Gomez-Pando, Luz Rayda, Enrique Aguilar-Castellanos, and Martha Ibañez-Tremolada. "Quinoa (Chenopodium Quinoa Willd.) Breeding." In *Advances in Plant Breeding Strategies: Cereals,* edited by Jameel M. Al-Khayri, Shri Mohan Jain, and Dennis V. Johnson, 5:259–316. Cham: Springer International Publishing, 2019.

Goodman, David. "The Quality 'Turn' and Alternative Food Practices: Reflections and Agenda." In "International Perspectives on Alternative Agro-Food Networks: Quality, Embeddedness, Bio-Politics," special issue, *Journal of Rural Studies* 19, no. 1 (January 1, 2003): 1–7.

Gootenberg, Paul Eliot. *Between Silver and Guano: Commercial Policy and the State in Postindependence Peru.* Princeton, NJ: Princeton University Press, 1989.

Gotkowitz, Laura, ed. *Histories of Race and Racism: The Andes and Mesoamerica from Colonial Times to the Present.* Durham, NC: Duke University Press, 2011.

Graeber, David. *Toward an Anthropological Theory of Value.* New York: Palgrave, 2001.

Greene, Shane. "Entre Lo Indio, Lo Negro, y Lo Incaico: The Spatial Hierarchies of Difference in Multicultural Peru." *Journal of Latin American and Caribbean Anthropology* 12, no. 2 (2007): 441–74.

———. "Getting Over the Andes: The Geo-Eco-Politics of Indigenous Movements in 21st Century Inca Empire." *Journal of Latin American Studies* 38, no. 2 (2006): 327–54.

———. "The Shaman's Needle: Development, Shamanic Agency, and Intermedicality in Aguaruna Lands, Peru." *American Ethnologist* 25, no. 4 (November 1, 1998): 634–58.

———. "Todos Somos Iguales, Todos Somos Incas: Dilemmas of Afro-Peruvian Citizenship and Inca Whiteness in Peru." In *Comparative Perspectives on Afro-Latin America*, edited by Kwame Dixson and John Burdick, 282–304. Gainesville: University Press of Florida, 2012.

Grey, Sam, and Lenore Newman. "Beyond Culinary Colonialism: Indigenous Food Sovereignty, Liberal Multiculturalism, and the Control of Gastronomic Capital." *Agriculture and Human Values* 35, no. 3 (September 1, 2018): 717–30.

Grillo, Ralph David, and Roderick L Stirrat. *Discourses of Development: Anthropological Perspectives.* New York: Berg, 1997.

Guillet, David W. "Reciprocal Labor and Peripheral Capitalism in the Central Andes." *Ethnology* 19, no. 2 (1980): 151–67.

Guthman, Julie. *Agrarian Dreams: The Paradox of Organic Farming in California.* Berkeley: University of California Press, 2004.

———. "Fast Food/Organic Food: Reflexive Tastes and the Making of 'Yuppie Chow.'" *Social & Cultural Geography* 4, no. 1 (2003): 45–58.

———. *The Problem with Solutions: Why Silicon Valley Can't Hack the Future of Food.* Oakland: University of California Press, 2024.

———. "'A Really Good Story Behind It': Moringa Bars and Venture Capital Funding." In *Critical Approaches to Superfoods*, edited by Emma McDonell and Richard Wilk, 79–94. London: Bloomsbury, 2020.

Guy, Kolleen. *When Champagne Became French.* Baltimore, MD: Johns Hopkins University Press, 2003.

Hall, Derek. "Where the Streets Are Paved with Prawns: Crop Booms and Migration in Southeast Asia." *Critical Asian Studies* 43, no. 4 (December 1, 2011): 507–30.

Haraway, Donna. "Anthropocene, Capitalocene, Plantationocene, Chthulucene: Making Kin." *Environmental Humanities* 6, no. 1 (May 1, 2015): 159–65.

Haushofer, Lisa. *Wonder Foods: The Science and Commerce of Nutrition.* Oakland: University of California Press, 2022.

Hayden, Cori. *When Nature Goes Public: The Making and Unmaking of Bioprospecting in Mexico.* Princeton, NJ: Princeton University Press, 2003.

Hayes-Conroy, Jessica, Adele Hite, Kendra Klein, Charlotte Biltekoff, and Aya H. Kimura. "Doing Nutrition Differently." *Gastronomica: The Journal of Food and Culture* 14, no. 3 (August 2014): 56–66.

Heldke, Lisa. *Exotic Appetites: Ruminations of a Food Adventurer*. New York: Routledge, 2003.

Hester, Jessica Leigh. "Save The Fleet, Eat Less Wheat: The Patriotic History of Ditching Bread." *NPR*, February 23, 2016. www.npr.org/sections/thesalt/2016/02 /23/466956650/save-the-fleet-eat-less-wheat-the-patriotic-history-of-ditching -bread.

Hetherington, Kregg. *Guerrilla Auditors: The Politics of Transparency in Neoliberal Paraguay*. Durham, NC: Duke University Press, 2011.

Higuchi, Angie, Rocío Maehara, Roger Merino, Franklin Ibáñez, and María Matilde Schwalb. "Presence of Internationally Banned Pesticides in Domestic Peruvian Quinoa during COVID-19 Pandemic." *Agrociencia* 57, no. 3 (2023): 564–88.

Higuchi, Angie, L. Emilio Morales, L. A. Sánchez-Pérez, and Rocío Maehara. "The Influence of Ethnic Identity on Peruvian Quinoa Consumption: A Top Lima and Modern Metropolitan Lima Approach." *Journal of Ethnic Foods* 9, no. 1 (September 23, 2022): 39.

Hirsch, Eric. *Acts of Growth: Development and the Politics of Abundance in Peru*. Stanford, CA: Stanford University Press, 2022.

Ho, Soleil. "#FoodGentrification and Culinary Rebranding of Traditional Foods." *Bitch Media*, January 23, 2014. www.bitchmedia.org/post/foodgentrification-and -culinary-rebranding-of-traditional-foods.

Hobart, Hiʻilei Julia. "A 'Queer-Looking Compound': Race, Abjection, and the Politics of Hawaiian Poi." *Global Food History* 3, no. 2 (2017): 133–49.

Hobsbawm, Eric, and Terence Ranger. *The Invention of Tradition*. New York: Cambridge University Press, 1983.

Hopkins, Terrence, and Immanuel Wallerstein. "Commodity Chains in the World Economy Prior to 1800." *Review* 10, no. 1 (1986): 157–70.

———. "Patterns of Development of the Modern World-System." *Review* 1, no. 2 (1977): 11–145.

IICA. *El mercado y la producción de quinua en el Perú*. Lima: Instituto Interamericano de Cooperación para la Agricultura, 2015.

INDECOPI. *Productos banderos del Perú*. Guia informativa. Instituto Nacional de Defensa de la Competencia y de la Protección de la Propiedad Intelectual, 2013.

INEI. *Censo nacional agropecuario*. Lima, Peru: Instituto Nacional de Estadística e Informatica, 2012.

Instituto Interamericano de Cooperación para la Agricultura. *Curso de quinua*. Lima: Fondo Simón Bolivar, Ministerio de Alimentación, Instituto Interamericano de Ciencias Agricolas, Universidad Nacional Técnica del Altiplano, 1977.

Instituto Nacional de Estadística e Informática. *Perú: Evolución de la pobreza monetaria, 2011–2022*. Informe Técnico. Lima: Instituto Nacional de Estadística e Informática, 2023.

———. *Puno: Resultados definitivos.* Lima: Instituto Nacional de Estadística e Informática, 2018.

Instituto Peruano de Economía. "Puno: Radiografía económica de la región del sur." January 11, 2023. www.ipe.org.pe/portal/puno-radiografia-economica-de-la-region-del-sur/.

International Development Research Centre. *Scaling up Quinoa Value Chain to Improve Food and Nutritional Security in the Rural/Poor Communities of Morocco.* July 15, 2022. https://idrc-crdi.ca/en/project/scaling-quinoa-value-chain-improve-food-and-nutritional-security-ruralpoor-communities.

International Trade Centre. "Product 100850: Quinoa "Cheonopium Quinoa." *Trade Statistics,* 2023. https://intracen.org/resources/data-and-analysis/trade-statistics#export-of-goods.

ITINTEC. *Norma técnica peruana: Quinua y cañihua.* Instituto de Investigación Tecnológica Industrial y de Normas Técnicas 205.036:1982, issued 1982.

Ives, Sarah. *Steeped in Heritage: The Racial Politics of South African Rooibos Tea.* Durham, NC: Duke University Press, 2017.

Jacobsen, Nils. *Mirages of Transition: The Peruvian Altiplano, 1780–1930.* Berkeley: University of California Press, 1993.

Jacobsen, Sven Erik. "The Worldwide Potential for Quinoa (Chenopodium Quinoa Willd.)." *Food Reviews International* 19, nos. 1–2 (2003): 167–77.

Janer, Zilkia. "(In)Edible Nature: New World Food and Coloniality." *Cultural Studies* 21, nos. 2/3 (2007): 385–405.

Jarvis, David E., Yung Shwen Ho, Damien J. Lightfoot, Sandra M. Schmöckel, Bo Li, Theo J. A. Borm, Hajime Ohyanagi, et al. "The Genome of Chenopodium Quinoa." *Nature* 542, no. 7641 (February 2017): 307–12.

Jasanoff, Sheila. "Biotechnology and Empire: The Global Power of Seeds and Science." *Osiris* 21, no. 1 (January 2006): 273–92.

Johnston, Josée, and Shyon Baumann. "The Culinary Other: Seeking Exoticism." In *Foodies: Democracy and Distinction in the Gourmet Foodscape*, edited by Josée Johnston and Shyon Baumann, 97–118. New York: Routledge, 2010.

———, eds. *Foodies: Democracy and Distinction in the Gourmet Foodscape.* London: Routledge, 2014.

Johnston Taylor, Susan. "Cooking for a Cleaner Environment." *The Hub,* 2020. https://phys.org/news/2020-04-cooking-cleaner-environment-biomass-health.html.

Jones, Bradley M. "Producing Heritage: Politics, Patrimony, and Palatability in the Reinvention of Lowcountry Cuisine." *Food, Culture & Society* 20, no. 2 (2017): 217–36.

Jordan, Jennifer A. "The Heirloom Tomato as Cultural Object: Investigating Taste and Space." *Sociologia Ruralis* 47, no. 1 (2007): 20–41.

Jovanovic, Zorica, Radmila Stikic, and Sven-Erik Jacobsen. "Climate Change: Challenge of Introducing Quinoa in Southeast European Agriculture." In *Biology and Biotechnology of Quinoa: Super Grain for Food Security*, edited by Ajit Varma, 345–71. Singapore: Springer, 2021.

Judkis, Maura. "'This Is Not a Trend': Native American Chefs Resist the 'Columbusing' of Indigenous Foods." *Washington Post*, April 9, 2023. www.washingtonpost.com /lifestyle/food/this-is-not-a-trend-native-american-chefs-resist-the-columbusing -of-indigenous-foods/2017/11/21/a9ca5be6-c8ba-11e7-b0cf-7689a9f2d84e_story .html.

Kerr, W. A. "Enjoying a Good Port with a Clear Conscience: Geographic Indicators, Rent Seeking and Development." *Estey Centre Journal of International Law and Trade Policy* 7, no. 1 (2006): 1–14.

Kerssen, Tanya M. "Food Sovereignty and the Quinoa Boom: Challenges to Sustainable Re-Peasantisation in the Southern Altiplano of Bolivia." *Third World Quarterly* 36, no. 3 (2015): 489–507.

Kimura, Aya Hirata. *Hidden Hunger: Gender and the Politics of Smarter Foods.* Ithaca, NY: Cornell University Press, 2013.

King, A., M. Lenox, and M. L. Barnett. "Strategic Responses to the Reputation Commons Problem." In *Organizations, Policy and the Natural Environment: Institutional and Strategic Perspectives*, edited by A. J. Hoffman and M. J. Ventresca, 96–109. Stanford, CA: Stanford University Press, 2002.

Kloppenburg, Jack. *First the Seed: The Political Economy of Plant Biotechnology, 1492–2000.* New York: Cambridge University Press, 1988.

Kobayashi, Orion, and Mariano J. Beillard. *Peru Quinoa Price Fluctuation.* Global Agricultural Information Network. Lima: United States Department of Agriculture, Foreign Agricultural Service, July 6, 2016.

La Vanguardia. "Entrevista con Diego Muñoz." n.d.

Lane, Kris. *Potosí: The Silver City That Changed the World.* Oakland: University of California Press, 2021.

Latorre Farfán, Jean Paúl. "Is Quinoa Cultivation on the Coastal Desert of Peru Sustainable? A Case Study from Majes, Arequipa." Master's thesis, Aarhus Universitet, 2018.

Laudan, Rachel. *Cuisine and Empire: Cooking in World History.* Berkeley: University of California Press, 2013.

Lauer, M., and V. Lauer. *La revolución gastronómica peruana.* Lima: Universidad de San Martín de Porres, 2006.

Lauer, Mirko. *La cocina francesa y el Perú.* Lima: Universidad de San Martín de Porres., 2017.

LeBlanc, Hannah. "What Makes Food Super? The Post-Eugenic Promises of Fish Flour and Other Super Powders." In *Critical Approaches to Superfoods*, edited by Emma McDonell and Richard Wilk, 119–34. London: Bloomsbury, 2020.

Lewis, David, and David Mosse, eds. *Development Brokers and Translators.* Bloomfield, CT: Kumarian Press, 2006.

Li, Fabiana. "Materiality and the Politics of Seeds in the Global Expansion of Quinoa." *Food, Culture & Society* 26, no. 4 (August 8, 2023): 867–85.

———. *Unearthing Conflict: Corporate Mining, Activism, and Expertise in Peru.* Durham, NC: Duke University Press, 2015.

Li, Tania Murray. "Articulating Indigenous Identity in Indonesia: Resource Politics and the Tribal Slot." *Society for Comparative Study of Society and History* 42, no. 1 (2000): 149–79.

———. *Land's End: Capitalist Relations on an Indigenous Frontier*. Durham, NC: Duke University Press, 2014.

———. "What Is Land? Assembling a Resource for Global Investment." *Transactions of the Institute of British Geographers* 39, no. 4 (2014): 582–602.

———. *The Will to Improve: Governmentality, Development, and the Practice of Politics*. Durham, NC: Duke University Press, 2007.

Lipper, Leslie, and David Zilberman. "A Short History of the Evolution of the Climate Smart Agriculture Approach and Its Links to Climate Change and Sustainable Agriculture Debates." In *Climate Smart Agriculture: Building Resilience to Climate Change*, edited by Leslie Lipper, Nancy McCarthy, David Zilberman, Solomon Asfaw, and Giacomo Branca, 13–30. New York: Springer International Publishing, 2018.

López-Canales, Jorge. "Peru on a Plate: Coloniality and Modernity in Peru's High-End Cuisine." *Anthropology of Food*, no. 14 (June 6, 2019). https://doi.org/10.4000/aof.10138.

Loyer, Jessica, and Christine Knight. "Selling the 'Inca Superfood': Nutritional Primitivism in Superfoods Books and Maca Marketing." *Food, Culture & Society* 21, no. 4 (August 8, 2018): 449–67. https://doi.org/10.1080/15528014.2018.1480645.

Lyon, Sarah. "Just Java: Roasting Fair Trade Coffee." In *Fast Food/Slow Food: The Cultural Economy of the Global Food System*, edited by Richard Wilk and Melissa Caldwell, 241–58. Lanham, MD: Altamira, 2006.

Maliro, M. F. A., M. M. Abang, C. Mukankusi, M. Lung'aho, B. Fenta, S. Walderi, R. Kapa, O. A. Okiro, E. Koma, C. Mwaba, M. M. Isse, and D. Bazile. *Prospects for Quinoa Adaptation and Utilization in Eastern and Southern Africa: Technological, Institutional and Policy Considerations*. Addis Ababa: FAO, 2021.

Manrique, Nelson. *La piel y la pluma: Escritos sobre literatura, etnicidad y racismo*. Lima: Sur, 1999.

Mansfield, Becky. "Spatializing Globalization: A 'Geography of Quality' in the Seafood Industry." *Economic Geography* 79, no. 1 (2003): 1–16.

Marca Vilca, Saturnino, Wilber Chaucha Jove, Juan Carlos Quispe Quispe, and Vladimir Mamani Centón. *Comportamiento actual de los agentes de la cadena productiva de quinua en la región Puno*. Proyecto: Desarrollo de Capacidades de la Cadena Productiva de Quinua en la Región Puno. Puno: Gobierno Regional Puno, Dirección Regional Agraria Puno, 2011.

Mariátegui, José Carlos. *Siete ensayos de interpretación de la realidad peruana*. Lima: Biblioteca Ayacucho, 1928.

Markowitz, Lisa. "Highland Haute Cuisine: The Transformation of Alpaca Meat." In *Reimagining Marginalized Foods: Global Processes, Local Places*, edited by Elizabeth Finnis, 34–48. Tucson: University of Arizona Press, 2012.

Mathews, Andrew. "Scandals, Audits, and Fictions: Linking Climate Change to Mexican Forests." *Social Studies of Science* 44, no. 1 (2014): 82–108.

Matta, Raúl. "República gastronómica y país de cocineros: Comida, política, medios y una nueva idea de nación para el Perú." *Revista Colombiana de Antropología* 50, no. 2 (2014). www.scielo.org.co/scielo.php?script=sci_arttext&pid=S0486-65252014000200002.

———. "Unveiling the Neoliberal Taste: Peru's Media Representation as a Food Nation." In *Taste, Power, Tradition: Geographical Indications as Cultural Property*, edited by Sarah May, Katia Laura Sildali, Achim Spiller, and Bernhard Tschofen, 103–18. Göttingen Studies in Cultural Property, vol. 10. Göttingen: Göttingen University Press, 2017.

———. "Valuing Native Eating: The Modern Roots of Peruvian Food Heritage." *Anthropology of Food* 8 (2013). https://doi.org/10.4000/aof.7361.

Mayer, Enrique. *The Articulated Peasant: Household Economies in the Andes*. Cambridge, MA: Westview Press, 2002.

———. *Ugly Stories of the Peruvian Agrarian Reform*. Durham, NC: Duke University Press, 2009.

Mayer, Enrique, and Manuel Glave. "Alguito Para Ganar (a Little Something to Earn): Profits and Losses in Peasant Economies." *American Ethnologist* 26, no. 2 (1999): 344–69.

McDonell, Emma. "Creating the Culinary Frontier: A Critical Examination of Peruvian Chefs' Narratives of Lost/Discovered Foods." *Anthropology of Food*, no. 14 (June 6, 2019). https://doi.org/10.4000/AOF.10183.

———. "La Despensa Nacional: Quinoa and the Spatial Contradictions of Peru's Gastronomic Revolution." *Latin American Research Review* 59, no. 1 (March 2024): 84–104.

———. "The Miracle Crop as Boundary Object: Quinoa's Rise as a 'Neglected and Under-Utilized Species.'" In *Critical Approaches to Superfoods*, edited by Emma McDonell and Richard Wilk, 95–117. New York: Bloomsbury, 2020.

———. "Miracle Foods: Quinoa, Curative Metaphors, and the Depoliticization of Global Hunger Politics." *Gastronomica: The Journal of Critical Food Studies* 15, no. 4 (2015): 70–85.

———. "Nutrition Politics in the Quinoa Boom: Connecting Consumer and Producer Nutrition in the Commercialization of Traditional Foods." *International Journal of Nutrition* (January 2016). http://dx.doi.org/10.15436/2377-0619.16.1212.

McDonell, Emma, and Richard Wilk, eds. *Critical Approaches to Superfoods*. New York: Bloomsbury Academic, 2020.

McFarlane, C. "Translocal Assemblages: Space, Power and Social Movements." *Geoforum* 40, no. 3 (2009): 561–67.

Medina, G. *Formalización de la minería en pequeña escala: Porque? Y como?* Lima: Better Gold Initiative Project, 2014.

Megyesi, Boldizsár, and Károly Mike. "Organising Collective Reputation: An Ostromian Perspective." *International Journal of the Commons* 10, no. 2 (September 9, 2016): 1082–99.

Mendelson, Anne. *Chow Chop Suey: Food and the Chinese American Journey*. New York: Columbia University Press, 2016.

Méndez, Cecilia. "Incas Sí, Indios No: Notes on Peruvian Creole Nationalism and Its Contemporary Crisis." *Journal of Latin American Studies* 28, no. 1 (February 1996): 197–225.

Mercado, Waldemar, and Karina Ubillus. "Characterization of Producers and Quinoa Supply Chains in the Peruvian Regions of Puno and Junin." *Scientia Agropecuaria* 8, no. 3 (2017): 251–65.

Mesa de Trabajo de la Quinua, Puno. *Plan Operativo de La Quinua Región Puno.* Puno, Perú: Ministerio de Comercio Exterior y Turismo; Kipu Internacional, 2006.

Miklavcic, Alessandra, and Marie Nathalie LeBlanc. "Culture Brokers, Clinically Applied Ethnography, and Cultural Mediation." In *Cultural Consultation: Encountering the Other in Mental Health Care,* edited by Laurence J. Kirmayer, Jaswant Guzder, and Cécile Rousseau, 115–37. International and Cultural Psychology. New York: Springer, 2014.

Ministerio de Agricultura. *Análisis económico de la producción nacional de la quinua.* Boletin. Lima: Dirección General de Políticas Agrarias/Dirección de Estudios Económicos e Información Agraria, 2017.

———. *Aspectos económicos en el cultivo de la quinua (provincios de Puno, Chucuito, Lampa, San Román, Dpto. de Puno), Zona Agraria XII.* Aspectos Económicos. Lima: Ministerio de Agricultura, Oficina General de Estadística, 1973.

———. "MINAGRI y FDA de EEUU coordinan acciones para asegurar inocuidad de agroexportaciones de quinua." Lima: Ministerio de Agricultura, December 18, 2014. www.midagri.gob.pe/portal/notas-de-prensa/notas-de-prensa-2014/11879-senasa-y-fda-de-eeuu-coordinan-acciones-para-asegurar-inocuidad-de-agroexportaciones-de-quinua.

———. *La quinua: Producción y comercio del Perú.* Boletín. Lima: MINAGRI, 2017.

———. *Quinua peruana: Situación actual y perspectivas en el mercado nacional e internacional al 2015.* Lima: Ministerio de Agricultura/Dirección de Políticas Agrarias/Dirección de Estudios Económicos e Informacion Agraria, 2015.

Mintz, Sidney W. *Sweetness and Power: The Place of Sugar in Modern History.* New York: Penguin Books, 1985.

Mishan, Ligaya, Patricia Heal, and Martin Bourne. "The Humble Beginnings of Today's Culinary Delicacies." *New York Times,* November 26, 2021, sec. T Magazine. www.nytimes.com/2021/11/26/t-magazine/humble-foods-poverty.html.

Mitchell, Jerry T., and William C. Terry. "Contesting Pisco: Chile, Peru, and the Politics of Trade." *Geographical Review* 101, no. 4 (October 1, 2011): 518–35.

Molinié, Anotoinette. "The Resurrection of the Inca: The Role of Indian Representations in the Invention of the Peruvian Nation." *History and Anthropology* 15, no. 3 (2004): 233–50.

Molz, Jennie Germann. "Eating Difference: The Cosmopolitan Mobilities of Culinary Tourism." *Space and Culture* 10, no. 1 (February 1, 2007): 77–93.

Montenegro de Wit, Maywa. "Stealing into the Wild: Conservation Science, Plant Breeding and the Makings of New Seed Enclosures." *Journal of Peasant Studies* 44, no. 1 (January 2, 2017): 169–212.

Moore, Jason W. "'Amsterdam Is Standing on Norway' Part II: The Global North Atlantic in the Ecological Revolution of the Long Seventeenth Century." *Journal of Agrarian Change* 10, no. 2 (2010): 188–227.

———. "Transcending the Metabolic Rift: A Theory of Crises in the Capitalist World-Ecology." *Journal of Peasant Studies* 38, no. 1 (2011): 1–46.

Morales, Luis Emilio, and Angie Higuchi. "Who Is Eating Quinoa? How Consumer Characteristics and Beliefs Affect the Expenditure on This Functional Food versus Traditional Staple Items." *Journal of Sensory Studies* 37, no. 2 (2022): e12725.

Morán, Iker. "Gastón Acurio: 'todos hacemos política, y yo la hago desde la cocina.'" *20 Minutos* (blog), February 9, 2016. http://blogs.20minutos.es/la-gulateca/2016/02/09/gaston-acurio-todos-hacemos-politica-y-yo-la-hago-desde-la-cocina/.

Morgan, Kevin, Terry Marsden, and Jonathan Murdoch. *Worlds of Food: Place, Power, and Provenance in the Food Chain.* Oxford: Oxford University Press, 2009.

Mozaffarian, Dariush, Irwin Rosenberg, and Ricardo Uauy. "History of Modern Nutrition Science—Implications for Current Research, Dietary Guidelines, and Food Policy." *BMJ* 361 (June 13, 2018): k2392.

Mudry, Jessica, Jessica Hayes-Conroy, Nancy Chen, and Aya H. Kimura. "Other Ways of Knowing Food." *Gastronomica: The Journal of Food and Culture* 14, no. 3 (August 2014): 27–33.

Muehlmann, Shaylih. "How Do Real Indians Fish? Neoliberal Multiculturalism and Contested Indigeneities in the Colorado Delta." *American Anthropologist* 111, no. 4 (2009): 468–79.

Mujica, A., S. E. Jacobsen, J. Izquierdo, and J. P. Marathee. *Resultados de la prueba americana y europea de la quinua.* Puno: UN Food and Agriculture Organization, Universidad Nacional del Altiplano, Centro Internacional de la Papa, 2001.

Münster, Daniel. "'Ginger Is a Gamble': Crop Booms, Rural Uncertainty, and the Neoliberalization of Agriculture in South India." *Focaal* 71 (2015): 100–113.

Murdoch, James. "Co-Constructing the Countryside: Hybrid Networks and the Extensive Self." In *Country Visions*, edited by Paul Cloke, 263–80. London: Prentice Hall, 2003.

Murdoch, Jonathan. "Inhuman/Nonhuman/Human: Actor-Network Theory and the Prospects for a Nondualistic and Symmetrical Perspective on Nature and Society." *Environment and Planning D* 15, no. 6 (1997): 731–56.

Murra, John V. "El 'control vertical' de un máximo de pisos ecológicos el la economía de las sociedades andinas." In *Formaciones ecónomicas y políticas del mundo andino*, 2nd ed., edited by J. V. Murra, 427–76. Huánuco, Peru: Universidad Nacional Hermilio Valdizán, 1972.

Mutersbaugh, Tad. "Serve and Certify: Paradoxes of Service Work in Organic-Coffee Certification." *Environment and Planning D: Society and Space* 22, no. 4 (2004): 533–52.

Neimark, Benjamin, Sarah Osterhoudt, Lloyd Blum, and Timothy Healy. "Mob Justice and 'The Civilized Commodity.'" *Journal of Peasant Studies* 48, no. 4 (June 7, 2021): 734–53.

New York Times. "Charming Botanical Strangers to Be Naturalized." January 5, 1913, sec. M.

———. "Paraguay Gains in Fight on Malnutrition, An Economic Paradox in South America." January 4, 1949.

Nolte, Gaspar E. *Quinoa Outlook*. Global Agricultural Information Network. Lima: United States Department of Agriculture, Foreign Agricultural Service, December 23, 2014.

Nonini, Donald M. "The Global Idea of 'the Commons.'" *Social Analysis: The International Journal of Social and Cultural Practice* 50, no. 3 (December 1, 2006): 164–77.

NRC. *Lost Crops of the Incas: Little-Known Plants of the Andes with Promise for Worldwide Cultivation*. Washington, DC: National Research Council, 1989.

———. *Underexploited Tropical Plants with Promising Economic Value*. Report of an Ad Hoc Panel of the Advisory Committee on Technology Innovation, Board on Science and Technology for International Development, Commission on International Relations. Washington, DC: The National Academies Press, 1975.

Ødegaard, Cecilie Vindal. "Border Multiplicities: At the Cross-Roads between Improvisation and Regulation in the Andes." *Journal of Borderlands Studies* 31, no. 1 (January 2, 2016): 23–38.

Ofstehage, Andrew. "The Gift of the Middleman: An Ethnography of Quinoa Trading Networks in Los Lipez of Bolivia." Master's thesis, Wageningen University, 2010.

———. "Nusta Juira's Gift of Quinoa: Peasants, Trademarks, and Intermediaries in the Transformation of a Bolivian Commodity Economy." *Anthropology of Work Review* 32, no. 2 (2011): 103–14.

O'Hagan, Lauren Alex. "Celebrity Greens Kale and Seaweed Were Long Considered Food of Last Resort." The Conversation, November 21, 2019. http://the conversation.com/celebrity-greens-kale-and-seaweed-were-long-considered-food -of-last-resort-124663.

Orlove, Benjamin S. *The Allure of the Foreign: Imported Goods in Postcolonial Latin America*. Ann Arbor: University of Michigan Press, 1997.

———. *Alpacas, Sheep, and Men: The Wool Export Economy in Regional Society in Southern Peru*. New York: Academic Press, 1977.

———. "Down to Earth: Race and Substance in the Andes." *Bulletin of Latin American Research* 17, no. 2 (1998): 207–22.

———. "The Past, the Present, and Some Possible Future of Adaptation." In *Adapting to Climate Change*, edited by Neil Adger, Irene Lorenzoni, and Karen O'Brien, 131–63. Cambridge: Cambridge University Press, 2009.

———. "Stability and Change in Highland Andean Dietary Patterns." In *Food and Evolution: Toward a Theory of Human Food Habits*, edited by Marvin Harris and Eric B. Ross, 481–515. Philadelphia: Temple University Press, 2009.

Osterhoudt, Sarah, Shaila Seshia Galvin, Dana J. Graef, Alder Keleman Saxena, and Michael R. Dove. "Chains of Meaning: Crops, Commodities, and the 'In-between' Spaces of Trade." *World Development* 135 (November 1, 2020): 105070.

Osterhoudt, Sarah R. "'Nobody Wants to Kill': Economies of Affect and Violence in Madagascar's Vanilla Boom." *American Ethnologist* 47, no. 3 (August 2020): 249–63.

———. *Vanilla Landscapes: Meaning, Memory and the Cultivation of Place in Madagascar*. New York: New York Botanical Garden Press, 2017.

Ostrom, E. *Governing the Commons: The Evolution of Institutions for Collective Action*. New York: Cambridge University Press, 1990.

Padulosi, Stefano, Vernon Heywood, Danny Hunter, and Andy Jarvis. "Underutilized Species and Climate Change: Current Status and Outlook." In *Crop Adaptation to Climate Change*, edited by Shyam S. Yadav, Robert J. Redden, Jerry L. Hatfield, Hermann Lotze-Campen, Anthony E. Hall, 507–21. New York: John Wiley & Sons, 2011.

Palomino Gonzales, María Mercedes. "Gourmetización del alimento andino y la estetización del agricultor como parte del boom gastronómico peruano." *Razón y Palabra* 20, no. 94 (2016): 581–95.

———. "Quinua gourmet: Raza, estética y evolución del uso de la quinua en la alta cocina peruana." In *Sabores, Saberes: Comunicación y conocimientos en la cultura alimentaria*, edited by Karina Herrera Miller and Alfonso Gumucio Dagron, 119–38. La Paz, Bolivia: Plural Editores, 2019.

Pantaleón, Alberto Luis, Jose Carlos Montes, Liliana Milagros Portilla, Pedro Otoniel Morales, Ramiro Azañero, and Richard Ignacio Montes. "Dinámica de la producción y exportación de quinua (Chenopodium quinoa) en Perú." *Revista Alfa* 8, no. 22 (January 20, 2024): 84–94.

Parasecoli, Fabio. *Knowing Where It Comes From: Labelling Traditional Foods to Compete in a Global Market*. Iowa City: University of Iowa Press, 2017.

Parrott, Nicholas, Natasha Wilson, and Jonathan Murdoch. "Spatializing Quality: Regional Protection and the Alternative Geography of Food." *European Urban and Regional Studies* 9, no. 3 (July 1, 2002): 241–61.

Parry, Elsie. "Staff of Life—Peruvian Style." *Nature Magazine* 47 (1954): 16–18, 50.

Paxson, Heather. "Locating Value in Artisan Cheese: Reverse Engineering Terroir for New-World Landscapes." *American Anthropologist* 112, no. 3 (2010): 444–57.

Paz, Alejandro. "The Circulation of Chisme and Rumor: Gossip, Evidentiality, and Authority in the Perspective of Latino Labor Migrants in Israel." *Journal of Linguistic Anthropology* 19, no. 1 (2009): 117–43.

Pilcher, Jeffrey. *Que vivan los tamales: Food and the Making of Mexican Identity*. Albuquerque: University of New Mexico Press, 1998.

Ponte, Stefano. "Bans, Tests, and Alchemy: Food Safety Regulation and the Uganda Fish Export Industry." *Agriculture and Human Values* 24, no. 2 (April 26, 2007): 179–93.

Ponte, Stefano, and Peter Gibbon. "Quality Standards, Conventions and the Governance of Global Value Chains." *Economy and Society* 34, no. 1 (February 1, 2005): 1–31.

Popkin, Samuel L. *The Rational Peasant: The Political Economy of Rural Society in Vietnam*, Berkeley: University of California Press, 1979.

Pratt, Mary Louise. *Imperial Eyes: Travel Writing and Transculturation*. New York: Routledge, 1992.

Price, Lisa L., Gisella S. Cruz-Garcia, and Nemer E. Narchi. "Foods of Oppression." *Frontiers in Sustainable Food Systems* 5 (2021). www.frontiersin.org/articles/10 .3389/fsufs.2021.646907.

Power, Michael. *Audit Society: Rituals of Verification*. Oxford: Oxford University Press, 1999.

Quark, Amy A. *Global Rivalries: Standards Wars and the Transnational Cotton Trade*. Chicago: University of Chicago Press, 2013.

Quijano, Anibal, and Michael Ennis. "Coloniality of Power, Eurocentrism, and Latin America." *Nepantla: Views from South* 1, no. 3 (2000): 533–80.

Radcliffe, Sarah, and Sallie Westwood. *Remaking the Nation: Identity and Politics in Latin America*. London: Routledge, 1996.

Ramos, Julio, Jorge Reinoso, and Hugo Torres. *Estudio de factibilidad*. Fomento de la producción agroindustrial de la quinua. Lima: Ministerio de Agricultura y Alimentación, Instituto Interamericano de Ciencias Agrícolas, Instituto Nacional de Investigación Agraria, Instituto de Investigaciones Agroindustriales, Universidad Nacional Técnica del Altiplano, 1979.

Rao, Nanduri K. "Quinoa: A Future-Proof Crop for Climate-Smart Agriculture." Paper presented at the Global Forum for Innovations in Agriculture, Abu Dhabi, United Arab Emirates, 2016.

Rao, Sheila, and Chris Huggins. "Sweet 'Success': Contesting Biofortification Strategies to Address Malnutrition in Tanzania." In *Agronomy for Development: The Politics of Knowledge in Agricultural Research*, edited by James Sumberg, 104–20. London: Routledge, 2017.

Riles, Annelise. *Documents: Artifacts of Modern Knowledge*. Ann Arbor: University of Michigan Press, 2006.

Renique, José Luis. *La batalla por Puno: Conflicto local y nación en los andes peruanos*. Lima: Instituto de Estudios Peruanos, 2004.

———. "Puno es la otra cara de la historia limeñizada de nuestro país: Entrevista con José Luis Rénique." *La República*, December 13, 2004, sec. Redes Sociales. https://larepublica.pe/tendencias/312033-jose-luis-renique-puno-es-la-otra-cara -de-la-historia-limenizada-de-nuestro-pais/.

Rissing, Andrea, and Bradley M. Jones. "Landscapes of Value." *Economic Anthropology* 9, no. 2 (2022): 193–206.

Robinson, R. G. "Amaranth, Quinoa, Ragi, Tef, and Niger: Tiny Seeds of Ancient History and Modern Interest." In *Station Bulletin*. Minneapolis: Agricultural Experiment Station, University of Minnesota, 1986.

Rogers, Richard A. "From Cultural Exchange to Transculturation: A Review and Reconceptualization of Cultural Appropriation." *Communication Theory* 16, no. 4 (November 1, 2006): 474–503.

Romero, Simon. "Quinoa's Global Success Creates Quandary at Home." *New York Times*, March 19, 2011.

Roseberry, William, Lowell Gudmundson, and Mario Samper Kutschbach, eds. *Coffee, Society and Power in Latin America*. Baltimore, MD: Johns Hopkins University Press, 1995.

Ruiz, Karina B., Stefania Biondi, Rómulo Oses, Ian S. Acuña-Rodríguez, Fabiana Antognoni, Enrique A. Martinez-Mosqueira, Amadou Coulibaly, Alipio Canahua-Murillo, Milton Pinto, Andrés Zurita-Silva, Didier Bazile, Sven-Erik Jacobsen, and Marco A. Molina-Montenegro. "Quinoa Biodiversity and Sustainability for Food Security under Climate Change: A Review." *Agronomic Sustainable Development* 34 (2013): 349–59.

Salvatierra, Svetlana. "Reducir el precio de la quinua enfrenta el costo de producirla." *La Razón*, April 7, 2013. www.la-razon.com/financiero/2013/04/07/reducir-el-precio-de-la-quinua-enfrenta-el-costo-de-producirla/.

Sarreal, Julia J. S. *Yerba Mate: The Drink That Shaped a Nation*. Oakland: University of California Press, 2023.

Schaffer, Amanda. "The Quinoa Evangelist." *MIT Technology Review*, December 18, 2020. www.technologyreview.com/2020/12/18/1013014/the-quinoa-evangelist/.

Schlick, G., and D. L. Bubenhein. "Quinoa: Candidate Crop for NASA's Controlled Ecological Life Support Systems." In *Progress in New Crops*, edited by J. Janick, 632–40. Arlington, TX: American Society for Horticultural Sciences Press, 1999.

Scott, James C. *Seeing Like a State: How Certain Schemes to Improve the Human Condition Have Failed*. New Haven, CT: Yale University Press, 1998.

Scrinis, Gyorgy. "On the Ideology of Nutritionism." *Gastronomica* 8, no. 1 (2008): 39–48.

Seligmann, Linda J. *Quinoa: Food Politics and Agrarian Life in the Andean Highlands*. Urbana: University of Illinois Press, 2022.

———. "To Be In Between: The Cholas as Market Women." *Comparative Studies in Society and History* 31, no. 4 (October 1989): 694–721.

Shiva, Vandana. *Monocultures of the Mind: Perspectives on Biodiversity and Biotechnology*. London/Penang: Zed Books, 1993.

Simmel, Georg. "Fashion." *American Journal of Sociology* 62, no. 6 (1957): 541–58.

Skarbø, Kristine. "From Lost Crop to Lucrative Commodity: Conservation Implications of the Quinoa Renaissance." *Human Organization* 74, no. 1 (February 23, 2015): 86–99.

Slow Food International. "Good Practices." n.d. www.fondazioneslowfood.com/en/good-practices/.

Slow Food USA. "The Ark of Taste." n.d. https://slowfoodusa.org/ark-of-taste/.

Smith, Stephen, and Carolina Trivelli. *El consumo urbano de alimentos andinos tradicionales*. Lima: Instituto de Estudios Peruanos, 2001.

Solorio, Fortunata, and Esther Revilla. *Enfoques sobre alimentación andina*. Puno, Perú: Centro de Proyectos Integrales Andinos, 1992.

Soluri, John. *Banana Cultures: Agriculture, Consumption, and Environmental Change in Honduras and the United States*. Austin: University of Texas Press, 2009.

Soto, J., E. Valdivia, R. Valdivia, A. Cuadros, and R. Bravo. "Descripción de sistemas de rotación de cultivos en parcelas de producción de quinua en cuatro zonas
(siete distritos) del altiplano peruano." *CienciAgro* 2, no. 3 (2012): 391–402.

Soto Mendizábal, José Luis, Roberto Valdivia Fernández, and Claudia Solano Oré.
"Normas técnicas para quinua y su contribución al comercio." Paper presented at
the Congreso Mundial de la Quinua, Ibarra, Ecuador, July 8–12, 2013.

Stanford, Lois. "Constructing 'Quality': The Political Economy of Standards in Mexico's Avocado Industry." *Agriculture and Human Values* 19, no. 4 (December 1,
2002): 293–310.

Star, Susan L. "This Is Not a Boundary Object." *Science, Technology and Human
Values* 35 (2010): 601–17.

Star, Susan Leigh, and James R. Griesemer. "Institutional Ecology, 'Translations' and
Boundary Objects: Amateurs and Professionals in Berkeley's Museum of Verte-
brate Zoology, 1907–39." *Social Studies of Science* 19, no. 3 (1989): 387–560.

Starn, Orin. "Missing the Revolution: Anthropologists and the War in Peru." *Cultural Anthropology* 46, no. 1 (1991): 63–91.

Stevens, William. "Rediscovering the Lost Crop of the Incas." *New York Times*, October 31, 1989.

Strathern, Marilyn. *Audit Cultures: Anthropological Studies in Accountability, Ethics
and the Academy*. New York: Routledge, 2000.

Sumberg, James. *Agronomy for Development: The Politics of Knowledge in Agricultural
Research*. London: Routledge, 2017.

SUNAT, *Estadísticas de Comercio Exterior*. Superintendencia Nacional de Aduanas y
Administración Tributaria, 2020. www.sunat.gob.pe/estad-comExt/modelo_web
/web_estadistica.htm.

Tally, Steve. "National New Crops Symposium to Be Held Oct. 22 25." *Purdue News*,
July 1995.

Tapia, Mario E. *Cultivos andinos subexplotados y su aporte a la alimentatión*. Rome:
Food and Agriculture Organization, 1990.

———. *La quinua y la kañiwa: Cultivos andinos*. Bogotá: Instituto Interamericano
de Ciencias Agrícolas (IICA) y el Centro Internacional de Investigaciones para el
Desarrollo (CIID), Oficina Regional para América Latina, 1979.

Terrio, Susan. *Crafting the Culture and History of French Chocolate*. Berkeley: University of California Press, 2000.

Thier, Dave. "The Story of a Cursed Crop." *Atlantic*, January 20, 2010.

Thrupp, Lori Ann, ed. *Bittersweet Harvests for Global Supermarkets: Challenges in
Latin America's Agricultural Export Boom*. Washington, DC: World Resources
Institute, 1995.

Tilghman, Laura M. "Matoy Jirofo, Masaka Lavany: Rural–Urban Migrants' Livelihood Strategies through the Lens of the Clove Commodity Cycle in Madagascar."
Economic Anthropology 6 (2019): 48–60.

Tinsman, Heidi. *Buying into the Regime: Grapes and Consumption in Cold War Chile
and the United States*. Durham, NC: Duke University Press, 2014.

Trapp, Micah M. "You-Will-Kill-Me-Beans: Taste and the Politics of Necessity in Humanitarian Aid." *Cultural Anthropology* 31, no. 3 (August 9, 2016): 412–37.

Trienekens, Jacques, Aad van Tilburg, Ruben Ruerd, and Martinus van Boekel, eds. *Tropical Food Chains.* Wageningen Academic Publishers, 2007.

Trubek, Amy B. *The Taste of Place: A Cultural Journey into Terroir.* Berkeley: University of California Press, 2008.

Tsing, Anna. *Friction: An Ethnography of Global Connection.* Princeton, NJ: Princeton University Press, 2005.

———. *The Mushroom at the End of the World: On the Possibility of Life in Capitalist Ruins.* Princeton, NJ: Princeton University Press, 2015.

———. "Sorting Out Commodities: How Capitalist Value Is Made through Gifts." *HAU: Journal of Ethnographic Theory* 3, no. 1 (2013): 21–43.

Tsing, Anna Lowenhaupt. *In the Realm of the Diamond Queen: Marginality in an Out-of-the-Way Place.* Princeton, NJ: Princeton University Press, 1993.

Turetsky, Matthew. "Quinoa: Rise of an Andean Superfood." *JSTOR Daily,* November 24, 2023. https://daily.jstor.org/quinoa-rise-of-an-andean-superfood/.

Turner, Frederick Jackson. *The Frontier in American History.* New York: Penguin, 1893.

Ulloa, Antonio de, and Jorge Juan. *Relación histórica del viaje a la America Meridional.* Madrid, 1748.

Urdanivia, Claudia. "Andean Quinoa: Local Farmers in a Global Market." *Anthropology Now* 6, no. 2 (2014): 35–43.

Urrutia, Carlos E., and Carolina Trivelli. "Entre la migración y la agricultura: Limitadas opciones laborales para los jóvenes rurales en el Peru." Documento de Trabajo, Estudios sobre desarollo, 34. Instituto de Estudios Peruanos, Lima, 2019.

Van Esterik, Penny. "From Hunger Foods to Heritage Foods: Challenges to Food Localization in LAO PDR." In *Fast Food/Stow Food: The Cultural Economy of the Global Food System,* edited by Richard Wilk and Melissa Caldwell, 83–96. Lanham, MD: Altamira Press, 2006.

Vandecandelaere, Emilie, Filippo Arfini, Giovanni Belletti, and Andrea Marescotti. *Linking People, Places and Products: A Guide for Promoting Quality Linked to Geographical Origin and Sustainable Geographical Indications.* Rome: FAO and SINER-GI, 2010.

Vandecandelaere, Emilie, Catherine Teyssier, Dominique Barjolle, Philippe Jeanneaux, Clermont Ferrand, and Olivier Beucherie. *Strengthening Sustainable Food Systems through Geographical Indications: An Analysis of Economic Impacts.* Directions in Investment. Rome: Food and Agriculture Organization of the United Nations (FAO) and European Bank for Reconstruction and Development, 2018.

Veblen, Thorstein. *The Theory of the Leisure Class.* Harmondsworth: Penguin Books, 1899.

Vich, Cynthia. "29 de julio de 2001: Toledo en el Cusco o Pachacútec en el mercado global." In *Batallas por la memoria: Antagonismos de la promesa peruana,* edited by Maria Hamman, Santiago López Maguiña, Santiago Portocarrero, and Victor

Vich, 451–63. Lima: Red para el desarrollo de las Ciencias Sociales en el Perú, 2003.

Vich, Víctor. "Dinámicas de racismo en el Perú: La perspectiva cultural de Gonzalo Portocarrero." *Debates en Sociología* 47 (2018): 219–32.

———. "Magical, Mystical: 'The Royal Tour' of Alejandro Toledo." *Journal of Latin American Cultural Studies* 16, no. 1 (March 1, 2007): 1–10.

Viñas, E., C. Días, A. Roca, P. L. White, H. S. White, E. Alvistur, R. Urquieta, and J. Vásquez. "Comprobación del valor alimenticio de la quinua." *Salud y Bienestar Social* 2 (1953): 17.

Wade, Peter. *Race and Ethnicity in Latin America*. London: Pluto Press, 1997.

Walsh, Andrew. "After the Rush: Living with Uncertainty in a Malagasy Mining Town." *Africa* 82, no. 2 (May 2012): 235–51.

Watts, Michael J. "The Agrarian Question in Africa: Debating the Crisis." *Progress in Human Geography* 13, no. 1 (March 1, 1989): 1–41.

Weber, Edward J. "The Inca's Answer to Food Shortage." *Nature* 272, no. 6 (1978): 486.

Weismantel, Mary J. *Cholas and Pishtacos: Stories of Race and Sex in the Andes*. Chicago: University of Chicago Press, 2001.

———. *Food, Gender, and Poverty in the Ecuadorian Andes*. Philadelphia: University of Pennsylvania Press, 1988.

West, Paige. *From Modern Production to Imagined Primitive: The Social World of Coffee from Papua New Guinea*. Durham, NC: Duke University Press, 2012.

Whatmore, Sarah. *Hybrid Geographies: Natures, Cultures, Spaces*. London: Sage, 2002.

White, Philip L., Enrique Alvistur, César Dias, Eduardo Viñas, Hilda S. White, and Carlos Collazos. "Nutritive Values of Crops, Nutrient Content and Protein Quality of Quinua and Cañihua, Edible Seed Products of the Andes Mountains." *Journal of Agricultural and Food Chemistry* 3, no. 6 (June 1, 1955): 531–34.

Wilk, Richard. *Home Cooking in the Global Village: Caribbean Food from Buccaneers to Ecotourists*. New York: Berg, 2006.

———. "Loving People, Hating What They Eat: Marginal Foods and Social Boundaries." In *Reimagining Marginalized Foods: Global Processes, Local Places*, edited by Elizabeth Finnis, 15–33. Tucson: University of Arizona Press, 2012.

Williams, Raymond. *The Country and the City*. New York: Oxford University Press, 1975.

Willow, Anna, Rebecca Zak, Daniella Vilaplana, and David Sheeley. "The Contested Landscape of Unconventional Energy Development: A Report from Ohio's Shale Gas Country." *Journal of Environmental Studies and Sciences* 4, no. 1 (2014): 56–64.

Winterhalder, Bruce, Robert Marsen, and Brooke Thomas. "Dung as an Essential Resource in a Highland Peruvian Community." *Human Ecology* 2, no. 2 (1974): 89–104.

Wolf, E. R. "Aspects of Group Relations in a Complex Society-Mexico." *American Anthropologist* 58 (1956): 1065–78.

Wood, Rebecca Theurer. *Quinoa, the Supergrain: Ancient Food for Today.* Tokyo: Japan Publications, 1989.

Woods, Michael. "Engaging the Global Countryside: Globalization, Hybridity and the Reconstitution of Rural Place." *Progress in Human Geography* 31, no. 4 (2007): 487–507.

Worboys, Michael. "The Discovery of Colonial Malnutrition between the World Wars." In *Imperial Medicine and Indigenous Societies,* edited by David Arnold, 208–25. Manchester: Manchester University Press, 1988.

Yapura Balboa, Rodolfo Jesús. "Caracterización del contrabando de la quinua (Chenopodium quinua) en Bolivia." Thesis, Universidad Mayor de San Andrés, 2011.

Zhang, Cici. "The Quinoa Genome Could Help Scientists Get It out of the Health Food Aisle." *Popular Science* (blog), February 8, 2017. www.popsci.com/quinoa -genome-sequenced/.

Zhu, Fan. "Can Quinoa Help Us to Survive Climate Change?" Newsroom, December 27, 2022. http://newsroom.co.nz/2022/12/27/can-quinoa-help-us-to-survive -climate-change/.

Zimmerer, Karl S. *Changing Fortunes: Biodiversity and Peasant Livelihood in the Peruvian Andes.* Berkeley: University of California Press, 1996.

———. "Vertical Environments." In *Mapping Latin America: A Cartographic Reader,* edited by Jordana Dym and Karl Offen, 263–68. Chicago: University of Chicago Press, 2011.

Zurita-Silva, Andrés, Francisco Fuentes, Pablo Zamora, Sven-Erik Jacobsen, and Andrés R. Schwember. "Breeding Quinoa (Chenopodium Quinoa Willd.): Potential and Perspectives." *Molecular Breeding* 34, no. 1 (June 2014): 13–30.

Zurita-Silva, Andrés, Sven-Erik Jacobsen, Fatemeh Razzaghi, Ricardo Álvarez Flores, Karina B. Ruiz, Andrea Morales, and Herman Silva Ascencio. "Quinoa Drought Responses and Adaptation," in *State of the Art Report on Quinoa around the World in 2013,* edited by D. Bazile, D. Bertero, and C. Nieto, 157–71. Rome: FAO and CIRAD, 2015.

INDEX

Açaí berries, 60
acopiadores, 22, 91, 111, 112, 113, 165, 167, 170, 187
Acurio, Gastón, 74–75, 76, 77
Adriana, 66, 84
aesthetic transformation of foods, 61–62
Africa: quinoa demand in, 72; quinoa production in, 48, 49; teff and fonio as new "superfoods," 237
agrarian land reforms, 45; Peru's Agrarian Reform (1969), 96
agriculture: adapting new crops to Andean highlands, 44–45; Andean agricultural livelihoods, 95–96, 163–66; Andean crop rotation, 8–9; Andean spiritual values and, 127–28; boom and bust cycles, effects of, 16–20, 163–66, 234–38; changing production geographies, 157–62, 158*fig*; coastal quinoa production, 160–61, 182–87; in coastal regions, 4; colonialism, shaping of food systems by, 32–33, 36, 37; crop rotation practices, 100–101; diet and social hierarchies, 32–33, 36, 41, 63–67; furrows, use of, 103–5, 104*fig*; global grain crisis and food insecurity, 42–44; green revolution, 6, 34; heterogeneity of quinoa, 126–27, 127*fig*, 128*fig*; livestock, role of, 8–9; miracle crops, 10–11, 27–31; neglected crops, revalorization of, 4–6, 34–39, *35*, 60–61, 238; peasant logics, 95; pesticide use, US rejection of quinoa

shipments, 177–81; in Puno Region, 3–4, 11–14; quinoa, plant characteristics, 8–10, 9*fig*; quinoa as adaptation to climate change, 47–49; traditional techniques as chemical free, 183–87; traditional techniques as "lower quality," 129–30. *See also* chemical residues, container shipments and
agriculture, the quinoa frontier: CIMA's zonification plan, 89–91, 91*fig*; commercialization and transforming agricultural landscape, 92–94; commodity frontiers, creation of, 92; crop rotation practices, 100–101; envisioning an agriculture of legibility, 96–101, 119–21; making an orderly social landscape, 110–14, 120–21; modernization of farming techniques, 92, 147–49; organic certification, 114–19, 118*fig*; quinoa production in context, 94–96; sustainability concerns, 100–101; technical assistance and the politics of knowledge, 101–5, 104*fig*, 120–21; técnicos and the politics of translation, 105–9. *See also* quality standards for quinoa
Agro Rural program, Peru's Ministry of Agriculture: funding for marca startup costs, 225–26; marca, beginnings of, 213–17; marca fee structure proposal, 223–24
Alan (marca member), 223, 227, 228, 230–31, 232

Alberto (buyer-exporter), 184, 198
Albes, Edward, 27–28, 29, 251n3
Alcázar, Jorge, 32, 42
Alejandro (técnico), 171
Alex (técnico), 164
alfalfa crops, 100–101
alpaca: fiber from, 17; as livestock in Andes, 8; meat from, 65, 256n45
Alter-Eco brand, 71
Altiplano: capitalism in, 95–96; changing production geographies, 157–62, 158*fig*; climate and quinoa production fluctuations, 99; defining of Quinoa Aynok'a, 217–20; environment of, 2; envisioning an agriculture of legibility in, 96–101; heterogeneity of quinoa, 126–27, 127*fig*, 128*fig*; INIA 431 quinoa variety, 138; Puno Region as quinoa heartland, 11–14; quinoa, characteristics of, 8–10, 9*fig*; risk and opportunity for buyers and processors, 169–72. *See also* agriculture; Puno Department
amaranth, 69
Ámaz restaurant, 56
Amazon region, 13–14
American and European Test of Quinoa, 43
Ancient Harvest brand, 46, 69, 70
Andes: farming in, as a spiritual act, 127–28; modernization and development of, 4, 46, 235, 236; poverty and malnutrition in, 28–29, 31, 32–33, 38–42, 44–47, 52, 54; quinoa as native plant, 2–3, 14, 32, 37, 217; quinoa branding using Andes, 71–72; race and class configurations in, 32, 65–67, 107, 130; social and ecological landscapes, 11–14; trade networks for agricultural products, vertical integration and, 95
anti-politics machine, 125
Arequipa Department, 102, 160; agro-export experience in, 114; risk and opportunity for buyers and processors, 169–72
Argentina, 1, 32, 216, 217
Arguedas, José María, 11, 63–64
artichoke crops, 159
Asia, quinoa demand in, 72
asparagus crops, 102, 114, 159

Association for Ecological Andean Grain Agroindustrials (Asociación de Agro-industriales Ecológicos de Granos Andinos), 216
Astrid y Gastón restaurant, 75, 76
Atlantic Magazine, 41
atrazine, 178
audit culture, 200
"authentic food," 70–71
avocados, 131, 158

Bair, Jennifer, 21
banana trade, 129
Banzer, Hugo, 40–41
barley crops, 100–101
Baumann, Shyon, 210
Belaúnde Terry, Fernando, 45
Bellemare, Marc, 18
bell pepper crops, 102
Benites, Juan Manuel, 159
Berlant, Lauren, 7
Besky, Sarah, 129, 131
biodigesters, 174
biodiversity: bioprospecting and, 56–57; commercial production of quinoa and, 93; contrasting grains and the politics of varietal purity, 134–40, 135*fig*, 136*fig*; global concerns about, 38; INIA certified seed producers, 137–40; International Year of Quinoa (2013), 51; quinoa heterogeneity, 43, 126–28, 127*fig*, 128*fig*, 130
Biodiversity International, 6, 39, 50, 51, 210
BioFach Expo, 201–2
biol fertilizer, 117–19, 118*fig*
biopower, 138
bioprospecting, 56–57. *See also* culinary bioprospecting
biotechnology, quinoa as adaptation to climate change, 48–49
Bob's Red Mill brand, 71
Bolivia: branding of Quinoa Real, 216; import substitution industrialization, 40–41; nutrition research on quinoa, 31–32, 33; quinoa as solution to malnutrition and poverty in the Andes, 39–42, 44; quinoa export market development, 46; quinoa from, 22;

CIMA (*continued*)
  plant equipment, quality standards and, 142–44; quinoa bust, effects of, 153–54, 175–76; quinoa bust and tensions with farmers, 166–68; quinoa purchases outside of Puna region, 114; technical assistance and the politics of knowledge, 101–5, 104*fig,* 120–21; técnicos, reputation, risk, and opportunity during bust, 172–76; técnicos and the politics of translation, 105–9; zonification plan, 89–91, 91*fig*
city, as loaded concept, 107
climate change: International Year of Quinoa (2013), 51; miracle crops and solutionist logic, 29; quinoa as future-proof crop, 47–49
coastal Peru, 13–14; agriculture in, 4; quinoa production in, 159–61, 182–87; risk and opportunity for buyers and processors, 169–72
Codex Alimentarius, 182
coffee trade, 129
collard greens, 60
Collazos, Carlos, 32–33
collective branding: in countries other than Peru, 216–17; origin verification requirements, 214–15. *See also* marca colectiva (marca) branding effort
colonialism: decolonial projects, 63; diet and social hierarchies, 32–33, 63–67; *hacienda* system, 96; neocolonial projects, 63; power dynamics in modern commerce, 112; quality standards and uneducated farmer tropes, 129; revalorizing indigenous foods, 60–63, 238; shaping of food systems by, 36, 37; unique crops, devaluation of, 5
coloniality of power, 60
Colorexa, 172
commodity chains, 20–23; commodity frontiers, creation of, 92; quinoa production in context, 94–96; técnicos and the politics of translation, 106–9. *See also* global commodity chain
commodity frontier. *See* agriculture, the quinoa frontier
commodity quinoa, 205

common-pool resources, 208–9; defining Quinoa Aynok'a, 217–20; scholarly framework for, 211–13. *See also* marca colectiva (marca) branding effort
Confederación Nacional Agraria, 131
Conference on Malnutrition (1948), 44
consumer preferences, changes in, 59–63; ease of incorporating into existing meal categories, 70; place-based foods as development tools, 209–13
contamination scandals. *See* chemical residues, container shipments and
contrasting grains (*puntos negros*), 134–40
convention theory, 125–26
Cook, Ian, 209
cooperatives, 22, 113–14; bust and tensions between farmers and buyer-processors, 166–68; marca, continuing contamination concerns, 229–33; marca, fluctuating interest in participation, 227–28. *See also* marca colectiva (marca) branding effort; QCOOP
copper, 19
corn hybrids, 139
Costco, 161
cotton, 158
countryside, as loaded concept, 107
Crang, Philip, 209
Cronon, William, 131
cruel optimism, 7
culinary bioprospecting, 84–86; defined, 56–57; gastronomic revolution and, 75–76; nutritional primitivism and global superfoods, 67–72; quinoa and, 57–63
culinary cosmopolitanism, 70–71
culinary nationalism, 4–6
culinary tourism, 56
cultural traditions: concepts of pollution and contagion, 136; global commodity chain, 21–23; "Indian problem" and, 12–14; indigenous foods, commercialization of, 13–14, 56–63; International Year of Quinoa (2013) and, 51–55; miracle crops and, 10–11; neglected crops and, 5–6; nutritionism and, 82–83; racial and ethnic social classifications and, 65–67; racialized imaginative geographies, 107;

técnicos and the politics of translation, 105–9; técnicos as cultural brokers, 94
culture brokers, 105–9
Cusack, David, 46
Cusco region, 13
cuy (guinea pig), 61, 65, 66
Cuzqueña Quinua beer, 72–73, 81
Cuzqueños, 80–81

Danish Development Agency, 43
de calidad (quality quinoa), 123, 134–40, 135*fig*, 136*fig*. See also quality standards for quinoa
decolonial projects, 63
demand: boom and bust, use of terms, 162. *See also* quinoa boom; quinoa bust
development agencies: promotion of organic certification by, 193–94; técnicos, reputation, risk, and opportunity during bust, 172–76; waning support for quinoa as development tool, 226. *See also* agriculture, the quinoa frontier; international development work
dietary modernization, 41; whiteness and nutritional authority, 81–84, 83*fig*
documents: chemical analysis for quinoa purity, 199–202; organic certification, delegitimized document and, 192–97; performative nature of bureaucracy, 194; representational view of, 195
domingal (open-air markets), 78–79
Doña Felicita (farmer), 192–93, 194
Doña Maria (farmer), 122–23, 125–26, 147
Don Lolin (farmer), 190–91
Don Roberto (farmers' association president), 145
Douglas, Mary, 136

Earle, Rebecca, 65
Ecoandina brand, 81–84, 83*fig*
Ecologist, 46
ecology of region: geographies of inclusion and exclusion, quality standards and, 144–47; heterogeneity of quinoa, 126–27, 127*fig*, 128*fig*; landscape, use of term, 94; quinoa production and climate fluctuations, 99; state power and capitalist value making, 98

economies of scale, 162
economy: boom and bust cycles, effects of, 16–20, 153–57, 163–66, 175–76, 234–38; capitalist economies, 95–96, 98, 234–38; coastal quinoa production, growth of, 160–61; global commodity chains, 20–23; global demand for quinoa, data for, 58–59; import substitution industrialization, 40–41; miracle crops as development solution, 10–11, 27–31; place-based foods as development tools, 210–13; in Puno region, 3–4, 12–14; quinoa as a global commodity, 6–7; quinoa as solution to Andean poverty, 44–47; reciprocity-based economies, 95; revalorization, use of term, 60–61, 238; Superfoods Peru campaign, 5–6, 159–60; vertical integration, Andean agricultural trade, 95. *See also* agriculture, the quinoa frontier
Ecuador, 217
Edith (farmer), 163, 164
Edwin (trainer in organic certification), 114–15
eel, 60
El Correo, 183
Emiliano (CIMA CEO), 89–90, 236; on 2014 seed shortage, 139–40; making an orderly social landscape, 110–14; organic certification challenges, 119; quinoa bust, effect on CIMA, 154; technical assistance and the politics of knowledge, 101–5, 104*fig*; zonification plans to meet market demand, 96–101
endangered foods, 218
entrepreneurs, as quinoa advocates, 58
Environmental Protection Agency (EPA), US, 177–79, 182
environmental regulatory bodies, 177–79, 182. *See also* chemical residues, container shipments and
Erma (farmer), 191
ethnic classifications, 65–67
ethnographic research: boom and bust cycles, effect on research, 156–57; limits of ethnographic ways of knowing, 180–81, 197
ethnography of decline, 155

Europe: banned agricultural chemicals, 178–79, 182; demand for quinoa, impact on Andean production, 133; origin-based labels in, 207, 210, 211; quinoa commercial production, 161; quinoa demand in, 72, 161; quinoa production in, 17

European Commission, SWUP-MED project, 48

export industry: boom and bust cycles, effects of, 155–57, 175–76, 234–38; chemical analysis for quinoa purity, 197–202; chemical residues, distrust throughout the supply chain, 187–92; global commodity chain, 22–23; global demand for quinoa, data for, 58–59, 161; organic certification, delegitimized documents, 196–97; pesticide use, US rejection of quinoa shipments, 177–81; Proquinua Program, Ministry of Agriculture, 158–62, 158*fig*; quinoa as version of Peruvian identity, 77; quinoa export data, 245*fig*, 246*fig*; quinoa market segmentation, 188–89; quinoa production and export data, 160–61, 245*fig*, 246*fig*; risk and opportunity for buyers and processors, 169–72; standards and power relationships, 131; Superfoods Peru campaign, 5–6, 159–60; US quinoa import data, 179. *See also* chemical residues, container shipments and; global commodity chain; marca colectiva (marca) branding effort

Fabio (CIMA processor), 143

Fabricant, Florence, 69

fair-trade certification, 194

farmers and farmer networks: bust and tensions with buyer-processors, 166–68, 237; chemical analysis for quinoa purity, 199–202; chemical residues, conflicting tales of blame, 181–87; chemical residues, distrust throughout the supply chain, 187–92; CIMA's zonification plan, 89–91, 91*fig*; coastal quinoa production, 160–61, 182–837; geographies of inclusion and exclusion, quality standards and, 144–47; INIA certified seed producers, 137–40; making an

orderly social landscape, 110–14, 120–21; marca, continuing contamination concerns, 229–33; marca fee structure decisions, 224–25; marca participation, exclusion from, 222–23; merma and the work ethic of quality, 140–41, 142*fig*; organic certification, delegitimized documents, 196–97; price for quinoa, 91; producer associations and cooperatives, 113–14; quality standards as judgment on farmer's worth, 125–26, 140–41, 142*fig*, 147–49; quinoa bust, effect on, 154, 155–57, 234–38; reevaluation of commercial quinoa production, 163–66, 175–76; shrinking margins and perishability politics, 162–66; standards, lack of incentive to follow, 133; standards development, lack of involvement in, 131; technical assistance and the politics of knowledge, 101–5, 104*fig*, 120–21; técnicos, reputation, risk, and opportunity during bust, 172–76; técnicos and the politics of translation, 105–9. *See also* marca colectiva (marca) branding effort

farm-gate price, 161, 249n56

Ferguson, James, 125, 155

Ferguson, Maes, 19

fertilizer, organic certification and, 117–19, 118*fig*

fonio, 237

Food and Agriculture Organization (FAO), United Nations, 6, 38, 182, 210

Food and Drug Administration (FDA), US, 177–79, 182

food gentrification, 61

food labels: Ancient Harvest (Quinoa Corporation), 68–69; defining Quinoa Aynok'a, 207–209, 208*fig*, 217–20, 229; IncaSur, 79; organic and fair-trade certifications on, 118–19, 194. *See also* origin-based labels

forage crops, 100–101

Foucault, Michel, 138

France: collective branding projects, 217–18; quinoa commercial production, 161

Francisco (técnico), 166

Friedberg, Susanne, 200

frontier. *See* agriculture, the Quinoa frontier

fungicides. *See* chemical residues, container shipments and

furrows, use of, 103–5, 104*fig*

Galvin, Shaila, 194

García, Mariá Elena, 75

gastronomic revolution, 5, 56, 74–78, 84–86

Genaro (farmer), 109

General Mills, 161

Gereffi, Gary, 20–21

Gestión, 183

global commodity chain, 20–23; boom and bust cycles, effects of, 154–57, 234–38; commodity frontiers, creation of, 92; fragmented knowledge of supply chain participants, 179–81; global demand and production data, 161, 245*fig*, 246*fig*; pesticide use, US rejection of quinoa shipments, 177–81; quality standards and power dynamics of supply chains, 125–26; quality standards and remaking of landscapes of production, 123–26, 147–49; quinoa production in context, 94–96; standards and power relationships, 131–33; técnicos and the politics of translation, 106–9; traceability, technology for, 201–2; trust, breakdown of, 202–3; uneven geographies, production of, 155; US quinoa import data, 179; zonification plans to meet market demand, 96–101. *See also* chemical residues, container shipments and; export industry; marca colectiva (marca) branding effort; quality standards for quinoa

Global North, quinoa demand in, 72

global value chain, 21–23

Globenatural, 172

gluten-free starches, 70

Gómez, Luz, 183

goosefoot plants, 8–10, 9*fig*

Gorad, Steven, 46, 67–69

grape crops, 158

Graziano da Silva, José, 50, 53

Greene, Shane, 81

green revolution, 6, 34, 40

Griesemer, James, 30

guano boom, 17

Guardian, 41

Guide to Collective Brands (Agro Rural), 213

Guillermo (buyer-processor), 141

guinea pig (*cuy*), 61, 65, 66

Gustavo (técnico, marca member), 197, 220, 228

Guthman, Julie, 29, 198–99

Gutsche, Astrid, 74–75

hacienda system, 96, 112

Haushofer, Lisa, 10

Hayden, Cori, 57

"healthy foods," 70–71

heirloom tomatoes, 69, 79

Heredia, Nadine, 1–3, 3*fig*, 49–50, 50*fig*, 157–58, 158*fig*

Ho, Soleil, 61

Hobart, Hi'ilei, 61

honey, 213

Hopkins, Terrence, 20

Huaca Pucllana Restaurant, 57–58

Humala, Ollanta, 1

Humboldt, Alexander von, 12

Ica Department, 160

IICA study: local market consumer preferences, 129; quality standards, development of, 130–34

imagined primitive, 69, 71–72, 79, 80; quinoa as a primitive grain, 31–34

imitation crab industry, 143

Inca Empire, 13; Cuzqueños, 80–81; imagined primitive as symbol, 71; IncaSur marketing and, 79–81; New Age spiritualism and appeal of quinoa, 68–69; rebranding of marginalized foods, 62–63, 79–80, 85, 236

Inca Kola, 81

IncaSur, 79–81

income, for farmers of quinoa, 4, 6, 28–29, 45, 46, 47, 49, 91–92, 95, 113, 147, 164–65

India: organic certification efforts in, 194; quinoa demand in, 161

India, tea trade, 131

processors, 168–70; certification apparatus, legitimacy of, 180; chemical
analysis for quinoa purity, 197–202;
chemical residues, rejected container
shipments and, 177–81; defining
Quinoa Aynok'a, 217–20; delegitimized
documents, 192–97; Julie Guthman on
the industrial organic, 198–99; labor
required and price considerations,
163–66; marca, continuing contamination concerns, 229–33; marca, traceability system, 231–32; traceability,
201–2. *See also* chemical residues, container shipments and; quality standards
for quinoa
origin-based labels, 206–9, 208*fig*; in
countries other than Peru, 216–17;
origin verification requirements,
214–15; place-based foods as development tools, 209–13; scholarly framework for study, 211–13. *See also* marca
colectiva (marca) branding effort
Ortiz, Teodoro, 79
Ostrom, Elinor, 212–13, 220, 221

panicles, 8
Paolo (quinoa processor, marca member),
68, 185, 187, 198, 214–15, 216, 218, 219,
223, 225, 230, 231–32, 234–35
paprika, 159
Parra, Violeta, 63–64
Parry, Elizabeth, 8
Parts Unknown, 56
Pasankalla, INIA 415 quinoa variety, 138
peasant agriculture: commercialization of
peasant food staples, 60; peasant, use of
term, 262n26; peasant logics, 95; resistance to legibility projects, 97–101,
119–21
pepper crops, 158
Peru, xii*map*; civil war (1980-1992), 45;
commodity boom and bust cycles,
effects of, 16–20, 234–38; import substitution industrialization, 40–41; nutrition research on quinoa, 32, 33; quinoa,
acceptance by upper class consumers, 72;
quinoa as malnutrition palliative in the
Andes, 28–29, 31, 32–33, 38–42, 44–47,

52, 54; quinoa export data, 245*fig*,
246*fig*; quinoa production and price
data, 244*fig*; rediscovering authentic
Peruvian food, 72–78; tripartite schema,
coast/Andes/Amazon, 13–14
Peruvian Association for Gastronomy, 63
Peruvian identity, food as core element,
72–78
pesticides, 177–81, 229–33. *See also* chemical residues, container shipments and
Piura Department, 185
place-based products, 206–9, 208*fig*; defining Quinoa Aynok'a, 217–20; as development tools, 209–13; scholarly
framework for study, 211–13. *See also*
marca colectiva (marca) branding effort
placeless commodity, 161
poi, 61
political landscape: chemical residues,
conflicting tales of blame, 181–87;
chemical residues, effects of container
rejection, 179–81; coastal quinoa production, growth of, 160–61; global
commodity chain, 21–23; marca, the
politics of exclusion, 220–25; origin-
based labels, success of, 211–13; quinoa
boom and, 59–63; standards and power
relationships, 131; standards and the
depoliticization of agricultural transformation, 125–26; technical assistance and
the politics of knowledge, 101–5, 104*fig*,
120–21
pollera, 1, 214, 247n4
pollination of quinoa, 135–40, 260n12,
260n14
potato crops, 100–101, 213
poverty: miracle crops and solutionist logic,
29; quinoa as solution to Andean
poverty, 44–47
poverty foods: diet and social hierarchies,
32–33, 36, 41, 59–67, 84–86; "lost" foods
as, 76–78; quinoa as, 16, 91, 234;
rebranding of for new audiences, 56–63,
79–80, 84–86; as superfoods, 82; use of
term, 250n57
power relationships: biopower, 138; boom
and bust cycles, effects of, 155–57, 175,
234–38; buyers and processors, risk and

power relationships (*continued*)
    opportunity during bust, 168–72; in
    changing agricultural landscape, 93, 96,
    98, 112–13; coloniality of power, 60, 67,
    72, 95–96, 112; in commodity chains, 21,
    125–26; common-pool resource manage-
    ment, 212–13; imagined primitive,
    symbolic power of, 71–72; Inca imagery,
    use of, 80; individual farmers and
    cooperatives, 190–91; in marca branding
    effort, 221–25, 233; marginalized foods
    and social hierarchies, 66; miracle crops
    and superfoods, power of, 10–11, 29, 30,
    51–52; neglected crops and, 36; place-
    based foods as development tools,
    210–11; quinoa boom, farmer's bargain-
    ing power during, 92; in quinoa boom,
    17–18, 50; sociopolitical networks and,
    51–54, 58, 59, 63, 73, 75, 85, 236, 237, 238;
    standards and, 126, 131–32, 138, 149
price of quinoa, 16, 244*fig*, 249n56; during
    boom (2008-2014), 90–92; boom and
    bust, use of terms, 162; boom and bust
    cycles, effects of, 16–20, 154–57, 175–76,
    234–38; during bust (2017), 163; bust
    and tensions between farmers and
    buyer-processors, 166–68; farmer loyalty
    to buyers, 110–14; farmers' reevaluation
    of commercial quinoa production,
    163–66; farm-gate price, 161; global
    demand and over production data, 161,
    245*fig*, 246*fig*; incompatible visions of a
    miracle crop, 28–29; marca, interest in
    and price fluctuations, 227; organic
    certification and, 193–94; shrinking
    margins and perishability politics,
    162–66; as symptom of social, political,
    and material processes, 59
primitive, images of, 69, 71–72, 79, 80;
    quinoa as a primitive grain, 31–34
processing equipment, quinoa-specific, 169
processors. *See* buyer-processors
producer associations, 113–14; Mesa
    collective branding efforts and, 213–17;
    standards and power relationships, 131.
    See also marca colectiva (marca) brand-
    ing effort

production process: commodity chain and,
    20–23; remaking of landscapes of
    production, 123–26, 147–49. *See also*
    quality standards for quinoa
promissory narratives, 28–29
Proquinua Program, 158–62, 158*fig*
protein: charismatic nutrients, 10–11; in
    quinoa, 9; quinoa as malnutrition
    palliative in the Andes, 28–29, 31, 32–33,
    38–42, 44–47, 52, 54
Puno Department, 249n40, xii*map*; boom
    and bust status in 2018, 234–38; com-
    mercial quinoa production, early history
    of, 46–47; defining Quinoa Aynok'a,
    217–20; economy and living conditions,
    3–4; marca, continuing contamination
    concerns, 229–33; Puno quinoa as
    distinct from other quinoa, 215; quinoa
    boom and bust cycles, effects of, 16–20,
    91–92, 154–55, 234–38; as quinoa heart-
    land, 11–14, 215; quinoa production
    data, 160–61; reevaluation of commer-
    cial quinoa production, 163–66; tradi-
    tional agricultural practices as chemical
    free, 183–87. *See also* agriculture, the
    Quinoa frontier; marca colectiva
    (marca) branding effort
puntos negros (contrasting grains), 134–40
Purdue University, 38
Purity and Danger (Douglas), 136

Qali Warma Program, 41
QCOOP, 14–15, 109, 111, 113–14, 157, 223;
    boom and bust status in 2018, 235; bust
    and tensions with farmers, 166–68, 175;
    chemical residues in shipments, distrust
    throughout the supply chain, 189–92;
    farmer decisions on selling or storing
    crops, 163–64; marca, continuing
    contamination concerns, 229–33; marca
    participation and, 228; merma and the
    work ethic of quality, 140–41, 142*fig*;
    técnicos, reputation, risk, and opportu-
    nity during bust, 172–76
quality standards for quinoa: chemical
    analysis for quinoa purity, 199–202;
    colonial export market tropes, 129;

construction of quinoa standards, 126–34, 127*fig*, 128*fig*; contrasting grains and the politics of varietal purity, 134–40, 135*fig*, 136*fig*; defining Quinoa Aynok'a, 218–20, 222; delegitimized documents, 192–97; depoliticizing the transformation of agricultural systems, 125–26; geographies of inclusion and exclusion, 144–47; heterogeneity and scale-up challenges, 129; INIA certified seed producers, 137–40; labor required and price considerations, 163–66; local quinoa market channels, 128–29; marca, continuing contamination concerns, 229–33; merma and the work ethic of quality, 140–44, 142*fig*; quality control tests, 122–23; state-sanctioned standards, quality grade categories, 131–34; as tool for remaking the landscapes of production, 123–26, 147–49; traceability, 201–2. *See also* organic certification

Quark, Amy, 125

Quijano, Aníbal, 60, 67

quinoa: consumption of in Peru, data on, 66, 186; cross-pollination of, 127, 127*fig*, 128*fig*; export data, 245*fig*, 246*fig*; heterogeneity of, 126–27, 127*fig*, 128*fig*; as ingredient in highland cuisine, 9–10; long-term storage of, 162–63; as malnutrition palliative in the Andes, 28–29, 31, 32–33, 38–42, 44–47, 52, 54; as a miracle crop, 10–11, 27–31; as new tool for global hunger, 42–44; nutrients in, 9–10; pesticide use, US rejection of quinoa shipments, 177–81; plant characteristics, 8–10, 9*fig*; pollination of, 135–40; processing required for, 9; production and price data, 244*fig*; Puno quinoa as distinct from other quinoa, 215; quinoa-specific processing equipment, 169. *See also* quinoa boom; quinoa bust

Quinoa, the Supergrain: Ancient Food for Today (Wood), 69

Quinoa4Med, 48

quinoa advocates, 58

Quinoa Aynok'a, 204–9, 208*fig*; abandonment of marca project, 232–33; defining of, marca and, 217–20; logo and packaging designs, 214, 215; marca, continuing contamination concerns, 229–33; quality standards for, 218–20, 222. *See also* marca colectiva (marca) branding effort

quinoa boom: as adaptation to climate change, 47–49; as boundary object, peak and fall of, 49–55, 50*fig*; changing production geographies, 157–62, 158*fig*; demand for various colors, fluctuations in, 98–101, 143; Edward Albes 1918 vision of a global crop, 27–28; gastronomic revolution, role in, 76–78; global demand, data for, 58–59, 90–91, 161; per capita consumption data, 58; in Peru's coastal areas, 159–61, 182–87; price fluctuations over time, 16, 90–91, 110–11, 153–54, 175–76, 234–38; production and export data, 160–61, 245*fig*, 246*fig*; production in context, 94–96; Puno Region as quinoa heartland, 11–14, 215; rise of neglected crops, 34–39, 35; as solution to Andean poverty, 44–47; in value added products, 58. *See also* global commodity chain; quality standards for quinoa

quinoa bust, 153–57, 175–76, 234–38; buyers and processors, risk and opportunity for, 168–72; changing production landscapes, 157–62, 158*fig*; effect on ethnographic research, 156–57; global demand and production data, 161, 245*fig*, 246*fig*; price fluctuations over time, 153–54; shrinking margins and perishability politics, 162–66; técnicos, reputation, risk, and opportunity, 172–76; tensions between farmers and buyer-processors, 166–68. *See also* chemical residues, container shipments and; global commodity chain; reputation, (re)building of

Quinoa Corporation, 46, 68–69

quinua fea (ugly quinoa), 134

"Quinua Mama" Festival, 1–3, 3*fig*

race: Inca as distinct racial imaginary, 80;
race and class configurations in the
Andes, 65–67, 74, 78–79, 179, 236;
racialized imaginative geographies, 107;
regionalization of, 13, 260n39; whiteness
and nutritional authority, 81–84, 83*fig*

radical Otherness, 69

ramen, 60

reciprocity-based economies, 95

Regional Agricultural Administration
(Dirección Regional Agraria, DRA), 117

Renique, José Luis, 12

representational view of documents, 195

reputation, (re)building of, 204–5; defining
Quinoa Aynok'a, 217–20; marca, abandonment of effort, 232–33; marca, beginnings of, 213–17; marca, continuing
contamination concerns, 229–33; marca,
fluctuating in interest in participation,
226–29; marca, the politics of exclusion,
220–25; place-based foods as development tools, 209–13; reputation as a
collectively managed resource, 208–9

restaurants, 56, 57–58; establishing Peruvian identity, food as core element,
73–78

revalorization, use of term, 60–61, 238

rice crops, 158, 159

Rigoberto (founder of CIMA nonprofit),
100, 101, 113, 220; on contaminated
quinoa containers, 183–84; making an
orderly social landscape, 112; quinoa
bust, effect on CIMA, 153–54; on
standards for quinoa, 133; on training
programs for farmers, 103

Roca Rey, Bernardo, 63, 73–74

Rolando (farmer), 137–38, 167

Román (QCOOP member), 190–92

rural development: place-based foods as
development tools, 207, 210–13; quinoa
boom and, 3–4, 39, 45, 46, 49, 100, 113

rural land tenure system, 45

rural population, racialized imaginative
geographies, 107

Salcedo District, 89

Salcedo INIA quinoa variety, 138, 219

saponin, 9, 129, 130, 133, 134

Schiaffino, Pedro Miguel, 56, 57–58, 62, 63

Scott, James, 98

Scrinis, Gyorgy, 82

seeds: commodification of, 139; cross-
pollination and, 135–36; IICA study,
standards and, 130; INIA certified
seeds, 137–40; Proquinua Program,
certified seeds from, 159; quinoa quality
standards, 141; saving of, heterogeneity
and, 126–28, 127*fig*, 128*fig*, 130; seed
suppliers, 216, 228; shortage in 2014,
price spikes and, 139–40; sowing of,
agricultural cycle and, 157–58, 158*fig*

Seeing Like a State (Scott), 98

*Seven Interpretive Essays on Peruvian
Reality* (Mariátegui), 13–14

Sierra Exportadora, 235

silver, 16–17

Simmel, Georg, 59

Simón Bolivar Foundation, 45

Simón Bolivar Fund, 126

Slow Food International, 51, 218

social class. *See* social landscape

social landscape: Andean spiritual values
and agriculture, 127–28; boom and bust
cycles, effects of, 155–57, 234–38; buyers
and processors, risk and opportunity
during bust, 166–68; chemical residues,
conflicting tales of blame, 181–87;
chemical residues, effects of container
rejection, 179–81; concepts of pollution
and contagion, 136; diet and social
hierarchies, 32–33, 36, 41, 59–67, 84–86;
global commodity chain, 21–23; landscape, use of term, 94; local quinoa
market channels, 128–29; making an
orderly social landscape, 110–14,
120–21; organic certification process
and, 119; Peruvian identity, food as core
element, 72–78; in Puna's agricultural
landscape, 97–101; race and class configurations in the Andes, 65–67; revalorization, use of term, 60–61, 238;
sociopolitical networks, 51–54, 58,
59–63, 73, 75, 85–86, 236, 237, 238;
técnicos, reputation, risk, and

United Nations (*continued*)
(FAO), 6, 182, 210; International Year
of Quinoa (2013), 1, 49–53, 50*fig*, 162
United States: demand for quinoa, impact
on Andean production, 133; FDA and
EPA rejection of quinoa containers,
177–81, 182; quinoa commercial production, 161; quinoa demand in, 161; quinoa
import data, 179
University of Minnesota Agricultural
Experiment Station, 38
urban population, racialized imaginative
geographies, 107
U.S. Department of Agriculture, 33, 42
U.S. National Research Council (NRC),
33, 34–39, *35*

value chain, global, 21–23
vanilla trade, 129
Veblen, Thorstein, 59
Vega, Garcilaso de la, 64
Velasco Alvarado, Juan, 40–41, 45
vegetarian / vegan diets, 69–70
vertical integration, 95
Victor (Puno-based técnico), 54, 106–7,
111, 139
Viñas, Eduardo, 40
vitamins: as charismatic nutrients, 10–11;
in quinoa, 9–10

Wallerstein, Immanuel, 20
water scarcity, 48
Weber, Edward, 40
Weber, Max, 78
West, Paige, 69, 71
Western diet, 32–33, 252n25
wheat trade, 36, 131
whiteness: hierarchical spectrum of,
65–67; Inca mythmaking and, 80–81;
nutritional authority and, 81–84, 83*fig*
Wilberto (técnico), 186, 192–93, 194
Wildlife Conservation Society, 174
Williams, Raymond, 107
The Will to Knowledge (Foucault), 138
Wolf, Eric, 95, 106
wonder foods, 10–11. *See also* superfoods
Wood, Rebecca, 69
World Bank, 6, 51
World Food Day, 49–53, 50*fig*
World Intellectual Property Organization,
214
world-system theory, 20–23

Zambian Copper Belt, 19, 155
Zhu, Fan, 48
zonification, 89–91, 91*fig*, 96–101

CALIFORNIA STUDIES IN FOOD AND CULTURE

Founded in 1893,
UNIVERSITY OF CALIFORNIA PRESS
publishes bold, progressive books and journals
on topics in the arts, humanities, social sciences,
and natural sciences—with a focus on social
justice issues—that inspire thought and action
among readers worldwide.

The UC PRESS FOUNDATION
raises funds to uphold the press's vital role
as an independent, nonprofit publisher, and
receives philanthropic support from a wide
range of individuals and institutions—and from
committed readers like you. To learn more, visit
ucpress.edu/supportus.

www.ingramcontent.com/pod-product-compliance
Lightning Source LLC
Chambersburg PA
CBHW020824270326
41928CB00006B/429